98

3000 800029 829
St. Louis Community College

D0079285

WITHDRAWN

 St. Louis Community College

Forest Park
Florissant Valley
Meramec

Instructional Resources
St. Louis, Missouri

The Critical Response
to John Cheever

St. Louis Community College
at Meramec
Library

The Critical Response to John Cheever

Edited by
FRANCIS J. BOSHA

Critical Responses in Arts and Letters, Number 6
Cameron Northouse, *Series Adviser*

Greenwood Press
Westport, Connecticut • London

Library of Congress Cataloging-in-Publication Data

The Critical response to John Cheever / edited by Francis J. Bosha.
    p.   cm.—(Critical responses in arts and letters, ISSN
1057-0993 ; no. 6)
  Includes bibliographical references (p.) and index.
  ISBN 0-313-28355-9 (alk. paper)
  1. Cheever, John—Criticism and interpretation—History.
I. Bosha, Francis J. II. Series.
PS3505.H6428Z634 1994
813'.52—dc20   93-8974

British Library Cataloguing in Publication Data is available.

Copyright © 1994 by Francis J. Bosha

All rights reserved. No portion of this book may be
reproduced, by any process or technique, without the
express written consent of the publisher.

Library of Congress Catalog Card Number: 93-8974
ISBN: 0-313-28355-9
ISSN: 1057-0993

First published in 1994

Greenwood Press, 88 Post Road West, Westport, CT 06881
An imprint of Greenwood Publishing Group, Inc.

Printed in the United States of America

The paper used in this book complies with the
Permanent Paper Standard issued by the National
Information Standards Organization (Z39.48-1984).

10 9 8 7 6 5 4 3 2 1

Copyright Acknowledgments

The author and publisher gratefully acknowledge permission to quote from the following:

"John Cheever's Sense of Drama" by Struthers Burt, *Saturday Review* 26 (24 April 1943): 9. Reprinted by permission of Omni International, LTD.
"New Fiction from the Atlantic to the Pacific" by Rose Feld. From *New York Herald Tribune*, 14 March 1943, p. 12; (c) 1943, New York Herald Tribune Inc. All rights reserved. Reprinted by permission.
"Fiction in Review" by Diana Trilling, *The Nation* 156 (10 April 1943): 533. Reprinted by permission of *The Nation* magazine/The Nation Co., Inc., (c) 1943.
"Snapshots in the East Fifties" by Taliaferro Boatwright. From *New York Herald Tribune*, 24 May 1953, p. 16; (c) 1953, New York Herald Tribune Inc. All rights reserved. Reprinted by permission.
"Esthetics of the Story" by William Peden, *Saturday Review* 36 (11 April 1953): 43-44. Reprinted by permission of Omni International, LTD. and the author.
"Cheever's Use of Mythology in 'The Enormous Radio'" by Burton Kendle, *Studies in Short Fiction* 4 (Spring 1967): 262-64. Reprinted by permission. Copyright by Newberry College.
"'Young Goodman Brown' and 'The Enormous Radio'" by Henrietta Ten Harmsel. *Studies in Short Fiction* 9 (Fall 1972): 407-08. Reprinted by permission. Copyright by Newberry College.
"Yankee Gallimaufry" by Carlos Baker, *Saturday Review* 40 (23 March 1957): 14. Reprinted by permission of Omni International, LTD.
"Out of an Abundant Love of Created Things" by William Esty, *Commonweal* 66 (17 May 1957): 187-88. Reprinted by permission.
"End of the Line" by Maxwell Geismar, *New York Times Book Review*, 24 March 1957, p. 5. Copyright (c) 1957 by The New York Times Company. Re-

printed by permission.
"John Cheever's Photograph Album" by Donald Malcolm, *The New Republic* 136 (3 June 1957): 17-18. Reprinted by permission of *The New Republic*, (c) 1957, The New Republic, Inc.
"Four Views of Love" by David L. Stevenson, *The Nation* 184 (13 April 1957): 329. Reprinted by permission of *The Nation* magazine/The Nation Co., Inc., (c) 1957.
"Dante of Suburbia" by Richard Gilman, *Commonweal* 69 (19 December 1958): 320. Reprinted by permission.
"Cheever and Others" by Granville Hicks. *Saturday Review* 41 (13 September 1958): 33, 47. Reprinted by permission of Omni International, LTD.
"Realities and Fictions" by Irving Howe, *Partisan Review* 26 (Winter 1959): 130-31. Copyright 1959 by Irving Howe. Reprinted by permission.
"Mr. Cheever's Sleights-of-Mood Performed with Consummate Skill" by Gene Baro. From *New York Herald Tribune*, 30 April 1961, p. 29; (c) 1961, New York Herald Tribune Inc. All rights reserved. Reprinted by permission of Albert Stadler.
"A Celebration of Life" by Joan Didion, *National Review* 10 (22 April 1961): 254-55; (c) 1961 by *National Review*, Inc., 150 East 35th Street, New York, NY 10016. Reprinted by permission.
"Cheever's Inferno" by Frank J. Warnke, *The New Republic* 144 (15 May 1961): 18. Reprinted by permission of *The New Republic*, (c) 1961, The New Republic, Inc.
"Sugary Days in Saint Botolphs" by Hilary Corke, *The New Republic* 150 (25 January 1964): 19-21. Reprinted by permission of *The New Republic*, (c) 1964, The New Republic, Inc.
"The Way We Feel Now" by Benjamin DeMott, *Harper's Magazine* 228 (February 1964): 111-12. Copyright (c) 1964 by *Harper's Magazine*. All rights reserved. Reprinted from the February issue by special permission.
"From Christmas to Christmas--A Ramble with the Wapshots" by George Greene, *Commonweal* 79 (24 January 1964): 487-88. Reprinted by permission.
"The Family Way" by Elizabeth Hardwick, *The New York Review of Books* 1 (6 February 1964): 4-5. Reprinted with permission from *The New York Review of Books*. Copyright (c) 1964 Nyrev, Inc.
"Cheever's Yankee Heritage" by Cynthia Ozick. Copyright (c) 1964 by The Antioch Review, Inc. First appeared in the *Antioch Review*, Vol. 24, No. 2 (Summer 1964). Reprinted by permission of the Editors.
"Tradition and Desecration: The Wapshot Novels of John Cheever" by Kenneth C. Mason, *Arizona Quarterly* 43 (Autumn 1987): 231-50. Reprinted by permission.
"Where Life Is but a Dream-World" by John W. Aldridge. From *New York Herald Tribune*, 25 October 1964, pp. 3, 19; (c) 1964, New York Herald

Tribune Inc. All rights reserved. Reprinted by permission of the author.

"Domestic Manners" by Frederick C. Crews, *The New York Review of Books* 3 (22 October 1964): 7-8. Reprinted with permission from *The New York Review of Books*. Copyright (c) 1964 Nyrev, Inc.

"Change Is Always for the Worse" by David Segal, *Commonweal* 81 (4 December 1964): 362-63. Reprinted by permission.

"John Cheever's Surreal Vision and the Bridge of Language" by Wayne Stengel. Reprinted from *Twentieth Century Literature* 33 (Summer 1987): 223-33, by permission.

"You Wouldn't Believe It" by Anatole Broyard, *The New Republic* 160 (26 April 1969): 36-37. Reprinted by permission of *The New Republic*, (c) 1969, The New Republic, Inc.

"A Grand Gatherum of Some Late 20th-Century American Weirdos" by Benjamin DeMott, *New York Times Book Review*, 27 April 1969, pp. 1, 40-41. Copyright (c) 1969 by The New York Times Company. Reprinted by permission.

"Salvation in the Suburbs" by Charles Nicol, *Atlantic Monthly* 223 (May 1969): 96, 98. Reprinted by permission.

"Cheever's People: The Retreat from Chaos" by Joyce Carol Oates, *Chicago Tribune Book World*, 20 April 1969, pp. 1, 3. Copyright (c) 1969 by Ontario Review, Inc. Reprinted by permission.

"Witchcraft in Bullet Park" by John Gardner, *New York Times Book Review*, 24 October 1971, pp. 2, 24. Reprinted by permission of Georges Borchardt, Inc. Copyright (c) 1971 by John Gardner.

"Victories of Happy Madness" by Charles Bazerman, *The Nation* 217 (10 September 1973): 218-19. Reprinted by permission of *The Nation* magazine/The Nation Co., Inc., (c) 1973.

"Cheever to Roth to Malamud" by John Leonard, *Atlantic Monthly* 231 (June 1973): 112-14. Reprinted by permission.

"The World of Apples" by D. Keith Mano, *Washington Post Book World*, 1 July 1973, pp. 1, 10; (c) 1973 The Washington Post. Reprinted with permission.

Review of *The World of Apples* by Robert Phillips, *Commonweal* 99 (30 November 1973): 245-47. Reprinted by permission.

"Fiction Chronicle" by William Peden, *Sewanee Review* 82 (Fall 1974): 719-21. Reprinted by permission of the author.

"Escape Within Walls" by Hope Hale Davis, *The New Leader* 60 (25 April 1977): 14-15. Reprinted with permission of The New Leader, 1977. Copyright (c) the American Labor Conference on International Affairs, Inc.

"Falconer" by Joan Didion, first appeared in the *New York Times Book Review*, 6 March 1977, pp. 1, 22, 24. Copyright 1977 by Joan Didion. Reprinted by permission of the author.

"Cheers for Cheever" by Janet Groth, *Commonweal* 104 (10 June 1977): 374-

76. Reprinted by permission.
"An Airy Insubstantial World" by Joyce Carol Oates, *Ontario Review* 7 (Fall-Winter 1977): 99-101. Copyright (c) 1977 by Ontario Review, Inc. Reprinted by permission.
"Up the River" by Robert Towers, *The New York Review of Books* 24 (17 March 1977): 3-6. Reprinted with permission from *The New York Review of Books*. Copyright (c) 1977 Nyrev, Inc.
"Two Good Fictions" by Geoffrey Wolff, *New Times*, 1 April 1977, pp. 63-64. Reprinted by permission of the author.
"The Moral Structure of Cheever's *Falconer*" by Glen M. Johnson, *Studies in American Fiction* 9 (Spring 1981): 21-31. Reprinted by permission.
"Literary Waifs" by Pearl K. Bell. Reprinted from *Commentary* 67 (February 1979) by permission; all rights reserved.
"The Cheerless World of John Cheever" by Isa Kapp, *The New Leader* 61 (11 September 1978): 16-17. Reprinted with permission of The New Leader, 1977. Copyright (c) the American Labor Conference on International Affairs, Inc.
"The World of WASP" by Perry Meisel first appeared in *Partisan Review*, Vol. 47, No. 3, 1980. Copyright 1980 by Perry Meisel.
"Light Touch" by Robert Towers, *The New York Review of Books* 25 (9 November 1978): 3-4. Reprinted with permission from *The New York Review of Books*. Copyright (c) 1978 Nyrev, Inc.
"Chance-taker" by Robert M. Adams, *The New York Review of Books* 29 (29 April 1982): 8. Reprinted with permission from *The New York Review of Books*. Copyright (c) 1982 Nyrev, Inc.
"Lonely Nomads" by Ann Hulbert, *The New Republic* 173 (31 March 1982): 42-45. Reprinted by permission of *The New Republic*, (c) 1982, The New Republic, Inc.
"Seeking Paradise" by George W. Hunt, *America* 146 (27 March 1982): 238-40. Reprinted by permission.
"The Optimistic Imagination: John Cheever's *Oh What A Paradise It Seems*" by Michael Byrne, *CEA Critic* 45 (March & May 1983): 38-42. Reprinted by permission.
"Grossness and Aspiration" by Ann Hulbert, *The New Republic* 200 (6 March 1989): 35-38. Reprinted by permission of *The New Republic*, (c) 1989, The New Republic, Inc.
"Our Lives Are Not Well-Told Stories" by Robert Kiely, *New York Times Book Review*, 18 December 1988, pp. 12-13. Copyright (c) 1988 by The New York Times Company. Reprinted by permission.
"The Cheever Chronicle" by Ted Solotaroff, *The Nation* 253 (18 November 1991): 616-20. Reprinted by permission of *The Nation* magazine/The Nation Co., Inc., (c) 1991.
"Cheever on the Rocks" by John Updike, first appeared as "The Waspshot Chronicle" in *The New Republic* 205 (2 December 1991): 36-39. Copyright 1991 by John Updike. Reprinted by permission.

From "The Enormous Radio" by John Cheever. Copyright (c) 1947 by John Cheever, reprinted with the permission of Wylie, Aitken & Stone, Inc.
From *The Wapshot Chronicle* by John Cheever. Copyright (c) 1957 by John Cheever, reprinted with the permission of Wylie, Aitken & Stone, Inc.
From "A Vision of the World" by John Cheever. Copyright (c) 1962 by John Cheever, reprinted with the permission of Wylie, Aitken & Stone, Inc.
From *The Wapshot Scandal* by John Cheever. Copyright (c) 1964 by John Cheever, reprinted with the permission of Wylie, Aitken & Stone, Inc.
From *Bullet Park* by John Cheever. Copyright (c) 1967, 1968, 1969 by John Cheever. Reprinted by permission of Alfred A. Knopf, Inc., and reprinted with the permission of Wylie, Aitken & Stone, Inc.
From *Falconer* by John Cheever. Copyright (c) 1975, 1977 by John Cheever. Reprinted by permission of Alfred A. Knopf, Inc., and reprinted with the permission of Wylie, Aitken & Stone, Inc.
From *Oh What a Paradise It Seems* by John Cheever. Copyright (c) 1982 by John Cheever. Reprinted by permission of Alfred A. Knopf, Inc., and reprinted with the permission of Wylie, Aitken & Stone, Inc.
From *The Letters of John Cheever*, edited by Benjamin Cheever. Copyright (c) 1988 by Benjamin Cheever. Reprinted by permission of Simon and Schuster, Inc. and International Creative Management, Inc.
From *The Journals of John Cheever* by John Cheever. Copyright (c) 1990, 1991 by Mary Cheever, Susan Cheever, Benjamin Cheever, and Federico Cheever. Reprinted by permission of Alfred A. Knopf. Inc., and reprinted with the permission of Wylie, Aitken & Stone, Inc.

Every reasonable effort has been made to trace the owners of copyright materials in this book, but in some instances this has proven impossible. The author and publisher will be glad to receive information leading to more complete acknowledgments in subsequent printings of the book and in the meantime extend their apologies for any omissions.

In memory of my father and mother,

Philip and Bridget Bosha

Contents

Contents

Series Foreword

Critical Responses in Arts and Letters is designed to present a documentary history of highlights in the critical reception to the body of work of writers and artists and to individual works that are generally considered to be of major importance. The focus of each volume in this series is basically historical. The introductions to each volume are themselves brief histories of the critical response an author, artist, or individual work has received. This response is then further illustrated by reprinting a strong representation of the major critical reviews and articles that have collectively produced the author's, artist's, or work's critical reputation.

The scope of *Critical Responses in Arts and Letters* knows no chronological or geographical boundaries. Volumes under preparation include studies of individuals from around the world and in both contemporary and historical periods.

Each volume is the work of an individual editor, who surveys the entire body of criticism on a single author, artist, or work. The editor then selects the best material to depict the critical response received by an author or artist over his/her entire career. Documents produced by the author or artist may also be included when the editor finds that they are necessary to a full understanding of the materials at hand. In circumstances where previous, isolated volumes of criticism on a particular individual or work exist, the editor carefully selects material that better reflects the nature and directions of the critical response over time.

In addition to the introduction and the documentary section, the editor of each volume is free to solicit new essays on areas that may not have been adequately dealt with in previous criticism. Also, for volumes on living writers and artists, new interviews may be included, again at the discretion of the volume's editor. The volumes also provide a supplementary bibliography and are fully indexed.

While each volume in *Critical Responses in Arts and Letters* is unique, it is also hoped that in combination they form a useful, documentary history of the critical response to the arts, and one that can be easily and profitably employed by students and scholars.

Cameron Northouse

Preface

While this project has been the work of one editor, it could not have been completed without the help of others. Even though I had copies of a good deal of the vast corpus of Cheever criticism when I began this book, I am indebted to Hajime Wada and Professor Hiroshi Ishikawa of the library of Kawamura Gakuen Woman's University, Chiba, Japan, and Hisaharu Yoshida of the library of the University of the Sacred Heart, Tokyo, for their help in securing a number of interlibrary loans. I am also grateful to Professor Ronald R. Janssen of Hofstra University, Kuniko Koseki, Dr. Rhoda Sirlin, and Philip J. Bosha, whose efforts to locate reference material for me were indispensible.

For graciously granting me reprint permissions, I would like to thank the following authors: John W. Aldridge, Pearl K. Bell, Joan Didion, Irving Howe, George W. Hunt, Perry Meisel, Joyce Carol Oates, Cynthia Ozick, William Peden, John Updike, and Geoffrey Wolff.

Thanks also to the following representatives of authors or publishers: Diana M. Daniels, Edgar A. Dryden, Robert S. Fogarty, Michael Greaves, Diane Kraft, Ann Leopold, Lourdes Lopez, Bridget Love, Marion Magrid, William McBrien, James Nagel, Josh Neufield, Laura Obolensky, Michael J. O'Shea, Barbara Shapiro, Raymond Shapiro, Raymond Smith, Albert Stadler, Kevin J. Sullivan, Marcia Taylor, Amanda Urban, John J. Virtes, Rob Walker, Peggy Walsh, and Jeff Zelmanski.

I am grateful to four Cheever scholars for their contributions to this volume, all of which are published here for the first time, with their permission: Professor Samuel Coale of Wheaton College and Professor Robert A. Morace of Daemon College, who wrote original essays expressly for this volume; Professor Lynne M. Waldeland of Northern Illinois University, who updated and expanded a paper she presented at the MLA Convention in 1982 for original publication here; and Robert G. Collins, who recently left a long-time professorial post at the University of Ottawa (Canada) to devote full-time to writing, has generously permitted me to include in this volume the text of an interview he conducted with John Cheever less than a year before the author's death. This interview is now, as Professor Collins writes, "almost certainly the last to be publicly heard."

I would like to give special thanks to this Series' adviser, Cameron Northouse, whose suggestions and advice have been most helpful and appreciated. My thanks also go to my editors at Greenwood Press, Marilyn Brownstein, Ann LeStrange and, especially, Maureen Melino, with whom I have worked closely since the outset, and who has helped me span the great geographic distances that separated us through our, at times, daily fax correspondence.

Finally, I owe an enormous debt to my wife, Michiyo, who has helped me in so many aspects of this project, including the tasks of proofreading and indexing, and who has consistently encouraged and supported my efforts throughout my career.

While credit is due to all these and more, any errors or omissions in this book remain entirely my own.

                                        Francis J. Bosha
                                        Chiba, Japan

Introduction

In the course of a writing career that spanned more than half a century, from 1930 to his death in 1982, John Cheever published nearly 200 short stories--including a number which rank among the finest in American literature--as well as five novels. He received such accolades as the National Book Award, the Howells Medal and, late in life, the Pulitzer Prize, culminating what had been a slowly but steadily growing literary reputation.

One factor which seems to have delayed early serious critical response to Cheever was that some 121 of his stories were published in the *New Yorker*, between 1935 and 1981. From virtually the outset of his career Cheever's name was associated with that of the *New Yorker*, which regularly set his fiction in its narrow columns amid the droll cartoons and (as one critic put it) the advertisements "for solid gold taxi whistles and for the sports jacket that will really make you feel casual."[1] As a result, there developed a concensus among certain reviewers that Cheever was "a *New Yorker* writer": his work, while clever, was light and tended toward the cynical or satirical.[2] In the words of *The New Republic*'s Ann Hulbert, writing six years after Cheever's death, his reputation suffered from a form of "guilt by association" (p. 200). It was to take time, then, for more penetrating reviewers and critics to see beyond the glossy pages to his seriousness of purpose and celebratory vision of the world. Eventually, John Updike would write of the "radiance" of Cheever's fiction, and Saul Bellow would praise Cheever's "power of transformation, his power to take the elements given and work them into something new and far deeper than they were at the outset" (p. 190).

Indeed, for more than half of his career, the critical response to John Cheever's work was often so cursory and dismissive that John Aldridge felt compelled to point out as late as 1964 that Cheever was "one of the most grievously underdiscussed important writers we have at the present time" (p. 77).

Yet, while Cheever's work may have been "underdiscussed," it was never neglected, beginning with the publication of the thirty-year-old author's first book, *The Way Some People Live* (1943). By far the most positive--and, it turns out, prescient--critical reaction to this collection of short stories was that of Struthers Burt in the *Saturday Review*. Burt, himself the author of a number of short stories, saw, in Cheever's ability to capture the drama and "universal importance" in "ordinary events and people" (p. 3), a potential to distinguish himself in the novel and the drama--genres at which Cheever would later, and to varying degrees,[3] try his hand. Burt's enthusiasm for this collection, which struck him as "the best volume of short stories I have come across in a long while," was tempered by two warnings: Cheever should be careful not to develop the affectations of "an especial style . . . and a deliberate casualness and simplicity" (p. 5).

Scarcely a week earlier, however, *The New Republic*, which had publish- ed Cheever's first story, "Expelled," in 1930 (inspired by the author's own expulsion from high school at the age of seventeen), ran a review by the novelist Weldon Kees which was among the earliest to cite what would become the recurrent criticism of Cheever as a *New Yorker* writer. That magazine, Kees maintained, hobbled its contributors' creativity, since it "demands a patina of triviality spread over those themes and situations which its policy allows." He praised the non-*New Yorker* stories--which accounted for only six of the thirty in this collection--yet he felt that Cheever accomplished little more than "episodic notation and minor perceptive effects" (p. 7).

Between these two poles fell the other contemporary reviews. The *New York Times'* William DuBois attributed the stories' "peculiar epicene detachment, and facile despair" to the *New Yorker*'s influence. He also contended that the characters shared too much of a "tortured similari- ty,"[4] while Diana Trilling saw them as being, simply, "inarticulate" (p. 8). Mark Schorer echoed Burt's view of Cheever as being "among the most promising"[5] writers of his generation, and praised his "eloquence" and ability to achieve a tight focus, whereas Rose Feld approached Kees' position. Writing in the *New York Herald Tribune*, Feld maintained that the stories, many of which were less than ten pages in length, were "interesting as fragments" but lacked "artistic fulfillment" (p. 5).

Cheever's reaction to Feld was that she didn't have "any idea of what I'm writing about."[6] As for DuBois and the rest, he observed that "the Times is very funny. But all in all--even though they don't like me--the reviewers seem to be very diligent and earnest people, anxious to help a gloomy young writer onto the right path, and to safeguard the investments of their readers" (*Letters*, 101).

It should be noted that when he compiled sixty-one stories for his Pulitzer Prize-winning *The Stories of John Cheever* in 1978, Cheever

chose not to include anything from this first collection, perhaps
indicating, as his biographer Scott Donaldson suggested, that "no critic
could have been harder on this first book of stories than Cheever
himself."[7] As Cheever himself remarked to an interviewer in 1979 about
the excluded stories, "they were embarrassingly immature."[8]

Cheever's second book, *The Enormous Radio* (1953), is distinguished by
its title story, which may well be his most widely read piece, and also
by "Goodbye, My Brother," in which he continued to develop the dark
theme of extreme fraternal love/hate relationships he had pursued as
early as 1937, in "The Brothers," and which would reach its apogee in
the fratricide in his 1977 novel, *Falconer*. Yet the fact that the
fourteen stories that make up this collection all originally appeared in
the *New Yorker* was not lost on its reviewers. Consequently, the
critical response to *The Enormous Radio* was largely negative, and Arthur
Mizener's reaction was indicative. To him, Cheever, quite simply, was
"not a writer of any great talent" (p. 10), just a skilled mannerist, "a
clever short-story manufacturer" (p. 11). William DuBois gave Cheever
the backhanded compliment of being a "top-drawer" contributor to the *New
Yorker* who epitomized the magazine's "brilliant, bitter essence."[9]
Cheever's Upper East Side milieu was to DuBois "amazingly narrow" and
resulted in a restricted range of "chillingly" drawn characters who
struck DuBois as "emotional dwarfs." These characters, added Taliaferro
Boatright, were all "trapped" (pp. 9-10) and "cut from the same
pattern--the middle-class, upper middle-brow, white collar people" (p.
9). Others, such as Paul Pickrel in the *Yale Review*, identified
Cheever's tone as "a kind of wistful humanism that has become intel-
lectually shabby-genteel; a kind of whimsical, unassertive, astringently
sentimental faith in the ability of people to assert their humanity."[10]

William Peden came to the defense of not only Cheever but also the *New
Yorker*, arguing against the existence of any "magic formula known as the
'*New Yorker* story'" (p. 12). Peden also became the first of several
critics who would lament what they saw--even this early in Cheever's
career--as the fact of Cheever being "one of the most undervalued
American short story writers" (p. 13).

Years later, in several interviews, Cheever himself was quick to rebut
the contention that he wrote stories expressly for the *New Yorker*,
observing, on one occasion, "one didn't write for *The New Yorker*"
(*Conversations*, 74). He amplified this view in 1977: "I never wrote *for*
The New Yorker, and I never stopped writing for *The New Yorker*--they
bought my stories" (*Conversations*, 123).

Commentary's Morris Freedman, however, did move beyond the *New Yorker*
fixation, and instead set Cheever's achievement in larger context: he
saw the author as "a product of the Hebraic New England conscience,
implacable as a Kafkaesque judge." Yet, Freedman found Cheever capable
of transcending "the bleakness of Kafka."[11]

The lukewarm reception of *The Enormous Radio* led Cheever to tell his friend Malcolm Cowley: "The fact that no one found the story collection worth while reviewing has reaffirmed the importance of writing a novel . . . " (*Letters*, 162). Within four years, he would do precisely that, and *The Wapshot Chronicle* appeared in early 1957.

Just a few months before that debut, in December, 1956, Cheever, along with his *New Yorker* colleagues Jean Stafford, Daniel Fuchs and William Maxwell, brought out a book--"somewhere between a collection and an anthology" (Donaldson, 155)--they called *Stories*. It contained fifteen pieces, four of them by Cheever.

The few reviews the book received were brief but uniformly positive. While *Time* considered Stafford "the biggest name"[12] of the quartet, Cheever was described elsewhere as "entertaining,"[13] and as a writer of "deft psychoanalytic stories which sunder the suburbanites where they wake or sleep."[14] William Peden, consistently an admirer of Cheever, found that there was "no finer present-day American writer of short fiction than John Cheever."[15]

The following month, in January, 1957, Cheever was elected to the National Institute of Arts and Letters, establishing him "among the nation's literary elite" (Donaldson, 156).

Two months later, in March, 1957, *The Wapshot Chronicle* was published. Maxwell Geismar's *New York Times* review was representative of the critical response to Cheever's first novel: it was "not quite a novel." Its parts did not "quite hang together, and the story as a whole becomes rather fragmentary and episodic. . . . a series of related 'sketches.'" Furthermore, it "hovers on the edge of a more serious purpose" (p. 23). The view of Cheever as being unable to write a cohesive novel would be voiced with each subsequent novel by a succession of reviewers. As Carlos Baker put it, "architectonics" (p. 20) was not Cheever's forte. He also felt the novel was "gamy" (p. 19), though David Stevenson took issue with that judgment, preferring to see the book's sexual aspect as illustrative of the author's "wry and compassionate view of human behavior" (p. 26). Others who shared this positive view and even noted the celebratory aspect of Cheever's writing included, perhaps appropriately enough, the *New Yorker*'s Maeve Brennan, who saw *The Wapshot Chronicle* as celebrating "mortal love."[16] Also, Joan Didion, writing a few years later, described Cheever's fiction of this period as "a celebration of life" (p. 38). William Esty ingenuously defended the work against the Geismar/Baker charge of structural weakness by noting of *The Wapshot Chronicle* that perhaps neither was *The Fall* a novel, "but who has snubbed Camus for that?" (p. 20) Still, another recurrent critical theme had been established: Cheever's characters could "shine in individual episodes," according to *The New Republic*'s Donald Malcolm, but they seemed "to stagger at times under the burden of supporting a full-length novel" (p. 25).

Writing four years later, Ihab Hassan took Cheever's measure and found his characters to be mere "caricatures" who move "in a cartoonist's world."[17] His Wapshots "show life to be at worst a kind of whimsical Puritan purgatory." However, later criticism found more to praise than pillory. Richard Rupp[18], writing in 1970, returned to the celebration motif which he found runs through Cheever's first novel. In 1980, James O'Hara contended that "in the sense in which dreams have meaning and shape as well as substance, *The Wapshot Chronicle* follows a definite internal logic."[19]

Although Cheever told an interviewer in 1976 that because he was in Italy, he "didn't see the reviews and wouldn't know of Maxwell Geismar's disapproval for nearly ten years" (*Conversations*, 97), a notation in his journal of this period when he was in Italy tersely states: "The reviews come, but this is a nothing."[20] Another, slightly later entry, provides an affecting insight: "I dream about the White House. It is after supper. . . . Ike and Mamie are alone. Mamie is reading the Washington *Star*. Ike is reading 'The Wapshot Chronicle'" (*Journals*, 84).

Despite its mixed critical reception, *The Wapshot Chronicle* did earn Cheever the National Book Award for fiction in 1958, selected over such contenders as Bernard Malamud's *The Assistant* and James Gould Cozzens' *By Love Possessed*.

In September, 1958 Cheever brought out his third collection of stories, *The Housebreaker of Shady Hill*. The locus of these stories shifted from Manhattan to the New York suburbs, and this became the setting with which Cheever would thereafter be closely associated, especially in the eyes of his reviewers. Some, in fact, would try to outdo each other in giving Cheever what struck them as apt sobriquets, and among the earliest was Richard Gilman, who coined "Dante of Suburbia" to describe Cheever's "prophetic role" in calling "suburbia to repentence" (p. 29). Gilman, however, chided Cheever for the "adolescent values" of his characters, and he felt that Cheever was, at bottom, "a sentimentalist" (p. 30). Irving Howe took this line of thought further to render one of the harshest judgments: Cheever was a "toothless Thurber, he connives in the cowardice of contemporary life" (p. 33). Yet, such notable stories in this collection as "The Country Husband," "The Sorrows of Gin," and "O Youth and Beauty!" received scant contemporary critical attention.[21]

In March, 1961 came *Some People, Places and Things That Will Not Appear in My Next Novel*, which a surprising number of critics took literally as Cheever's declaration of independence from relying on certain character types. Various facets of the dark tone underlying many of these stories (which, as it turned out, anticipated that of *The Wapshot Scandal*, which Cheever was then writing), became a focal point for a number of critics. In Melvin Maddocks' view, Cheever wrote "haunted rhetoric,"[22] and the result was "as if Marquand had somehow been crossed with Kafka, and the standard New Yorker flavor of a twist of lemon suddenly interrupted by a mouthful of ashes." In Frank Warnke's phrase, too, Cheever was "a haunted chronicler of the impingements of an inexplicable malevolence on ordinary life" (p. 41), and David Boroff saw Cheever as a "Gothic writer whose mind is poised at the edge of terror."[23] Beyond that, reviewers such as David Ray felt Cheever to be an "enlightened Puritan"[24] and the collection a work "of the first magnitude." Joan Didion took the opportunity in her review to articulate the first serious estimation of Cheever's women characters whom, she found, were "disinherited . . . [living] in that trackless country of lost money and lost families" (p. 37). Gene Baro proved to be among the least sympathetic of this book's reviewers. He maintained that Cheever's "virtuoso performance" was indicative of his lack of "intellectual passion or an enlarged vision of reality" (p. 36), a contention which renewed the old charge of Cheever's lack of seriousness.

Cheever's second novel was *The Wapshot Scandal*, a sombre sequel to the celebratory *Chronicle*. Soon after it was published in January, 1964, it enjoyed a more favorable and more deeply considered response than did its predecessor. It also went on to win the Howells Medal as the best novel of 1960-1965. Front page reviews in the *New York Times Book Review,* the *New York Herald Tribune* and the *Chicago Sunday Tribune* were uniformly effusive, and saw this novel as having a "mythic element,"[25] and Cheever as being capable of understanding suffering without moralizing. Glenway Wescott went as far as to call Cheever an "existentialist" and *The Wapshot Scandal* as "visionary."[26] William Barrett, too, saw a visionary quality in that Cheever had moved from realism "into the fantastic and grotesque," becoming a "latter-day Nathaniel Hawthorne."[27] Both George Greene's review and George Garrett's essay (the longest and most fully developed of the contemporary responses), disagreed with those who had seen Cheever as a whimsical writer: as Garrett put it, "Cheever is an author who must be taken quite seriously."[28] Furthermore, *The Wapshot Scandal* was Cheever's "best book" to date, and his characters were not at all the caricatures that Hassan had earlier decried. Elizabeth Hardwick tempered her praise, in part due to her dismay at the novel's "unavoidable bits of Our-Townism" (p. 54). She also added that if Cheever "has a master, it is probably F. Scott Fitzgerald" (p. 56).

But on the two significant points of structure and substance there emerged disagreement. Hilary Corke spoke most forcefully for those, such as Cynthia Ozick and Benjamin DeMott, who maintained that yet again Cheever had written an episodic novel, the whole of which, in Corke's phrase, was "fatally flawed" (p. 44). As for substance, DeMott and Ozick took the position opposite Greene and Garrett by asserting that Cheever was a "minor" writer. Ozick detailed her position in *two* reviews of this novel, criticizing Cheever for recording "not societies

. . . but vapid dreams and pageants of desire" (p. 56). To her, Cheever's nostalgic evocation of the fictional village of St. Botolphs was fraudulent and baseless because such a place never existed: "Nobody can inherit it because nobody had a grandfather who lived there." Thus, "on this myth . . . Cheever as social critic finally crashes."[29] However, Joan Didion, in her review "The Way We Live Now"--a title allusive to Cheever's first book-- had no problem with Cheever's mythic port town, seeing this "twilight world of the old American middle class" as indeed being "a lost world."[30]

Cheever was all too well aware of the frequent criticism of the structural weakness of his novels and noted in his journal in 1963: "A great many people felt that the 'Chronicle' was not a novel, and the same thing is bound to be said about this [The Wapshot Scandal], perhaps more strongly" (Journals, p. 179). It is interesting to note that whereas Ozick found St. Botolphs a fraud and a contributing factor to Cheever's "minor" status, other critics would chide Cheever for abandoning that village setting in Bullet Park (1969). Cheever addressed this ironic turn of events in a 1976 interview: "Did I tell you about the review of Bullet Park in Ramparts? It said I missed greatness by having left St. Botolphs. Had I stayed, as Faulkner did in Oxford, I would have probably been as great as Faulkner. But I made the mistake of leaving this place, which, of course, never existed at all. It was so odd to be told to go back to a place that was a complete fiction" (Conversations, 101).

Soon after The Wapshot Scandal appeared, Time featured Cheever on its March 27, 1964 cover. Considering the alliterative appeal of the name of the Hudson River town Cheever lived in, the editors called him "Ovid in Ossining" and concluded that "at bottom he is a New England moralist."[31] However, appearing on Time's cover was to many intellectuals even more damning than writing for the New Yorker. While George Garrett found the publicity a "mixed blessing," John Aldridge saw it, along with Cheever's 1958 National Book Award, as being perhaps "the best conceivable reason for withholding" serious critical attention. Those two magazines, in Aldridge's view, "have helped to obstruct his breakthrough into genuine excellence and serious reputation" (pp. 79-80). But to Cheever, his friend Alwyn Lee's Time cover piece, "in its discretion, its cunning, rendered me as a serious and likable person when I could, on the strength of the evidence, be described as a fat slob enjoying an extraordinary run of luck" (Journals, 191).

Then, in October, 1964, another collection of stories, The Brigadier and the Golf Widow, was published. It contained one of his best stories, "The Swimmer," as well as "The Angel of the Bridge," "The Ocean," and several of his Italian stories. As with Cheever's 1961 collection, the haunted, nightmarish quality of some of the pieces caught the reviewers' attention. Adrian Mitchell, writing in the New

York Times Book Review, covered nearly the identical ground as John Gardner would in 1971: to both, Cheever's work said "a good deal about witchcraft, mainly in . . . Bullet Park."[32] The tone of various pieces ranged, for Mitchell's *Times* colleague Orville Prescott, from "only melancholy" to one of "dismay" to the "definitely grim."[33] However, the "horror" that David Segal found "beneath the surface" was lessened by its having been "recollected in detachment." Thus, he wrote, Cheever's stories "belong where they are usually found, in a thin column in the New Yorker" (p. 84).

Others, such as Aldridge, Frederick Crews and George Elliott were vexed by what seemed the fact (as Aldridge put it) that Cheever "does not yet disturb us enough" (p. 81). Crews could not "take this Miniver Cheever seriously" (p. 82), and Elliott returned to the criticism of Cheever as being merely whimsical, even though he made the questionable decision of using "The Swimmer" to illustrate his point.[34] Yet, Crews did offer a sympathetic rebuttal to one of the older charges against Cheever: "if we are tempted to think of him as a *New Yorker* writer, it is worth remembering that to a great extent he has given *The New Yorker* its fictional tone for twenty years, not vice-versa" (p. 82).

Meanwhile, Cheever had begun to receive serious academic attention: in 1963 Frederick Bracher published his essay, "John Cheever and Comedy," and the following year, "John Cheever: A Vision of the World," in which he argued (among other points) that Cheever's work is characterized by "moral earnestness."[35]

In April, 1969 Cheever's third novel, *Bullet Park*, was published. It had been five years since his last novel appeared and, with both Wapshot novels earning prestigious awards, expectations of a favorable reception for *Bullet Park* were "very high," according to Susan Cheever.[36]

The critical response to Cheever's departure from St. Botolphs was disappointing, however, with the most severe and damaging criticism being leveled by Benjamin DeMott on the front page of the *New York Times Book Review*. To DeMott, this novel was not "a first-rate addition to the man's *oeuvre*." Structurally, he found it "broken-backed, [with] parts tacked together." In addition, the book was plagued by "carelessness, lax composition, perfunctoriness"; yet, "most important . . . [was] the problem of story style vs. novel style" (p. 99): Cheever could handle the short sprint of the story but could not go the distance required by the longer form.

Other negative reviews followed, but none had quite the impact of DeMott's. As Cheever remarked a few years later, "The manuscript was received enthusiastically everywhere, but then Benjamin DeMott dumped on it in the *Times*, everyone picked up their marbles and ran home" (*Conversations*, 97). Cheever also wrote a friend on October 3, 1969 about the reason for the harsh reception: "I may have made a mistake in using a suburb as a social metaphor" (*Letters*, 277). Pearl K. Bell joined in the negative reaction to the book, finding "something strangely misguided and botched, fundamentally wrongheaded" about it, and concluded it was attributable to its author's lack of a point of view.[37]

Still, a number of reviewers were more appreciative though restrained in their praise. Anatole Broyard found Cheever "almost helplessly carried away by . . . his imagination" (p. 95). He also felt that Cheever was "determined to be surprising or original, even at the cost of incredulity" (p. 97). In a journal entry from 1972, Cheever commented: "I read 'Bullet Park,' which is an extract of my most intimate feelings, and wonder why it should have antagonized Broyard" (*Journals*, 282).

Joyce Carol Oates' front page review in the *Chicago Tribune Book World* appeared one week before DeMott's and, while she felt the work was "really not a novel at all," she did praise it for being "a series of eerie, sometimes beautiful, sometimes overwrought vignettes" (p. 109). John Leonard, whose review appeared in the *New York Times* two days after DeMott's, wrote: "'Bullet Park' is John Cheever's deepest, most challenging book."[38] Still, such varied critics as Guy Davenport, Charles Nicol, and Warren Sloat found the book's ending too implausible to accept.[39] Charles Shapiro's review in *The Nation* also cited what appeared to him as structural problems, but still maintained that *Bullet Park* was a "beautiful book" in which Cheever went "beyond satire to truth."[40] John Updike, writing in the London *Sunday Times* five months after the novel appeared, defended the book's "broad streak of the fantastic" and found that it succeeded "as a slowly revolving mobile of marvellously poeticized moments."[41]

In a somewhat belated effort to redress the negative response, John Gardner offered a reconsideration of *Bullet Park*, in the *New York Times Book Review* in 1971, and forthrightly declared that those who attacked or dismissed Cheever over this novel were "dead wrong" (p. 110). He instead chose to explore *Bullet Park* as a work of religious affirmation. Later, other critics would take a similar approach in discussing Cheever's final two novels.

The World of Apples, which appeared in the spring of 1973, was Cheever's first collection of short fiction in nearly a decade. Despite his reputation as a *New Yorker* writer, from 1964 to his death only eleven stories were accepted by that magazine. As a result, six out of the ten stories that make up the *The World of Apples* originally appeared in publications as diverse as *The Saturday Evening Post*, *Esquire* and *Playboy*. The warm response that met *The World of Apples* stands in marked contrast to the nadir of critical opinion that *Bullet Park* received.

One of the most consistently enthusiastic reviewers of Cheever's work, John Leonard, sought to replace the Dante or Ovid comparison with one that finally caught on: "Chekhov of the exurbs." He furthermore called Cheever "our best living writer of short stories" (p. 125). Larry Woiwode, in the *New York Times Book Review*, agreed with Leonard, and noted that Cheever "shares Chekhov's gentility, ingenuous warmth, humor, universality and all-seeing eye for the . . . weaknesses of human-kind."[42] For D. Keith Mano, no writer since Proust had been so concern-ed with memory (p. 129). Nelson Algren, following a line of thought Morris Freedman developed twenty years earlier, wrote that Cheever "shares with Hawthorne a heritage of Puritan demons, as well as the ne-cessity of exorcising them thru writing."[43] Another novelist, Geoffrey Wolff, saw that this new collection brought Cheever's career, as he in-dicated in the title of his *Los Angeles Times* review, "back in focus."[44]

Less effusive though nonetheless positive response came from both John Wain[45] and Thomas R. Edwards,[46] who considered the title story to be the best piece in the book, and focussed their reviews almost exclusively on it. Yet, Ronald DeFeo found that, compared to the *The Brigadier and the Golf Widow*, the present collection "seems rather tired,"[47] and Robert Phillips added that this work was "as important to the Cheever canon as a carbon copy is to its bright original" (p. 131).

Later in 1973, Cheever was honored by being elected to the American Academy of Arts and Letters. In his nominating petition a few months earlier Robert Penn Warren had written, "In a series of stories unsurpassed in his generation and in his excellent novels, John Cheever has reported faithfully a segment of modern America and at the same time has created a world that embodies his personal vision" (Donaldson, 269).

If *Bullet Park* struck some critics as a departure for Cheever from the world of the Wapshot novels, the prison setting of *Falconer*--which was published in March, 1977--was more radically so. It is little wonder that Cheever wrote in his journal after this novel had gone to press: "The strain of waiting for the publication, I mean the reception, of 'Falconer' . . . is not too difficult to bear, but it is, nonetheless, a strain. So the most you can do is fill in the time" (*Journals*, 327).

Nonetheless, the critical response to this fourth novel was, by and large, far more favorable than it was to *Bullet Park*. Also, whereas *Time* had profiled Cheever in the wake of his second novel's appearance, *Newsweek* featured him on its cover of March 14, 1977, accompanied by an interview which had been conducted by his daughter Susan, and an article by Walter Clemons which hailed *Falconer* as both a masterpiece and his "best sustained long narrative."[48] This opinion was later seconded by Elizabeth Hardwick, writing two years after Cheever's death, despite her overall estimation that he was "a disappointing novelist."[49]

Joan Didion's front page review in the *New York Times Book Review* saw *Falconer*'s Farragut, of all Cheever's "characters who have suffered nostalgia," to be the first to realize that the home for which he longs is not on any map. This novel is thus "a meditation on the abstraction Cheever has always called 'home'"(p. 141). Others, such as *Commentary*'s John Romano and *Commonweal*'s Janet Groth, also welcomed Cheever's concern for redemption and "spiritual renewal"[50] in this "stunning meditation on all the forms of confinement" (p. 142).

Geoffrey Wolff viewed *Falconer* as part of a pattern of Cheever's later work which "inclined increasingly toward the odd perspectives and dimensions of the dream state" (p. 152). This novel also demonstrated how far its author had come, in Wolff's view, from the genteel world of the *New Yorker*. John Leonard, too, saw that "Shady Hill has been reversed, turned inside out,"[51] which is akin to D. Keith Mano's observation that this novel "is Cheever upside down."[52]

Hope Hale Davis considered the homosexual aspect of the novel and detected a message she had seen implicit in Cheever's earlier work. She suspected, given the current trend in "'alternative life styles,'" that "Cheever, in his own sly way, may be offering one" (p. 137). Robert Towers, too, commented on this issue, noting that in *Falconer* there was a marked shift from the earlier work, where "the straight characters invariably respond [to homosexuality] with fear or distaste" (p. 151).

It should also be noted, in this context, that three years earlier, in November, 1974, Cheever had published "The Leaves, the Lion-Fish, and the Bear" in *Esquire*[53], which included an explicitly homosexual vignette. Furthermore, according to Dennis Coates, when he asked Cheever about the "homosexual strains" in his fiction, Cheever responded, "It's always been there, for all the world to see" (Donaldson, 281). The subsequent posthumous revelations by Susan Cheever in *Home Before Dark*, as well as those found in the *Letters* and *Journals*, will no doubt fuel further critical speculation along the lines originally suggested by Davis and Towers.

Superlatives characterized the assessments of both the *Washington Post*'s William McPherson ("moving and excellent")[54] and the novelist Anne Tyler, who described *Falconer* as a "concentration of all that is wonderful and sad and astonishing in everyday life."[55] John Gardner held the novel in such high regard that he deemed it "an extraordinary work of art."[56] Considering the high praise *Falconer* received in the spring of 1977, Bruce Allen noted that fall, in the *Sewanee Review*: "I don't believe it has been overrated."[57]

Yet, Joyce Carol Oates viewed the novel in the negative terms a number of earlier critics had applied to Cheever's other novels: *Falconer* was "a fable, a kind of fairy tale; near-structureless, it has the feel of an assemblage of short stories . . . " (p. 146). Furthermore, its serious intent was undercut, as had been the case with his other novels, by a "whimsical impulse" (p. 147).

The following year, on June 8, 1978, Cheever was awarded an honorary doctorate from Harvard, of which Richard Schickel observed: "He seems to find something Cheeveresque in the ultimate university's honoring of a failed preppie."[58] Such recognition presaged the honors and acclaim that were soon to come.

Buoyed by the warm reception of *Falconer*, Cheever agreed with the suggestion of his editor, Robert Gottlieb--who would also edit Cheever's posthumously published *Journals* in 1991--and brought out a comprehensive collection of his stories. In October, 1978 *The Stories of John Cheever* appeared, consisting of sixty-one stories dating from the end of World War II. The response to this 700-page magnum opus was nearly unanimously congratulatory and exuberant, with a number of reviews taking a valedictory tone in their assessments of the then 66-year-old author's career.

While many critics, such as Robert Towers and Anne Tyler, used such terms as "brilliant" (p. 181) and "dazzling"[59] to describe this collection, John Leonard went as far as to term the publication "a grand occasion in English literature."[60] Geoffrey Wolff described the work as containing "the stories of our civilization,"[61] and a number of reviewers invoked what had, by then, become the inevitable comparisons to Hawthorne, Henry James and Chekhov.

So widespread was reviewers' enthusiasm that this spawned a response *to* the critical response. In a long, contentious essay that apeared in *Harper's* the following year, Bryan Griffin felt compelled to take the reviewers to task for "having made fools of themselves."[62] He wrote that "the middlebrow American literary community" was just "trying to be friendly," and this widespread critical approval was little more than the granting of "retroactive profundity," in the light of *Falconer's* appearance, to a "minor" writer. A more evenhanded assessment of the reception was made by the poet Robert Shaw, who candidly pointed out that "without a doubt," Cheever's four novels had "led critics to pay him serious attention."[63]

Among the reviewers to offer qualified praise, was Isa Kapp, who took issue with the Cheever/Chekhov analogy: "We sense the Russian writer's intuitive sympathy with all of his characters. Cheever's sympathies," she pointed out, "spring unaccountably back to the observer, as if he were personally affronted . . . " (p. 169).

Estimations of Cheever's Christian sensibility appeared in William Rickenbacker's review[64] and, at more length and depth, in George Hunt's essay, "Beyond the Cheeveresque: A Style Both Lyrical and Idiosyncratic."[65] Father Hunt later published the insightful book-length study, *John Cheever: The Hobgoblin Company of Love*, in 1983.

Reviewers, such as Joy Williams, also felt the need to determine Cheever's dominant tone, which to her was sad: he "knows that the essentiality of human loneliness remains constant."[66] To Pearl K. Bell, Cheever's "abiding theme" was "the private pain of disappointment" (p. 166). Irwin Shaw preferred to describe his colleague and friend of forty years as "a prober of the hidden, and a judge of stern moral standards."[67]

The Stories of John Cheever went on to win the National Book Critics' Circle Award in 1979, the first prize Cheever had received in over twenty years. In his remarks at the January 25 awards ceremony Cheever expressed satisfaction and relief that the collection had been so well received and that it had not been a "horrendous clinker," the sort of book one finds on a shelf in "the houses we rent for the summer."[68]

In April, 1979 he was then awarded the Pulitzer Prize. As he told an interviewer that year, "I'm pleased to receive prizes . . . because it makes life so much easier for other people. When one meets a stranger, he's inclined to be anxious, but if you've got the Pulitzer Prize, you're rather like Shredded Wheat. They don't worry."[69]

In the midst of this recognition there was speculation, as there had been in 1976 and again in 1977, that Cheever might be awarded a Nobel Prize. "When the house fills up with Swedish reporters," he said, "then I'll know damned well that I'm up for the Nobel" (*Conversations*, 187).

While the Nobel did not materialize, Cheever did receive the Edward MacDowell Medal on September 9, 1979, for "outstanding contribution to the arts." Cheever remarked that day that "writers have very little to say about continuing to write. I did wake one morning and think 'Ahh, but I don't *have* to write another novel.' And then I realized I had no choice. The need to write comes from the need to make sense of one's life and discover one's usefulness. For me, it's the most intimate form of communicating about love and memory and nostalgia."[70]

He continued to write what he thought would be "another bulky book,"[71] but what turned out to be--largely due to his deteriorating health--the 100-page novella, *Oh What a Paradise It Seems*.

Published in March, 1982, three months before his death, this book was received respectfully. John Updike felt it "too darting, too gaudy in its deployment of artifice and aside, too disarmingly personal in its voice" to be labelled a novel or novella. For him, it was "a parable and a tall tale."[72] While it was "minor art"[73] to John Leonard, and its ending made Anatole Broyard[74] uncomfortable (as Cheever's earlier reviewers frequently said of certain of his other endings), it also struck Paul Gray as a "coda to other works, a spontaneous riff on some people, places and things that have appeared elsewhere in Cheever's fiction."[75] What Updike found as "sparkling," in the novella, however, Ann Hulbert saw as "eerie" and believed the color of Cheever's writing "to have faded somewhat" (p. 186). Furthermore, even the criticism of structural weakness which dogged his previous four novels surfaced in Rachel Hadas' otherwise appreciative assessment. Despite the fact that "the book is true to the integrity of its mood," she maintained that "in certain ways the novella tends to split in two."[76]

The most strident note in the critical response came from Thomas Mallon in *The National Review*. Reviving the decades-old criticism, Mallon called the book "a piece of whimsey."[77] He also asked a question which Cheever had already answered years before: "Why does he so often send his nostalgic characters in search of homes that never existed . . . ?"

A far more penetrating analysis was made by George Hunt, who shared Updike's view of Cheever as a gifted "yarn-spinner" (p. 189), but who also saw "[s]alvage and salvation . . . at the heart of this story" (p. 190). He furthermore found much to praise in Cheever's simultaneous "vivid sense of transcendence and an equally vivid sense of humor" (p. 191). The following year Michael Byrne considered the novella along similar lines, and found it to be informed by Cheever's "vision of regeneration and redemption" (p. 197).

The month after *Oh What a Paradise It Seems* was published, Cheever was given the National Medal for Literature. At the April 27th award ceremony William Styron spoke of him as "undislodgeably established in the wonderful firmament of American literature." Styron went on to include Cheever among "the greatest of writers" and called him "a lord of the language" (Donaldson, 349).

Since John Cheever's death on June 18, 1982, a collection of his letters (1988) and an edition of his journals (1991) have been published. Also, Susan Cheever has written a biographical memoir of her father, *Home Before Dark* (1984), as well as *Treetops* (1991), in which she chronicled her mother's family and her father's relationship with them. Furthermore, Scott Donaldson's *John Cheever: A Biography*, the first such full-length study, was published in 1988.

The response to *The Letters of John Cheever*, which was edited by his elder son Benjamin, was indeed mixed. Whereas *Time*'s Paul Gray found the collection engaging and amusing,[78] and *The Nation*'s William McPherson felt that it, along with *Home Before Dark*, constituted "about as much biography as most people will need,"[79] a more thoughtful view was expressed by Robert Kiely in the *New York Times Book Review*. Kiely thought that the *Letters*, "now colorful and witty, now crude and routine--has a hole at the center" (p. 207), and he hoped for publication, one day, of documents that would fill that gap. Ann Hulbert, too, found that this collection did "not . . . raise the curtain on the private self" (p. 202). With rare exceptions, she maintained, the *Letters* offers only "a veiled self-portrait, full of ambivalence" (p. 203).

A major step toward filling the hole Kiely wrote of was made in October, 1991 with the publication of *The Journals of John Cheever*, though it should be noted that this volume was preceded by the appearance of sizeable excerpts, published in a series of six installments between August, 1990 and August, 1991 in the *New Yorker*. The compilation was culled from twenty-nine notebooks Cheever left, representing only about one-twentieth of the total, according to its editor, Robert Gottlieb. The *Journals*' entries date from the late 1940s to just a few days before Cheever's death.

Five years before the *Journals* were published, Ted Solotaroff was permitted "to look through" the "unstrung prose" (p. 209) which he felt constituted Cheever's notebooks. He was consequently impressed by the published edition: "Not since *Look Homeward, Angel* has there been an editorial feat like this" (p. 210).

Mary Gordon described this book as a "treasure-trove" of Cheever's sketches and notes concerning "four main subjects: nature, God, home and sex." Yet she felt at times like a voyeur and saw little point to the repetitive details of Cheever's obsessions; nonetheless, she noted that when "Cheever is writing about writing . . . there is nowhere else I'd like to be."[80]

John Updike found that the journals told him "more about Cheever's lusts and failures and self-humiliations and crushing sense of shame and despond than I can easily reconcile with my memories of the . . . man" (p. 223). Reflecting on the revelations Cheever's children have made public, Updike observed that he hoped they "have indeed benefitted. Like Noah's, they have gazed upon their father naked" (p. 222). He also speculated, as Kiely had done, on the likelihood of additional work being done with the yet-unpublished Cheever papers, and concluded that Cheever's literary standing will determine whether "a scholarly edition of the complete journals, as has been done for Hawthorne's notebooks, will seem warranted. . . . For now, we have . . . bile and melancholy, clean style and magical impressionability" (p. 224).

In the fifty years that have passed since the publication of John Cheever's first book, *The Way Some People Live* (1943), his stories and novels have generated a wide range of critical response. Some ten books, nearly as many doctoral dissertations, scores of scholarly articles and hundreds of reviews have appeared and, with the prospect of the publication of Cheever's previously uncollected stories, further critical evaluation can be expected. In addition, retrospective evaluation of the Cheever canon in light of the recently published *Letters* and *Journals* will no doubt continue, as indicated by the essays of Samuel Coale and Robert Morace which appear in this volume.

John Cheever's place in what William Styron referred to as "the wonderful firmament of American literature," is due in part to his unique lyrical vision of the world which he conveyed in his fiction, as well as to that "shadowy and troubled undergrowth" of his stories that Elizabeth Hardwick and others have found reminiscent of Melville and Hawthorne. It is impossible to plot the course his repute may take in the next century but, if the literary reputation of F. Scott Fitzgerald--to whom Cheever has also been compared[81]--offers any indication, Cheever's position may well be "undislodgeable", as Styron put it. It does seem likely that we will long continue to read and appreciate the fiction of John Cheever which, as he wrote in one story, "celebrate[d] a world that lies spread out around us like a bewildering and stupendous dream."

This volume makes available a representative selection of major contemporary reviews and later assessments, spanning five decades of the critical response to John Cheever's writing. Most of this material has not been previously collected. In addition, new essays have been commissioned to cover areas that had been, to date, either insufficiently discussed or, as yet, unaddressed. Also, the text of one of the last interviews John Cheever gave is published here for the first time.

It should also be noted that *Stories*, the collection of short fiction which Cheever and his three *New Yorker* colleagues published in 1956, has not been afforded a place in the Documentary Section primarily because the critical response it generated was exiguous. Beyond the overview of this collaborative effort's reception in the foregoing pages, the supplementary bibliography covers the principal contemporary reviews and lists a number of recommended studies.

Finally, a word on the Documentary Section: all texts reprinted there are neither critical nor corrected versions, but are reproductions of the original published material; however, in the few instances where egregious errors of fact have occurred in the originals, they have been noted and corrected within the text in brackets. The texts are complete, with the exception of reviews in which Cheever was just one of the authors under discussion. In such cases, the Cheever material is reprinted in full, the excised part is indicated by an ellipsis, and the title is followed by an asterisk. Any other ellipses that appear in this section are those of the author of the specific piece and not of this volume's editor.

It is hoped that readers will find *The Critical Response to John Cheever* a useful companion to their study and understanding of the achievement of John Cheever.

NOTES

1. David Segal, "Change Is Always for the Worse," *Commonweal* 81 (4 December 1964), 363. This review has been reprinted in this volume, and this quotation appears on page 84. Hereafter, all references to material reprinted in this volume will be noted parenthetically in the text by number of the page on which it appears.
2. In 1980, when an interviewer mentioned that some people felt Cheever's stories were cynical, Cheever replied: "Well, time seems to have changed the way the stories are perceived. I like to think people thought they were cynical because they used to run in narrow columns

between pages of the most expensive advertising in the world. They're thought to be quite compassionate now. And I expect presently I'll be charged with sentimentality. I've never thought of myself as being particularly cynical. I can be nasty." See Jo Brans, "Stories to Comprehend Life," *Southwest Review* 65 (Autumn 1980): 339.

3. Cheever's few forays into the genre of drama included a script for CBS's prospective television series, *Life with Father and Mother*, in 1952; a screen treatment of a D.H. Lawrence novel for a film that was never made, in 1960; and, the teleplay, *The Shady Hill Kidnapping*, for PBS, which was first broadcast on January 12, 1982.

4. William DuBois, "Tortured Souls," *New York Times Book Review*, 28 March 1943, p. 10.

5. Mark Schorer, "Outstanding Novels," *The Yale Review* 32 (Summer 1943): xii.

6. John Cheever, *The Letters of John Cheever*, ed. by Benjamin Cheever (New York: Simon and Schuster, 1988), p. 99. References to this work will hereafter be noted parenthetically in the text as *Letters*.

7. Scott Donaldson, *John Cheever: A Biography* (New York: Random House, 1988), pp. 99-100. References to this work will hereafter be noted parenthetically in the text as Donaldson.

8. Scott Donaldson, ed., *Conversations with John Cheever* (Jackson: University Press of Mississippi, 1987), p. 173. References to this work will hereafter be noted parenthetically in the text as *Conversations*.

9. William DuBois, "Books of The Times," *New York Times*, 1 May 1953, p. 19.

10. Paul Pickrel, "Outstanding Novels," *The Yale Review* 42 (Summer 1953): xii.

11. Morris Freedman, "New England and Hollywood," *Commentary* 16 (October 1953): 389-90, 392. Reprinted in R. G. Collins, ed., *Critical Essays on John Cheever* (Boston: G.K. Hall, 1982), pp. 25, 26.

12. "News from the Defeated," *Time* 68 (3 December 1956): 107.

13. William Hogan, "Prize Stories That Have Won No Prizes," *San Francisco Chronicle*, 6 December 1956, p. 25.

14. Ramona Maher Martinez, "Book Reviews," *New Mexico Quarterly* 26 (Winter 1956-57), 407.

15. William Peden, "Four Cameos," *Saturday Review* 39 (8 December 1956): 16.

16. Maeve Brennan, "Mortal Men and Mermaids," *New Yorker* 33 (11 May 1957): 154.

17. Ihab Hassan, *Radical Innocence: Studies in the Contemporary American Novel* (Princeton: Princeton University Press, 1961), p. 188.

18. Richard H. Rupp, *Celebration in Postwar American Fiction, 1945-1967* (Coral Gables: University of Miami Press, 1970), pp. 27-39.

19. James O'Hara, "Cheever's *The Wapshot Chronicle*: A Narrative of Exploration," *Critique* 22 (1980): 20.

20. John Cheever, *The Journals of John Cheever*, ed. by Robert Gottlieb (New York: Knopf, 1991), p. 81. References to this work will hereafter be noted parenthetically in the text as *Journals*.

21. Alfred Kazin did refer to "The Country Husband" on p. 54 of "Our Middle-Class Storytellers," a wide-ranging essay he wrote for the *Atlantic Monthly* (August 1968), and which he then developed into his section on Cheever in his *Bright Book of Life* (Boston: Little Brown, 1973), p. 112. Since, to Kazin, the husband was "brainwashed" and "the interchangeable suburban nobody," he asked, "who cares about this fellow?" In 1977 Joan Didion criticized him for these remarks in her review of *Falconer* (see p. 139 of this volume).

22. Melvin Maddocks, "Cheever's Latest Collection," *Christian Science Monitor*, 4 May 1961, p. 11.

23. David Boroff, "A World Filled With Trapdoors Into Chaos," *New York Times Book Review*, 16 April 1961, p. 34.

24. David Ray, "The Weeding-Out Process," *Saturday Review* 44 (27 May 1961): 20. Reprinted in *Critical Essays on John Cheever*, p. 28.

25. Elizabeth Janeway, "Things Aren't What They Seem," *New York Times Book Review*, 5 January 1964, p. 1.

26. Glenway Wescott, "A Surpassing Sequel," *New York Herald Tribune Book Week*, 5 January 1964, p. 1.

27. William Barrett, "New England Gothic," *Atlantic Monthly* 213 (February 1964): 140.

28. George Garrett, "John Cheever and the Charms of Innocence: The Craft of *The Wapshot Scandal*," *Hollins Critic* 1 (April 1964): 1-4, 6-12. Reprinted in *Critical Essays on John Cheever*, p. 51.

29. Cynthia Ozick, "America Aglow," *Commentary* 38 (July 1964): 67.

30. Joan Didion, "The Way We Live Now," *National Review* 16 (24 March 1964): 237-38, 240. Reprinted in *Critical Essays on John Cheever*, p. 68.

31. [Alwyn Lee], "Ovid in Ossining," *Time* 83 (27 March 1964): 66.

32. Adrian Mitchell, "Haunted and Bewitched," *New York Times Book Review*, 18 October 1964, p. 5.

33. Orville Prescott, "John Cheever's Comedy and Dismay," *New York Times*, 14 October 1964, p. 43.

34. George P. Elliott, "Exploring the Province of the Short Story," *Harper's* 320 (April 1965): 114.

35. Frederick Bracher, "John Cheever's Vision of the World," in *Critical Essays on John Cheever*, pp. 168-80. This essay incorporates material from his 1963 *Critique* and 1964 *Claremont Quarterly* articles.

36. Susan Cheever, *Home Before Dark* (Boston: Houghton Mifflin, 1984), p. 179.

37. Pearl K. Bell, "Taker of Notes," *The New Leader* 52 (26 May 1969): 11.

38. John Leonard, "Evil Comes to Suburbia," *New York Times*, 29 April 1969, p. 43.

39. See Nicol, p. 107. Also: Guy Davenport, "Elegant Botches," *National Review* 21 (3 June 1969): 550; Warren Sloat, Review of *Bullet Park*, *Commonweal* 90 (9 May 1969): 242.

40. Charles Shapiro, "This Familiar and Lifeless Scene," *The Nation* 208 (30 June 1969): 837.

41. John Updike, "Suburban men," London *Sunday Times*, 14 September 1969, p. 62. Reprinted as "And Yet Again Wonderful" in *Picked-Up Pieces* (New York: Knopf, 1975), p. 428.

42. L[arry] Woiwode, "The World of Apples," *New York Times Book Review*, 20 May 1973, p. 26.

43. Nelson Algren, Review of *The World of Apples*, *Chicago Tribune Book World*, 13 May 1973, p. 1.

44. Geoffrey Wolff, "Cheever's Career Back in Focus with *Apples*," *Los Angeles Times Book Review*, 24 June 1973, p. 1.

45. John Wain, "Literate, Witty, Civilized," *New Republic* 168 (26 May 1973): 24-26. Reprinted in *Critical Essays on John Cheever*, pp. 28-32.

46. Thomas R. Edwards, "Surprise, Surprise," *New York Review of Books* 20 (17 May 1973): 35.

47. Ronald DeFeo, "Cheever Underachieving," *National Review* 25 (11 May 1973): 536.

48. Walter Clemons, "Cheever's Triumph," *Newsweek* 89 (14 March 1977): 61.

49. Elizabeth Hardwick, "Cheever, or The Ambiguities," *New York Review of Books* 31 (20 December 1984): 6.

50. John Romano, "Redemption According to Cheever," *Commentary* 63 (May 1977): 68.

51. John Leonard, "Crying in the Wilderness," *Harper's* 254 (April 1977): 88-89. Reprinted in *Critical Essays on John Cheever*, p. 80.

52. D. Keith Mano, "Exhaustion," *National Review* 29 (22 July 1977): 833.

53. John Cheever, "The Leaves, the Lion-Fish, and the Bear," *Esquire* 82 (November 1974): 110-11, 192-96.

54. William McPherson, "Lives in a Cell," *Washington Post Book World*, 20 March 1977, p. 2.

55. Anne Tyler, "Life in Prison With a Sunny Innocent," *National Observer* 16 (12 March 1977): 19.

56. John Gardner, "On Miracle Row," *Saturday Review* 4 (2 April 1977): 20-23. Reprinted in *Critical Essays on John Cheever*, p. 81.

57. Bruce Allen, "Dream Journeys," *Sewanee Review* 85 (Fall 1977): 695.

58. Richard Schickel, "The Cheever Chronicle," *Horizon* 21 (September 1978): 31.

59. Anne Tyler, "Books Considered," *The New Republic* 179 (4 November 1978): 47.

60. John Leonard, "Books of The Times," *New York Times*, 7 November 1978, p. 43.

61.   Geoffrey Wolff, "Cheever's Chain of Being," *New Times*, 27 November 1978, p. 86.
62.   Bryan F. Griffin, "Literary Vogues: Getting Cheever while he's hot," *Harper's* 258 (June 1979): 90-93.
63.   Robert B. Shaw, "The World in A Very Small Space," *The Nation* 227 (23 December 1978): 705.
64.   William F. Rickenbacker, "Visions of Grace," *National Review* 31 (13 April 1979): 491-93.
65.   George Hunt, "Beyond the Cheeveresque: A Style Both Lyrical and Idiosyncratic," *Commonweal* 106 (19 January 1979): 20-22. Reprinted in *Critical Essays on John Cheever*, pp. 38-42.
66.   Joy Williams, "Meaningful Fiction . . . John Cheever's Stories are memorable," *Esquire* 90 (21 November 1978): 36.
67.   Irwin Shaw, "Cheever Country," *Bookviews* 2 (October 1978): 56.
68.   John B. Breslin, "John Cheever in the Critics' Circle," *America* 140 (17 February 1979): 115.
69.   Jesse Kornbluth, "The Cheever Chronicle," *New York Times Magazine*, 21 October 1979, p. 28.
70.   Michiko Kakutani, "In a Cheever-Like Setting, John Cheever Gets MacDowell Medal," *New York Times*, 11 September 1979, p. C7.
71.   Kornbluth, p. 102.
72.   John Updike, "On Such a Beautiful Green Little Planet," *New Yorker* 58 (5 April 1982): 189. Reprinted in *Hugging the Shore* (New York: Knopf, 1983), p. 293.
73.   John Leonard, "Cheever Country," *New York Times Book Review*, 7 March 1982, p. 25.
74.   Anatole Broyard, "Books of The Times," *New York Times*, 3 March 1982, p. C28.
75.   Paul Gray, "Coda," *Time* 119 (1 March 1982): 85.
76.   Rachel Hadas, "La Grand Poésie De La Vie," *Partisan Review* 50 (1983): 622.
77.   Thomas Mallon, "No Place Like Kansas," *National Review* 34 (30 April 1982): 496.
78.   Paul Gray, "Grace Notes," *Time* 132 (28 November 1988): 98.
79.   William McPherson, "'The Geometry of Love'," *The Nation* 247 (5 December 1988): 610.
80.   Mary Gordon, " The Country Husband," *New York Times Book Review*, 6 October 1991, pp. 1, 21, 22.
81.   See Elizabeth Hardwick, p. 56 of this volume; Stanley Kaufmann, "Literature of the Early Sixties: Cheever, Fitzgerald, Hemingway," *Wilson Library Bulletin* 39 (May 1965): 766-67; and Donaldson, *John Cheever: A Biography*, pp. 351-53.

Chronology

1912   John Cheever born to Frederick and Mary Cheever in Quincy, Massachusetts, 27 May.

1924-26   Attends Thayerlands, the junior school of the Thayer Academy, South Braintree, Massachusetts.

1926-28   Attends Thayer Academy

1928-29   Attends Quincy High School

1929   Returns to Thayer Academy but is expelled.

1930   Publishes first story, "Expelled," in *The New Republic*, 1 October.

1930-34   Pursues writing career. Shares apartment with his older brother Fred in Boston.

1931   Takes a walking tour of Europe with Fred.

1934   Moves to New York City. Supports himself in part by writing synopses of novels for MGM. Visits Yaddo, the Sarasota, New York artists' colony, for the first of what would be many visits, and attempts a novel, 4 June to 28 July.

1935   Publishes "Brooklyn Rooming House," his first *New Yorker* story, 25 May.

1937-38   Employed by the WPA's Federal Writers' Project, first in

Washington, D.C., in May, then in November returns to New York to work as an Editorial Assistant on the New York City Guide.

1939   Meets Mary Winternitz, who was then working in the office of his first agent, Maxim Lieber.

1941   Marries Mary Winternitz in New Haven, 22 March. Receives O. Henry Award for "I'm Going to Asia."

1942   Enters the Army at Fort Dix, New Jersey, 7 May. Assigned to Camp Croft, South Carolina for infantry training, and then transferred to Camp Gordon, Georgia.

1943   Publishes first collection of short stories, *The Way Some People Live*, March. Daughter Susan born, 31 July. Transferred to Signal Corps, Astoria, Queens and works on scripts for the film series, *Army-Navy Magazine*.

1945   Sent to Guam and the Philippines on research and writing assignment for a little over two months. Honorably discharged from Army, 27 November.

1945-50   Lives in New York City and expands the range of his fiction, writing such stories as "The Enormous Radio." Makes another unsuccessful attempt at writing a novel.

1948   Son Benjamin born, 4 May. A Broadway production of his "Town House" series of stories runs for only twelve performances and closes 30 September.

1950   Receives O. Henry Award for "Vega."

1951   Leaves New York for Scarborough. Receives Guggenheim grant. Receives O. Henry Award for "The Pot of Gold."

1952   Writes a script for CBS television's prospective series, *Life with Father and Mother*

1953   Publishes second volume of stories, *The Enormous Radio and Other Stories*, February.

1954-56   Teaches creative writing at Barnard College.

1955   Receives both the Benjamin Franklin Magazine Award and an O.
            Henry Award for "The Five-Forty-Eight."

1956   Receives O. Henry Award for "The Country Husband." Receives
            grant from the National Institute of Arts and Letters. Sails
            to Italy for one year with his family, October. Publishes
            four stories in *Stories*, an anthology of fifteen short stories
            by four *New Yorker* writers.

1957   Publishes first novel, *The Wapshot Chronicle*, March. Son
            Federico born, 9 March. Elected to National Institute of Arts
            and Letters. Receives O. Henry Award for "The Journal of an
            Old Gent."

1958   Receives National Book Award for *The Wapshot Chronicle*.
            Publishes *The Housebreaker of Shady Hill and Other Stories*,
            September.

1959   Receives O. Henry Award for "The Trouble of Marcie Flint."

1960   Receives second Guggenheim grant to write his next novel.

1961   Moves to Ossining, New York. Publishes the collection, *Some
            People, Places, and Things That Will Not Appear in My Next
            Novel*, April.

1964   Publishes second novel, *The Wapshot Scandal*, January. Featured
            on cover of *Time* magazine, 27 March. Travels to Russia as
            part of a State Department cultural exchange program, in the
            fall. Publishes the collection, *The Brigadier and the Golf
            Widow*, October. Receives O. Henry Award for "The Embarkment
            for Cythera."

1965   Receives Howells Medal of the American Academy of Arts and
            Letters for *The Wapshot Scandal* as the best novel, 1960-1965.

1968   Frank and Eleanor Perry's film of "The Swimmer," starring Burt
            Lancaster, released.

1969   Publishes third novel, *Bullet Park*, April.

1971-72   Teaches creative writing to inmates at Sing Sing prison.

1973   Publishes the collection, *The World of Apples*, May. Teaches
            at the University of Iowa Writers Workshop in the fall.
            Elected to the American Academy of Arts and Letters. Receives
            O. Henry Award for "The Jewels of the Cabots."

1974-75   Teaches creative writing at Boston University. Severe
            alcoholism leads him to enter the Smithers Alcoholism Rehabil-
            itation Center in New York City, where he overcomes his
            addiction.

1977   Publishes fourth novel, *Falconer*, March. Featured on cover of
            Newsweek magazine, 14 March. Receives O. Henry Award for
            "President of the Argentine."

1978   Awarded honorary doctorate from Harvard, 8 June. Publishes
            The Stories of John Cheever, November.

1979   Receives National Book Critics' Circle Award, January, and
            Pulitzer Prize, April, for *The Stories of John Cheever*.
            Receives the Edward MacDowell Medal, 9 September. Adaptations
            of "The Sorrows of Gin," "O Youth and Beauty!" and "The
            Five-Forty-Eight" are broadcast on PBS television's *Great
            Performances* series, 24 October, 31 October, and 7 November,
            respectively.

1980   Receives Lincoln Literary Award of the Union League Club.
            Suffers a grand mal seizure at Yaddo, October.

1981   Receives American Book Award for *The Stories of John Cheever*
            (paperback). Cancer is detected during kidney surgery, July.

1982   His teleplay, *The Shady Hill Kidnapping*, is broadcast for the
            first time, on PBS, 12 January. Publishes the novella, *Oh
            What a Paradise It Seems*, March. Receives National Medal for
            Literature, 27 April. Dies at his home in Ossining, 18 June.
            Buried in Norwell, Massachusetts, 22 June.

The Writings
of John Cheever

The Way Some People Live. New York: Random House, 1943.

The Enormous Radio and Other Stories. New York: Funk & Wagnalls, 1953.

Stories [with Jean Stafford, Daniel Fuchs, and William Maxwell]. New York: Farrar, Straus and Cudahy, 1956.

The Wapshot Chronicle. New York: Harper & Brothers, 1957.

The Housebreaker of Shady Hill and Other Stories. New York: Harper & Brothers, 1958.

Some People, Places, and Things That Will Not Appear in My Next Novel. New York: Harper & Brothers, 1961.

The Wapshot Scandal. New York: Harper & Row, 1964.

The Brigadier and the Golf Widow. New York: Harper & Row, 1964.

Homage to Shakespeare. Stevenson, CT: Country Squire Books, 1968. [limited edition]

Bullet Park. New York: Alfred A. Knopf, 1969.

The World of Apples. New York: Alfred A. Knopf, 1973.

Falconer. New York: Alfred A. Knopf, 1977.

The Day the Pig Fell Into the Well. Northridge, CA: Lord John Press, 1978. [limited edition]

The Wapshot Chronicle. Franklin Center, PA: The Franklin Library, 1978. [limited edition]

The Stories of John Cheever. New York: Alfred A. Knopf, 1978.

The Stories of John Cheever. Franklin Center, PA: The Franklin Library, 1980. [limited edition]

The Leaves, the Lion-Fish and the Bear. Los Angeles: Sylvester & Orphanos, 1980. [limited edition]

The National Pastime. Los Angeles: Sylvester & Orphanos, 1982. [limited edition]

Oh What a Paradise It Seems. New York: Alfred A. Knopf, 1982.

Atlantic Crossing. Cottondale, Alabama: Ex Ophidia, 1986. [limited edition]

The Letters of John Cheever. Ed. Benjamin Cheever. New York: Simon and Schuster, 1988.

The Journals of John Cheever. Ed. Robert Gottlieb. New York: Alfred A. Knopf, 1991.

DOCUMENTARY SECTION

The Way Some People Live
1943

John Cheever's Sense of Drama

Struthers Burt

Unless I am very much mistaken, when this war is over, John Cheever--he is now in the army--will become one of the most distinguished writers; not only as a short story writer but as a novelist. Indeed, if he wishes to perform that ancient triple-feat, not as popular now as it was twenty years ago in the time of Galsworthy and Bennett and their fellows, he can be a playwright too, for he has all the necessary signs and characteristics. The sense of drama in ordinary events and people; the underlying and universal importance of the outwardly unimportant; a deep feeling for the perversities and contradictions, the worth and unexpected dignity of life, its ironies, comedies, and tragedies. All of this explained in a style of his own, brief, apparently casual, but carefully selected; unaccented until the accent is needed. Meanwhile, he has published the best volume of short stories I have come across in a long while, and that is a much more important event in American writing than most people realize.

The short story is a curious and especial thing; a delicate and restricted medium in which many have walked, but few succeeded. It is like the sonnet in poetry; the only artificial (I mean in technique, not content) form of poetry that has ever been able to make itself thoroughly at home within the realms of that magnificent, impatient, sensible, and beautiful mode of human expression, the English language, and, like the sonnet, the short story has, or should have, the same limitations of space, of concentrated emotion, of characters, of theme and events. Never by any chance should it be the scenario, the skeleton, of something longer. Its strength, like the sonnet's, comes from deep emotion and perception, and, when necessary, passion, beating against the inescapable form that encircles it. As in the sonnet, as indeed in all good poetry, not a word or line, or figure of speech, or simile, must be amiss or superfluous. The author has just so many minutes in which to be of value, and the contest--the selection--in his mind is between what he would like to say, and what he should say; the search is for the inevitable phrase and sentence and description that contain the final illumination but which, at the same time, seem inevitable and natural.

As a result, probably not more than a score of truly great short stories have ever been written. The same holds true of sonnets. Even the great masters of the short story, Chekhov, Turgeniev, Maupassant, Kipling, O. Henry in his better moments, and others, only reached their culmination in a few instances. The short story, like electricity, gains its power through its amperage. It is a bullet whose penetration is due to a force poured through a narrow channel. Of all forms of writing it is the most difficult.

The present volume consists of thirty short stories most of which have appeared in the *New Yorker*, the *Yale Review*, and *Story* magazine, and one can see the compression used, for the book is only two hundred and fifty-six pages long. Many of the stories are only a few pages in length, a thousand, twelve hundred words; and at least half of them are eminently successful; a quarter are far above the average; all are well done; and only a couple fail. "Of Love; A Testimony," except for its title, is one of the best love stories I have ever read. There is a curious and interesting development in the book, and in the procession of the stories--the way they are placed--that ties the volume together and gives it almost the feeling of a novel despite the inevitable lack of connection between any short stories. The earlier stories have to do with the troubled, frustrated, apparently futile years of 1939 and 1941; and then there are some beautifully told stories of the average American--the average American with a college degree, the same suburbanite--actually at war, but still in this country. This gives the book the interest and importance of a progress toward Fate; and so there's a classic feeling to it.

No one can tell how many artists, musicians, writers, painters, sculptors, are in our armed forces. They will not emerge for some years yet. When they do there should be something interesting, for these younger men have learned a lot, apparently, and apparently it's part of their make-up. They are just as honest and ruthless as their predecessors, perhaps even more so, but they have regained in some mysterious way their belief in irony and pity and the catharsis, which, despite the Greeks, and Anatole France, the last who announced their necessity, have for some time been regarded as sentimental clichés.

John Cheever has only two things to fear; a hardening into an especial style that might become an affectation, and a deliberate casualness and simplicity that might become the same. Otherwise, the world is his.

Saturday Review 26 (24 April 1943): 9.

New Fiction from the Atlantic to the Pacific

Rose Feld

To the extent that in the writing world any material—sketch, article, newspaper report, fiction—is called a story, John Cheever's book, "The Way Some People Live," may be called a collection of stories. But in the conventional sense, only a few of the thirty pieces that make up the volume fulfill the ordinary requirements of the short-fiction form. The rest are moments or moods caught in the lives of his characters, pointed in quality but inconclusive in effect. They give the feeling, very often, of being notes made on a contemplated larger work which has remained unfinished. While they are interesting as fragments and show a subtle and sensitive talent at irony and satire, they leave the reader suspended in anticipation that has no artistic fulfillment.

That Mr. Cheever can bring a story to a satisfying conclusion, however unconventional his pattern, is evidenced by some of the pieces in the book. His story called "The Cat" succeeds notably in presenting a crisis in the lives of a young married couple. When Hannah Bannister thought her pet was lost she became a woman demented, deprived of everything that meant a home to her. To comfort her, her husband threw over all his objections against their having a child, promising her to save his money, to stay on the wagon, to buy a house in Westchester. Mr. Cheever's penetration into the emotional conflict, past as well as present, gives the story its distinction.

He accomplishes the same thing in "The Edge of the World," this time in describing the desperation and loneliness of a boy. The lad is an only child, aware of the fact that neither of his parents ever wanted him. They wound and lacerate him with their quarrels and mutual accusations of infidelity. What brings them to a feverish reconciliation is not the anguish of their child but an insignificant accident to the woman.

The search for a husband makes the theme of "Summer Remembered." "I'm twenty-five years old," declares Grace to her friend Betty who had boasted of having an admirer at Lake George the summer before, "and I'm

not getting any younger and I have two weeks off to find a man and all
I find is a lot of old women looking at the mountains." The pay-off in
this piece is Betty's confession that all she has said about her man was
a parcel of lies.

"The Man Who Was Very Homesick for New York" is a penetrating story of
a soldier, a former lawyer, who hated the life of the army, who had a
chance to get a medical discharge and return to the city he loved and
discovered that he didn't want to.

In "A Border Incident" Mr. Cheever most closely approaches the
conventional story with a surprise ending but unlike his other pieces it
lacks his integrity of characterization. The prude who gave herself, as
the saying goes, to a man in order to discover his activities as a Nazi
spy, makes neither sense nor satire.

But, mainly, however slight his material, Mr. Cheever brings sympathy
and irony to characters in the bleak moments in which he catches them.
He explores various kinds of relationships, that between husbands and
wives, between brothers, between parents and children, between lovers,
between friends. It would be interesting to see what he could do with a
task that required a more sustained effort than the contributions in the
present book.

New York Herald Tribune Weekly Book Review, 14 March 1943, p. 12.

John Cheever's Stories

Weldon Kees

In 1930, when he was seventeen, John Cheever severed his connections
with an Eastern preparatory school, and not long afterwards appeared in
this magazine with a sensitive and precocious account of the institution
in which he had been a most unhappy student. It was a very promising
piece of work. Cheever went on to publish stories at infrequent
intervals in the little magazines of the early nineteen-thirties; but it
was not until The New Yorker, shrewdly detecting a writer of talent,
took him up only a few years ago that he suddenly displayed an
unexpected knack for rapidly turning out neatly tailored sketches for
that magazine, most of them acid accounts of pathos in the suburbs.

As examples of fiction from The New Yorker, these stories of Mr.
Cheever's are among the best that have appeared there recently, and this
is particularly true of those which exploit a cool and narrow-eyed
treatment of tensions arising from the war. Mr. Cheever's drunken
draft-dodger and his young draftee are particularly well managed, and
the sketches in which they appear are quite unblemished by the pieties

and embarrassments which ordinarily mark war fiction published while a war is on. Many of the other stories--and if my count is right, all but six of the thirty included here are from The New Yorker--have not improved by their being collected in a book. As individual magazine stories they seemed better than they are; read one after another, their nearly identical lengths, similarities of tone and situation, and their somehow remote and unambitious style, produce an effect of sameness and eventually of tedium. The formula has been flourished too obviously and too often.

Mr. Cheever is not alone. He bathes in that same large municipal pool where all New Yorker short-story writers swim and sink. As Lionel Trilling remarked, one feels that almost any one of them might write another's story. Their characters live in an identical and tidy world which the magazine's editors have laboriously created by a set tone and by an elaborate hierarchy of taboos. It is a milieu which the writers stray from only at their peril. From Mr. Cheever's bleak suburban homes to Sally Benson's nurseries, or to John O'Hara's night clubs (Chicago, Hollywood and New York), or to Edward Newhouse's bars, it is only a step. The reader need scarcely move. Few magazines of the time have had so bright and professional an air, and fewer others have attained so high a level of general skill in their prose. But it is skill expended on what is more often than not the essentially trivial; it would even seem that the magazine's character demands a patina of triviality spread over those themes and situations which its policy allows. Its writers must frequently entertain themselves by concentrating on the merely decorative qualities of a scene, a restriction brought on by an understandable hesitancy to explore their material deeply. Thus, in such a story as Mr. Cheever's "Forever Hold Your Peace," the exhaustively reported small talk of guests at a wedding performs the services of a more consequential and telling method of viewing the situation.

Some of Mr. Cheever's best stories, which were written during his less fettered pre-New Yorker phase--particularly "The Teaser" and "The Princess," which came out in this magazine some years ago, and "Behold a Cloud in the West," from New Letters--have been mysteriously omitted. So have a number of others that would stand up better than many that are here. But one long story, "Of Love: A Testimony," which is seven or eight years old, has been retained. It is an excellent example of what this writer is capable of doing when he is his own man, when he has room enough in which to work for something more than episodic notation and minor perceptive effects.

The New Republic 108 (19 April 1943): 516-17.

Fiction in Review*

Diana Trilling

. . . To read the even better-than-average short story nowadays is to
have an experience so tangential to the real thing that it is rather
like having a conversation in a language in which one has had
considerable training but in which one is still not fluent. John
Cheever's stories, which for the most part have appeared in the *New
Yorker* and which are even more talented than the average stories printed
in that magazine, are now collected in a volume called "The Way Some
People Live" (Random House, $2): to read them one after another is to
end with an intense feeling of frustration. For even the best of Mr.
Cheever's pieces, such as The Pleasure of Solicitude [*sic*: Solitude] or
The Edge of the World, are strongly worded hints rather than completely
communicated statements, and I am led to the conclusion that one of the
troubles with short-story writers today, even more than with novelists,
is that they not only choose inarticulate characters to write about but
then refuse to be articulate *for* them. It is an artificial and
completely self-imposed limitation, of the same order as the fashionable
time-limitation in the short story, and I suspect that the sooner it is
got rid of, the better for this branch of contemporary fiction. . . .

The Nation 156 (10 April 1943): 533.

The Enormous Radio and Other Stories

1953

SELECTED REVIEWS

Snapshots in the East Fifties

Taliaferro Boatwright

In "The Enormous Radio," the title story of John Cheever's collection of short stories, Jim Westcott buys his wife a new radio which unaccountably tunes in the quarrels, love-making, conversations, and routine living noises of the other apartments in his apartment house. It's an apt keynote for the whole collection, for here are the lives--laid bare, unwrapped--of the people in your apartment house and mine, that is, if you live on the East Side, about the Fifties, or a little higher. Oh, the Pommeroys may be at "Laud's Head," off the coast of Massachusetts, for the summer, and the Hartleys at "Pemaquoddy," skiing. And the unnamed victim in "The Cure" may be a commuter. But basically the characters are cut from the same pattern--the middle-class, upper middle-brow, white collar people who subscribe to "The New Yorker," in which all fourteen of the stories in "The Enormous Radio and Other Stories" have appeared.

All of these stories are competently done, some are excellent. Many of them, notably "The Season of Divorce"--that beautiful and despairing study of the early middle years of a middle-class marriage, and the "Pot of Gold," an examination of what makes that same white collar worker tick, have been anthologized. Practically all, individually, are candidates for anthologies. Unfortunately, in the aggregate, as here, they present a rather overpowering picture. This collection is definitely for dipping in, not sustained cover-to-cover reading.

Mr. Cheever's basic situation is that urban, literate New Yorker trap-

ped in his environment. In his enormous apartment house there are many
varieties of experience, and several nicely appreciated expositions of
the basic situation. Nevertheless, he is not overtly indicting his
society, although most of his characters succumb to, or come to terms
with, their fate. As Laura Whittemore, in "The Pot of Gold," saw, after
a few years there began to be at parties and gatherings, the "missing":
"the platoon that divorce, drink, nervous disorders and adversity had
slain or wounded." So it is with the protagonists of most of the
stories--the Mackenzies, in "The Children," accept their fate as
constant children, dependent on the largesse of those to whom they have
trained themselves to be subservient; Lawrence Pommeroy fights the
criminal emptiness of that society, but his foolish brother, its agent,
casts him out; the Westcotts, the Hartleys, in the story of the same
name, the couple in "The Cure" who had separated for the third time, and
the couple in "The Season of Divorce" are all caught in it.

Even the servitors of apartment-land are trapped--Clancy, the elevator
operator, in his Tower of Babel; the rather wise Chester Coolidge, the
superintendent, and Charlie, the elevator operator in "Christmas Is a
Sad Season for the Poor." It must be said, however, that these
characters are not as well realized as their masters, the tenants. One
feels that Mr. Cheever knows them only externally, that what they say
and do is only a projection of what he thinks they may feel and think.

Even though this is a specialized sort of society, and totally outside
the experience of, say, the Shamrock Hotel, hillbilly music, pro
football, and even the subway, it comes frighteningly alive. John
Cheever's competence and craftsmanship are a constant delight.

New York Herald Tribune Book Review, 24 May 1953, p. 16.

In Genteel Traditions*

Arthur Mizener

Both these writers [John Cheever and J. D. Salinger] are *New Yorker*
authors. It is fashionable, I gather, to be a little superior to the *New
Yorker* story, and no one would want to maintain that making a living
writing for *The New Yorker* would in the long run be the best thing that
could happen to a talented man like Mr. Salinger. But I suspect *The New
Yorker's* standards are better than we admit; they set high requirements
of observation, understanding, and composition. If their limitations on
subject matter are in the long run dangerous to real talent, they
nonetheless provide a stiff course in the craft.

Mr. Cheever, for example, is not a writer of any great talent, but the

stories in his book are all skillfully worked out and loaded with
carefully observed manners. Congreve, who might, for a while at least,
have been a great success in *The New Yorker*, once remarked that he
selected a moral and then designed a fable to fit it. It seems unlikely,
though great works have been written in even queerer ways than that. It
is the glaring fault of Mr. Cheever's stories that they all appear to
have been produced in that way. He does not so much imagine experience
as have clever ideas for stories. There are the ingenious camera-angles,
the elevator operators (two of these) and the apartment-house
superintendents, very cute and innocent and staring wide-eyed at quality
folk. There are the neat discoveries of commonplace morals in
sophisticated lives. When Mr. Cheever tries for the big idea, his
stories waver toward a formally--and therefore morally--ambiguous
melodrama, as in "Torch Song" where a girl who appears, magically, never
to grow old (shades of Dorian Gray) turns out to love dying people, or
in "O City of Broken Dreams," where a pair of hicks who are said to be
from Indiana but are really from Ring-Lardner-land are fantastically
diddled by blasé theatrical people. These are the stories of a clever
short-story manufacturer, a man who has ideas about experience but has
never known these ideas in experience. Their language and technique are
highly refined; their feeling is crude. They are as well-made as any
conscientious editor could demand; you cannot blame the doctor for their
having been born with a very minimum of vitality. . . .

The New Republic 128 (25 May 1953): 19-20.

Esthetics of the Story*

William Peden

In the wondrous world of the academe, there tend to be two schools of
thought concerning *The New Yorker*. There are those who love it, and
there are those who hate it. Similar intensity exists concerning "*New
Yorker* short stories," a term which evokes comments like "magnificent"
or "abominable," "admirable verisimilitude" or "pretentious eyewash," as
the case may be. The editors, meanwhile, continue to deny that there is
a *New Yorker* type of short story; aspiring writers continue to deluge
the office with what they hope *are New Yorker* stories; and the magazine
continues to publish more good short fiction than any other magazine now
in print. Whether one likes the idea or not, *The New Yorker* has altered
some of our boundary lines, literary and otherwise. Nowhere, probably,
has it been more influential than in the field of the short story.
    The first number of *The New Yorker* appeared on February 21, 1925. It

was not until several years later, however, that the fictional type later to be called the *"New Yorker* short story" began to emerge. To simplify a complex matter, this "new" fiction was a breakaway from the unrealistic, mechanically plotted story which the imitators of the imitators of O. Henry and Kipling had reduced to a kind of literary garbage unrelated to life and unconcerned with truth. Among its ancestors were Henry James, who believed in the short story as a great art form with truth as its goal; Chekhov, who depicted real men and women in characteristic day-by-day actions; and James Joyce, who developed the story centering around an epiphanal, all-revealing incident which reveals the essence of a character or a situation beneath the facade of daily existence, the flash of lightning which suddenly illuminates an entire moral landscape.

Some time before Harold Ross conceived his idea of a weekly magazine "not edited for the old lady in Dubuque," the battle for freedom of form and idea had been fought and to a large degree won--in the pages of the little magazines and through the efforts of many writers and editors who had never heard of Kay Boyle or James Thurber or E. B. White.

The New Yorker, then, did not consciously effect a revolution in American short fiction. Rather, it helped shape a literary form which had already asserted its independence, and had already established its own direction. As *The New Yorker* grew (circulation, for example, rose from 77,500 in 1929 to 125,000 in 1934, during a period which saw the death of many small magazines with valid claims to literary respectability), its influence inevitably widened. The magazine possessed both snob appeal and legitimate prestige honestly won by publishing good fiction which did not depend for success upon a falsely rosy picture of American life or which did not rely heavily on literary hocus-pocus and legerdemain. Equally or even more important, it offered financial rewards virtually unheard of in the field of anything resembling serious magazine fiction. More and more good writers appear-ed in its pages, although frequently not with their best work: Sherwood Anderson, Erskine Caldwell, Rhys Davies, Nancy Hale, Shirley Jackson, Christopher and Oliver La Farge, Frank O'Connor, John O'Hara, Dorothy Parker, Marjorie Kinnan Rawlings, Irwin Shaw, Jean Stafford, Peter Taylor, James Thurber, Thyra Winslow, Jessamyn West, E. B. White, Thomas Wolfe. It is foolish to deny the significance of a magazine which has published good work by these and many other authors, or to suggest that such writers have produced fiction according to a magic formula known as the *"New Yorker* story." On the other hand, the magazine has published hundreds of mistakes by good and bad writers alike, a long and dreary procession of self-consciously plotless sketches of people talking brightly or cynically in hamburger stands or cocktail lounges or subway trains, a series of smugly sophisticated or annoyingly oblique commen-taries as unappetizing in their own way as is the trash of the big slick magazines. But over the long haul, issue in and issue out, *The New Yorker* has consistently published the best short fiction of any of the nationally circulated magazines either in this country or abroad.

A well-known critic a few years ago complained that most of the books he had been forced to review during a certain period of time had been either anthologies edited by Louis Untermeyer or books by *New Yorker* authors. His dismay to the contrary notwithstanding, one indication of the real importance of *The New Yorker* is the impressive number of significant volumes of stories by authors who are frequent contributors to its pages, collections such as J. D. Salinger's "Nine Stories" and John Cheever's "The Enormous Radio." . . .

John Cheever's stories are less spectacular than Salinger's, but at their best--and Cheever is usually very good--they improve with re-reading, which is not usually true of a Salinger piece. In contrast to Salinger's informal narrative methods, Cheever's stories of New York's apartment dwellers--young college graduates on their way up, or slightly older ones on their way down--are extremely conservative. Cheever shuns the melodramatic, but his stories, beneath their placid surfaces, seethe with a kind of restrained excitement often not far removed from violence, "the peculiar excitement with which the air of the city seems charged after midnight, when its life falls into the hands of watchmen and drunks . . . the bus brakes, the remote sirens, and the sound of water turning high in the air."

John Cheever possesses an absolute genius for taking the usual and transforming it into the significant. His situations are, indeed, commonplace: a lonely husband whose wife and children have left him, a wholesome looking girl from the Middle West who comes to New York to attend a school for models, a respectable young man who buys his wife an enormous radio. But the lonely husband develops suicidal tendencies; the big, splendid girl becomes a masochistic, drunken ghoul; the fingers of the radio reach behind the bland facade of an apartment house to pick up details of lust, violence, and disease among its dwellers. Few writers have delineated more skilfully than Cheever the loneliness and sickness of a segment of contemporary society; his stories are permeated with a sense of vague regret not far removed from fright, the feeling one might have were he to awaken, alone, at three in the morning in a strange room in a strange city. "I cry," speaks the central character of "The Season of Divorce," "I cry because I saw an old woman cuffing a little boy on Third Avenue . . . I cry because my father died when I was twelve . . . I cry because of some unkindness that I can't remember . . . I cry because I'm tired--because I'm tired and I can't sleep."

John Cheever is one of the most undervalued American short story writers; it is good to have another volume of his work in print.

Saturday Review 36 (11 April 1953): 43-44.

LATER CRITICISM

Cheever's Use of Mythology in "The Enormous Radio"

Burton Kendle

Though much less overt in its use of mythology than his recent "Metamorphoses," and "Mene, Mene, Tekel, Upharsin," John Cheever's "The Enormous Radio" derives much of its power from an ironic reinterpretation of the Eden story that helps to universalize what might otherwise appear to be merely a brilliant study of mid-century urban discontent. The chief characters, Jim and Irene Westcott, are appropriately typical representatives of their class and "seem to strike that satisfactory average of income, endeavor, and respectability that is reached by the reports in college alumni bulletins." Their life is comfortably commonplace, except for their sensitivity to classical music that both precipitates and explains their response to the radio. Eve's *hubris* seems ironically paralleled by Irene's somewhat self-consciously developed sensitivity. Significantly, the purchase of the radio is attributed to Jim's uxoriousness; he wants not only to keep his promise, but also to produce "a surprise for her. . . ."

Cheever develops the motif of innocence by details like Irene's "wide, fine forehead upon which nothing at all had been written," and Jim's youthfulness: "he dressed in the clothes his class had worn at Andover, and his manner was earnest, vehement, and intentionally naive." The radio, an appropriately ugly instrument that looks "like an aggressive intruder" to Irene, is the Satanic invader of the Westcotts' world of apparent innocence. Like her archetypal parallel, Irene is the first to become aware of the radio's "mistaken sensitivity to discord," though not of the significance of this discord. Eve's momentary illusion of godhead, and Irene's brief elation over the possibilities of supposed omniscience are similarly undercut by later occurrences in their lives.

Initially, Jim seems less disturbed by the knowledge revealed through the radio than by the effect of this knowledge on his wife, but gradually the combined forces of the radio and Irene's growing anxiety cause him to articulate an insight into the nature of evil more searching than any Irene can experience. Even before the radio starts broadcasting conversations from neighboring apartments, its mere presence in the household oppresses the atmosphere: "Jim was too tired to make even a pretense of sociability, and there was nothing about the dinner to hold Irene's interest, so her attention wandered from the food to the deposits of silver polish on the candlesticks. . . ."

Once the radio does begin to tune in to the lives of the Westcotts' neighbors, the conversations of an elderly couple, overheard at night, make clear to Irene the sinister implications of the knowledge she is acquiring: "The unrestrained [*sic*: restrained] melancholy of the dialogue and the draft from the bedroom window made her shiver, and she went back to bed." The next morning, further conversations transmitted by the radio "astonished and troubled her," and this increasing disillusion about the hidden lives of her neighbors carries over to a luncheon, where she "looked searchingly at her friend and wondered what her secrets were."

Irene's interest in the Salvation Army band during the couple's walk to a dinner party, like her obsession with the Sweeney's nurse, is a desperate, if shallow attempt to maintain a belief in the reality of human goodness, ultimately her own. Predictably, the attempt fails: at the dinner, Irene "interrupted her hostess rudely and stared at the people across the table from her with an intensity for which she would have punished her children." A self-righteous aversion to the possible covert evil of others, and an intensifying conviction of her own virtue impede any meaningful learning experience for her.

The final scene of the story, carefully foreshadowed by the growing tensions in the household, reveals the unstable basis of the Westcotts' edenic world. Jim's anxieties indicate that the initial portrait of him was ironically misleading: "I'm not getting any younger, you know. I'm thirty-seven. My hair will be grey next year. I haven't done as well as I'd hoped to do. And I don't suppose things will get any better." The phrase "intentionally naive," used in the introductory description of Jim, had unobtrusively exposed his air of innocence as a rather desperate pose. In a passage reinforcing mythic parallels, Jim stresses Irene's guilt as the major cause of his grief and ridicules her assumptions of personal virtue: "Why are you so Christly all of a sudden? What's turned you overnight into a convent girl? You stole your mother's jewelry before they probated her will. You never gave your sister a cent of that money that was intended for her--not even when she needed it. You made Grace Howland's life miserable, and where was all your piety and your virtue when you went to that abortionist? I'll never forget how cool you were. You packed your bag and went off to have that child murdered as if you were going to Nassau."

Irene's final futile attempt to tune in the Sweeneys' nurse, the positive image of humanity needed to reinforce a belief in her own goodness, illuminates the terrors of assumed omniscience and the inevitable defeat of human pride. The detached voice of the announcer, mingling disasters with weather reports, is a twentieth-century version of a divine edict that permanently exiles the Westcotts, but offers no parallel to the ultimate promise traditionally associated with the original pair. The ironic reinterpretation given the myth by Cheever suggests that the expulsion from Eden does not symbolize the fall from good to evil, or from innocence to experience, but the fall from assumed innocence to awareness, specifically self-awareness, and its attendant anguish. Cheever's irony implies that man's knowledge of his personal evil, no matter how painfully acquired, does not bring the power conventionally attributed to such insight, but only additional difficul- and frustrations. Both Adam and Jim are exiled to a life of constant anxiety and fruitless bickering.

Studies in Short Fiction 4 (Spring 1967): 262-64.

"Young Goodman Brown" and "The Enormous Radio"

Henrietta Ten Harmsel

Burton Kendle's analysis of Cheever's "The Enormous Radio" (*Studies in Short Fiction*, 4 [1967], 262-264) perceptively clarifies the change from apparent innocence to disturbing self-knowledge in Jim and Irene Westcott. Comparing the malevolent radio to a powerful Satanic intruder is also very sound. However, associating "The Enormous Radio" with the Eden story seems to me less enlightening than comparing it with Hawthorne's "Young Goodman Brown." In both of these stories the "innocent" protagonists are made aware of an evil that already quite definitely exists, in themselves as well as their societies. In both it is partly the deceptive façades of their societies—certainly not Edenic—that have made honest acknowledgement of evil impossible. And in both, the leading protagonist is left finally in this deep dilemma: the necessity and yet the apparent impossibility of maintaining love when the corruption of both the individual and his society has been overwhelmingly exposed.

In the two stories the development from innocence to self-knowledge is amazingly similar. Initially Irene's pleasantly blank forehead and Jim's intentional naiveté resemble the pretty "pink-ribboned" head of Faith and Goodman Brown's dubious affirmation of his innocent intentions. The mysterious, black-clad figure whom the uneasy Goodman meets in the forest is hard for him to recognize in spite of the devil's snake-like staff. So also Irene becomes immediately uneasy at the malevolence of the "aggressive intruder" but fails to comprehend its power as she turns the "dials and switches . . . disappointed and bewildered." As the radio progresses from violently amplified music to crackling static to electric razors, Irene meets each new development with the decision to "turn it off." In a similar manner Goodman Brown punctuates each deeper move into the evil forest with his determination to "go no farther." The radio's "mistaken sensitivity to discord" is like the devil's recounting of only the evils in Goodman's society: the lashing of Quaker women and the secret burial of illegitimate infants. These revelations of unrecognized evils parallel the obscenity, the dishonesty, and the lechery that the radio reveals to Irene in her neighbors. As young Goodman Brown slowly recognizes Goody Cloyse, Deacon Gookin, and the "confused and doubtful . . . voices" from the "depths of the cloud" above him, so Irene begins to identify the voices of Miss Armstrong, the Fullers, and the Osborns in 16-C.

Just as the "horrible laughter" of Goodman Brown changes later to the sadness of "a darkly meditative, a distrustful, if not a desperate man," so Irene's laughter changes later to furtive guilt and hysterical tears. Goodman Brown's self-righteous hesitations and his final desperate advice to Faith to "resist the wicked one" are also somewhat reflected in Irene's actions: her sad attempt to do "a good deed in a naughty world," her desperate plea to Jim to intervene in the Osborn's struggles, and her painful insistence that she and Jim "have never been like that." Indeed Hawthorne's forest music that "seemed a hymn" but proved to be the "awful harmony" of individual and social corruption is not unlike the soothing classical music that the enormous radio changes to the thin scratchy music of "The Missouri Waltz" and the horrible cacophony of life in the surrounding apartments. Finally, in both stories the malevolent intruder is suddenly removed: the radio is fixed and the devil of Goodman Brown's "vision" disappears. But things are no longer the same. Young Goodman Brown now sees only evil in those whom he formerly loved, even in Faith, into whose face he looks "sternly and sadly." All harmony has also disappeared for Jim and Irene: he reveals his financial insecurity, resentfully shouts "turn it off" to Irene's guilty fears, and finally enumerates cruelly all the secret sins of her past. But, like the Goodman, Irene can no longer suppress her vision of her pervasive guilt. "Disgraced and sickened" she stands, unable to turn the radio off.

Although both stories do somewhat resemble the Eden tale, they both reveal also a basic difference from it: that a perverted society is partially responsible for the individual's unrealistic "innocence" and isolation. Hawthorne is obviously exposing the hypocritical purity of a community that refuses to acknowledge its sin, making honest human relationships impossible. Cheever is obviously criticizing a society in which technology and compartmentalized urban living are making human understanding and communication impossible. The old radio at the beginning of the story is still "sensitive, unpredictable," and responsive to a human strike of the hand. But when it is "beyond repair," it is replaced by the enormous, ugly radio whose confounding "number of dials and switches" makes it a fitting symbol of the burgeoning forces of uncontrollable technology. In such a society "scratchy music" and the superficial "Whiffenpoof Song" replace the classics. The real sig-

nificance of human relationships seems to be "lost forever" like the
Schubert melody.   Instead, Jim's purchasing of a   more intricately
technological machine is supposed to   bring   satisfaction: "I bought
this damned radio to give you some pleasure. . . . I paid a great deal
of money for it.   I thought it might make you happy."   Although the re-
paired radio finally does broadcast Schiller's "Ode to Joy," it is
obvious from their bickering that Jim and Irene have paid too high a
price for technological advancement.   Even more than hypocritical
Puritanism, growing technology engenders devils which dehumanize men.
   Like Hawthorne's story, Cheever's also proceeds and concludes in
ambiguities.   One hardly knows whether the radio--like Hawthorne's devil
--represents a surrealistic nightmare or "the real thing." Does the
radio's final noncommittal announcement of catastrophe--but also of
charity "by nuns"--suggest that some remnant of "Faith" may live on to
accompany Irene Westcott to her grave?   Like Goodman Brown she may
remain "distrustful" and even "desperate."   But like him she has learned
something significant: the reality of evil cannot be hypocritically or
technologically "turned off."   Like Hawthorne, Cheever deals basically
with the universal dilemma of maintaining a balanced humanity in a world
where evil seems to overwhelm the good.

Studies in Short Fiction 9 (Fall 1972): 407-8.

The Wapshot Chronicle
1957

SELECTED REVIEWS

Yankee Gallimaufry

Carlos Baker

When Moses Wapshot decided to leave his native village of St. Botolphs to seek his fortune in the great world, his mother gathered up a few mementos for him to take along. These included his confirmation certificate (the Wapshots were lukewarm Episcopalians), a souvenir spoon from Plymouth Rock, the drawing of a battleship made when Moses was six, his football sweater, prayer book, muffler, and two of his better report cards. Although she knew perfectly well that he would not carry these artifacts away with him, she had enjoyed trotting them out for the occasion. Her heart was light enough when she put them back where they came from.

So is the reader's when he puts down John Cheever's gay, wistful, gamy fistful of a book. For, like the mother of Moses Wapshot, he has been able to lift and briefly examine a whole gallimaufry of loosely related episodes, characters, letters, signs, diaries, skulduggeries, conversations, houses, gift shops, amorous adventures, hotels, boarding-houses, boat rides, harridans, carp dinners, courtships, delicatessens, fishing trips, windbreakers, psychiatric interviews, and strip-tease acts. "The Wapshot Chronicle" is an antique bureau filled with everything and apparently everybody under the sun.

It is no accident, it is indeed a Cheeverian plan, that the chronicle should open with an Independence Day parade which is broken up when a wag sets off a firecracker under the mare which pulls the float on which the members of the Woman's Club are riding, complete with folding chairs, lectern, water carafe, and tumbler. Independence is in fact the very mark and emblem of the Wapshots. Miss Honora Wapshot, an eccentric old widgeon who holds the purse strings of the tribe; her improvident cousin, Leander his wife, Sarah (President of the Woman's Club), and their sons, Moses and Coverly, represent the family as it was in the period 1890-1950 or thereabouts. Honora's independence shows in her browbeating of her faithful cook, whose brows can take it, withholding money from Leander, reaching barehanded for live lobsters in a lobster pound, and seeing a movie through twice to get her money's worth. Leander's independence asserts itself in sailing the *Topaze*, a decrepit launch, back and forth between Travertine and Nangasakit, and Sarah's in performing good works for the improvement of the public weal in Botolphs.

Roughly the first third of the book is devoted to life in this charming old river town. Most of the rest is about the fortunes and misfortunes of the two sons, Moses and Coverly, in Washington, New York, San Francisco, Island 93 in the South Pacific, a rocket launching settlement in the West, and an imported castle inhabited by an ancient Wapshot cousin named Justina and her toothsome ward, Melissa.

As readers of Cheever's short stories know, he is a wonder with the limited scene, the separate episode, the overheard conversation, the crucial confrontation. "The Wapshot Chronicle" reflects these powers with immense vitality, largesse, and profusion. But it is held together largely by spit and wire. It shows that while John Cheever's fortes are many, amusing, touching, and admirable, one of them is not architectonics.

Saturday Review 40 (23 March 1957): 14.

Out of an Abundant Love of Created Things

William Esty

The Wapshot Chronicle must have been fun to write; it is wonderful fun to read. The reviewers on the whole have not been kind to it, pointing out that the book is not "really" a novel. No more is *The Fall* really a novel, but who has snubbed Camus for that? As a matter of fact, *The Wapshot Chronicle* is the perfect book to read right after one has done one's duty and finished the Frenchman's brilliant, depressingly masochistic monologue. Irving Howe, in an excellent *New Republic* review, noted that "Camus seems to have lost the affection for created things that the novelist must have if he is to be a novelist and men must have if they are not simply to expire from boredom."

Well, John Cheever possesses the love of created things in abundance, and in his pages you will discover what things a New England evening wind smells of, which ingredients to add to carp before boiling, how it feels to traverse, naked and at night, the multiple roofs of a millionaire's castle in search of your lover's terrace, or to swim, again naked, through the vivifying waves off a Northern beach to the rock where your bride sits combing her hair like a siren. *The Wapshot Chronicle* abounds in lights and colors and smells, but especially in the lights, colors and smells of water--a bay, a trout lake--for "all things of the sea belong to Venus," and Venus with her son Eros are the true heroine and hero of Mr. Cheever's novel.

The Wapshots have always lived in St. Botolphs, a decaying New England port town. As St. Botolphs has declined the Wapshot men have lost their ability to cope with the world, and old Leander Wapshot, whose ancestors sailed their ships to Java and lechered in Samoa on the home voyage, is reduced to plying a bay in a decrepit launch, carrying tourists to an amusement park. He lives on the bounty of his eccentric Cousin Honora, the last Wapshot with "the wherewithal," and when his launch founders in a storm his wife Sarah inflicts the final indignity by converting the raised hulk into New England's Only Floating Gift Shoppe. Leander, like many a Yankee captain before him, dies at sea--as the result of swimming too far from the beach one morning.

But if Leander Wapshot is an absurd old man, his philosophy, his joy in created things, is the book's message. "He would like them (his sons Moses and Coverly) to grasp that the unobserved ceremoniousness of his life was a gesture or a sacrament toward the excellence and the continuousness of things." And if Leander's ceremoniousness includes the avoidance of sleeping in moonlight, his last message to his sons ends with the injunction "Fear tastes like a rusty knife and do not let her into your house. Courage tastes of blood. Stand up straight. Admire the world. Relish the love of a gentle woman. Trust in the Lord."

The quaintness of Leander's prose style is part of "the rich dark varnish of decorum and quaintness" that overlays St. Botolphs. The first part of *The Wapshot Chronicle* is a wonderfully funny exploration of St. Botolphs and its "characters": Theophilus Gates who put a For Sale sign on his lawn to convince the town he was losing money; the undertaker who "like any good Yankee . . . had never trimmed the bereaved without remarking on The Uncertainty of All Earthly Things"; Uncle Peepee Marshmallow; but above all the Wapshots, Leander and his Cousin Honora and Aunt Adelaide.

We see Leander, who hates "foreigners," trying to raise money by offering his pure-Yankee-stock body to the local doctor for "an experiment." We watch Cousin Honora systematically avoiding signing the form signifying approval of the bank's management of her trust, and sending the bus company a Christmas check in lieu of depositing her fares. All this is a feast for the reader, but Mr. Cheever also knows that "if we accept the quaintness of St. Botolphs we must also accept the fact that it was the country of spite fences and internecine quarrels" and respect for craft and dishonesty. And he knows that Moses and Coverly Wapshot must seek their fortune and their manhood away from this woman-dominated town, much as they and Mr. Cheever love it. In any case, Cousin Honora has decided they "might go to someplace like New York or Washington, someplace strange and distant," in the tradition of the Wapshot men.

The rest of the novel is concerned with the brothers' adventures and misadventures in those exotic cities. The eccentricities of the New England port town yield to the vagaries of the Great World, the world of psychological tests for jobs and security firings and womanless islands in the Pacific where rockets are launched. The craziness of St. Botolphs is found to be preferable to that of the world, for the former is simple and traditional like the town's whole way of life, while the latter is more damaging, more impersonal, and is not even recognized as madness.

Fans of Mr. Cheever's short stories laid in Manhattan know how this bottomlessly sophisticated writer can use the device of an innocent eye to reveal the grotesqueries inherent in what we all see and live every day. That grotesquerie is present in *The Wapshot Chronicle*, and also Cheever's awareness of the loneliness and sense of defeat that visit most of us; but all is overlaid with the gently reassuring atmosphere of a fairy tale for grownups. Mr. Cheever permits himself eighteenth-century asides—"it is not my fault that New England is full of eccentric old women," "we cannot endow him with wisdom and powers of invention that he does not have"—that a carping critic would call coyly self-indulgent, but which are justified by the enchantment of the tale. We know that Moses and Coverly will remain faithful through all their trials to their father's credo and to lovely Venus, Mr. Cheever's good fairy; and that she will guide the brothers safely at last to fortune, love and happiness.

The Commonweal 66 (17 May 1957): 187-88.

End of the Line

Maxwell Geismar

The New Yorker school of fiction has come in for so many critical strictures lately that one almost wishes John Cheever, a talented member of this group, would confound the critics and break loose. One reads the present novel, which is not quite a novel either, but which starts out so well, with this hope--but at the end I am not quite sure whether Mr. Cheever has broken loose, or hasn't. The story is entertaining, for the most part, which hovers on the edge of a more serious purpose.

The Wapshots are a run-down New England family founded in Revolutionary times and now reduced to the lowest circumstances. Their town, St. Botolphs, has descended the scale with them. The father, Leander, commands a venerable excursion boat, in order to feel useful to himself, but exists through the courtesy (and cash) of his rich relative, Honora. (This society is a matriarchy where the women, by outliving the shipbuilders, ship captains and prosperous merchants, now exercise a sterile and capricious power.) The two young Wapshot boys, Moses and Coverly, are the heirs of a decaying dynasty.

The story opens with an entertaining Independence Day parade in the old-fashioned manner, and Mr. Cheever constantly evokes the illustrious past of the town--and of nineteenth century New England--and contrasts this with its dingy and mediocre prospects. The "modern girl" of the chronicle is Rosalie Young, who has run away from her religious family, and who has no further interests or values of her own beyond her cheerful and abundant sexuality. But Rosalie is really seeking something else, love and friendship, through the only path she knows. When she yields herself to Moses, and the horrified Honora is trapped in a closet by the frolicsome couple, the true action of the story begins.

This is also a central theme in Mr. Cheever's work: the power of human love and desire, which turns out to be a shield for human loneliness and melancholy--along with a note of broad farce, or of downright burlesque at times, which accompanies the tragicomedy of sex. It is at this point that the chronicle of the Wapshots breaks through the proper confines of "sensibility" in the typical New Yorker story. The depth of the narrative lies in the accent on human "unrequital," and in the lyrical apostrophes to the sea-born Venus, to love and women. The ironic twist lies in the antics of lovers.

There is another high point when Moses sets out to make his fortune in Washington and meets the "higher morality" of the reform administration. There is a brilliant bit of satire when his brother, Coverly, an innocent small-town adolescent, is subjected to a battery of psychological tests in the world of business. But this suggests also that the last half of the book is a picaresque of modern times set against the earlier, nostalgic background of the New England past. The two parts don't quite hang together, and the story as a whole becomes rather fragmentary and episodic. One has the final impression of a series of related "sketches," which do not quite achieve either the impact of the short story proper or the inner growth and development of a novel.

The New York Times Book Review, 24 March 1957, p. 5.

John Cheever's Photograph Album

Donald Malcolm

It is really remarkable how many contemporary writers seem to regard psychiatrists with distaste. Whatever the psychiatrists themselves may think about the matter, this feeling is a healthy one for literature, since it is based, to a great extent, on professional pride. After all, the art of throwing light on the darker side of man was practiced by writers whole centuries before Sigmund Freud and his doughty followers descended on the Republic of Letters to rob and pill. Is it any wonder, then, that the writer is inclined to look upon the psychologist with the sort of baleful gaze an Italian Irredentist might turn upon the Yugoslavs in Trieste?

This natural and wholesome resentment has led a number of writers to introduce psychologists into their fiction for the purpose of holding the profession up to ridicule. But these portrayals, or at least the ones I have seen hitherto, have been uniformly unsuccessful because, in offering a comic psychologist, the writers have only poked fun at an incompetent practitioner, and not at the practice itself. Much as I felt the justice of the writer's cause, I found it hard to avoid the suspicion that he was no match for the professional psychologist, even on his own home grounds.

And that is why I relish, out of all proportion to its prominence in the novel, John Cheever's wholly successful spoof of industrial psychology. A young man named Coverly Wapshot, applying for a job in a New York carpet factory, is given a routine psychological interview. The questions asked by Mr. Cheever's psychologist are by no means extravagant. But Coverly, who finds the psychologist "as strange and formidable as a witch doctor," ingenuously rakes over his past for the sort of thing he believes a psychologist might wish to know: that his father is afraid of fire and spends most of his off-days walking around the house sniffing for smoke; that his mother once laid his back open with a buggy whip for peeking in the women's bathhouse; that he often dreams of "doing it," with women, sometimes dreams of "doing it," with men and: "Once I dreamed I did it with a horse." Coverly does not get the job. That is all, but, without belaboring the point, Mr. Cheever makes it abundantly evident that Coverly, for all his eccentricity, is not one tenth so crazy as a society which considers a psychological examination a proper prelude to employment in a carpet factory.

The fact is, Mr. Cheever is very partial to eccentrics, and his writing draws much of its strength from that crochety side of human nature which finds its highest expression, not on the psychiatrist's couch, but in the closets of old houses and in cluttered bureau drawers.

When he wishes to acquaint us with Coverly's father, for instance, the author invites us to pry into ". . . Leander's bureau drawer, where we find a withered rose--once yellow--and a wreath of yellow hair, the butt end of a Roman candle that was fired at the turn of the century, a boiled shirt on which an explicit picture of a naked woman is drawn in red ink, a necklace made of champagne corks and a loaded revolver."

The characters that Mr. Cheever creates in this fashion are at once very brilliant and very fragile. They shine in individual episodes, but seem to stagger at times under the burden of supporting a full-length novel. It is certain, at any rate, that they appeared to greater advantage in the short stories that were excerpted from the novel and published in *The New Yorker*, than they do in the novel itself. Mr. Cheever seems to have room at the center of his stage for only one person at a time, and the place of honor is occupied alternatively by Leander Wapshot, his cousin Honora, and his two sons Coverly and Moses. Each, in his moment of triumph, tends to crowd the others into the wings. Moses, for instance, does not begin to emerge as a distinct person until he is clean away from the family and clambering over the slates of a grotesque old mansion to reach the bedroom of his fiancee. Leander is only slightly more mindful of his obligations to the novel. He makes a dutiful effort to interest himself in the lives of his sons and in his own disasters as captain of an excursion launch. But his real enthusiasm (and ours) is reserved for the journal which records the memories of his youth and the death of his first wife--events, typically, in which the other important characters took no part.

If the novel successfully resists the centrifugal movement of its characters, credit is due more to Mr. Cheever's comic spirit than to his craftsmanship. Every episode in this extremely episodic book is stamped with the author's special view of life--a blend of gusto, nostalgia and profoundly innocent ribaldry that is unique to him. It is this that loosely binds the whole together, and provides the necessary links between the memories of Leander and the highly individual courtships of his two wandering sons. I realize that I have given the reader no clear conception of these various story lines and, with his permission, I don't intend to. They follow such picaresque and various courses that adequate summary has been put out of the question. I can further plead, in defense of this abdication of duty, that *The Wapshot Chronicle* is a book that will be remembered more for its episodes and digressions than for its total effect. By way of evidence and example, I conclude with this small jewel:

> "Yesterday afternoon," says Aunt Adelaide, "about three o'clock, three or three thirty--when there was enough shade in the garden so's I wouldn't get sunstroke, I went out to pull some carrots for my supper. Well, I was pulling carrots and suddenly I pul-

led this very unusual carrot." She spread the fingers of her right hand over her breast--her powers of description seemed overtaken, but then she rallied. "Well, I've been pulling carrots all my life but I never seen a carrot like this. It was just growing in an awdinary row of carrots. There wasn't no rocks or anything to account for it. Well, this carrot looked like--I don't know how to say it--this carrot was the spit and image of Mr. Forbes' parts." Blood rushed to her face but modesty would not halt nor even delay her progress. . . . "Well, I took the other carrots into the kitchen for my supper," Aunt Adelaide said, "and I wrapped this unusual carrot up in a piece of paper and took it right over to Reba Heaslip. She's such an old maid I thought she'd be interested. She was in the kitchen so I give her this carrot. That's what it looks like, Reba, I said. That's just what it looks like."

The New Republic 136 (3 June 1957): 17-18.

Four Views of Love: New Fiction*

David L. Stevenson

John Cheever's *The Wapshot Chronicle* is a specialty number, an adult entertainment tenuously but amiably held together by its author's casual wit. In part, it is a series of loosely related sketches of the more eccentric members of the Wapshot family, living and dead, who have inhabited the New England town of St. Botolphs since 1630.

In the main, though, it is a rather aloof look at the fretful anxieties and the pleasant rewards of sex--both as they are recorded in his journal and mulled over by the somewhat lecherous, present-day Leander Wapshot, and as they are experienced by Leander's two sons, Moses and Coverly.

Reviewers' adjectives of praise have begun to pile up around *The Wapshot Chronicle*, and I find myself in disagreement with only one. Both Jean Stafford in her dust-jacket comments and Carlos Baker in *The Saturday Review* refer to the novel as "gamy." I think this word misses the point. Leander's debaucheries and his terse description of them, Moses' sentimental journeys across the roof tiles of his aunt's Victorian castle to assignations with Melissa, and Coverly's temporary fright, when his wife leaves him, that he is a homosexual virgin, completely lack the flavor of the smoking-room story. They rather illustrate Cheever's wry and compassionate view of human behavior. Cheever insists that we take a cosmic point of view toward love. And it is his great achievement, in *The Wapshot Chronicle*, that we find ourselves (in his company) for once outside the clinic, in the open air, taking the complexities of sex in a cheerful, twentieth-century stride. . . .

The Nation 184 (13 April 1957): 329.

The Housebreaker
of Shady Hill
and Other Stories

1958

SELECTED REVIEWS

Dante of Suburbia

Richard Gilman

Paul Valery has spoken of the ideal reader whom each writer addresses
and to whom he submits himself for judgment. Fortunate is the man who
finds actual readers resembling the image he has carried in his heart.
And it must follow that the worst thing that can befall a writer is to
have his work taken up by the image's opposite, by a sewing circle, for
instance, when his ideal is a confidence-man.

Consider the situation of John Cheever, whose prophetic role it is to
call suburbia to repentance, but whose artist's soul must kick against
the pricks. Are we to believe that he puts his sorrowing heart and
dry-eyed perceptions in the service of an image native to Westchester or
Fairfield County, that the people he writes about are, by some inner
triumph of magnanimity, also the ones by whom he wishes to be judged?

He is more likely uncomfortable in the role of culture-hero to the
barbecue and Volkswagen set, though whatever distress he feels he keeps
to himself. Still, that is what he is, the Dante of the cocktail hour,
and if he deserves, for his craftsmanship and uncommon satirical gifts,
another name to go under, it is also true that he has laid himself open
to his followers.

There is a curious masochistic streak in Cheever's most devoted, or
professional, readers. They await each new exposé of their follies and
lovelessness with the tingling sensations usually associated with anticipated praise or the preliminaries to a liason. It is, I think, essen-

tially a non-literary phenomenon, and the masochism is only apparent.
What Cheever's well-heeled admirers want is what, by an ultimate failure
of sensibility, he recedes into giving them: an exercise in
sophisticated self-criticism, together with a way back into the
situation as before. This isn't to say that he has nothing else to
give; only that the extravagance of the esteem for him has
psychological, not esthetic, origins.

The tension in these stories about the mythical suburban community of
Shady Hill arises, as in all art, from the space between appearance and
reality, or the data of existence and its possibilities. In this town
where existences receive the most brittle nourishment, like paper
flowers in a martini glass, there storms up the dream of love. Here
where the good life is pursued as by sleep-walkers there supervenes,
like a hand on the shoulder, the temptation of a shattering about-face.

"God preserve me," a character in one story prays, "from women who
dress like toreros to go to the supermarket, and from cowhide dispatch
cases, and from flannels and gabardines. Preserve me from word games
and adulterers, from basset hounds . . . and Bloody Marys and smugness
and syringa bushes and P.T.A. meetings."

And "amen" the readers on the 5:18 may say. And an amen at each
moment in these chapters of the moral history of Shady Hill when with
grace and economy the revelation is offered--that all is sand, that no
felicity has been snared, that life has reneged on its promises. But
they do not get off in the Bronx and throw their attaché cases away, and
who could expect them to? Still, literature has been known to bring
about such things.

Cheever's will not bring it about, nor anything symbolic of it,
because if you wait patiently enough and hearken between the lines you
will hear, often faintly it is true, the all-clear sounding.

For Cheever, with all his wit and sophistication and his coldness of
eye, is essentially a sentimentalist and usually contrives to let his
fish off the hook. It is never clearer than when he is opposing
something to the toreador pants and sterile parties and waspishness of
suburban marriages. The land of deliverance he prays for is wholesome
and American: "the trout streams of our youth," a light-hearted game of
softball, bright welcoming lights behind the picture window. Or else it
is romantic and "deep"--the "churches of Venice" or islands in the
"purple autumn sea."

Cheever's women are always loved for their blondeness or bosom line
and his men because they are lithe. They have a nostalgic need for
mountains (not high), sailboats at twilight and tennis with new balls.
It is all adolescent at bottom and not simply because Cheever is
portraying a world of adolescent values. In the end he shares them. At
least he shares them enough so that in these stories sadness never
mounts to tragedy or feeling to passion. To smell red meat is a vague

hope in a universe of frozen canapés, and the jungle is far, far from the cropped lawns.

The Commonweal 69 (19 December 1958): 320.

Cheever and Others*

Granville Hicks

. . . Worthy as the contents of "Short Story 1"** are, they aren't as much fun to read as the eight stories in John Cheever's "The Housebreaker of Shady Hill" (Harper, $3). Cheever, of course, is an old hand. He must have begun publishing stories in *The New Yorker* as a relatively young man, for it seems to me I have been reading them there for at least twenty years, and they had given him a reputation in certain circles long before the success of his first novel, "The Wapshot Chronicle." For years every discussion of what constitutes a typical *New Yorker* short story has got around to Cheever, the common view being that he is quite representative and yet a good deal better than average.

When one tries to explain why the stories in "The Housebreaker of Shady Hill" are so much livelier than most of the stories in "Short Story I," one is tempted to say that Cheever's people are just intrinsically more interesting people. They have greater opportunities, and more things happen to them. He has chosen, one is tempted to say, a more exciting segment of American life than is represented in the other book.

But what is Cheever's chosen segment? It is suburbia, than which nothing, according to a widely held opinion, can be duller. Nor can it be said that Cheever seeks to contradict the general impression. Saturday night parties and Sunday hangovers figure in several of the stories, and he does not suggest that they are particularly glamorous. As for the other side of life in Shady Hill--"a regular Santa Claus's workshop of madrigal singers, political discussion groups, recorder groups, dancing schools, confirmation classes, committee meetings, and lectures on literature, philosophy, city planning, and pest control"--the glimpses he gives of it are not inviting.

If, then, Cheever's stories are rich and exciting, the explanation lies not in his material but in what he is able to make of it. In one of the stories, describing Shady Hill at night, he writes: "The village hangs, morally and economically, from a thread; but it hangs by its thread in the evening light." The figure of speech suggests his vision of the quality of the life he is writing about. For his characters, life in Shady Hill, whatever its limitations, represents stability. The

hero of the title story sees this clearly: "Shady Hill is, as I say, a
banlieue and open to criticism by city planners, adventurers, and lyric
poets, but if you work in the city and have children to raise, I can't
think of a better place." Thus Johnny Hake is awakened to an
appreciation of what Shady Hill means to him because he has become, in
his own mind, an outcast. He knows he can lose what he has, and it is
therefore dear to him. But of course everyone is vulnerable; every life
"hangs, morally and economically, from a thread."

The best of the stories are concerned with this vulnerability. Johnny
Hake loses his job and finds himself a common thief. Francis Weed in
"The Country Husband" is subjected to a series of unusual emotional
experiences, and is able to re-achieve stability only by virtue of a
psychiatrist's advice and woodwork as therapy. Marcie Flint is led into
adultery by the least predictable of paths. Cash Bentley in "O Youth
and Beauty!" and Will Pym in "Just Tell Me Who It Was" are victims of
the encroaching years. The thread breaks or it almost breaks, and the
result is a crisis that absorbs the reader's attention.

I am not suggesting that Cheever's success can be explained solely in
terms of his sense of vulnerability. He is one of the sharpest of
observers, and some of his descriptions of suburban scenes are a pure
joy. He has also developed an admirable technique for handling a
complex series of incidents, so that such a story as "The Trouble of
Marcie Flint" has a remarkable density. But his great gift is for
entering into the minds of men and women at crucial moments. Johnny
Hake's relief when he is pulled back from the abyss, Charles Flint's
euphoric state just before disaster hits him, Francis Weed's delayed
response to an airplane accident—it is in such passages as these that
Cheever shows his mastery. Cheever knows where drama is to be found,
and he has taught himself how to make the most of it.

**[Editor's note: by Richard Yates, Gina Berriault, B.L. Barrett, and
Seymour Epstein]

Saturday Review 41 (13 September 1958): 33, 47.

Realities and Fictions*

Irving Howe

. . . John Cheever is one of the *New Yorker's* most canny and skillful
hands, an expert at regulating the delicate psychic relations between
the magazine and its public. Undeceived as to the troubles of suburbia,
Cheever stands before his readers somewhat like a cautious therapist

making sure the patients don't fly into a rage and tear apart the modern furniture.

The stories in *The Housebreaker of Shady Hill* have a recurrent pattern. They start with a release of some trouble in the life of a suburbanite: the hero is short of cash, he wants to neck with the babysitter, he is ready to vomit up a throatful of boredom. Reading the first page or two leads to a surge of expectation—the sense of danger is genuine enough, reality is breaking past the world of gadgets and ranch houses, even past the surface of Cheever's greying prose. But, alas, this reality proves to be a canary, not an eagle, and a canary soon caged. The adorable fantasy of escape is squashed in a mild whimsy of resignation; the emotion that had been pinched into vitality becomes a mere dribble of weariness. And though defeat may well be the greatest of literary subjects, Cheever never allows his characters to face either the desperateness or dignity of defeat: he murders their vital core before they have a chance to.

Cheever really knows a great deal about suburban life; but he cheats. He systematically refuses to face the meaning of the material he has himself brought to awareness and then suppressed. A toothless Thurber, he connives in the cowardice of contemporary life; the resignation which constitutes his stock of wisdom is nothing but advice to his readers that, dying slowly, they also die quietly. . . .

Partisan Review 26 (Winter 1959): 130-31.

A Pluralistic Place*

Martin Tucker

. . . While Malamud's world is peopled with the tender and adolescent of all ages, and Purdy's with lost souls trafficking down the corridors of hell, John Cheever's world is gaily inhabited by mature inhibited people who have good senses of humor, a knowledge of the latest fashions, and an awareness of the irony of their very busy lives. Cheever is justly famous for his amusing representation of this upper-middle-class milieu. In his latest book, a series of stories tied together by the common setting of Shady Hill, Cheever never disappoints his readers who expect an intelligent and ironic comment about the joys of life in a moderately well-heeled society. In the title story Cheever takes his hero, Johnny Hake, through one of the most grueling crises in his life. Characteristically it has to do with money. Hake has lost his job and in desperation he becomes a night prowler who robs the houses of his friends at three a.m. Dostoievsky might have made a tragedy of redemption of this material; Cheever cooks up a comedy. Hake is a successful crook, but he has no heart for dishonesty. In spite of all his sardonic cracks about Boy Scouts, honesty, middle-class morality and the attitudes by which he lives, Hake is loyal to his beliefs. He gives up his clandestine night life and returns to the bosom of his family; he gets back his job, and all is right in Shady Hill again.

In *The Country Husband*, another husband who errs, Francis Weed, also makes his return journey home without too much struggle. Weed has fantasies of raping his beautiful young baby-sitter, he nastily refuses a job for the baby-sitter's fiance, he insults a leading social arbiter of Shady Hill, but none of these acts profoundly affect him, although they disturb him to the point of seeing a psychiatrist. Within a week, however, Cheever has Francis "happy" again in the basement workroom of his house.

It would be unfair to suggest that Cheever is either flippant or superficial. In *The Five-forty-eight* he contrasts an inhuman businessman-philanderer with a female psychopath who has the capacity to love. In *O Youth and Beauty!* he mercifully pokes fun at Cass [*sic*: Cash] and Louise Bentley who live in the past glory of Cass' athletic fame. Cass breaks his leg one night but recuperates, goes back to practicing his high-jumps, and is killed by his adoring wife who misunderstands his instructions about firing the starter's gun.

Never sentimental, Cheever is always urbane. His main theme is the beauty of companionship shared by two adults. While his characters may separate, they always return to each other. Indeed, in all eight stories, the main characters are married couples, and in four of the stories, the plots involve at least one scene in which the husband or wife threatens to go off. They do not go, however. If they do, it is only for a dreary hour at the railroad station, and then back to the warmth of their comfortable home.

If Cheever's tales are wise and sane and witty, they are also contrived. The heroes have the saving grace of humor and tolerance, and even their crises are dealt with sardonically; but all this good will and tolerant amusement prevents them finally from giving their situations an importance outside their own milieu. Such an attitude on Cheever's part is commendably modest, but it also shuts the door on a developing sense of greater significance. For in choosing a standardized irony and characters who are self-satisfied, Cheever has saved himself from the danger of having to deal with possibly dreary, confused people, but he may also have cut off larger issues of humanity.

[Editor's note: also reviews Bernard Malamud's *The Magic Barrel* and James Purdy's *The Color of Darkness*.]

Venture 3 (1959): 71-73.

Some People, Places, and Things That Will Not Appear in My Next Novel

1961

SELECTED REVIEWS

Mr. Cheever's Sleights-of-Mood Performed with Consummate Skill

Gene Baro

There is something of the virtuoso performance in the writings of John Cheever, particularly in his short stories. The reader is seldom, if ever, allowed to forget the author or to lose himself in the matter of the work; instead, he is invited at almost every turn to recognize the shaping intelligence and subtle sensibility of the writer himself. For instance, at one telling point in "Boy in Rome," a first person narrative, Mr. Cheever breaks in, "But I am not a boy in Rome but a grown man in the old prison and river town of Ossining, swatting hornets on this autumn afternoon with a rolled up newspaper." And again, "Why, never having received from my parents anything but affection and understanding, should I invent a grotesque old man, a foreign grave and a foolish mother."

In story after story, the reader is gripped by poignance or terror or surrenders himself to a humanitarian idealism or to a social criticism expressed as ironic comedy, only to have the rug pulled out from under him by Mr. Cheever. Suddenly, the reverse of what appeared to have been affirmed seems true. The roué in the story, "Brimmer," is not to be pitied or despised but to be accepted and even admired for living the full life of the senses, that is, for the very qualities that were alienating the narrator in the first place. In "The Scarlet Moving Van," a suburbanite husband is first kind to a rowdy ex-neighbor, then cruel, but is essentially so guilty in his total relationship that the pattern of his life comes to resemble that of the man he has wanted to help.

Almost entirely, Mr. Cheever is concerned with middle-class values, with the orderly and comfortable life that has been made apparently by rational self-interest. We meet well-to-do families at home and abroad; we see the promise of privileged lives; but somehow the promise is not working out; the dark pressures of the irrational underlie the everyday performance. The civic zeal of the Wrysons for upzoning is unhappily the combined product of their individual neuroses; their habits compel them to miss the one moment when they might have communicated importantly with one another. The television writer living with his family in an Italian castle and passing himself off as a poet is reassured as to the value of his television work by the very Italian neighbors whose finer standards he feels he is corrupting.

At the same time, there are moments in virtually all of these stories when, so to speak, the promises of suburbia, of the orderly life of the monied middle class, seem real, seem truly to point to something more desirable just ahead. In fact, Mr. Cheever plays variations on what this life might be and on what it seems to be. His stories are parables of some complexity, and his rather teasing methods with the reader are an admirable means of showing us on yet another level how gullible we are, how disposed to believe readily in the surface of things.

One does not need to point out that Mr. Cheever writes very well indeed. A less than first-rate talent could not manage convincingly these quick changes of appearance, these sleights-of-mood. In practice, we are always taken in; Mr. Cheever's disciplined imagination is one move ahead of us; for the moment, he so controls his material and our interest that everything seems possible.

Mr. Cheever is addressing the very audience he is writing about; it is a weakness of his method--virtuoso performance though it is--that he seems to be playing at writing. All the problems he points to are real, all the values, with their implications, are in genuine debate, yet the result is of an intricate trick performed with consummate skill. It is as if the writer were saying, "Watch me! I can make you feel this or that about the life you lead, the things you cherish." At the end, the world of Mr. Cheever's concern remains intact. This is because he does not follow his insights far enough; his work lacks intellectual passion or an enlarged vision of reality--though it suggests both these qualities. In the final analysis, it is as if he had hypnotized us at a suburban house party rather than compelled our greater understanding of ourselves.

New York Herald Tribune Book Review, 30 April 1961, p. 29.

A Celebration of Life

Joan Didion

"She's one of those John Cheever women," someone said to me of a friend's wife not long ago; I knew exactly what he meant, precisely what to expect of her. She would be a gentle woman, long on neither imagination nor wit, faithful unless pressed by sudden pity beyond some point of no return; she would have come from a place like Morristown, New Jersey, from a family that had once--a generation prior to that of anyone now living--had money. She would be a warrior about schools, be given to tears in the middle of the night, be loved by habit; she would have vague but urgent longings for some daffodils planted by a neighbor, for a house barely glimpsed, some ten years ago (before either of the children was born), on a back road near Marblehead.

She would be, in short, one of the disinherited, one of those who live in that trackless country of lost money and lost families charted by no one so well as by John Cheever. Like all of his stories and like his single novel, *The Wapshot Chronicle*, Cheever's new book, a collection of stories and fragments called *Some People, Places, and Things That Will Not Appear in My Next Novel*, is an anatomy of disinheritance. There is in it one story, for example, about a couple, Peaches and Gee Gee, condemned by Gee Gee's genius for antagonisms to wander from unincorporated town to unincorporated town. (*"He remembered Peaches standing in the hallway at the Watermans' calling, 'Come back! Come back!' . . . She seemed to call after the sweetness of a summer's day--roses in bloom and all the doors and windows open in the garden. It was all there in her voice; it was like the illusion of an abandoned house in the last rays of the sun. A large place, falling to pieces, haunted for children and a headache for the police and fire departments, but, seeing it with its windows blazing in the sunset, one thinks that they have all come back."*)

There is another about a television writer making believe, on a holiday in a Tuscan castle, that he is a poet (*"Our ideas of castles, formed in childhood, are inflexible, and why try to reform them? Why point out that in a real castle thistles grow in the courtyard, and the threshold of the ruined throne room is guarded by a nest of green adders? Here are the keep, the drawbridge, the battlements and towers that we took with our lead soldiers when we were down with the chicken pox"*) another about a man drawn inexorably into the past by the reconstruction of a scene from childhood: a lowboy on a certain carpet, a silver pitcher full of chrysanthemums. (*"Out they go--the Roman coins, the sea horse from Venice, and the Chinese fan. We can cherish nothing less than our random understanding of death and the earth-shaking love that draws us to one another. Down with the stuffed owl in the upstairs hall and the stctue of Hermes on the newel post! Hock the ruby necklace, throw away the invitation to Buckingham Palace, jump up and down on the perfume atomizer from Murano and the Canton fish plates.")*

I suppose that Cheever and my mother and I belong to the last generations in America with a feeling for the unbearable pull of the Chinese fan, the Canton fish plates; I am told that this sense of inextricable involvement with the past occurs infrequently even in my own generation. All of this means, perhaps, that Cheever is the matchless chronicler of a world that my children will never understand, a world caught in the ruins of a particular stratum of American society that somewhere along the way, probably during the 1920s, lost its will. But the point about Cheever is that he is doing something more than that chronicle; he has during the past few years been doing something that can only be described as (and I do not use such words easily) a celebration of life.

Although the urgency of this celebration has crept up gradually in Cheever's fiction, its elements were there early; two of his early stories, "Torch Song" and "The Season of Divorce," are as delicate and brilliant and suggestive and unforgettable as any written in English. They were, of course, *New Yorker* stories; that Cheever has written almost exclusively for the *New Yorker* has tended to trail red herring across his real intentions. One expects, there among the reminiscences of a childhood in South Africa and the heady aura of Patou's "Joy," a story of manners, a great tale about the day the 6:10 to Greenwich was delayed, about a girl seen once that afternoon and never again in the Oyster Bar at Grand Central. Cheever delivers that particular merchandise, but Cheever, somewhere between the Oyster Bar and the Upper Level, gets involved, and that involvement is the difference between a *New Yorker* story and a Cheever story.

Almost overcome by the variousness of life, he writes as if people and places and things crowded in upon him; he lives in a world that seems to have been already transmuted into fiction. Probably one of the few really first-rate pieces of fiction (along with J.D. Salinger's *Catcher in the Rye*, Flannery O'Connor's *Wise Blood*, and William Styron's *Lie Down in Darkness*) written in America since the thirties, *The Wapshot Chronicle* surprised some, troubled others, seemed not even a novel to those brought up on twentieth-century fiction. What it was not was a sentimental novel; what it was not was a novel of manners. It was a novel more like *Tom Jones* than *Madame Bovary*, more like *Tristam Shandy* than *Pride and Prejudice*. (And more like any one of them than like the novels commonly written by "*New Yorker* writers.")

Cheever's compulsive perception of everything on the scene leads him down roads he cannot possibly follow, into *cul-de-sacs*, across rivers that do not, finally, interest him. In this new collection, each story is a kind of irrelevancy, a claim upon the attention as tenuous and yet urgent as that of the Chinese fans, the Canton fish plates. In one story, Cheever roughs in two endings: one that happened, one that "did not happen, and if it had, it would have thrown no light on what we know." He produces Aunt Louisa, smoking a cigar and wearing a fringed Spanish shawl ("She was an artist. . . . She tackled all the big subjects--the Rape of the Sabines, and the Sack of Rome"); he trots out a pretty girl wandering behind the crowds along the foul line at a Princeton-Dartmouth rugby game. (*"She seemed very shy. Someone opened a can of beer and passed it to her, and she stood and wandered again along the foul line and out of the pages of my novel because I never saw her again."*)

He introduces Royden Blake, a writer who (not unlike Cheever) goes through a period in which "he memorized the names of the Groton faculty and the bartenders at '21.'" On his deathbed, Blake tells a story about three travelers (*"a tall bald-headed man, wearing a sable-lined coat that reached to his ankles . . . a beautiful American woman going to Isvia to attend funeral services for her only son . . . a white-haired, heavy Italian woman in a black shawl, who was treated with great deference by the waiter"*) waylaid in an Alpine railroad station. Scarcely into his story, Royden Blake *"put his head on the pillow and died--indeed, these were his dying words, and the dying words, it seemed to me, of a generation of storytellers, for how could this snowy and trumped-up pass, with its trio of travelers, hope to celebrate a world that lies spread around us like a bewildering and stupendous dream?"*

In Cheever's own fiction, there may be *cul-de-sacs* and wrong turns, a Canton plate and a girl at a rugby game, an Aunt Louisa and a Royden Blake; but there are *no snowy passes, no trio of travelers.*

National Review 10 (22 April 1961): 254-55.

Cheever's Inferno

Frank J. Warnke

It is easy to be put off by the archness of the title attached to this collection of stories, and by the author's sporadic attempts to maintain that there is unity behind the collection:

> "In order to become readable again, to say nothing of recoup-
> ing some of its lost importance, fiction can no longer operate

> as a sixth-rate boardinghouse. And in a world that changes more
> swiftly than we can perceive . . . the process of eviction, of
> selecting characters of stature, can be as interesting as the
> final cast."

One suspects in this apologia something more dangerous than gimmickry;
one fears nothing less than a failure of belief in the validity of the
imagination--and some developments later in the volume seem to bear out
the fear. It would be a pity, though, to be completely alienated by
either the pretensions or the wrong-headedness of the book, for Mr.
Cheever is a writer whose talents enforce respect, and some of the
stories in this volume are excellent. In "The Death of Justina," for
example, the commonplaces of suburban life--zoning laws and supermarkets
and virtuous attempts to give up smoking--take on the lurid colors of
nightmare, and in "Brimmer" an ordinary respectable man's shipboard
encounter with an archetypal satyr becomes an ironic observation on the
complexities of experience.

In these, as in other stories, Mr. Cheever presents memorable
transformations of conventional modern life into an infernal commentary
on itself: in "The Scarlet Moving Van" a decayed athlete disrupts a
fashionable community and, by imposing an unmet moral challenge on him,
corrupts one of its citizens; in "The Wrysons" a suburban couple,
monstrous in their typicality, are brought to a brief and inconclusive
epiphany by their mutual hitherto-disguised oddity. But the latter of
these stories is vitiated by the author's failure of nerve: for his own
reasons, near the end, he deliberately tears the veil of illusion,
comments wryly on the Wrysons as fictional creations, and suggests
alternative destinies which he might have imposed on them. The reader
would be completely puzzled by this seeming abdication of fictional
responsibility (which occurs markedly also in "Boy in Rome") if it were
not for some hints contained in the last, and archest, selection in the
volume--"A Miscellany of Characters that Will Not Appear." Here Cheever
flings at us a number of half-drawn fictional people, together with his
reasons for dismissing them from his serious artistic attention--lushes,
homosexuals, "explicit descriptions of sexual commerce," "scornful
descriptions of American landscapes"--all must go, people and scenes
alike. If the dismissal were based simply on the dreary fact that such
figures and descriptions have become clichés in modern fiction, one
could only sympathize and agree. But, by his own admission, they have
haunted Mr. Cheever, and his rejection--almost his exorcism--of them is
based on his belief that they "throw so little true light on the way we
live" or that they "are the temporary encampments and outposts of the
civilization that we--you and I--shall build." The final exorcism--of
romantic exoticism--concludes thus:

> ". . . how could this snowy and trumped-up pass, with its trio
> of travelers, hope to celebrate a world that lies spread out
> around us like a bewildering and stupendous dream?"

The words echo the conclusion of "Dover Beach," but one remembers that
Matthew Arnold goes on to observe that this world

> "Hath really neither joy, nor love, nor light,
> Nor certitude, nor peace, nor help for pain;
> And we are here as on a darkling plain
> Swept with confused alarms of struggle and flight,
> Where ignorant armies clash by night."

Cheever's vision is more of nightmare than of promise, and his struggle
against the terms of his vision has made this book less than what it
might have been.

  The nightmare vision points up an affinity between Cheever and a whole
important aspect of the American tradition in fiction. Like Hawthorne
and Melville, he is a haunted chronicler of the impingements of an
inexplicable malevolence on ordinary life; like Hawthorne and James, he
is obsessed by the contrast between American rawness and innocence and
European culture and experience. (The least convincing passages in the
volume occur when, as in "The Duchess" or "The Golden Age," he tries to
lay this particular ghost by pointing out that castles are leaky and
that Italians like television.) These are great names which I have
conjured up, but Mr. Cheever is not wholly unworthy of their company:
for one thing, he is the master of a prose style as natural, clear, and
luminous as any currently to be found among our writers; for another, he
has the quality of invention without which fiction becomes merely documentation. It will be a disaster if the desire to be true to the
surface of "the way we live" and the impulse to achieve a positive
statement of social values prevent him from following--wherever it may
lead him--the inner vision which is both his burden and his birthright.

The New Republic 144 (15 May 1961): 18.

The Wapshot Scandal
1964

SELECTED REVIEWS

Sugary Days in Saint Botolphs

Hilary Corke

The hardened review-reader knows what to expect from a notice that
begins with praises; he will be quite aware of the giant BUT lurking in
the wings. It can only be ominous therefore, that I start by observing
that John Cheever is an intelligent, original and in many respects
brilliant man; that he is one of the best living short-story writers in
the language; that he has a remarkably acute nose for the significantly
fascinating relation or situation, and a remarkably acute ear for the
thing said, as such and such a person says it. He is possessed, in
fact, of almost all the talents.

So it is that *The Wapshot Scandal*, like its predecessor *The Wapshot
Chronicle*, is full of plums. The characters (inhabitants of the small
New England port of St. Botolphs) are much the same as those in the
Chronicle, apart from those who died there and were committed to the
sepulchre with full literary honors. There are the two Wapshot
brothers: Moses--the handsome and pushing, quick to succeed and, as we
now learn, quick to degenerate too; and Coverly--the honest and dubious,
who doesn't "make good" but all the same is the better sort of apple.
Cousin Honora, the embodiment of the eternal youth of old age, is still
with us--until the last pages, when she too receives a fine interment.
Moses' wife, Melissa, deteriorates like her husband, going down roughly
the same slope of the same hill and finally running off with the
grocer's boy to live in sin in Rome. Coverly's wife, Betsey, is her old
complaining, disappointed--indeed pointless--self of the *Chronicle*, only

more so, And so on; *The Wapshot Scandal* is not less of a "chronicle" than the other. It is frankly episodic.

So episodic, in fact, that a large number of readers will already have encountered substantial chunks of it in the pages of *The New Yorker*. If they share my tastes, moreover, they will have admired and enjoyed those chunks, and have been predisposed to admire and enjoy the whole picture as well as the magnified details. BUT. I find the whole fatally flawed, and by some cause that it is not very easy at first to identify. It is, I think, that Mr. Cheever is what, if one were counsel for his defense, and trying to stretch a point as far as it would go without parting in the middle, one would describe as "too relaxed"; and what the prosecutor would term "sloppy."

There is a lack of grip, even of the will to grip, and it seems to adversely affect the Wapshot books in two main ways: it leads to unredeemable carelessnesses and loosenesses of construction--and, on the emotional or even (it may be) moral side, to bouts of arrant sentimentality.

Take the constructional side first. *The Wapshot Scandal* can hardly claim the proud title of novel. Whole episodes seem simply glued in in order to swell the bulk--as if they were short stories (and good short stories too), pressed into service by altering the name of some minor figure in them into "Wapshot" and leaving it at that. There is, for instance, a long section on the Roman holiday of a rocket physicist, a Dr. Cameron, and another recounting his hearing before a Congressional security committee. Neither has more than the most formal connection with the main body of the book. The second (but not the first) is also couched in a fanciful satirical vein that is quite out of key with most of the remainder. Worse still, these two interpolated pieces don't even tie up with each other: for instance, in the first Cameron's character is described in terms of "cleanliness," "decency," "a good man"--whereas in the second he appears as a fiend in human shape who has destroyed his small son's reason by continual beatings. (And this, as it appears in context, is unmistakably a careless, not an ironic, discrepancy).

One begins to speculate on whether Mr. Cheever writes a lot of short stories and then sews them together; or whether he takes care to write the sort of novel from which a number of complete short stories can be painlessly extracted. I don't mean to sound pedantically narrow here; there is an honorable place for the novel-of-episodes, even though that form, in order to make its short-term gains of apparent breadth of canvas and quick effects, is obliged to surrender the novel's fundamental dynamic (which is that we are carried on, not transported for short distances and then set down to await the next vehicle). But there is not a place for the novel of contradictory episodes: particularly if it is written in such a way as to promise an over-all unity, and if the cracks are so carefully pasted over with decorative tinsel. *The Wapshot Scandal* (and after a careful reading, I remain completely in the dark as to what incident may be referred to in the title) would have been much better issued as a volume of short stories.

Furthermore: this looseness is not confined to construction. It runs right through, down to the small details. For instance, in an incident which has neither antecedent nor after-history, Coverly Wapshot puts the vocabulary of Keats through a computer:

> The vocabulary was eight thousand five hundred and three and the words in the order of their frequency were: "Silence blendeth grief's awakened fall / The golden realms of death take all . . ."
> "My God," Coverly said. "It rhymes. It's poetry."

And he goes on to philosophize about this. But one doesn't have to be anything of a statistician, one needs no more than an elementary sense of the way the world, and its languages, are put together, to be sure that a frequency count yields something of the nature of *the and of that to it*. If one is going to fool about with science, and then draw wise conclusions, one has to make one's science, if not accurate, then at least conceivable. Or, if one is going to be frankly fantastic, one must not embed one's fantasy in a wholly realistic context.

Irrelevancies. Contradictions. Unrealities. Hiatuses, if we are to consider the *Scandal* as a follow-on from the *Chronicle* (what for instance of Cousin Justina, and how did Moses and Melissa get themselves where the beginning of this second book finds them?). And repetitions. Mr. Cheever has a number of tricks that he happily repeats, even applying the same psychological quirk to quite different characters (for instance, pages 50-52 give an account of how Melissa used to pretend that things that had happened hadn't; and page 69 details exactly the same peculiarity in Coverly). Goodness knows how many of the male characters (in both books) lie on the beds bursting with desire while listening to the maddening, deliberate ablutions of their women in the bathroom. Betsey's disastrous attempt to give a party (none of the guests come) is a re-write of a similar occasion in the *Chronicle*. On the tiniest scale (contradictions again), the St. Botolphs watch-repairer is called Spofford on page 15 and Sturgis on page 31; and one could fill half a page with discrepancies of that sort. All these leap out in glaring contrast to the loving and exact care that Mr. Cheever brings to his characters, their speech, his descriptions, and the always sensitive and often dazzling texture of his writing.

Mr. Cheever has plenty of feeling and isn't frightened to show it, and I for one am prepared to cheer him all the way for that: if it is a fault, it is a fault on the right side. But sentimentality, I take it, means feeling that is out of control, feeling that no longer troubles to relate properly to its object or cause but detaches itself from reality and begins to feed on itself and to exist solely for its own sake. It leads Mr. Cheever at times into scenes that might have made Dickens, at his absurdest, pause and blush: such as when Coverly, on Christmas Eve, goes to rescue Moses from the whore-house in which he is busily degenerating--

> Then Coverly opened the door. "Come home, Moses," he said. "Come home, brother. It's Christmas Eve." (End of paragraph, end of scene).

So too, in the *Chronicle*, we have the set scene of the "burning of the great house," a purely sentimental cliché-event that goes straight back, through *Rebecca*, to *Jane Eyre*, to take it no further.

But it is not merely individual scenes: the whole atmosphere is just one shade of baby-pink warmer than life. The general purpose of these books is presumably to draw a picture of a certain form of society, a certain way of life--the *modus vivendi* of a small and ancient Massachusetts port which is earthy, eccentric, individualistic, innocent, passionate, rich, as contrasted with the smooth, impoverished, sophisticated uniformity of the city. Fine: but the vision gets over-simple, over-stressed, over-ripe--and, finally and disastrously, self-indulgent. It sets out to be social history but, the fatal specter of the Great American Novel hovering somewhere near, becomes an anatomy not of a life as it is, or recently was, but of a dream-life as a basically conventional and sentimental literary sense would have it be.
To put it another way, Mr. Cheever unluckily falls in love with his theme, and falls in love with it in a hopelessly uncritical way. He falls in love with his characters too. And again that's a fault on the right side, but he goes too far: he tends to introduce them with haloes of lovableness about their brows. It is as if he were saying "Look! this man is great, he's adorable, he's splendid, you just take my word for that, I know." Well, as a matter of fact he is dead right: Leander Wapshot, of the *Chronicle*, is lovable and all the rest, there's no denying it. Only one feels that Mr. Cheever ought to conceal his confidence, his love-affair, more discreetly.

The trouble about sentimentality is that it debases the coinage. The whole tone of Mr. Cheever's mind is attractive: intelligent, sympathetic, exploring, sweet, clean. But in the end, feeling flows too readily, taps are dripping all over the place. Emotion gives way to acrobatics and the crises become unreal, unurgent, because we are so certain that all will happily be resolved in a page or two. Even such

an incident as poor old Cousin Honora's determination to hang herself in
her attic is all great fun and even Mr. Cheever can't be bothered to
consider the tragic implications of it. All tends to the facile, the
quick trick, and often to archness--

> And now we come to the unsavory or homosexual part of our tale
> and any disinterested reader is encouraged to skip.

Don't worry, reader, nothing naughty happens, it's all a false alarm.
Just relax. You are safe with John Cheever.
   I seem to descry the hooves and horns of the deliberately contrived
best-seller. "I think the whole book is marvelous," says Malcolm
Cowley, and thousands and thousands of readers are going to feel the
same way.

The New Republic 150 (25 January 1964): 19-21.

The Way We Feel Now

Benjamin DeMott

It is Saturday afternoon. Betsey Wapshot, a figure in John Cheever's
The Wapshot Scandal (Harper & Row, $4.95), is sitting in her living room
looking at TV. Her husband is away shopping with their young son.
Glancing outside Betsey notices a neighbor taking down storm windows and
putting up screens. The man appears to be having trouble with one of
the windows. Perched on a ladder, he yanks at it, loses his footing,
falls two stories onto a cement terrace. Betsey watches long enough to
see that the body on the terrace is inert, and returns to her TV
program. Twenty minutes later an ambulance carts off the body (the
alarm has been given by passing children), and in the evening Betsey
learns that the neighbor was killed instantly in the fall. Now, as
earlier, she has no reflections.
   Viewed in the garish light cast by the Standard Modern Authors,
creators who regard the present age as a living hell, this snippet of
fiction looks unoriginal. Its subject, feelinglessness, haunts nearly
all their work. And, given the density of genius among them--among
Kafka, Gide, Joyce, Eliot, Camus, Faulkner, and Lawrence, that is--the
chance seems slim that anyone similarly haunted in the 1960s could avoid
being repetitive or dull.
   That the inventor of the Wapshot clan is never dull is traceable in
part to his success in updating hell. The props and furnishings of
modern life change fast, as everybody knows; finding the present look of

the world in the work of the older modern masters already demands an act of imagination. Cheever rarely demands imaginative acts of this kind. His first novel and best book, *The Wapshot Chronicle* (1957), was decorated with lively quotations from an old New Englander's autobiography, but its hero was a rocket technician. His four volumes of short stories tell of marital agonies and failures of love not wholly unheard-of in the past, but invariably these agonies have a spot news quality. (Wayward husbands steal kisses not from buxom tarts but from baby-sitting teen-agers, and are consigned not to Hades but to hobbies—a therapeutic lathe, say, in a cellar workshop.)

The Wapshot Scandal, an episodic tale which follows young Moses and Coverly Wapshot through disastrous marriages to the final breakup of their Massachusetts family camp, suggests that this writer's determination to Stay Abreast is increasing in intensity. The book's memorable narrative sequences—an airliner hijacking, a Senate hearing about the Bomb, an uproarious special Easter promotion by a store manager drunk on avant-garde market research—are briskly in the current. The talk is ahead of the times. ("I'm keen on chicken," says a scientist at supper, "and when I get my appetite dialed up I can put away a very satisfactory payload.") The lesser characters on the sidelines are, to a man, people with their feet planted in the weightless mush of the Space Age—witness Mr. Armstrong, whose accomplishment is that of developing "a dry, manly and monosyllabic prose style for ghosting the chronicles of astronauts."

And as for the central characters—at their backs, too, the wingless rockets and ziptop cans of the 'sixties are always popping near. Coverly Wapshot (pr. WARP-SHART) lives in a development at a missile site, and works for a mad scientific administrator who believes in the inevitability of hydrogen warfare; Coverly's dawns are lit by launchings and his off hours are spent studying Keats on a computer. Melissa, his sister-in-law, lives a life of terror in a New York suburb and ends her wild pilgrimages in a Roman Supra-Marketto Americano, where she is seen "chant[ing], like Ophelia, snatches of old tunes. 'Winstons taste *good* like a cigarette should. Mr. Clean, Mr. *Clean* . . .'" And stately, aged Honora Wapshot, relic of gentler days and a Red Sox fan, flies the country to avoid prosecution for income-tax evasion.

There is more to Cheever's gift, though, than an eye for last night's news and commercials: there is a remarkable comic inventiveness. Apathetic Betsey, observer of death by storm window, has no response to that event, as just indicated. But elsewhere in the book, unconcern at the fall of man finds its true voice, and the stream of solecisms that issues from it is hilarious. ("I want something for a deceased," says a customer in a florist's shop. "The marriage was no go. We couldn't optimize," says a divorced engineer to a stranger.) On page after page ancient commonplaces about lonely Yankees are translated into zany drama

showing how American ingenuity undertakes to fill the human void it
helped to create. (A husband, defeated in his effort to produce local
mourners to attend his wife's funeral, turns resourcefully away to the
vacation life of their marriage, and musters a clutch of near strangers
met on cruise ships years before.) More important than any of this, the
author of *The Wapshot Scandal* has worked out, over the years, a
fictional gambit--"point of view" is the received expression--that is
shrewdly adapted to his theme, and bound to be imitated in the future.

The value of the gambit, not entirely easy to grasp, is that it
enables its user to describe behavior without describing the feelings
that accompany it--but without lapsing into embarrassing silences. In
good, or non-suspense fiction, Tolstoy said, interest in details of
feeling predominates over interest in events. John Cheever doesn't
write stories of suspense. And, since he means to portray feelingless
men, figures whose emotional life consists only of generalized terror
and vague sexual need, he can hardly focus on details of feeling. A
careful account of Coverly Wapshot's reasons for studying Keats, an
analysis of Betsey Wapshot's feelings as she resumes viewing instead of
aiding her neighbor--these can't be offered except at the risk of
blurring the essential point, namely that individual reasons and
feelings no longer count.

Yet the novelist does have to speak; his traditional obligation is to
comment on the behavior he reports. Cheever's solution is to present
behavior as a scientific problem; he adopts the stance of a social
psychologist. Before introducing the storm window incident, for
example, he says a word about the quality of life in a
government-managed, Cold War suburb:

> Security was always a problem. Talifer [the missile site] was
> never mentioned in the newspapers. It had no public existence.
> This concern with security seemed to inhabit life at every
> level.

And after the fatal crash to the terrace he asks the expected question:
Why didn't Betsey Wapshot care about her neighbor's accident? But
instead of probing his character's consciousness for an answer, instead
of revealing the means by which some momentary sense of guilt was
squashed, Cheever delivers a psychosociological generalization, and
thereby folds little Betsey neatly into a trend:

> The general concern for security seemed to be at the bottom of
> her negligence. . . . Presumably her concern for security had
> led her to overlook the death of a neighbor.

The word "presumably" not only announces that the novelist means to keep his nose out of the character's head and heart, it implies--to repeat--that individual heads and hearts are insignificant. Similar announcements occur everywhere in *The Wapshot Scandal* and in Cheever's recent stories. The objection to them, or rather to the fictional method of which they stand as an outward sign, is that the method is antihuman in effect. One defense of the method is that a sound way to teach the worth of feelings is to tell what the world would be like if there were no feelings. Another defense is that comic writers have always mechanized their characters.

The latter argument isn't completely convincing, for the final impression left by this writer's work is not simply of comedy but of pathos. But that his books raise a serious question is the measure of their interest. Their limits are plain enough. Cheever is never angry, merely sad; his own range of feeling extends only to a generalizing pity for human helplessness; he neither claims nor possesses a massive power of intellect. And, as should be added, unrelenting contemporaneousness is, in his fiction, a form of built-in obsolescence. (The march of events is already overtaking some of Cheever's newsy tales--"The Enormous Radio" for one.) But if this writer is what is called a minor figure, he is also an American original: witty, suggestive, intelligent, aware of the endless fascination of the junk with which his world and ours is furnished, and able almost at will to make his audience laugh out loud. There are fewer than half a dozen living American writers of fiction for whom more than this can be said.

Harper's 228 (February 1964): 111-12.

From Christmas to Christmas—A Ramble with the Wapshots

George Greene

Mr. Cheever should have called his new book *The Education of Coverly Wapshot*, for already I can hear the critical establishment lining up to praise its technical skill while gently, paternally, dismissing its graver implications. Some hint of Henry Adams, that earlier and indisputably serious citizen of the South Shore of Boston, might take off the curse. I grant that this parallel demands not only decorum, but also that dexterity which comes with consummate art. If John Cheever does not handle words with requisite skill, I know of no American writer better equipped to imply without offense.

Early in *The Wapshot Scandal*, Coverly reads from Tristram Shandy. Not long afterwards, alone in the family house, he sees the ghost of his father Leander, whom readers of *The Wapshot Chronicle* will know as tra-

veler, lover, skipper of the launch *Topaze*. The scene is important for
both the Wapshots and their author. Critics have long admired the
Tristram Shandy side of Mr. Cheever--wry, wild exposures of delusion and
erratic sexuality among members of our country club set. Surely he has
earned the right to be judged on a more ambitious level? For he is now
more involved in reassessing the claims of ghosts than in relaying
scandal.

Mr. Cheever is a member of the varsity squad among masters of the
American short story. He figures, not only as contributor, but also as
oracle as to how the tale was achieved, in that most revered Creative
Writing Bible, *Understanding Fiction* by Brooks and Warren. Apparently
this very success causes reservations whenever Mr. Cheever embarks on
longer journeys. One thinks of Carlos Baker's observation about *The
Wapshot Chronicle* of 1957, when, after praising its invention and
variety, he concluded that "architectonics" was not among its author's
gifts.

This sequel also explores a regional state of mind, and its
voices go beyond the common range in contemporary fiction, which most
often mirrors some existential victim in frontline trench, prison, or
mental hospital. Mr. Cheever studies the generation of Moses and
Coverly, though an older age group figures importantly through Cousin
Honora, who courts trouble by her failure to pay income taxes. In the
town of St. Botolphs children still phone the general store to inquire
whether the proprietor has Prince Albert in the can, then gleefully
demanding that he be freed.

In this bucolic crossroads Honora Wapshot occupies an imposing, indeed
solemn, position. She insists on wearing white, except for Labor Day,
when she dons the color of mourning. Yet sad lapses overshadow comedy.
Moses' wife, distraught by the limits of suburbia, takes a delivery boy
as her lover. Miles away from New England Coverly, tempted also by
selfishness and lust, resists the destructive relativism of Dr. Cameron,
head of the Talifer Missile Site, a revolt symbolized by Coverly's
campaign to do a word count of the poetry of John Keats on a computer.

Explosions of wild antics relieve more weighty moments when members of
the Wapshot clan seek with something like desperation to define
themselves, or to revive the sense of security once provided by their
family's image of itself. The *Chronicle* began with Independence Day.
The Wapshot Scandal starts--and ends--with Christmas. We have moved
beyond those decades of self-congratulation when we could loudly indulge
ourselves in parochial oratory. The missile site, grotesque and
frightening, looms like some set for a horror film after midnight.

Dr. Cameron reads *Western Romances*. During a Senate investigation, he
plays a Bach air for solo violin, hoping to prove he is cultured. At
this same session one learns about the retarded son he once confined in
a locked closet. Dr. Cameron represents the modern enemy of the

Wapshots, who have long been disqualified for theological debate and too fallible to issue social edicts. Such a man projects an atmosphere "where we seem to regard one another with the horror and dismay of a civilization of caricaturists."

No one can accuse the Wapshots of being caricaturists, which accounts for their edification as well as their entertainment. Old Leander possessed that indestructible youthfulness found in certain Yankee faces, but his face--at least in old age--was the face of a boy who had seen the Gorgon. This is his bequest to the next generation, and the question raised by one of his daughters-in-law underlines the most central paradox. ". . . why, in this most prosperous and equitable world, should everyone seem so bored and disappointed?"

No one will be surprised anymore at Mr. Cheever's tactical successes in portraiture and dialogue that exposes like an x-ray. The bar of the Viaduct House, St. Botolph's solitary hotel, "smelled like a soil excavation." Mr. Williams keeps a picture of Woodrow Wilson framed in a mahogany toilet seat. "'My husband's family came over on the *Arbella*,'" says Coverly's wife. "'That's the ship that came after the *Mayflower* but it had a higher class of people.'" Almost all of the participants are fond of using the name of Christ "out of its liturgical context." Mr. Applegate, the Episcopal pastor, hears the requests of his congregation as he distributes holy communion. "("Shall I buy a new icebox?" "Shall I send Emmett to Harvard?")" Yet sometimes even Mr. Applegate dreams about "a renaissance without brigands, an ecstasy of light and color, a kingdom!"

Mr. Cheever is dramatizing the radical melancholy as well as the peripheral laughter as modern Americans, moreso than their ancestors, find themselves forced to forge in large part their own culture. His characters revive that most archetypal and, by now, pathetic solution of flight. Not only do Honora but Melissa and her lover escape to Europe, while Dr. Cameron flies for appointments with a Roman tart. Coverly remains on the fighting line, for no "suspension of conscience" will reach him beyond the Atlantic.

Coverly is more conscious of the special problems of our era, one when, for the first time, "Total disaster seemed to be some part of the universal imagination." Like all of us, he wants more than a private solution to the war between "the head and the groin." It is in this area where a code, no matter how tainted by exaggeration and, worse still, pretense, comes to his aid.

No recent novel has more sharply verified the passion of loneliness which looms larger and larger on our American scene. Expatriates in Italy "seemed set apart by an air of total unpreparedness for change, for death, for the passage of time itself." Page after page exposes those imbalances, physical as well as mental, which distort our cities. Food markets, significantly, resemble temples or art exhibits, "galler-

ies and galleries of canned goods, heaps of frozen poultry and, over by
the fish department, a little lighthouse above a tank of sea water in
which lobsters swam." One individual suspects what may be wrong. "Could
it be true that his character was partly formed from rooms, streets,
chairs and tables?"

More than lobsters, and for better cause, human beings need an
environment, a loyalty. At length Coverly accepts the possibility that
his life, his portion of "some delight and some dismay," need not
condemn him to solitary confinement. Honora, home from Europe, slips
into death, but not before she has called Coverly back to New England.
And there his education, accidental, often comic, continues. There may
well be some discipline accessible only through long winters, enforced
introspection, such as that which once formed men where "the bitter cold
gave to the dark sky the acoustics of a shell."

Winter terrain is always harsh, but it possesses the inestimable
advantage of allowing us to hear others and to know that they can hear
us. "'Let us pray,'" Mr. Applegate lurches, half drunk, through another
Christmas service, "'for all alcoholics measuring out the days that the
Lord hath made in ounces, pints and fifths.'" His words evoke the
dilemma of the Wapshots and, through them, of many of the rest of us,
with our demands for rapture, our weakness for shortcuts, our national
sin of impatience. If John Cheever is not dealing with problems which
legitimately belong to the province of the novel, I know of no one who
may claim to be laboring in that privileged and dangerous vineyard.

The Commonweal 79 (24 January 1964): 487-88.

The Family Way

Elizabeth Hardwick

John Cheever's literary career is like one of those graphs of the
movements of the middle class after the war. He, like they, is seeking
some lonely corner of beauty and truth, some "real" place exempt from
the disfigurations he has fled. The compulsion, in Cheever, to move on
is perplexing since his most valuable bit of inventory is his knowledge
of the slummy asphalt alleys of the middle class. He began in New York
City and out of that came the gritty brilliance of the stories in *The
Way Some People Live* (written between 1935-43) and *The Enormous Radio*
(1947-53). These stories are tenderly and painfully urban in feeling
and usually in setting. They are truly observed, gently desperate, and
a selection from the two volumes would make one of the impressive
literary achievements of the period. Then the city seemed to become

more than Cheever felt anyone had to endure. He moved on to the shady, bankrupt suburbs of *The Housebreaker of Shady Hill* (1953-1958). That too, at last, seemed compromised beyond hope and he began to write stories with a European setting in *Somes Places & Things That Will Not Appear in My Next Novel*. His next novel instead, went back, back home, back to the roots, beyond the city, the suburb, to the old New England village, to the study of St. Botolph's (a sort of Newburyport, Mass.) and its leading family--the Wapshot family. (The names in his early work are the usual ones; they will now, in the novels, become old-fashioned, traditional: Honora and Leander and so on. The name Wapshot is itself a curiosity. The only thing plain about it is that in both syllables it threatens to become obscene unless uttered with the utmost vigilance.)

Both of the Wapshot novels are regional fantasies of a conventional sort. The old town serves as a moral rebuke to the present world; but of course one cannot look very closely at a moral rebuke. The romantic regionalism of the books is not so much a form as a mood, and a mood that will necessarily be more an attitude than an observation. Unavoidable bits of Our-Townism deform the style: "The village had like any other its brutes and its shrews, its thieves and its perverts, but like any other it meant to conceal these facts under a shine of decorum that was not hypocrisy but a guise or mode of hope." We are asked to take a special interest in the older members of the Wapshot family. They have not done anything notable nor stood for anything remarkable nor had devastating experiences; rather, they are sentimentalized figures of the American middle-class romance. They come, whole, with all their things, their tricks, their iconography, out of that busy little corner of genealogical longing that lies hidden in every ambitious unconscious. They are local, aggressively local. Their history in the town gives them snugness if not happiness. Their harmless eccentricities are the real claim they make upon our attention.

In the elders, in Honora and Leander Wapshot, we are given a form of moral beauty not based upon deed so much as upon a certain casual charm of manner. This charm is not only valued for itself; it is fundamentally a judgment upon the splintered psyche of the next generation, upon us all, upon the loss of place, clear connection, and personal dimension. How else to look at these characters and give their antics meaning? Even their many failures and absurdities are dressed, as it were, in real clothes. They are meant to be "authentic," like the old clapboard museum house preserved by the New England towns. As for the present generation: Coverly Wapshot marries a prosey girl and goes to live in a non-town, a literally secret place where missiles are made. He works for a sinister scientist named Dr. Cameron, a man whose nature is a secret too. The comparison with the "realness" of St. Botoloph's and the articulated place the Wapshots occupied there is clear. Moses

Wapshot moves to a suburb called Proxmire Manor, where his wife, Melissa, has a dispiriting affair with the boy who delivers groceries. Maule's curse is pronounced on poor Moses: God will give him whiskey to drink!

In these novels one has the sense that Cheever is in flight from the manners and belongings of the new middle class. Flee them most of us will, but they are, still, just a footnote. How can anyone think that our despair is contained in the decorative, the purely social mannerism? Fiction that sees modern horror in our manufactures and looks for redemption in the absurdities of funny, old, impossible people is not in despair but in a state of guilt over well-being. To yearn for the sense of "identity" that came from a fixed town and fixed family position is depressing; one cannot, in any case, avoid a sense of "identity." You can see eternity in a grain of sand, but not in the grain of the wood on the dining room table. In these two novels the strength of romantic fantasy clutches at everything, even the modern "realistic" half. When Moses Wapshot moves to Proxmire Manor we know that we are in a region, the suburbs, Cheever understands as well as any writer in America. But the events there have become as unreal as those in St. Botolph's. The affair of Melissa and the grocery boy is very much like one of those exotic, fantasy couplings in the plays of Tennessee Williams.

Of all Cheever's work, the stories collected in *The Enormous Radio* are the most memorable. Janitors, young couples, call girls, homosexuals, divorced people, miserable children, people moving from one apartment to another--many of the details of New York in the 1940s are preserved with great fidelity and beauty. The style is very pure, as in "A Pot of Gold." "Ralph was a fair young man with a tireless commercial imagination and an evangelical credence in the romance and sorcery of business success." This desolate story of the failed young executive has the simplicity and truth of some old American tale. In the suburban stories, mystification begins to fog the surface of things. The very plausibility, typicality of the scene invites it. "It was my bad luck to have to take the collection at early Communion on Sunday, although I was in no condition. I answered the pious looks of my friends with a very crooked smile and then knelt by the lancet-shaped-stained-glass windows that seemed to be made from the butts of vermouth and Burgundy bottles . . . . I knelt on an imitation-leather hassock . . ." Objects are beginning to represent the inner spirit. Both the seen and the unseen are full of menace. Rich people are bankrupt, the cocktail party ends in a shooting, the baby sitter drinks as much as the parents, suburban Othellos, businessmen, are crazed by jealousy. Doom, breakdown, fraud, alcoholism--and then something beyond, some further doom, not quite seriously presented, but played with, teased, as in a Charles Addams cartoon.

It is hard to place the stories of John Cheever. His special note is tenderheartedness: at his best he is given to suffering, not to satire, and that gives his suburban and city families their sweet, rather pitiful reality. If he has a master, it is probably F. Scott Fitzgerald. At least he has one disciple: John Updike.

New York Review of Books 1 (6 February 1964): 4-5.

Cheever's Yankee Heritage

Cynthia Ozick

What is the difference between a minor and a major writer? Certainly it is not subject-matter: *The Wapshot Scandal* and *Anna Karenina* are both about adultery. Nor is it a question of control--John Cheever has an aerialist's sly command over just how taut the line of a sentence should be, and just how much power must be applied or withheld in the risk of ascent. Nor can the disparity be uncovered, finally, in any theory of what sustains an original characterization--the plain fact is that Leander Wapshot and Honora Wapshot are among those figures who continue to stand even after the novels that housed them have disintegrated into total non-recall. They outlive and overwhelm every artifact and sunset on the premises, and the reason is the premises are exactly that--not merely a farm and a house in a New England port town called St.Botolphs, but the premises and hypotheses of Cheever's idea of America. It is not that major writers work from major premises and minor writers from minor ones--Chekov alone is evidence for the opposite. The difference is simply this: those writers we must ultimately regard (*regard*, not dismiss) as minor do not believe in what they are showing us. Major writers believe. Minor writers record not societies, or even allegories of societies, but vapid dreams and pageants of desire.

Now in an earlier, pre-Wapshot era, Cheever was celebrated as our supreme cicerone and Virgil of the suburbs--conductor on those commuters' trains carrying us to that eery but fine place known as Shady Hill, and, when we arrived, canny conductor once again, this time of the ladies' cocktail orchestra hidden in the forsythia. Everyone applauded, but everyone said: "Limited. Give us more; become major," and those prosperous, self-consciously self-improving communities along the New Haven tracks, with their amiable lusts, lawns, loves, lushes, and of course their babysitters and assembly nights and conjugalities, were abandoned for nothing less than the Yankee Heritage itself. Or so it seemed--*The Wapshot Chronicle* appeared to be both a Departure and a Widening-of-Compass. That Moses and Melissa Wapshot at length settled in Proxmire Manor, Shady Hill under another name, was only accident, and irrelevant; Cheever, in moving from the short story to the novel, had given up the breadth of a finger-nail for the roominess of all the Russian steppes. And as if that were not bravery enough, we have in *The Wapshot Scandal* a sequel, suggesting perhaps an American cycle, family epic, documentary, even, of the national or free-world tone: it is true that the *Scandal* chases us all the way from a missile center (with gantries on the horizon) somewhere in the "real" American West to a sale of male prostitutes just on the other side of the Bay of Naples, where Melissa buys her old lover (who happens also to be her old grocery-boy), to Rome, where, in good Yankee-heritage Edmund Wilson style, Honora is caught up with for non-payment of Federal taxes. The canvas looks wide enough at last--surely Shady Hill is finally too specialized to count, surely St. Botolphs is left far behind, veiled in its miasma of not-being-with-it?

But the canvas, just because it *is* so "contemporary," is deceptive; you can turn it upside-down and see something else, perhaps the very note the artist most needed to hide from himself and us--that suddenly clear figure in the abstraction which gives everything away. The *Chronicle* began overtly as an idyll, so that it might end cunningly as an idyll mocking at its own elements. But the *Scandal*, to prove its even shrewder ironies, begins with the mockery itself: Coverly Wapshot, spending the night in the empty house of his childhood, thinks he sees the ghost of Leander. "Oh, Father, Father, why have you come back?" he cries, and cries it still, even when he is safely back in the missile center which is his home, and which, like all appurtenances of the up-to-date, is thoroughly ghost-free.--"Oh, Father, Father, why have you come back?"

The answer is that in Cheever Father (Father Time, in fact) always comes back because he only pretended not to be there in the first place. Cheever's suburbs are not really suburbs at all; they are a willed and altogether self-deluding reconstruction of a dream of St. Botolphs. And St. Botolphs is not really what we are meant to take it for, a dying New England village redolent of its sailing-glory days--it too is a fabrication, a sort of Norman Rockwell cover done in the manner of Braque: Cheever's deliberately wistful, self-indulgent and sleight-of-hand dream of a ruined history and temperament. It is the history and temperament of the "quaint," commemorated and typified in fake widow's walks on top of those ubiquitous antique shoppes which seek to reproduce Our New England Legacy in places like Mojave Desert naval stations or the Florida swamps. Under this system of pretense we all landed at Plymouth Rock, and that is why Dr. Cameron, the missile master of the *Scandal*, is shamed by having to reveal that he was born not a Cameron, but a Bracciani. Cheever's Yankee Heritage, for most Americans, never existed, and even the few who are entitled to it have long ago repudiated it for the acceptable salvations of our coast-to-coast parking lot, with its separate traffic lanes for shopping carts and baby carriages. This is the supermarket America we all daily smell, and this is the America which the suburbs, those stage-sets of our grassy and decently small-town beginnings, play at forsaking and often denying. The trouble is not just homesickness, but meretricious homesickness. We long for the white clapboard house behind the picket fence, we have need of going to Grandma's for Thanksgiving, and in our plasterboard-walled version of the American Dream Past we tell each other lies about the land around us. The suburbs are not St. Botolphs, they cannot be St. Botolphs, because there is no St. Botolphs any more--and for most of us there never was. We too were born Bracciani.

All of this Cheever knows, and his knowledge is his irony--but there is no iron in it. The problem stems partly from the beauty of his prose--I can think of only four or five other novelists who match his crystal and perfectionist dedication to the weight of a word, and, except for Nabokov, they are all embossers, cameo-workers in the extreme. Cheever's is a prose on which the ironic has been forced by conscience and will: so that often enough the second half of a sentence will contrive to betray the first half--whether by anti-climax, an unexpected intrusion of the mundane or a sly shift of tonality from the oratorical to the humble, or a shudder of fatalism suddenly laid on the glory of the perceived world. "The maples and beeches had turned," he will begin, "and the moving lights of that afternoon among the trees made the path ahead of him seem like a chain of corridors and chambers, yellow and gold consistories and vaticans," and then the completion with "but in spite of this show of light he seemed still to hear the music from the television, and see the lines at Betsey's mouth and to hear the crying of his little son. He had failed. He had failed at everything." Or an elderly Senator at a Congressional investigatory hearing will rise and speak thus:

> Come, come, let us rush to the earth. It is shaped like an egg, covered with fertile seas and continents, warmed and lighted by the sun. It has churches of indescribable beauty raised to gods that have never been seen, cities whose distant roofs and smokestacks will make your heart leap, auditoriums in which people listen to music of the most serious import and thousands of museums where man's drive to celebrate life is recorded and preserved. Oh, let us rush to see this world! They have invented musical instruments to stir the finest aspirations. They have invented games to catch the hearts of the young. They have invented ceremonies to exalt the love of men and women. Oh, let us rush to see this world!

The next words are: "He sat down," and immediately afterward we learn that the witness, who is Dr. Cameron, is a sadist who has tortured his own son into idiocy. It is all chiaroscuro, all febrile play: play derived from the hints and darts of fantasy, from a yearning for the brightness that precedes disillusionment.

"This was the place where he [Coverly] had been conceived and born, where he had awakened to the excellence of life," Cheever says of St. Botolphs, "and there was some keen chagrin at finding the scene of so many dazzling memories smelling of decay; but this, he knew, was the instinctual foolishness that leads us to love permanence where there is none." This explicit rebuttal of all his charge of instruments, games, ceremonies, and exaltations of love is rare in Cheever; he eschews statement and leaves it to the falling tread of his elegiac lines. Among these his disbelief must be *detected*, for he covers everything over with a burden of beauty and sensibility. Exquisite apprehension of one's condition cancels failure; "some intensely human balance of love and misgiving" cancels brutality. Eloquence cancels all things inscrutable. All the same it is no surprise that Cheever does not believe in St. Botolphs and its cardboard replicas, including the houses and lives girdled by the gantries. He does not pretend to believe in them; he only wishes they were real. The luminiferous quality of his wishing follows his sentences like a nimbus, and in the end he fails to move because he moves us *all the time*, from moment to moment, from poignancy to poignancy. In Cheever, even adultery is less an act than an emblem of promise and peace. In every instance rapture overwhelms chagrin; over every person and incident he throws his coruscating net of allusion: to the past, to other lives, other possibilities, other hopes--so that his novels have no unitary *now* out of which the next event can naturally rise. I mentioned Chekhov as an example of a writer who, though self-limiting, is not minor, and it is Chekhov who gives the final word on the relation of manner to emotion. For language to be moving, Chekhov said, coldness is essential--a style should always be colder than its material. Cheever's infirmity is not that he is often episodic (he progresses like a radiant yet never static mediaeval triptych), and not even that his people are frequently tiresome innocents (through whom he has the terrifying trick of making evil seem picturesque); but he has not heeded Chekhov. It is no use arguing that he has justified and ameliorated his nostalgia by mocking it. The mockery is weaker than the nostalgia and is in every case overcome by it. And the nostalgia, like those wagon-wheels on suburban lawns, like old Mr. Jowett, the stationmaster of St. Botolphs with his yellow lantern, is fraudulent and baseless, a lie told not out of malice or self-interest, but worse, out of sentiment and wholesale self-pity.

It is all a part of the American piety. It is a ritual exercise in an emptied-out culture--the so-called Yankee Heritage has no willing legatees. "Oh, Father, Father, why have you come back?" But in reality, and in America especially, he does not come back, and Cheever, in his anguish over this absence, this unyielding and mutilating absence, settles for ghosts. There is no Yankee sociology, there is no Yankee anthropology, there is only a Yankee archaeology, and, perhaps, a Yankee mythology, more comic-strip cliché than compelling legend. The latter subsumes an image of a Europe ruined, brilliant, erotic, and past. It is on account of the abundant yet barren supermarket present that Cheever needs this sensuous and fertile make-believe past--how else can he complicate and enrich? Mere eccentricity, like Honora Wapshot's, will not do--eccentricity is a function of a secure and complacent society, but Cheever is so out of sorts and so out of sympathy with Happy America that he has been driven to invent a Happier America. It is a sad country where a decision--a return, a renewal, a reprieve--is made not because anything has *happened*, but because something is all at once *felt*: an epiphany of the spirit, a revelation without relevance. Smell the rain! see how the light slants!--and suddenly restoration is achieved, forgiveness flows from the spleen. It is a country so splendid and melancholy, so like an artificial (though thoroughly artistic) rose, that anyone writing in it can measure his stature by the inchworm. Oh, it is hard to be a Yankee--if only the Wapshots were, if not Braccianis, then Wapsteins--how they might then truly suffer! And we might truly feel.

Antioch Review 24 (Summer 1964): 263-67.

LATER CRITICISM

Tradition and Desecration: The Wapshot Novels of John Cheever

Kenneth C. Mason

A major article of the late John Cheever's faith as a writer was the portrayal of the attitude of sacrament by which we must approach our lives if we are to redeem them from despair and emptiness. Nothing is more clearly at the center of Cheever's moral vision than the fact that human life and the beauty of nature are mysteries, ineffable and unsearchable, and that human fulfillment lies only in the complete acceptance of and participation in these mysteries. Ceremony and a sense of the sacred are the foundation stones of Cheever's world view, upon which are built the houses of his fiction. *The Wapshot Chronicle* (1957) and *The Wapshot Scandal* (1964), taken together, are a grand baronial manor, resting solidly upon that moral foundation. The two novels are more than just successful book and sequel, or to continue our architectural metaphor, house and addition. They are a coherent whole, representing a family's fall from grace in mid-twentieth century America.

Morally, the two novels present a harsh critique of modern American materialism: the bland facelessness of a mass culture created by consumer advertising; the paranoid, unchecked scientism that has transformed the major world powers into nuclear arsenals; the foundering of modern marriage and the hopelessness of adultery as an answer to it; and most significant of all, the loss of a felt connection to the past--a loss, that is, of a sense of tradition and of the concomitant order and integrity such a sense implies.[1] The movement in the Wapshot novels is from order, stability, and the essential sanity of life to depersonalization, social incoherence, and rootless anomie--a fall, in short, from a living tradition to desecration.

Few novels open on such a note of wistful innocence as *The Wapshot Chronicle*. Cheever introduces us first to the town of St. Botolphs, certainly one of the most memorable towns in American fiction. Once a prosperous inland port, St. Botolphs now depends upon a table-silver factory for its survival. The sense of the past, however, is strong in the town. The local inhabitants, many of whose families have lived there for generations, still feel themselves a part of their rich heritage. Cheever details for us the businesses skirting the town green, noting even the smells of the buildings, and concludes that, "In a drilling autumn rain, in a world of much change, the green at St. Botolphs conveyed an impression of unusual permanence."[2] St. Botolphs, then, is a place where tradition is still vital, where a sense of historical continuity is a major part of its citizens' psychological inheritance. As Cheever first presents it to us, the town is decked in bunting for the Independence Day parade, a holiday aptly chosen for the novel's first pages, evincing as it does a people involved in commemorating an event from America's distant past.

We first see Moses and Coverly Wapshot as they await the parade's commencement. They have canoed from their farm home to the town, forced a window at Christ Church, and rung the bell--a ritual of many years' standing. Sarah Wapshot, their mother and an energetic, civic-minded woman--responsible, among other things, for a war memorial, which connects her to the town's past--is at the founder's lectern of the Woman's Club float. Sarah Wapshot's sad smile, the product not of nostalgic melancholy, but of her husband Leander's infidelities, is the first note of what becomes a veritable symphony of marital discord in the novels, discord that Cheever connects in the contemporary generation directly to his theme of desecration.[3]

Leander Wapshot's ancestors were mostly seagoing men, and this day finds Leander guiding the decrepit tourist launch *Topaze* (the third ship

of that name in the family) downriver, in an attempt to carry on, at
least in spirit, a family tradition. The *Topaze* is a diminishment from
the glory of the past, but that fact does not keep Leander from
investing heavily in her emotionally:

> The *Topaze* seemed to be his creation; she seemed to mirror his
> taste for romance and nonsense. . . . (*TWC*, p. 5) But the
> voyage seemed to Leander, from his place at the helm, glorious
> and sad. The timbers of the old launch seemed held together by
> the brilliance and transitoriness of summer. . . . (*TWC*, p. 6)

Cheever symbolically reveals in this last sentence the necessarily
ephemeral nature of Leander's link to the past, a caducity testified to
by Leander's later loss of the *Topaze*, which is perhaps the moment of
greatest pathos in the novel.

Cheever explodes his quaint idyll, and, emblematically, the life of
the Wapshots and of St. Botolphs, when he has an unseen prankster ignite
a firecracker under the horse pulling the Woman's Club float. Since the
street is unpaved, the ladies on the float disappear in "a pillar of
dust" (*TWC*, p. 8). Thus, Cheever makes the past and its traditions
vanish into dust, after having evoked them so forcefully. This symbolism
parallels the novel's conclusion, in which the past is buried with
Leander, while the present generation lives on, resigned to the virulent
materialism of modern life.

The Wapshot family history is told in brief in the second chapter of
the book. The family name has been traced, through several
permutations, back to the Vaincre-Chauds of ancient Normandy. Its
American history began when Ezekiel Wapshot emigrated aboard the *Arbella*
in 1630 and settled in Boston.[4] Between Ezekiel and Leander are five
generations of Wapshots. Ezekiel is remembered for turning down a
position in the royal government, starting a family tradition of never
accepting an honor, a tradition Cheever tells us "that would--three
hundred years later--chaff Leander and his sons" (*TWC*, p. 9). Strangely,
there is no evidence in the novel of this "chaffing"; it remains one of
the narrative threads that is left dangling.

Cheever informs us that the Wapshots were all "copious journalists"
(*TWC*, p. 11), and it is from the journal of Lorenzo Wapshot, Leander's
uncle, that we learn of another male Wapshot tradition: an initiatory
sailing voyage, to include venery with Samoan maidens. The sections
Cheever offers us of Lorenzo's journal are important, not only because
they prefigure the journal Leander keeps in Part Two, but also because
they reinforce the novel's theme: "By a retrospective view of the past
may I find wisdom to govern and improve the future more profitably"
(*TWC*, p. 13). As always for Cheever, the wisdom needed to prepare us to
face the future--a wisdom so elusive in modern America--is best sought

in a study of the past.

With wry wit Cheever has Thaddeus Wapshot, Lorenzo's younger brother, and his wife Alice sail to the Pacific "on what may have been a voyage of expiation" (*TWC*, p. 15) for his father Benjamin's Samoan debauches. They spend eighteen years as missionaries on the islands there. Honora Wapshot, Thaddeus's only daughter, inherits her parents' moral piety and Lorenzo's wealth, facts which later give her power over her cousin Leander and his sons. Samuel Coale observes that Honora "represents the strictly spiritual side of the Wapshot legacy,"[5] in distinct counterpoint to Leander's earthy lustiness. Because of her money and the force of her personality, Honora has equally as much influence as Leander upon the lives of Moses and Coverly, and Cheever uses her in important ways to connect them to the family's past.

Having placed the Wapshot family in a historical/traditional context, Cheever returns to the progress of Sarah Wapshot and the Woman's Club, glossing several of the town's eccentrics as the club float passes their homes, but using one family, the Brewsters, to strike through to a deeper thematic level. The Brewsters' two sons have left St. Botolphs for college and have made good lives for themselves, but they have never returned to the village, not even for a visit. The parallel to Sarah, who has two sons about to leave home to seek their fortunes in the greater world, is implicit, but Cheever generalizes the perception of the divergence between the lives of the generations to include all of the women on the float: "for while the ladies admired the houses and the elms they knew that their sons would go away. Why did the young want to go away? Why did the young want to go away?" (*TWC*, p. 21). The answer to this question is the burden of the novel. A strong hint at an answer, though, is apparent earlier in the chapter, when the women reach the top of Wapshot Hill: "There was beauty below them, inarguable and unique . . . and there was decadence--more ships in bottles than on the water. . ." (*TWC*, p. 17). St. Botolphs can offer the young a sense of tradition, but unfortunately, it cannot offer them a living. They must seek their livelihoods in a far different, far more desecrated world.

Modern urban America crashes quite literally into the lives of the Wapshots the night of that same July Fourth, when the car carrying Rosalie Young and her latest lover wrecks against a tree on the Wapshot's land. Rosalie is a young woman of an independent frame of mind, who, in the spirit of carpe diem, moves casually from affair to affair. Cheever tells us a good deal when he says Rosalie seeks in lovemaking "the only marriage of her body to its memories that she knew" (*TWC*, p. 25). Disconnected from any greater sense of the past than her body's memory of past couplings, or from any greater sense of purpose than present sensual pleasure, Rosalie becomes emblematic of a tradition-impoverished, morally displaced America.

It is therefore apt that Cheever employs Rosalie to engineer the exodus of Moses and Coverly from St. Botolphs. Honora overhears Moses and Rosalie making love, and, offended by the idea that Moses has succumbed to a life that, judged against her traditional values, seems "unsubstantial" (*TWC*, p. 75), demands that he leave St. Botolphs, that he "go out in the world and prove himself" (*TWC*, p. 86). Leander responds favorably to the idea, as Cheever reveals in a passage fraught with ironic foreshadowing:

> For Leander the world meant a place where Moses could display his strong, gentle and intelligent nature; his brightness. When he thought of his son's departure it was always with feelings of pride and anticipation. How well Moses would do! Honora had tradition at her back, for all the men of the family had taken a growing-up cruise. . . . (*TWC*, p. 88)

Cheever ironically uses the Wapshot's sense of tradition to send the two brothers out to be initiated into the rootless materialism of modern America, and so to begin his revelation of the modern world's desecration of the traditions of the past.

What Moses and Coverly take with them into the larger world are the instructions and example of their father's life. Every aspect of Leander's behavior and appearance, from the cold bath he takes each morning to the flower he wears in his buttonhole, is a ritualistic gesture. Leander "would like them [his sons] to grasp that the unobserved ceremoniousness of his life was a gesture or sacrament toward the excellence and the continuousness of things" (*TWC*, p. 53). Probably the most important ritual Leander has practiced with his sons is his annual spring fishing trip, north to the border country of French Canada. Moses' first trip with his father is a raw engagement in natural living, and Cheever fondly evokes its crudity and roughness. This is a magical scene in the novel, an incident begging comparison with Hemingway's famous fishing scene in *The Sun Also Rises*. The manner of life practiced at the fishing camp is so vastly different from the maternally dominated St. Botolphs that Moses feels that his world has broken "into two pieces or halves" (*TWC*, p. 56). Moses is very much his father's son, however, and he seems to relish the male ritual and to live up to Leander's expectations.[6]

It is entirely another matter with Coverly during his first trip to the camp. When Leander discovers a cookbook that Sarah has sent along with Coverly, he throws it out and Coverly suffers in quiet: "The sense

was not only that he had failed himself and his father by bringing a
cookbook to a fishing camp; he had profaned the mysterious rites of vir-
ility and had failed whole generations of future Wapshots. . . " (*TWC*,
p. 60). Referred to here, in Coverly's thoughts of future Wapshot
generations, is a highly significant condition of Honora's will: She has
left her fortune to Moses and Coverly, but only if they produce male
heirs. Nothing could reveal more Honora's sense of the importance of
tradition and of the family's continuity through time. This sense is
underscored by Honora's remarks to the family on the occasion of the
making of her will: "Lorenzo was very devoted to the family and the
older I grow the more important family seems to me. It seems to me that
most of the people I trust and admire come from good New England stock"
(*TWC*, p. 52). Honora's provincialism is on display here but also her
sense of moral guardianship of the Wapshot family.

The first third of *The Wapshot Chronicle*--to the point at which Moses
and Coverly leave home--shares a single locus of action: the town of St.
Botolphs. After the boys' departure the narrative breaks into three
alternating strands: Leander's autobiographical journal, Moses' marriage
and career, and Coverly's marriage and career. No other facet of the
novel has attracted so much critical attention as its supposed failure
to achieve strict structural unity after the twelfth chapter. Reviewers
and critics are nearly unanimously agreed that this lack of linear
cohesiveness in plot is a major weakness in the book, one which it
struggles, with charming futility, to overcome.[7]

Samuel Coale, however, while admitting the "episodic" and "disjointed"
nature of the book, makes a thematic apology for its structure:

> The more the novel deals with contemporary scenes and events,
> with the cities and the suburbs as opposed to the older New
> England landscape, the more episodic the structure of it
> becomes, suggesting that the very episodic form of the book
> parallels the fragmented experience of living in a traditionless
> and disoriented modern society.[8]

The preponderance of *The Wapshot Chronicle*'s thematic burden lies in
showing the disparity between the traditional values and the integrated
sense of community of a town like St. Botolphs and the generality of
modern America. Cheever manifests this glaring disparity by solidly
rooting a family into a rural port town and then forcing the family's
contemporary generation out into the greater world. Had Cheever restricted the point of view to one of the sons, omitting Leander and the
other son, the novel would have doubtless been more tightly constructed,
but it would have also been much the poorer in human incident and interest. Without the emphasis on Leander, there would have been no moral or

emotional counterweight to the loss of traditional values evidenced in the world beyond St. Botolphs, and without both sons, the thematic richness of the counterpointing of the brothers would have been lost.

That same spring that his sons leave home, Leander loses the *Topaze* in a rough sea. So ingrained is Leander's sense of connection to his family's past that he turns as if by instinct to the family tradition of keeping a journal to solace himself and to afford occupation for his hours. Leander is devastated by the loss of the ship, a loss that makes him aware of man's naked isolation in the universe. What turns his hurt to burning gall, however, is the fact that he does not qualify for a bank loan to repair the bow of the *Topaze*, but his wife, Sarah, is given a loan to turn the ship into "THE ONLY FLOATING GIFT SHOPPE IN NEW ENGLAND," a desecration of the once vital family tradition of sailing. For the first time Leander begins to think of death. He asks Honora to have Prospero's famous speech from Act IV of *The Tempest* ("Our revels now are ended. . . ") read at his funeral.

What makes Leander's personal misfortune particularly ironic is that Cheever has foreshadowed it earlier, in commenting on the rise of just such gift shops in St. Botolphs:

> Now in his lifetime Leander had seen, raised on the ruins of that coast and port, a second coast and port of gift and antique shops, restaurants, tearooms and bars where people drank their gin by candlelight, surrounded sometimes by plows, fish nets, binnacle lights and other relics of an arduous and orderly way of life of which they knew nothing. (*TWC*, pp. 138-39)

The rise of businesses that exploit the memories of a more robust past is not the only incursion of time on St. Botolphs and the Wapshot family. The Wapshot name has been "memorialized in many things" in the town, but Wapshot Avenue has now become, as Leander articulates it in his fragmented journal style, a "back street in honkytonk beach resort further south. . . . Such a street named after forebear who rode spar in Java Sea for three days, kicking at sharks with bare feet" (*TWC*, p. 97). Cheever poignantly evokes here the disturbing contrast between the dynamism of the past and the sordidness of the present.

Because Leander goes swimming alone one morning and vanishes, Waldeland believes that his death is ambiguous and may have been a suicide.[9] But Leander's pleasure in the church service the day before, his taking to the beach his binoculars and a sandwich, the statement that "he wanted to swim and sun himself" (*TWC*, p. 302), the splashing of water on his face and chest to prevent a heart attack--these things would all seem to indicate that his death is accidental, which is as it should be. The sea must claim Leander as one of its own, must take him while he is still strong and vigorous. With Leander's death a whole era

comes to a close, an era that in its simplicity had known something of
innocence, of the beauty and sacredness of the natural world, and of the
sense of tradition and ceremony necessary, in Cheever's view, to a
meaningful life.

As their father's life is approaching its mythic end, Coverly's and
Moses' are only beginning. The courses their lives take not only lend
to the novel its weight and force as social commentary, but they also
prepare us for the acerbic critique of modern American culture in *The
Wapshot Scandal*, a novel that is concerned in the main with the lives of
the sons. The dream Moses' Aunt Lulu has two nights before he leaves
home--in which she gives him a gold watch, only to see him break it on
some stones--is symbolically prophetic: Moses, the more aggressively
intelligent, the more handsome, and the more worldly of the two
brothers, should be able to achieve success with comparative ease. That
Moses fails, that he breaks the golden watch of opportunity, tells us
something about both his character and the world we live in.

Moses' work in the federal government in Washington is secret, and
because Moses' social life is rather seriously restricted, he begins to
feel the peculiar isolation of urban life. There is about Washington,
Cheever tells us, a "theatrical atmosphere of impermanence," a "latitude
for imposture" (*TWC*, p. 131) that is morally foreign to Moses. He is
out of place in the desecrated landscape of this impersonal world, and
he is soon fired as a security risk. The remaining chapters devoted to
Moses in *The Wapshot Chronicle* treat his courtship and marriage.

Melissa Scaddon, the woman Moses chooses for his bride, is more a
symbol of a certain kind of emotionally mercurial, erotically
fascinating woman, more an Aphrodite figure, than a real woman.
Cheever's first description of her evidences this: "She was beautiful
and it was that degree of beauty that fills even the grocery boy and the
garage mechanic with solemn thoughts" (*TWC*, p. 217). Melissa's ability
to attract the grocery boy is a salient fact, as it foreshadows her
behavior in *The Wapshot Scandal*, where she pursues an obsessive affair
with the grocery boy, Emile. Moses and Melissa do manage to produce a
son, fulfilling the demands of Honora's will. Other than this fathering
of a male heir, however, there is no evidence that Moses feels any real
connection either to St. Botolphs or to his Wapshot heritage.

When Coverly goes to New York after leaving St. Botolphs, he feels as
if he has entered an alien world, a world that does not recognize the
traditions within which he has been raised. Coverly is not especially
impressed with the city:

> . . . although you have come here to make your fortune you think
> of the city as a last resort of those people who lack the for-
> titude and character necessary to endure the monotony of places
> like St. Botolphs. It is a city, you have been told, where the

value of permanence has never been grasped. . . . (*TWC*, p. 105)

Impermanence is the nature of the world beyond St. Botolphs, according to Cheever, and it is painful to watch the innocent Coverly in his stumbling progress through this world.

Betsey MacCaffery, the young, rural Georgia woman who becomes Coverly's wife, is likewise displaced in the modern world. She is a simple, friendly, naive woman, who is chronically depressed because of her inability to make friends in the ultraimpersonal places in which she and Coverly must live. Coverly passes his Civil Service examinations, is trained as a computer operator, and is assigned to a rocket-launching station called Remsen Park, a small city of "four thousand identical houses" (*TWC*, p. 226). Sharing the same architectural floor plan has done nothing to promote fellow-feeling in Remsen Park. Suspicion and even gratuitous dislike of strangers are the standards of public behavior. Betsey becomes pregnant and manages to make one friend, but when this friend claims illness and does not show up for Betsey's birthday party, and when Betsey learns that she went to another party instead, Betsey is crushed. That night she suffers a miscarriage, an event symbolic of the life-destructive nature of Remsen Park. Fortunately, she later becomes pregnant again and bears Coverly a son, thus ensuring their financial future and the continuation of the Wapshot heritage.

Coverly shows his respect for this heritage when, against the minister's wishes, he recites at Leander's funeral the words that Leander requested be spoken over his grave. Waldeland argues that, while Moses has inherited Leander's physical lustiness, Coverly "becomes more of a real son to his father": "Coverly, differing more greatly from his father, seems to have a better vantage point really to see and appreciate the older man's life and values. . . ."[10] From the beginning of his adventure as an independent man, Coverly has taken as his goal "to create or build some kind of bridge between Leander's world and that world where he sought his fortune. . ." (*TWC*, p. 118).

It is appropriate, then, that it is Coverly and not Moses who returns to St. Botolphs the next Fourth of July to watch his mother in the parade, rounding the novel deftly back to the celebration of the past with which it began. Walking alone through the Wapshot house, Coverly has a realization of the strength of his connection to the family's history: "Then, before the rain began, the old place appeared to be, not a lost way of life or one to be imitated, but a vision of life as hearty and fleeting as laughter and something like the terms by which he lived" (*TWC*, p. 306). This realization demonstrates that Coverly has managed to build that bridge between Leander's world and his own.

Cheever cleverly contrives to allow Leander, from the water kingdom of his death, the last words in the novel. Coverly finds in his grand-

father Aaron's copy of Shakespeare a message in Leander's handwriting,
headed "Advice to my sons." Part pragmatism, part superstition, part
laws of social decorum, Leander's advice is also part moral encourage-
ment: "Stand up straight. Admire the world. Relish the love of a gentle
woman. Trust in the Lord" (*TWC*, p. 307). Such advice is the ultimate
Wapshot legacy. It is something real and true that Coverly can carry
with him wherever he goes, something that he can pass on to his own son.

Critics of *The Wapshot Scandal* agree that as a novel it is very
different from *The Wapshot Chronicle*. The major difference, however, is
one of tone. *The Wapshot Scandal* is excoriating in its social
criticism. As Scott Donaldson notes, "the attack on modernity implied
in *The Wapshot Chronicle* now takes an overt form."[11] The course of
events in Cheever's sequel is much darker: Moses loses his wife and
drinks himself into alcoholic vagrancy, and Honora, the last bulwark of
the older generation, starves herself to death.

In 1959, two years after finishing *The Wapshot Chronicle*, Cheever
wrote a brief statement about his world view for *Fiction of the Fifties*,
an anthology of the decade's short stories. The statement is not
reflective at all of the tone of his first novel, but is very much in
accord with the prevailing mood of *The Wapshot Scandal*:

> Halfway through the decade, something went terribly wrong. The
> most useful image I have today is of a man in a quagmire looking
> into a tear in the sky. . . . I fully expected the trout streams
> of my youth to fill up with beer cans and the meadows to be
> covered with houses; I may even have expected to be separated
> from most of my moral and ethical heritage; but the forceful
> absurdities of life today find me unprepared.[12]

It is little wonder, then, that Cheever has described his mood as
"happy" while writing the first novel and "suicidal" while writing the
second.[13]

Like its predecessor, *The Wapshot Scandal* opens with a survey of the
town of St. Botolphs, this time on Christmas Eve, symbolically a night
of spiritual hope for mankind. The snowfall is peaceful enough, and the
bells of Christ Church are a reminder of the sacredness of the night.
The decorating of trees is the occupation of the hour throughout the
village. But with the mention of the trees, Cheever begins his social
criticism: ". . . they [the citizens of St. Botolphs] treated their
chosen trees . . . with more instinctive respect than is the case today.
The trees were not, at the end of their usefulness, stuck into ashcans
or fired into the ditch. . . . The men and boys burned them ceremonious-
ly in the back yard. . . ."[14] What has been lost in the contemporary
world is precisely that sense of ceremony that meant so much to Leander.

Cheever says more about the trees, though: "Fancy illuminations, competitiveness and disregard for the symbols involved would all come, but they would come later" (*TWS*, p. 5). What becomes clear as we read *The Wapshot Scandal* is that St. Botolphs is relatively sheltered, that these desecrations of a world of beauty, ceremony, and coherence have already come to the world beyond.

In juxtaposition to a band of Christmas carolers, Cheever presents a young woman named Dolores, a stranger to the town, who calls her mother to wish her a Merry Christmas, only to end up weeping into the phone: "But the voice of Dolores, with its prophecy of gas stations and motels, freeways and all-night supermarkets, had more to do with the world to come than the singing on the green" (*TWS*, p. 13). The image with which Cheever leaves us in this opening chapter, an image which evinces the angry, despairing tone of the novel, is that of Mr. Spofford trying to drown some kittens he has been unable to give away, and himself falling in and drowning.

In the few years since that last July Fourth parade in *The Wapshot Chronicle*, Coverly has been transferred to the Talifer Missile Site, a complex of twenty thousand people, which, if anything, is even more impersonal and sterile than Remsen Park. There is a great concern for security at Talifer, and this concern so infects the populace that a widespread and acute sense of social anomie is created. Betsey sees a neighbor fall from a ladder to his death, but on noticing that his body is still, she goes back to her television. Betsey, the most natural, spontaneous, and friendly of young women in *The Wapshot Chronicle*, has fallen victim to her society.

Not only do the people who live at Talifer suffer the psychological consequences of an environment totally controlled and conditioned by a concern for security, but they also lose their freedom to the Talifer bureaucracy. When he is transferred to Talifer, Coverly is switched through a computer error to public relations, and there is no appeal open to him. Cheever symbolically emphasizes the suddenness of the rise of this depersonalized world of supertechnology by drawing attention to the fact that the computation and administration center for Talifer sits beside a deserted farm: ". . . the abandoned buildings with the gantries beyond them had a nostalgic charm. They were signs of the past, and whatever the truth may have been, they appeared to be signs of a rich and a natural way of life" (*TWS*, p. 37). The vaguely anthropological tone of this passage makes Cheever's point quite effectively: the cultural past has been sacrificed to mechanistic progress, and the richness of life has consequently been lost.

Things are no more pleasant socially for Betsey at Talifer than they were at Remsen Park. When Betsey sends out invitations to a cocktail party and no one comes, she is devastated by her failure to find any sense of community at Talifer: "She had offered her innocence, her vision of friendly strangers, to the community and she had been wickedly spurned. . . . It was a world that seemed to her as hostile, incomprehensible and threatening as the gantry lines on the horizon. . ." (*TWS*, pp. 41-42). Betsey, irrationally blaming Coverly for her unhappiness, begins to sleep alone and refuses to speak to him, a state of affairs that points up the socially pernicious atmosphere of Talifer.

Before he endures the temporary estrangement of Betsey's feelings, however, Coverly visits St. Botolphs, and feels there a release from his worries. But while staying in his old home, Coverly becomes terrified when he believes he has seen his father's ghost, and he leaves the town. The lament "Oh, Father, Father, why have you come back?" becomes a refrain in the Talifer chapters whenever Coverly is faced with the inhumanity of his new world. Whether or not Coverly actually sees a ghost is left ambiguous by Cheever, but either way the symbolism is clear: the spirit of the past cannot find rest when the world it loved is being desecrated.

Hilary Corke has complained that Cheever gives too much play to minor characters in the novel, impeding the forward progress of the main action.[13] Dr. Cameron, the director of the Talifer site, is one of these characters whose role is perhaps written too large for the plot but of whom Cheever makes powerful thematic use. Cameron is afflicted with gigantism of the ego and he rules his missile site like a man born to kingship. There are several other highly troubling aspects of his character. For example, he is essentially dishonest. Because Coverly has exhibited an interest in poetry, Cameron transfers him directly to his employ, where Coverly's first job is to write a commencement address for Cameron. Coverly remembers the first time he saw Cameron, on a ski lift near dusk. Cameron, a legendary skier, sent his companions on down the slope, and then rode the chair lift down the mountain.

Cameron is a man of many contradictions. He is a Catholic convert who also believes in the necessity of genetic engineering; he is an eminent scientist, whose pleasure reading consists of pulp westerns; he is a man who purports to approach the world only through the force of reason, but who must fly periodically to Rome to relieve his sexual frustration with a kept prostitute. Coverly is disillusioned, not only by the contradictions in Cameron's character, but by those found in other important Talifer scientists as well: "They could destroy a great city inexpensively, but had they made any progress in solving the clash between night and day, between the head and the groin?" (*TWS*, p. 178). Coverly wonders, in the face of these contradictions, what he can look to as a basis for his values and identity: "It seemed, in this stage of the Nuclear Revolution, that the world around him was changing with incomprehensible velocity but if these changes were truly incomprehensible what attitude could he take, what counsel could he give his son?" (*TWS*, p. 179). It is plain that the desecrated world Coverly inhabits offers no meaning, no moral vision, and little or no hope.

Cheever's social criticism becomes strident satire at this point in the novel. Cheever moves outward from Cameron and the nuclear science community to include all of middle America. He makes it clear that one cannot find a balm for man's troubled psyche in the contemporary world. At the Atlantic City airport Coverly overhears a family having lunch; their whole conversation is nothing more than a succession of fragments lifted from television commercials. Nevertheless, Cheever reserves his most acrimonious criticism for the nuclear scientists. Listening to Cameron's testimony at a Senate hearing, Coverly is frightened by what he hears. An old senator makes a plea to Cameron on behalf of humanity, a plea which is doubtless Cheever's own:

> We possess Promethean powers but don't we lack the awe, the humility, that primitive man brought to the sacred fire? Isn't this a time for uncommon awe, supreme humility? If I should have to make some final statement . . . it would be in the nature of a thanksgiving for stout-hearted friends, lovely women, blue skies, the bread and wine of life. Please don't destroy the earth, Dr. Cameron. . . . Oh, please, please don't destroy the earth. (*TWS*, p. 215)

Cameron is, however, quite unfazed by the senator's entreaty. With unswerving confidence he testifies that he believes in the inevitability of nuclear war and that he would choose to destroy the planet if it seemed that his nation would not survive such a war. More than any other scene in the novel, this Washington hearing evidences Cheever's deep concern about a society ruled by men whose values reflect an unrestrained and inhumane scientism, a society without any emotional or cultural center, a society whose attitude toward the earth and the human spirit is one of desecration.

Moses, whose future seemed so bright to Leander, fares far worse in *The Wapshot Scandal* than does Coverly. Cheever, intruding early in the novel, profiles Moses in a single sentence, a sentence that contains in germ the whole of Moses' tragic career: "Moses, when I knew him best, had the kind of good looks and presence that sweeps a young man triumphantly through secondary school and disappointingly enough not much farther" (*TWS*, p. 19). Moses has gone to work for Leopold and Company, "a shady brokerage house" (*TWS*, p. 20), an act that places him outside his ethical inheritance and virtually assures his fall from grace. Moses and Melissa live in Proxmire Manor, one of those overly comfortable but spiritually deficient suburbs for which Cheever is famous, and though Moses is satisfied with their life there, Melissa is unfulfilled and unhappy. She and Moses no longer have anything in common but sensual pleasure.

One of Cheever's master strokes in this novel is the introduction, after Melissa has begun her infidelities, of the small suburban allegory of the technologically victimized Gertrude Lockhart, which he uses as a symbolic foreshadowing of Melissa's own moral downfall. The primary difference between the two women is that, while Gertrude is a helpless, unthinking victim of suburban life, Melissa is neither helpless nor unthinking. She is, however, no less a victim. Unlike Gertrude, Melissa is not one to endure the shortcomings of her life in quiet desperation. She rebels against them, a courageous thing to do, but her rebellion takes a form that results perhaps in even greater unhappiness for her. Instead of divorcing Moses and making a new life for herself, Melissa opts for the simpler solution of adultery, a course also taken by Gertrude, though in her case, more by accident than by choice. Cheever's description of Melissa's transformation makes it clear that she has only exchanged one evil for another: "Her feelings had changed from boredom to a ruthless greed for pleasure" (*TWS*, p. 51). This greed soon leads Melissa to make love to her doctor in his office and to a consuming affair with Emile Cranmer, the nineteen-year-old grocery delivery boy. Emile is typical of his generation in that sex is a casual thing to him; for that reason he makes an appropriate partner in Melissa's fall into a voraciously erotic half-life.

Though Moses sinks overnight into financial ruin when his checks from Honora are cut off, Melissa, for her part, is wholly unbothered by their monetary plight. Through a series of masterfully comic incidents (the finest being Emile's hiding of his supermarket's Easter contest eggs), Cheever engineers Melissa's leaving of Moses for a life as an expatriate in Rome with Emile. When we last see Melissa, she is buying her groceries in a Supra-Marketto Americano, weeping to herself as she pushes her cart through the aisles. Cheever compares her to the drowning Ophelia, and concludes that she is "no less dignified a figure of grief than any other" (*TWS*, p. 298). Though admittedly a sad one, Melissa's fate is less tragic than either Honora's or Moses'.

Ironically, Honora is in Rome at the same time that Melissa is, though they never meet. Honora has withdrawn her money from her bank and fled to Rome, a fugitive from the IRS (through ignorance she has never paid an income tax). Honora is, as we might expect, a pathetic figure in Rome--so far from the rural New England she loves, so ashamed of her legal entanglements. Nonetheless, Cheever grants her a last moment of transcendent dignity. As she and the federal agent who has served her with an extradition notice walk the streets, she gives away all of her money to astonished and grateful passersby. Honora's act has little to do with charity, though. It is a moral purging, a cleansing of her soul from the taint of her money.

When Coverly arrives in St. Botolphs after receiving an urgent wire from Honora, he finds his once-corpulent cousin dying of starvation.

Honora, realizing that there is no longer any place for her in a world whose values and way of life have nothing to do with her own, has decided to take her life. Coverly feels a profound love and admiration for Honora, and it is evident that he will assimilate her example and values into his own life. His determination to do so is the single hopeful sign in the dark denouement of the novel.

When Coverly and his family return to the town again a few months later to celebrate a last Christmas there, Coverly finds a greatly reduced Moses, drunk and sexually carousing with the dissolute Widow Wilston (whose inclusion here makes for a pleasing symmetry in the novel, since we saw her similarly occupied on the Christmas Eve at the beginning of the novel). Coverly reclaims his brother, drying him out at least temporarily, so that they may fulfill Honora's final wish: that they play host for Christmas dinner, as Honora did in the past, to a delegation from the Hutchins Institute for the Blind.

Cheever closes *The Wapshot Scandal* in his own authorial voice (putatively, he has made a visit to St. Botolphs during the autumn of a later year). He says that he knows "how harshly time will bear down on this ingenuous place," and his farewell to the town is decidedly downbeat: "I will never come back, and if I do there will be nothing left, there will be nothing left but the headstones to record what has happened; there will really be nothing at all" (*TWS*, p. 309). Cheever's tale of the Wapshot family, begun so lyrically and exuberantly in *The Wapshot Chronicle*, in a world so rich in history and tradition, has concluded in a desecrated America.

NOTES

1. Clinton S. Burhans, Jr., comments insightfully on Cheever's view of the past: "For Cheever . . . man is a creature of the past both in his unchanging and unchangeable existential conditions and also in the tissue of historical, social, and familial forces and relationships which shape his response to these conditions ("John Cheever and the Grave of Social Coherence," *Twentieth Century Literature*, 14 [1969], 189. Rpt. *Critical Essays on John Cheever*, ed. R.G. Collins [Boston: G.K. Hall & Co., 1982], p. 111).

2. John Cheever, *The Wapshot Chronicle* (New York: Harper & Brothers, 1957), p. 3. Further references in the text are to this edition and are identified by TWC. It has been noted by George Garrett that the smells that play so large a part in the creation of atmosphere in *The Wapshot Chronicle* are noticeably absent in *The Wapshot Scandal*, which concentrates more on the technologically sanitized world outside St. Botolphs ("John Cheever and the Charms of Innocence: The Craft of *The Wapshot Scandal*," *The Hollins Critic*, 1, No.2 [1964], 8).

3. James O'Hara ("Cheever's *The Wapshot Chronicle*: A Narrative of Exploration," *Critique*, 22, No.2 [1980], 20) argues persuasively that one of the principal themes of *The Wapshot Chronicle* is "the fundamental irreconcilability of male and female temperaments," and he presents an extended discussion of the sexual warfare in the novel.

4. *The Wapshot Chronicle* is a loosely autobiographical novel, and Ezekiel Wapshot is based on Cheever's great-grandfather, Ezekiel Cheever. Susan Cheever sorts out the autobiography from the fiction very thoroughly in *Home Before Dark* (Boston: Houghton Mifflin Company, 1984).

5. Samuel Coale, *John Cheever* (New York: Frederick Ungar Publishing Co., 1977), p. 75.

6. Lynne Waldeland says of Moses and Leander: "Moses is almost like Leander incarnate and only the sensuous side of Leander at that" (*John Cheever* [Boston: Twayne Publishers, 1979], p. 47).

7. Carlos Baker speaks for many when he says that, "As readers of Cheever's short stories know, he is a wonder with the limited scene, the separate episode, the overheard conversation, the crucial confrontation. 'The Wapshot Chronicle' reflects these powers with immense vitality, largesse, and profusion. But it is held together largely by spit and wire. It shows that while John Cheever's fortes are many, amusing, touching, and admirable, one of them is not architectonics" ("Yankee Gallimaufry," rev. of *The Wapshot Chronicle*, *The Saturday Review*, March 23, 1957, p. 14).

8. Coale, p. 77.

9. Waldeland, p. 46.

10. Waldeland, p. 47.

11. Scott Donaldson, "John Cheever, 1912-- ," *American Writers: A Collection of Literary Biographies*, ed. Leonard Ungar et al., Supplement 1, Part 1 (New York: Charles Scribner's Sons, 1979), p. 181.

12. John Cheever, "A Word from the Writer," *Fiction of the Fifties: A Decade of American Writing; Stories*, ed. Herbert Gold (Garden City, NY: Doubleday & Company, Inc., 1959), p. 22.

13. Susan Cheever, "A Duet of Cheevers," *Newsweek*, March 14, 1977, p. 73.

14. John Cheever, *The Wapshot Scandal* (New York: Harper & Row, 1964), p. 5. Further references to this edition will be identified in the text by TWS.

15. Hilary Corke, "Sugary Days in Saint Botolphs," rev. of *The Wapshot Scandal*, *The New Republic*, January 25, 1964, pp. 19-21.

Arizona Quarterly 43 (Autumn 1987): 231-50.

The Brigadier and
the Golf Widow

1964

SELECTED REVIEWS

Where Life Is but a Dream-World

John W. Aldridge

If you have searched as I have for critical discussion of John Cheever that goes beyond the mere review and treats of his special gifts with some real thoroughness and force, you will probably already share my conviction that Cheever is one of the most grievously underdiscussed important writers we have at the present time. It is perfectly true that his first novel, *The Wapshot Chronicle*, won a National Book Award in 1958, and that he was the subject earlier this year of a cover story in *Time* magazine. But this scarcely constitutes critical attention. In fact, the receipt of either of these honors may be the best conceivable reason for withholding such attention.

Still, every now and then and perhaps altogether by accident, good writers, even distinguished writers, have been chosen to receive one or both, and however cheaply they may be valued in the intellectual world, they do represent a kind of good housekeeping seal of middlebrow literary approval; they signify that somebody up there, or down there, in the mass power complex likes you or at any rate finds you innocuous; and one would have thought that, if nothing else, the very wholesomeness of it all would have provoked some nasty young critic into coming forward before this with a blistering denunciation of Cheever as a paid moralist of the button-down collar Establishment, or at the very least, into finding out what the ballyhoo was all about. But thus far no critic has, to the best of my knowledge, been so provoked, with the result that Cheever remains secure in his position of official celebrity

curiously unsupported by real reputation, a writer whom a great many
people have obviously heard of and a good number must surely have read,
yet in whom nobody who genuinely matters seems to take very much
interest.

Cheever has of course all along been unfortunate in the company his
work has kept. His lengthy association with The New Yorker, in which
ever since the early Thirties the bulk of his fiction has appeared, has
not helped to attract serious critics to his work, and as his image has
come over the years to be more and more closely identified with that of
the magazine, he must long ago have resigned himself to the fact that,
if recognition should one day come, it would very probably take the form
of some such damning encomium as the Time profile. For The New Yorker
air of blase superciliousness and the Time air of blase
sanctimoniousness are both generated by the same wind machine, and a
writer can hardly expect to be buoyed up on the one without sooner or
later being borne off on the other. It was no accident that Time should
have offered Cheever to the world as a kind of crew-cut, Ivy-League
Faulkner of the New York exurbs, who could be both artistically sincere
and piously right-thinking about the eternal verities, and who was
somehow so stalwartly imaginative that he could parlay even the eternal
banalities into a disturbing yet comforting, whimsical yet tragic, fable
of immense significance for the present age.

But the question is not whether the Time profile was an accident, but
whether it was altogether mistaken, and one is compelled to admit that
it was not. There are moments, to be sure, when Cheever does indeed
seem to resemble Faulkner--in his distinguished story-telling gifts, his
obsession with, and creative mastery of, a cultural territory of which
he has made himself the sole owner and proprietor, even in his essential
integrity and toughness of mind which have enabled him to be
consistently better than the medium he writes for and more serious than
his middlebrow admirers would be able to recognize. There are also
moments when he seems extraordinary in his power to infuse the
commonplace and often merely dyspeptic metaphysical crises of modern
life with something of the generalizing significance of
myth--particularly at a time when it is precisely the ability to deal
with the modern social experience in terms of any principle of
imaginative coherence that seems to be missing in so many of our most
important writers.

Certainly, more thoroughly than anyone else now at work in the field
of the American short story, Cheever has explored the troubled surfaces
of the new affluent society in which so many of us now live and cannot
quite find our being. And as the best of the stories in The Brigadier
and the Golf Widow make clear, he has also penetrated beneath the
surfaces into the special conditions of psychic purgatory which we have

been able to afford to create for ourselves. He understands just what
happens when a man making too much money awakens to the fact that there
is nothing left to spend it on except some form of anesthesia against
the knowledge that there is nothing left to spend it on.

His people are all exempt, at least in his later stories, from the
problems of economic insufficiency; hence they are open to all the
torments of economic surfeit. They drink too much, fornicate when they
can, and then with all guilt and no pleasure, and the men ride commuter
trains with the feeling that they are being borne along on fur-lined
conveyor belts from somebody else's fabrication of Happiness to somebody
else's merchandising image of Success, with no chance that anything ever
again will happen to *them*. So they are obliged to take refuge in small,
arbitrary or merely ceremonial rebellions, in nostalgia for a past which
they may not particularly have liked but in which they at least had
something to feel, and in daydreams, not of Walter Mittyish grandiosity,
but of almost girlish modesty and poignance.

Yet on the rare occasions when they do open their eyes to the real
world, they tend to find themselves in another dream in which the most
incredible things are likely to happen or *appear* to be happening. A
beautiful woman without any clothes on combs her long golden hair in the
window of a passing Pullman car; a husband and wife, also naked, chase
each other around the terrace of the house across the street; the
teen-age babysitter suddenly turns into a siren of unspeakable
loveliness, awakening in them quaint, implacable longings to flee with
her across the Atlantic on the old *Mauretania* and settle down in some
sex-smelling Bohemian garret. Or just as incredibly, they feel their
identities slipping away, and *others* notice: the elevator operator
mistakes them for deliverymen; the train conductor thinks they are
waiters; when they arrive home, they are attacked in the driveway by
their own dogs. Or they decide it would be fun to swim home from a
party by way of various friends' pools, until they discover that
everything they had always taken for granted is beginning to seem
untrue, that they have all along been swimming from some crazy illusion
of the real into some horrible hallucination which just happens to *be*
the real, and in which the reassuring image of the four beautiful
daughters safely at home playing tennis, the popularity enjoyed in the
community, the affluence and the martini parties, are all revealed to be
a lie, part of some fantastic and unnamable hoax perpetrated, oddly
enough, on themselves by themselves.

These are some of the typical dramatic projections of Cheever's sense
of the contemporary world, and I hope I will not seem unfaithful to my
own sense of their importance if I say that showing through them are the
qualities which have made Cheever likable to The New Yorker and Time,
and which have helped to obstruct his breakthrough into genuine excel-

lence and serious reputation. Somehow the nightmare tonalities of his
work come to seem after a while a little too coy and cloying, the
postures of psychic torment a little too much like the smartly macabre
decor of some Fifth Avenue shop window in which creepy mannequins stand
around draped in the latest creations by Charles Addams.

For Cheever's vision of all the exactly right contemporary horrors
comes perilously close to expressing itself in the stereotypes and
platitudes, rather than in the perceived actualities, of experience, and
one wonders if he is any longer capable of dealing with his materials in
any other way, so that his characters and situations, his Proxmire
Manors,   Shady   Hills,   and   Bullet   Parks,   will   cease   to   seem
interchangeable, and his resolutions predictable and harmless because
stylish.   One also notices, particularly in his novels and more
particularly in *The Wapshot Scandal*, that his most aberrant effects are
not only represented in the cliches of aberration--in nymphomania, dip-
somania, paranoia, and sexual narcissism--but are often neutralized by
some last-minute withdrawal from the full implications of their meaning,
some abrupt whimsical detour into palliating fantasy. And while less
obvious in his stories, the same tendency is discernible in them. All
discordant extremes of conduct and perception are finally absorbed into
a fundamentally equable view of life, in much the same way The New
Yorker tends to substitute for the distasteful realities a kind of gloss
or meringued confection of the real, which provides us with a faint
sickening flavor without actually disturbing our psychic digestion.

It may be that Cheever is temperamentally the sort of writer who
prefers to give comfort rather than to educate and transform
consciousness. After all, he has been quoted as saying that "one has
the impulse to bring glad tidings to someone." Sometimes he even seems
to be registering certain grotesqueries simply because he thinks he
ought to, or that they are expected of a writer who wishes to be taken
seriously, or quite blatantly because he imagines them to be the going
literary thing this season. Certainly, his work always seems on the
verge of escaping from under its weight of nightmare into an almost
Dionysian celebration of the joys of clean living.

In any case, it is obvious that Cheever needs both to strengthen and
to expand his imaginative grasp, and there is some evidence in this new
collection that he has at least tried to do the latter. The stories
here are more varied in situation and locale than those in his previous
two volumes. Several have to do with expatriate life, and there are
some experimental pieces and character studies which show that he has
become aware of a world that is not entirely regulated by the arrival
and departure every weekday morning of the 9:14. But they are also more
uneven in quality, and the touch is very often unsure, even rather
mechanical, as if Cheever were writing at times from habit or falling
back on certain effects which have served him well in the past.

He also seems to be experiencing some difficulty in telling his good work from his bad. A really fine story like "The Swimmer" is followed by the group of vignettes in "Metamorphoses," some of which are vapid beyond belief, and the last and best story in the book, "The Ocean," is forced to work hard to overcome the pointlessness of "A Vision of the World," which immediately precedes it. Perhaps three or four of the stories at most come up to the level of the best in *The Enormous Radio* and *The Housebreaker of Shady Hill*.

There is, in short, still very little to convince one that Cheever is moving on. He still needs to find something more and, above all, something different to say about his subject. In fact, he needs to be more drastic than that. He needs to break out of his present mode and rearrange or retool his imaginative responses, not only so that he will be able to confront squarely the full implications of his vision, but so that his vision can become in fact a vision and not simply a congeries of shy and whimsical glances through a glass darkened by a pessimism not quite his own, not quite earned by his imagination.

One wishes to say to him now what Gertrude Stein once said to Hemingway: begin over again and concentrate. For he does not yet disturb us enough. He does not yet rouse enough fear. And, until he does, he seems destined to remain a writer best known and most admired by the wrong people for his comforting limitations.

New York Herald Tribune Book Week, 25 October 1964, pp. 3, 19.

Domestic Manners*

Frederick C. Crews

Most serious writers who work from an experience outside the main areas of strife in our society find themselves adopting an attitude of weary sarcasm toward the blandness of present-day American life. The irony of these three style-conscious books** seems directed largely against their authors' own innocence--innocence of history, innocence of tragedy--and their need for special mannerisms of style and plotting seems to grow from the absence of any compelling theme; compare, to take an extreme example, the awful simplicity of Schwarz-Bart's *The Last of the Just*. . . .

John Cheever is so cliché-shy that he once wrote a whole book purportedly in order to exorcise unworkable types from his "Next Novel" (which turned out to be *The Wapshot Scandal*). He has often spoken of the way American writers are thwarted by the drabness of their milieu, and he has lamented the unavailability of a tragic vision these days.

But there is little reason to take this Miniver Cheever seriously; his temperament and talent appear quite suited to the times. His four previous volumes of short fiction show a remarkably serene writer who has always been at home with his cast of wealthy neurotics and petty adventurers. In *The Brigadier* they are noticeably older and more entrenched in the suburban code, but Cheever's amused indulgence toward them remains constant. The most practiced of the three authors under review, he aims at modest effects and almost always achieves them. He is easy to underrate; if we are tempted to think of him as a *New Yorker* writer, it is worth remembering that to a great extent he has given *The New Yorker* its fictional tone for twenty years, not vice-versa.

Of course this tone--the jaunty but literate essay-style that seems to count on the reader's wish to take short views--ought to be pretty deadening by now. Not much passion or power can be inserted into a story that begins, "You may have seen my mother waltzing on ice skates in Rockefeller Center. She's seventy-eight years old . . ." and ends, "My brother is still afraid of elevators, and my mother, although she's grown quite stiff, still goes around and around and around on the ice." Curiously, however, most of the stories in this book manage to seem fresh.

Perhaps this is because Cheever has chosen frankly to celebrate his characters' banality, and from the literal details of suburbia and his knowledge of how desperately unreal that brightly busy world is has devised a kind of poetry. On close inspection his characters look more like mythological figures than the fund-raising housewives and polite lechers they are asserted to be; plausible motivation has been inconspicuously subtracted from them and replaced by godlike compulsions. One woman is absorbed in getting the key to her lover's bombshelter; a man wins back his cold wife by taking piano lessons from an enchantress and breaking down his wife's resistance by practicing intolerable scales; another man conceives the plan of swimming across the county by traversing all his neighbors' pools, only to remember at the end that he no longer lives in the house that was his goal. Still another tale is called "Metamorphoses," giving away Cheever's game; its characters are modern figures, with names like Actaeon and Nerissa, who suffer magical changes. Here Cheever comes dangerously near a Thorne Smith classicism; yet despite his often annoying tricks he succeeds in getting the atmosphere he wants, a sense of awakening from culturally induced delusion to the steady facts of senescence and death. Lest this awakening suggest tiresome social criticism, the recourse to magic helps to keep moralism at a safe distance.

Before the bland American scene Cheever strikes a pose of decadent acquiescence. The most he promises is to show us some amusing types --people who parody us but in such contrived ways that we needn't take offense. But he often fulfills the promise with slick professionalism, somewhat at the expense of sincerity and psychological interest. As one of Cheever's characters rightly complains, "I just have this terrible feeling that I'm a character in a television situation comedy. I mean I'm nice looking, I'm well-dressed, I have humorous and attractive children, but I have this terrible feeling that I'm in black-and-white and that I can be turned off by anybody." It is typical of the disarming Mr. Cheever to have put these words in his character's mouth just as the reader was about to say more or less the same thing.

**[Editor's note: also reviews Jeremy Larner's *Drive, He Said*; Richard G. Stern's *Teeth, Dying And Other Matters*.]

New York Review of Books 3 (22 October 1964): 7-8.

Change Is Always for the Worse

David Segal

When I was a boy I read a story that terrified me. It was about a child who declared that he needed the help of no living creature. That night the sheep came and took from him everything woolen, the tree came and took everything wooden, and so on until he was naked and cold under the sky. I remembered this fairy tale while reading *The Brigadier and the Golf Widow*, a collection of the short stories John Cheever has written over the last ten years. My children's story contains both Cheever's most successful technique and his obsessive theme. The technique is the use of magic progressing logically; the theme is the chanciness of possessions.

If Louis Auchincloss writes the best fiction about the rich these days, Cheever writes the best fiction about people living like the rich. Auchincloss' characters are at home with what they own, and are free to worry about moral questions; Cheever's live in constant terror that the paraphernalia of their lives will suddenly vanish. And they are right. "Things fall apart; the centre cannot hold," and the swimming pool goes down the drain.

Cheever's people tend to live in Connecticut. They are investment bankers, and the acquaintances they don't much like, but keep meeting at cocktail parties, manufacture tongue depressors. They are filled with unearned snobberies which are used as a bulwark against change, because in Cheever's world change is always for the worse. In "The Swimmer," Donald Westerhazy, at a pool-side party, realizes that he could swim home, by way of all the pools between the party and his house. As he goes from pool to pool his greeting from friends becomes less friendly, until it is downright hostile, and when he reaches his home he finds that no one has lived in it for a long, long time.

There are two notable things about this story, besides the tale itself, that make it memorable. The reader hardly notices that the seasons change from mid-Summer to Winter; the hero's reception from pool to pool charts his decline from bad manners to bad morals. Because of Cheever's technical mastery the ending is both unbelievable and prepared for; the logic within the magic makes it inevitable.

The implication is that Donald Westerhazy loses the world because of some flaw in himself; Larry Acteon (see "Bulfinch") is destroyed by a series of tiny erosions. His story is in another typical Cheever mode: the comfortable man living the comfortable life, whose comforts are suddenly removed after his sense of reality and sense of self are given a series of small but damaging blows. He is a partner in a conservative investment firm who enters the office of his senior partner without knocking. He finds the man nakedly entertaining a naked lady. Later that day, in a bar, he is barked at by a dog who never barks at strangers; still later he is mistaken for a deliveryman by an elevator operator. When he arrives home that night he is killed by his own dogs, who fail to recognize him.

Since Cheever's characters find their reality in their status and possessions, and since these are tightly held in a slippery grip, his people have a weak hold on their own reality. "I have this terrible feeling that I'm a character in a television situation comedy, I mean I'm nice looking, I'm well dressed, I have humorous and attractive children, but I have this terrible feeling . . . that I can be turned off by anybody" says a Cheever wife. And then the narrator says about her, "My wife is often sad because her sadness is not a sad sadness, sorry because her sorrow is not a crushing sorrow," which applies to all of Cheever's characters, and is true and damning about Cheever's work.

I have described these stories by their structure, these characters by their types, because his characters run to types and brilliant structure is his mainstay. Cheever is working with an attitude toward life, acutely observed and full of variation. But his people not only think they can be turned off, they can be. They are not fleshed out, their sadness is not a sad sadness. His stories belong where they are usually found, in a thin column in the New Yorker; they comment on the advertisements on either side for solid gold taxi whistles and for the sports jacket that will really make you feel casual. One finishes a book of them delighted by Cheever's suave style, dazzled by the necromancy of his invention, and aware that he is touching on the horror beneath the surface. But it is horror recollected in detachment.

The Commonweal 81 (4 December 1964): 362-63.

LATER CRITICISM

John Cheever's Surreal Vision and the Bridge of Language

Wayne Stengel

The 1984 publication of Susan Cheever's *Home before Dark*, a memoir by
John Cheever's novelist daughter about Cheever's thirty-year struggle
with alcoholism and bisexuality, reveals Cheever to be anything but a
glib writer of *New Yorker* short stories of manners. In *Home before
Dark*, Cheever emerges as a consistently brooding surrealist, a writer
whose novels and stories frequently return to images of exile, family
discord, and disruptive travel. The sense of displacement that these
situations evokes haunted Cheever throughout his career. His writing
therefore becomes the effort to bridge the gap, lessen the abyss between
appearance and reality in both the world he recorded and the life he
lived. As Susan Cheever quotes from the journal her father kept from
the early 1930s until his death in 1982: "The bridge of language,
metaphor, anecdote, and imagination that I build each morning to cross
the incongruities in my life seems very frail indeed."[1] Accordingly,
the sense of psychological disorientation that plagued Cheever in the
last five years of his life permeates all his art. This quality makes
Cheever a master of fragmentary, anecdotal short stories and, for some
critics, an unsatisfactory shaper of novelistic continuity and *durée*.

However, just this sense of obsolescence and disarray in the midst of
the seemingly familiar, affluent, and secure creates the collage effect
of much of Cheever's fiction. It also gives his writing as many
affinities to postmodernism as to the more realistic milieu of an Updike
or an Auchincloss. Moreover, *Home before Dark* should enable his
audience to see Cheever as an unfailingly surreal lyricist of
disorientation, a writer whose fictions are propelled by a perpetual
sense of fear. Similarly, Cheever's joyous ecstasy in the physical
world can be extinguished as quickly as a candle flame.

As Clinton S. Burhans, Jr., and Frederick Bracher have demonstrated,[2]
of all John Cheever's more than 100 short stories no single tale so
closely reveals his point of view and philosophy of composition as "A
Vision of the World," first collected in *The Brigadier and the Golf
Widow* in 1964. With this story, written in midcareer, Cheever
literalizes the compunction he feels to bridge the gap. Here he creates
a chain, arch, or bridge—and these are the words Cheever uses again and
again in his fiction—between an absurdly affluent world of material
possessions and the unsettling yet unifying force of his dreams. By
midcentury, Cheever was convinced that the quotidian, grotesque
realities of American life had grown uniformly hostile and threatening.

In the nature of dream experience, he felt, lay the meaning and explanation for the grating disjunctures and incongruities of middle-class suburban life.

Any reader intrigued by Cheever's thought and writing can find repeated instances of his metaphoric use of the concept of the chain, arch, or link. This structuring device bridges the distance between the increasingly horrifying American nightmare and an idealized, seemingly Jungian dreamworld of archetypes, doubles, light and shadows, personae, and masks. Cheever believed this realm might give individual lives a vision of completeness and transcendence. In describing the shaping of his fiction to Christopher Lehmann-Haupt in 1969, Cheever said: "It's almost like shaping a dream . . . to give precisely the concord you want . . . the arch, really. It's almost the form of an arch."[3] Or as R. G. Collins interprets Cheever's remark: "It seems an accurate description of Cheever's view of successful fiction, a dream that becomes an arch tying together the universe of the inner being."[4] However, when one begins to explore the implications of this linkage, a reader is surprised at how thoroughly the metaphor runs through Cheever's writing. Nonetheless, Cheever's protagonists have enormous difficulty in making these bridges connect their dream visions with reality.

"A Vision of the World" develops more like a transcendental essay by Emerson or Thoreau than a contemporary short story. The narrator, a suburban lord of the manor--much like Cheever in Ossining--describes a series of random events that frustrates all of his efforts to make order or purpose of his world. The absurd cha-cha musak that blares over the delicatessen counter of his neighborhood grocery induces the homely woman in front of him into his arms for a fleeting pas de deux. Gardening in his backyard, the narrator discovers a copperhead molting from its winter skin and suddenly experiences a prescience of the evil that his suburban enclave so wants to deny. Nearby, the narrator unearths a long-buried shoe-polish can containing a twenty-year-old note from a young social climber asserting that he will hang himself if he is not a member of the Gory Brook Country Club by the time he is twenty-five. Apprehensively, the narrator wonders how to make sense of this increasingly meaningless world. Interestingly, it is his wife, the dream-conscious, feminine principle who offers a solution:

> But I was grateful to my wife then for what she had said, for stating that the externals of her life had the quality of a dream. The uninhibited energies of the imagination had created the supermarket, the viper, and the note in the shoe-polish can. Compared to these, my wildest reveries had the literalness of double-entry bookkeeping. It pleased me to think that our external life has the quality of a dream and that in our dreams we find the virtues of conservatism.[5]

With the aid of the feminine imagination, the narrator suddenly understands how to interpret reality so as to make it less threatening and distorted. If the human imagination finds Sixties' suburban life bizarre and disorienting, that same imagination can be used to interpret those qualities of the narrator's dreams that suggest harmony, security, and triumph. Suddenly, the protagonist discovers a narrative method which will generate the events of the story to come while reconstructing the chain of situations through which the tale has evolved. The narrator will use imagination and language to describe not a bridge of events, but that essence of his dreams which suggests wholeness and harmony in a deeply fragmented world.

> What I wanted to identify then was not a chain of facts but an essence--something like the indecipherable collision of contingencies that can produce exaltation or despair. What I wanted to do was to grant my dreams, in so incoherent a world, their legitimacy. (p. 607)

Many of Cheever's narrators use their imaginations and speech as mediation between senseless reality and an ironically coherent dreamworld. This process involves them in two immediate problems. First, the arch, bridge, or chain that is the Cheever protagonist's device for conveying the quality of dream may convey situations and plot, but it is grossly inadequate to reproduce the texture and essence of dream. These Jacob's ladders fall before even the most superficial Jungian analysis. Secondly, the language--gesture, intonation, and semiotic--of the dream state is hardly the articulated speech of contemporary Westchester. Therefore Cheever's narrators are always confronted with the dilemma of translating the speech and thoughts of dream into the language of surreal Bullet Park. Thus the Cheever protagonist desperately clings to his bridges and wants to destroy them; he or she desires passage between dream and debilitating reality while sensing that no means of satisfactory translation may ever be attainable.

Nonetheless, this narrator doggedly pursues his tranquilizing dreams and his effort to translate them into tormenting reality. The protagonist of "A Vision of the World" first dreams of arriving with a group of men on a desert island and of mastering the difficult language of this world while ordering a meal in a restaurant. He next dreams of seeing a priest or bishop walking along the edge of a seashore and of being greeted by this holy man with the same sentence of this arcane language he used earlier in the restaurant. Finally, he dreams of playing on the winning team in a touch football game. Consistently, his wife and daughter, and the wives and daughters of the other team members who have formed a cheerleading squad for the players, hail their fathers

and husbands with the same cheering phrase. "Porpozec ciebie nie prosze
dorzanin albo zyolpocz ciwego" (p. 688) [*sic*: 608], says the narrator to
the waiter, the priest to the narrator, and the cheerleaders to the
players. Like many Cheever stories, this repeated speech act is a
linguistic attempt to carry the secure, unifying nature of dream to the
discordant collage of middle-class American experience.

Typically, the Cheever protagonist can maintain a shaky equilibrium
between dream essence and the baroque, discontinuous dreamland of
American life as long as this narrator restricts his dreams and their
uncommunicative language to his own consciousness. When these
individuals strive, as Cheever the writer did daily, to bridge the gap
between individual dream and desperate American dreamland, disaster
ensues. Emotional breakdown, or *cafard*, that compulsive sense of dread
that inflicts so many of Cheever's protagonists, results. In "A Vision
of the World" this apocalyptic moment occurs when the narrator enters
his wife's kitchen, a dreamland of "pink, washable walls, chilling
lights, built-in television (where prayers were being said), and
artificial potted plants" (p. 610). Fresh from his dream of being on
the winning side of the football game, the narrator writes his breakfast
order on the tablet the family reserves for their mealtime
transcriptions. Without hesitation, the narrator writes, "Porpozec
ciebie nie prosze dorzanin albo zyolpocz ciwego." Amused, then
concerned, his wife asks him what these words mean. The protagonist
responds by repeating the phrase over and over again. Immediately, his
wife calls for help. The family doctor arrives and gives the narrator
a sedative. Within hours, the narrator takes an afternoon plane to
Florida to recuperate from nervous exhaustion.

Inevitably, dreams and dreamland pursue the protagonist to Florida.
There the narrator transfers his frustration with his wife to a dream of
a beautiful, alluring woman kneeling in a field of wheat. He recounts
this dream in language that attempts to evoke the comfort of his dreams
while bridging the gap between confusing reality and transcendent
imagination. Describing this enticing, desirable woman much as Eliot
describes the hyacinth girl in *The Waste Land*, the narrator says:

> And yet she seems real--more real than the Tamiami Trail four
> miles to the east, with its Smorgorama and Giganticburger
> stands, more real than the back streets of Sarasota. I do not
> ask her who she is. I know what she will say. But then she
> smiles and starts to speak before I can turn away. "Porpozec
> ciebie . . ." she begins. Then either I awake in despair or am
> waked by the sound of rain on the palms. . . . I think of some
> plumber who, waked by the rain, will smile at a vision of the
> world in which all the drains are miraculously cleansed and
> free. Right-angle drains, crooked drains, root-choked and

rusty drains all gargle and discharge their waters into the sea.
. . . Then I sit up in bed and exclaim aloud to myself, "Valor!
Love! Virtue! Compassion! Splendor! Kindness! Wisdom! Beauty!"
The words seem to have the colors of the earth, and as I recite
them I feel my hopefulness mount until I am contented and at
peace with the night. (pp. 610-11)

As this passage eloquently demonstrates, Cheever's persona believes
many of the connecting links of twentieth-century life are inadequate to
men's and women's expressive needs. If these chains and links are still
in place, for many, they have become bonds and shackles rather than
pathways to communication or love. The garish Tamiami Trail and the
vulgar backstreets of Sarasota are convoluted thoroughfares for those
who travel them. The woman in the narrator's dream has more reality for
this dreamer than these roadways have. Moreover, Cheever's persona
questions the purpose of love or eroticism in the modern world if it
functions only as a dream. Often the communication attained with the
object of desire is the same nonsense syllables of social approval,
religious affirmation, or athletic victory the narrator has heard in
other dreams.

In despair, the protagonist turns to the practical world and thoughts
of a plumber wakened by rain from a pleasant dream of a world without
clogged drains. This vision could only occur in a world where
connections are made, arches arch, chains link, and our most soothing
dreams flow into reality. Its sheer sublimity enables the protagonist
to decode his linguistic puzzle. "Porpozec ciebie nie prosze dorzanin
albo zyolpocz ciwego" means valor, love, virtue, compassion, splendor,
kindness, wisdom, beauty. The narrator searches desperately for these
qualities in the modern world. Yet he finds them only in this ersatz,
Slavic language of his dreams. The tale ends with the narrator
repeating these invaluable but diminishing attributes. In an almost
religious epiphany, he forms an ecstatic chain of being reaching from
earth to the heavens above him. The narrator could bridge the gap
between the language of his dreams and the virtues those words represent
if only these qualities were more abundant in the modern world.

"A Vision of the World" serves as a paradigm of a kind of Cheever
story in which a narrator attempts to use his imagination to connect his
tranquilizing dreams with the wilderness of twentieth-century existence.
In these tales Cheever shapes fictive experience into the arch of a
dream. One can also see how this story suggests interesting
applications to other stories throughout Cheever's career. The
arch-chain-bridge metaphor has immediate affinity with a frequently
anthologized Cheever story, "The Angel of the Bridge," from *The
Brigadier and the Golf Widow* (1964). In this tale the bridge of the
title is the Tappan Zee Bridge, a contemporary New York thoroughfare

swirling with terrifying traffic and inhuman speed. The George Washington and the Triborough Bridges completely paralyze the protagonist's driving reflexes. However the Tappan Zee finally proves crossable when the narrator gives a ride to a female hitchhiker--a kind of angel--whose beautiful voice calms the narrator and enables him to travel the bridge.

What Cheever has done in this story is to forge a poetic bridge of correspondences that serves as a parallel to the frightening automotive bridges men and women have inherited from mid-twentieth century, machine-ridden technology. In "A Vision of the World" the protagonist attempts to translate the security of his dreams into the manic, incomprehensible dreamland of contemporary suburbia. Analogously in "The Angel of the Bridge," the preconscious fear of its protagonist becomes that all the bridges in New York will collapse as he drives over them. This hysteria describes the interior life of a man whose dreams have given way to nightmares. This traumatized protagonist must maintain an almost impossible equilibrium between the terror unleashed by the mechanizations of suburban America and the spiritual vertigo he feels as an individual driven by this society.

The ultimate horror of this story is that not only the narrator but his mother and older brother have been afflicted by a similar *cafard*, a fear of the mechanization and change inherent in midcentury America. This phobia so intensifies that it transforms its victims into machines, automatons ruled and programmed by their dread. While the narrator is partially sympathetic to their fates, he also feels their conditions are ridiculous. His brother has become a man terrified of elevators because he believes all the skyscrapers in New York will fall on one another as he ascends from floor to floor. His mother's situation is equally grotesque. She is a woman so frightened of change that she spends her days skating on the rink at Rockefeller Center since it reminds her of her childhood in St. Botolphs, Massachusetts. The narrator's jealousy of his brother's social standing and his hostility to his mother's nostalgia for the past make family ties too emotionally ambiguous a chain for him to accept their *cafards*.

Only when he arrives at the highest point in the arc of a bridge does the narrator exhibit his own *cafard*. His frenzy shows how his own dreams have become nightmares about the ugliness and duplicity of American life. Such moments also reveal how deeply he hates the flimsy, hypocritical chains of appearance we erect to bridge the gaps between surfaces and reality. On a trip to southern California, the narrator observes the chaos of Sunset Boulevard at three a.m. In this epiphany, he discovers the connecting link between his vision of the world and his fear of bridges:

But the height of bridges seemed to be one link I could not forge or fasten in this hypocritical chain of acceptances. The truth is, I hate freeways and Buffalo Burgers. Expatriated palm trees and monotonous housing developments depress me. The continuous music on special-fare trains exacerbates my feelings. I detest the destruction of familiar landmarks. I am deeply troubled by the misery and drunkenness I find among my friends, I abhor the dishonest practices I see. And it was at the highest point in the arc of a bridge that I became aware suddenly of the depth and bitterness of my feelings about modern life, and of the profoundness of my yearnings for a more vivid, simple, and peaceable world. (pp. 584-85)

The aesthetic tension of "The Angel of the Bridge" evolves from the emotion of a writer who realizes that despite his fear of bridges, he desperately needs these constructs. Cheever's consistent artistic quest was the effort to forge a bridge of correspondences between the grim, macabre realities of post-World War II American life and the dreams, aspirations, imaginative possibilities, and even nightmares that many Americans use to evade these actualities. The writer's task thus becomes the same as the individual dreamer's: to use the imagination to record the world of dreams and anxieties and to counterbalance a frighteningly technological world with structures of hope, imagination, and love.

"The Angel of the Bridge" is a particularly rich Cheever story. It examines the actual bridges of a menacing, industrialized world, the imaginative bridges of dream and language, and the hereditary bridges of family bonds and ties which haunted all of Cheever's life and art. At the highest arc of the Tappan Zee Bridge, the narrator confronts his most intense fear. All he can see before him is the sweating face of his brother in a claustrophobic elevator and his mother going around and around on the ice at Rockefeller Center. His family symbolizes those links that give him personal history but which also lock him into molds determined by blood and genes. He pulls to the side of the Tappan Zee and prays that his totally debilitating anguish will pass. Meanwhile he insists that all the bridges in the world are falling down. Yet as he relates the incident, this bridge of family weakness still stands, fixed in place before his harried consciousness:

I remember my brother's face, sallow and greasy with sweat in the elevator, and my mother in her red skirt, one leg held gracefully aloft as she coasted backward in the arms of a rink attendant and it seemed to me that we were all three characters in some bitter and sordid tragedy, carrying impossible burdens and separated from the rest of mankind by our misfortunes. My

> life was over and it would never come back, everything that I
> loved--blue-sky courage, lustiness, the natural grasp of things.
> It would never come back. I would end up in the psychiatric
> ward of the county hospital, screaming that the bridges, all the
> bridges in the world, were falling down. (p. 586)

Once again, the essential dilemmas for the Cheever protagonist remain.
Should he believe that the frail bridge of language he uses to recount
his trauma might be an adequate means of opposing the horrors of
reality? Is he justified in feeling that these bridges are inadequate,
or that they have all collapsed? Finally, should he fear any bridge
that attempts to link exterior, manufactured appearances with vulnerable
human yearnings? Moreover, if these bridges are functional, how does
the Cheever narrator translate the aspirations of his dreams? These are
the qualities that Cheever calls in the preceding passage, "blue-sky
courage, lustiness, the natural grasp of things." Unfortunately, they
are found nowhere in the story. To triumph, these virtues must become
forces that can effectively overwhelm the soulless mayhem of the
highways or the agonizing *cafards* of his family and himself.

Cheever resolves the seemingly insoluble problem in "The Angel of the
Bridge" with almost divine intervention. A young woman folksinger
hitchhiking on the Tappan Zee interprets the narrator's stopped car as
a sign that her signaling has been answered. She enters his car
carrying a small harp in a cracked oilskin. Then she proceeds to sing
to him the English folk ballad "I gave my love a cherry that had no
stone." Listening to her music, the narrator miraculously finds the
courage to cross the bridge. He records his almost ecstatic
transformation as a nearly religious conversion:

> She sang me across a bridge that seemed to be an astonishingly
> sensible, durable, and even beautiful construction designed by
> intelligent men to simplify my travels, and the water of the
> Hudson below us was charming and tranquil. It all came
> back--blue-sky courage, the high spirits of lustiness, an
> ecstatic sereneness. (p. 587)

Similarly, in "A Vision of the World," the repetition of a phrase in an
invented language becomes a mystical, religious epiphany. This
transformation parallels the appearance of the beautiful, pure-voiced
angel in "The Angel of the Bridge," whose song creates this story's
musical dream vision. In both cases, the language of these events
supplies the link, the bridge between the world of dream and the
terrifying emptiness of modern life. Moreover, Cheever translates his
protagonists' dreams. Their visions represent those sublime qualities
of love, courage, and compassion found in our dreams but dwindling in an

absurdly industrialized world.

Examining closely only these two stories nonetheless evokes the suggestiveness and depth of Cheever's vision of the world. In these tales and throughout his stories and novels, Cheever is a Jungian, neo-Transcendentalist writer who skillfully orchestrates chains of association that link unlikely realms of appearance and reality, cause and effect, behavior and emotion. Cheever seems more Jungian than Freudian not because he ridiculed psychoanalysis as his daughter states in her memoir,[6] or because he evades the force of family strife on the ego as we see in "The Angel of the Bridge" and other stories. Rather, in all his writing Cheever consistently avoids painstaking, psychological examination of his personae's identities and their family turmoils. Quite characteristically, Cheever told John Hershey [sic: Hersey] in a 1977 interview: "I have no memory for pain."[7] But as Susan Cheever's memoir so vividly chronicles, Cheever had vast reservoirs and storehouses of pain. Hence Cheever's writing floats on the shimmering surface of lives and consciously skirts the troubled, Freudian depths.

Fortuitously, Cheever's writing most frequently appeared in the *New Yorker* and emerged from the publishing world of the Thirties. This journalistic preserve was a male enclave in which direct hints of homoeroticism in a developing American writer might have created difficulties for this writer and the fashionable, reserved magazine in which his work was first acclaimed. For fifty years Cheever was so wedded to the *New Yorker* that much of his writing about sex and sexuality appears there as myth and code. Nonetheless, any serious reader of Cheever can find stories other than "A Vision of the World" and "The Angel of the Bridge" in which emasculating, harridan wives or mothers are transformed by stories' end into angels or chaste goddesses. These creations free the protagonists to translate their vision of beauty to the world. As feminists and psychologists are surely observing and as Susan Cheever's book confirms, Cheever was doubtlessly a writer who alternately feared, admired, and hated the women in his art. In them he found greater sources of control and creativity than in his male narrators and protagonists.

Ultimately, much of Cheever's writing as demonstrated in these two tales seems a continual search for the language and structure to contain his sacramental dream vision. As Clinton S. Burhans, Jr., defines Cheever's goal: "Cheever's writing since the mid-fifties . . . seems at its deepest levels of meaning and value to be his groping both for a conceptual framework to explain his apprehensions and also for a language and form to express them."[8] Therefore, dream becomes the medium, while song or heightened language serves as the expression of this quest. Congruently, the arch, bridge, or link functions as the overriding shape of his dream vision. Consistently, ecstatic religious sensation seems his stories' goal. Likewise, feminine intuition emerges as the spark or goad that enables Cheever's narrators to span their linguistic distances. Throughout his career Cheever attempted to suffuse his surreal suburbs with qualities of love, courage, faith, and compassion. He found these attributes vanishing in midcentury America, and he desperately sought the words and vision to translate these virtues across his bridge of language.

NOTES

1. Susan Cheever, *Home before Dark* (Boston: Houghton, 1984), p. 199.
2. Frederick Bracher, "John Cheever's Vision of the World," and Clinton S. Burhans, Jr., "John Cheever and the Grave of Social Coherence," in *Critical Essays on John Cheever*, ed. R. G. Collins (Boston: G.K. Hall, 1982), pp. 168-79 and pp. 109-22.
3. Christopher Lehmann-Haupt, "Interview with John Cheever," in *Critical Essays on John Cheever*, p. 12.
4. R. G. Collins, ed. and intro., *Critical Essays on John Cheever*, p. 12.
5. John Cheever, *The Collected Stories* (New York: Ballantine, 1980), pp. 606-07. All subsequent references are from this edition and are cited parenthetically in the text.
6. Susan Cheever, *Home before Dark*, pp. 163-65.
7. John Hershey [*sic*: Hersey], "Interview with John Cheever," in *Critical Essays on John Cheever*, p. 106.
8. Burhans, "John Cheever and the Grave of Social Coherence," p. 110.

Twentieth Century Literature 33 (Summer 1987): 223-33.

Bullet Park

1969

SELECTED REVIEWS

You Wouldn't Believe It

Anatole Broyard

There are people who believe that when writers pass middle age their imaginative power--like their sexual energy--tends to diminish. If they are good writers, the argument runs, they have learned their craft by this time, and so their later books have a carefully disciplined, if comparatively lifeless, quality.

In his short stories over the past several years, and in his new novel, John Cheever reverses this formula. In his late fifties, he appears to be almost helplessly carried away by the flood tides of his imagination.

The parts of Cheever's talent often seem to exceed the whole. His ear for speech, his eye for significant small actions, his polish, his boldness of invention illuminate almost every page of his work--but these gifts are often lavished on stories which seem, as a whole, unfinished, inchoate, even unserious. It is as if, in doing his little numbers, in running through the catalog of his many talents, Cheever loses interest in his characters and his story. He's like a brilliant talker whose sentences are so full of inspired digression and incidental felicities that he forgets what he has set out to say. In his last collection, for example, there are at least three fine stories--*The Swimmer*, *The Ocean* and *A View* [sic: Vision] *of the World*--which end in a blur that is all the more unsatisfying for the remarkable precisions that have preceded it.

"A revolution of things colliding"--Wallace Stevens' phrase--would be

an apt description of Cheever's vision, if one could but see the
revolution, if there were some sort of progression from one condition to
another. But after all the collisions, large and small, his characters
are still drinking martinis, still making middleaged love every night,
still catching the 8:11 in the morning, the only real difference being
that they have survived the collision. And if *that* is the meaning of
these stories, it is not enough, because the collisions themselves were
only catalytic occasions, not great crackings in the surface of the
human condition.

The plot of *Bullet Park* deserves to be called Gothic, with all the
reservations that term implies. Eliot Nailles, mouthwash salesman and
uxorious husband, meets Paul Hammer, a newcomer to his town, and the
accident of their names instantly links their fates. Though Nailles is
normal almost to the point of caricature, his son is stricken with
hysterical paralysis and cured by a self-styled swami hired by father.
While she seems to love him, Nailles' wife is prevented from betraying
him with three different men only by three separate acts of God: a fire,
indigestion and Nailles' being home with a cold. Nailles is no better
off, for all his normalcy: he develops train phobia and buys
unidentified tranquilizers from a mysterious pusher whom he meets in
public rest rooms and cemeteries.

Paul Hammer is born out of wedlock and his name is derived from the
circumstance of a handy man walking by with a hammer. Hammer's father
lifted weights and developed such a remarkable physique that, when he
travelled in Europe, sculptors used him as a model for the figures on
the facades of some of the Continent's best-known hotels. And Cheever
does not hesitate to have Hammer stumble over these figures--still
standing, or lying in bomb craters--when it is his turn to go abroad.

Hammer's mother has complicated musical dreams in which airplane
engines play Bach and Handel. She lives in Kitzbuhel, and says that if
she were to go back to the US, she'd settle in Bullet Park and "crucify"
someone whose life was less idiosyncratic than hers, i.e., a conformist.

This is what Hammer ultimately tries to do, but first he wanders about
taking planes from here to there for no apparent reason (other than
Cheever's passion for place-dropping), falling inexplicably in love with
women, men, children and dogs. He suffers from a feeling of anxiety--a
"cafard"--which can only be cured by inhabiting a yellow room he happens
to see in Italy. When he tries to rent this therapeutic room, the
tenant refuses to move. Falling back on his flying tic, he goes back to
America, where, miraculously, he happens upon another such room. This
tenant also refuses to decamp, but she is conveniently--or
cavalierly--killed in a highway accident.

Happy in his yellow room, Hammer resumes his translation of the poetry
of Montale. But his peace is soon disturbed by Marietta, a neighbor he
falls for and marries. The honeymoon is short-lived: Hammer discovers

that Marietta's moods are always the inverse of the weather or the political climate. Thunderstorms and assassinations turn her tender; blue skies and prosperity bring out the bitch in her.

With no discernible motive--except his mother's fantasy--Hammer moves to Bullet Park and sets about kidnapping Nailles' teen-age son, whom he proposes to set afire on the altar of the local church. Nailles, however, is warned by the swami, in whom Hammer has unwisely confided, and he cuts the church door down with his chain saw in the nick of time. Hammer then goes to an insane asylum and Nailles goes back to his every-day life, which is "as wonderful, wonderful, wonderful as it had been."

It is necessary to summarize the plot to this extent because no one would believe it of a writer as talented and sophisticated as Cheever. On almost every page, someone is doing something highly improbable for a remarkably obscure reason. The wildest turns of events are wantonly invoked simply to move a character from one mood to another, or to bring two people a half-step closer together. Dreams, visions, insanity, religious mania, sexual obsession--Cheever's palette seems to have nothing but screaming colors.

Minor characters who appear and disappear in the space of a few pages all have Pinter-like set speeches, center stage. Ordinary men and women ruminate poetically on philosophical or eschatological questions. People not only try to murder each other: they are killed by cars, trains, even, in one instance, castration fear. The book abounds in coincidences that would make Dickens blush. Blind passion and impulse are forever bursting the buttons or flies of Brooks Brothers suits.

In a peculiar way, Cheever seems to be championing exurbanites, who, he claims, all cultivate a more riotous garden than city slickers imagine. Under Thoreau's quiet desperation lies a different despera-tion, which turns each fake Colonial into an asylum, a temple of love or hate. It's as though Cheever is saying to New Yorkers, we're even wilder than you are; we live out here not in search of a pastoral peace, but because we need more room for our dervish evolutions; we need more intimate contact for our outrageous occasions. Everyone is secretly smoldering like a barbecue. Bullet Park is an emotional nudist colony, a cult or commune dedicated to eccentric sexual or religious practices.

Cheever's arbitrary manipulation of his characters betrays a deep contempt for--or at least a disinterest in--people's manifest motives and concerns; these, he seems to be saying, are hopelessly prosaic, not worth writing down. Or perhaps he regards them as mere screens, or rationalizations.

He is determined to be surprising or original, even at the cost of incredulity. *Bullet Park* is almost a morality play in which super-natural agents determine everyone's fate. But in morality plays, you at least had a general scheme--a morality--which helped you grasp the meaning. Cheever's book is like a bottle party where you have to bring your own.

The New Republic 160 (26 April 1969): 36-37.

A Grand Gatherum of Some Late 20th-Century American Weirdos

Benjamin DeMott

For half of its length, John Cheever's new novel is a collection of sketches of a suburban nuclear family named Nailles; the detached narrator's focus shifts from mother to father to son, with an occasional glance at some Bullet Park neighbors. In mid-course these people vanish and a new storyteller appears--an unappetizing melancholic named Paul Hammer, bastard son of an Indiana klepto and a socialist millionaire, who offers autobiographical-picaresque rumination. The parts are wedded at the end, when Hammer arrives in the suburb determined, for no intelligent reason, to commit an act of violence against the Nailles's son.

Looked at as a necessary fix for Cheever addicts--the latter are legion, for this writer is a topline fictional entertainer, whose best stories are powered by superbly continuous explosions of narrative surprise--"Bullet Park" earns points. Here, as elsewhere in his work, Cheever offers a grand gatherum of late 20th-century American weirdos--the suburban taxbreak nut who puts his firm's name on dinner-party invitations ("The Amalgamated Development Corporation and Mr. and Mrs. Thomas Lewellen cordially request the pleasure . . ."), the psychiatrist who specializes in drilling young men in how to disqualify themselves for the Army (fee: $500), the motorist who pots up in order to bear the freeway, the commuter waiting at the station amid a coffee-aspirin-tranquilizer high that gives him "the illusion [he's floating] upon a cloud like Zeus in some allegorical painting," the jailhouse vagrant who has theories about how to stay young ("Read children's books. You read novels, philosophy, stuff like that and it makes you feel old"), and leaves behind mounds of anthropological chat:

"'I've made a study of the customs and history of the Cherokee Indians and a great many people find this interesting. I once lived with them on a reservation in Oklahoma for three months. I wore their clothes, observed their customs and ate their food. They eat dogs, you know. Dogs are their favorite food. They boil them mostly although sometimes they roast them. They . . .'

"'Shut up,' said the Lieutenant."

Here as elsewhere, moreover, Cheever is brilliantly attentive to the discontinuity that nowadays butts anybody on earth who ventures off his

porch. Nellie Nailles, lace-and-carnation suburban mother interested in
flower arrangements and good works committees, goes to a Village loft to
report on an Off-Off show for her "class" in Modern Drama. At the
intermission curtain, the actors strip to starkers. Nellie leaves,
shaken, crosses Washington Square and sees male and female students
circling the pool, their picket signs emblazoned with basic
four-and-five-letter words, no supporting texts. Newsstands glare at
her, shots of naked men, and two young males in front of her on the bus
begin necking. Whereupon the true shocker, the reversal that confirms
the madness. The bus stops, a lady climbs on, sits beside Nellie and
talks--talks homey and cozy, talks reps and cretonnes! "I have good
English things and an English-type house and nubbly, stretchy reps look
completely out of place in my decorating scheme but nubbly, stretchy
reps are all you can get" and on and on and on.

There's more to "Bullet Park," of course, than mere notations of
nudies, nuts, non sequiturs. Again and again, there's the characteristic sound of this writer--a sad, licked lyricism that finds poetry
in the leaves blowing through headlight beams, that's forever gasping
under the burden of "another autumn" feeling, forever exulting in the
sweetness of physicality long gone: "He loved football, loved the
maneuvers, the grass work, the fatigue, and loved the ball itself--its
shape, color, odor and the way it spiraled into the angle of his elbow
and ribcage. He loved the time of the year, the bus trips to the other
schools, he loved sitting on the bench. . . ." And there are splendid
fantasy rebellions, wherein mass mania gets it from mass men--witness
Eliot Nailles firing his TV out the door into the rainy dark, hearing it
break on the cement with "the rich glassy music of an automobile
collision."

But although Cheever does turn up in its pages, this third novel can't
fairly be described as a first-rate addition to the man's *oeuvre*.
There's the structural problem to begin with--the book *is* broken-backed,
parts tacked together as flimsily as the Hammer-Nailles ploy suggests.
And there are characters who refuse to hold firm: when it helps the
scene of the moment to do so, the writer sees Nellie Nailles as a
proper, delicate lady, shockable by "Hair"; a minute later, when the
scene's over, the lady's demoted to the rank of mere knowing housewife
and her talk is all shrinks and drinks. And throughout there are marks
of carelessness, lax composition, perfunctoriness (it's Estoril,
Portugal, isn't it?--not "*the* Estoril?")--as though the writer hadn't
cared to tune himself to his own standard pitch.

And finally--most important, maybe--there's the problem of story style
vs. novel style. Except when tricked up in gothicism, fantasy or
allegory, the novel is a world of explanations, and the story is a world
of phenomena--and heretofore Cheever was a great respecter of the
difference. Sprinting and flashing, his stories--five volumes of them--

say that nowadays a man falls in love with his baby sitter and heals himself by buying a lathe ("The Country Husband")--or that nowadays a paramour doesn't want diamonds, just the *luxo* bombshelter key ("The Brigadier and the Golf Widow")--or that nowadays zoning laws against dying are a feature of some subdivisions ("The Death of Justine")--and by the time the reader of any of them thinks to ask, What? What was that? Why? he's into the next tale in the book. No explanations offered or required.

Whereas in his first two novels--"The Wapshot Chronicle" (1957) and "The Wapshot Scandal" (1964)--Cheever was a kind explainer in the familiar novelistic way, and traveled at a wholly different pace. A young executive at a computer center, otherwise a conventional husband, parent, teamplayer, fools about with a program on Keats's grammar--why? The answer is full and explicit: the man's a New England boy, and there is craziness in his past, and the precise nature of the craziness in past generations is laid out in slow, rich family-chronicle style.

Very little laying-out on this model in "Bullet Park" (despite considerable genealogy), hence small comfort for novel readers who still value accountings of motives, explanations of why people are sick or won't go to school or wish to commit murder. Hints about how and why the rage for inexplicability grinds the good writer down are scattered through Cheever's earlier work--see especially "Some People, Places, and Things That Will Not Appear in My Next Novel." And certainly, whether or not story style wrecks a novel, there's no denying its seeming congruency with contemporary life. And what, after all, is mysterious about a writer with dozens of swift, whippy tales to his name at last turning resentful of lumbering novelistic pedantry? Remembering how it went with those tales, how they curved like birds, dipped, slid, raced, vanished, never stopped for an answer, how could he not want it that way always?

But it's one thing to understand a defect and another to puff it up into a virtue. John Cheever's short stories are and will remain lovely birds--dense in inexplicables and beautifully trim. But in the gluey atmosphere of "Bullet Park" no birds sing. The impatience that drives this talent elsewhere, that seems a pure energy, light and free, here figures, sad and surprising to say, as an absence of energy--a sluggishness, a heaviness, a crude useless film slicking bright wings.

The New York Times Book Review, 27 April 1969, pp. 1, 40-41.

America's Nomads

Louis Grant

In *Bullet Park*, as in all of John Cheever's novels, "the setting seems
in some way to be at the heart of the matter." The town for which the
novel is named, a suburban commuter-stop near Manhattan, appears to be
a community but is not. This is at the heart of the matter, because the
book itself is about *appearances* and how they have come to supplant
reality in American life. The plot and the characters are organized to
develop this theme, which the setting represents.

The inhabitants of Bullet Park include a number of minor characters
who, rather than being essential to the action, are more or less
elements of the setting. To describe them is to describe Bullet Park.
Mrs. Trencham, for instance, is a "religious" woman: "Her genuflections
were profound and graceful . . . her Lamb of God was soulful . . . she
would throw in a few signs of the cross as a proof of the superiority of
her devotions." Charlie Stringer, although he publishes pornography,
still "wants to water his grass and play softball with the kids." The
rest could be summarized in these words: "The handful of men and women
who attended Holy Communion were all well known to Nailles . . . they
seemed invincible. Their honor, passion and intelligence were genuine."

Of course, they are no such thing. The central action of the
novel--acted out by the symbolic pair, Eliot Nailles and Paul Hammer,
and focusing on their struggle for the life and the soul of Eliot's son,
Tony--is a dramatic (possibly melodramatic) embodiment of the struggle
between appearance and reality. On the part of Paul Hammer it is a
conscious--perhaps mad--attempt to strip away appearances by an act of
violence: "Nothing less than a crucifixion will wake the world." For
Eliot Nailles it is an unconscious attempt to preserve appearances if
possible, but above all to preserve life--in this case, Tony's
life--without which there can be neither appearance nor reality.

"Lying in bed that night Nailles thought: Hammer and Nailles,
spaghetti and meatballs, salt and pepper, good and evil, life and death,
love and death." The struggle between these two characters--between
Nailles, who is a suburban Dad, a mouthwash chemist for Saffron Chemical
Corporation (producer of Spang) and Paul Hammer, a bastard son, an
intellectual and malcontent, sometime translator of poetry, pursued by
a cafard and seeking release from his anxieties--is in many ways the
struggle between love and death (Cheever seems to consider them opposites which, locked in battle, comprise the totality of modern life).
In fact, however, *Bullet Park* is symbolic narrative a la Nabokov, pasted
onto a very good contemporary problem play a la Playhouse 90.

The story of Eliot Nailles and his commuting double, Paul Hammer, is

like one of those X-rays in TV commercials--only this time the subject
is America's spiritual heartburn. And although it is a slightly
different, somewhat better X-ray than the one taken by John Updike in
his lascivious *Couples*, or that taken by Philip Roth in his malicious
Portnoy's Complaint, it is little more than an ad for the author's own
brand of aspirin. *Bullet Park* does differ from these two novels in one
sense: although the calibration of Human Sexual Response is as accurate
and clinical as it ought to be in a modern novel, the sexual organs are
not so large that the rest of human experience--also the rightful domain
of the novel--shrivels up and dies in their shadow. According to
Cheever, the rest of human experience died of other causes not long
before he wrote his novel. "He feels himself to be a hollow man, but one
who has only recently been eviscerated and who can recall what it felt
like to have a skinful of lively lights and vitals." *Bullet Park* is an
exploration of the cavity which remains.

Although Cheever's subject matter seems to have died off with Honora
Wapshot in *The Wapshot Scandal*, Cheever still has his fine eye for the
vulgar and the ridiculous. "Nailles was principally occupied with the
merchandising of Spang and he was definitely restive about this. It
seemed to reflect on his dignity. In Nailles's mythology the nymphs
complained among themselves about the bad breath of Priapus."

Eliot is as happily married to Nellie Nailles as Dagwood has been to
Blondie for so many comic strip years. As in most comic strips, soap
operas and video tape fairy tales, the hero has a problem. His son,
Tony, does not do well in school; he prefers football and observing the
ghost of nature which still haunts the countryside to French verbs. He
even threatens his sex-starved, hysterical French teacher with
extinction. In other words, the boy is not content to Grow Up Absurd
without a struggle. Of the modes of rebellion open to him, Tony chooses
prolonged bedrest after a funny-tragic scene with the old man at an
abandoned miniature golf course: "Then I lost my patience, my woolly
blanket, and said he ought to get off his ass and do something useful
and he said: 'What? Like pushing mouthwash?'" As Paul Goodman put it,
"It's hard to grow up when there isn't enough man's work."

Tony takes to his bed for an epic sleep-in of approximately 22 days.
He explains that although the real estate salesman claims Bullet Park is
here to stay, "I feel as if the house were made of cards." In other
words, Tony is overwhelmed by the temporariness, the provisionality and
the weakness of the world in which he lives. He does not realize it,
but he has seen through its appearances. Like a sleeping beauty,
however, he is revived by the magic of Swami Rutuola, a beautiful black
prince from the Bullet Park ghetto.

The grand finale of the novel includes a "Graduate"-like chase when
Paul Hammer kidnaps Tony and takes him to be sacrificed on the altar of
the American Identity Crisis. Eliot rushes to the church where Tony is

to be immolated, cuts through the locked doors with his sanctified power
saw and rescues his son. Eliot's weaknesses and foibles, we are tempted
to read, are outweighed by his love for his son. Paul Hammer's attempt
to kill Tony is an attempt through an act of violence to symbolize the
emptiness and meaninglessness of Bullet Park and to reveal
reality--blood and all. But it is motivated by spiritual desperation
and a death-wish.

At the beginning of the novel, a hypothetical adolescent who is both
"zealous and vengeful," states his case against the inhabitants of
Bullet Park: "Damn their shelves on which there rests a single book--a
copy of the telephone directory bound in pink brocade." The adolescent
has been unfair to the depth and dimension of the typical Bullet Park
family library. On that shelf would also be a paperback copy of *The
Graduate*, and the book club editions of *Couples*, *Portnoy's Complaint*,
and *Bullet Park*. Cheever would be one of the favorite novelists of his
hero, Eliot Nailles.

John Cheever has not become a public figure like certain other major
American authors. He is not the showpiece intellectual on the Merv
Griffin show like Norman Mailer. He probably would not like having his
writing career embalmed by becoming a "Man of Letters" at the hands of
the National Book Award Committee. He has not taken epic pisses at
radical rallies or claimed the role of Intellectual Master of Ceremonies
of the Revolution. He would seem, from the incriminating evidence of
Bullet Park, to be engaged in the national pastime of many of our
important novelists (e.g. John Updike and Philip Roth): he is destroying
his past, abandoning the landscape where his imaginative roots were
laid. Updike's sexy toddlers playing in their Tarbox lack something his
earlier characters'had; Roth's masturbating anti-Jew lacks something the
real Jews of his *Goodbye, Columbus* collection had. Cheever seems intent
on joining them in the composition of clever, bright, facile
commentaries on the suburban-urban void--chronicles of the homeless,
nomadic American without a past and therefore without a future.

"It would have troubled Leander," states the narrator of one of John
Cheever's early Wapshot stories, "to think that he would be buried in
any place as distant from West Farm as Yankee Stadium, but that is where
his bones were laid to rest." The story, "The National Pastime," is
about a young, modern man who is oppressed by the full, energetic spirit
of his large-dreamed father not only during his life but even after his
death. The narrator confesses, "I had never been able to build any kind
of bridge from Leander's world to the worlds where I lived." This is
Cheever's problem as well, and for him as for the narrator of the story,
learning to play baseball will not resolve it. It is clear that Cheever
had not laid Leander to rest when the story was written. He returned to
St. Botolph's and to Leander in *The Wapshot Chronicle*. No matter how

oppressive the myths and landscape of the Wapshot family may have been to him, they continued to be the fertile nexus of his most powerful associations.

From that material he wrote a novel which bears comparison with Faulkner's *Sartoris* (*The Sartoris Chronicle* it might have been called) in the realization of regional landscape, in the theme of family and social disintegration and in total imaginative impact. With *The Wapshot Chronicle* Cheever seemed very near to greatness—almost a Yankee Faulkner. And yet, Cheever's discovery of the North and of the Wapshot myths released in him none of the enormous fictional energies that Faulkner had attained with his discovery of the Sartoris family and the South. With his death at the end of the *Chronicle*, one might have expected that Leander, like John Sartoris, "freed as he was of time and flesh," would have become a "more palpable presence" in the subsequent fiction of John Cheever. One felt that Leander's injunction, "admire the world," might find Cheever admiring it best by rendering it most fully in the place he knew best, St. Botolph's, as Faulkner had done in the South in Jefferson.

However, the new generation of Wapshots in *The Wapshot Scandal* sense that if they ever return to St. Botolph's it will have disappeared. And the spirit of Leander has not survived in them. Coverly Wapshot foreshadows Eliot Nailles, and his brother Moses is a Paul Hammer. Now that Cheever has abandoned St. Botolph's, he persists in writing novels; but they are merely a form of literary baseball above the bones of Leander in which Cheever attempts to drive American Vulgarity, American Anxiety and American Complacency from the mound in disgrace.

The best of Cheever's work is rooted in West Farm on the rocky Massachusetts coast. That is the "dear perpetual place" which nourished his imagination. Bullet Park is no place, and any novelist who felt condemned to write about the humanoids who live there would have good reason to tell Christopher Lehmann-Haupt, as Cheever recently did: "Right now I'm working on a Reporter-at-Large piece for The New Yorker about a state highway they want to build through the valley near here. It's caused a lot of trouble." And to speculate on whether he would "ever write fiction" again.

Ramparts 8 (September 1969): 62, 64, 66.

Salvation in the Suburbs

Charles Nicol

John Cheever, cheerful believer in suburbia, champion of the upper middle class in lower middle age. He invokes the muse merely to describe a railroad station, then confidently explains that "the setting seems in some way to be at the heart of the matter. We travel by plane, oftener than not, and yet the spirit of our country seems to have remained a country of railroads." America's essence rides the commuter train.

St. Botolphs, Shady Hill, and now Bullet Park--the setting is indeed at the heart of the matter, and Cheever's genius is the genius of place, so much so that in this novel the first person we meet is a real-estate agent. Here are the $50,000 and $60,000 homes, each with its toilet seat cover of "pink plush" and its "telephone directory bound in pink brocade," each with its suffering, hangover-ridden commuter recovering from the weekend: "Finally he dresses and racked by vertigo, melancholy, nausea and fitful erections he boards his Gethsemane--the Monday-morning 10:48." Crucified middle class indeed; the main characters of this novel are named Hammer and Nailles. And Hammer, who is insane, intends to immolate brutally an arbitrarily chosen member of the middle class, on the altar of a suburban church, to awaken the world to the sins of suburbia.

According to Cheever, suburbia is the trickiest Paradise since Eden, full of traps and falls, demanding much of its inhabitants. One exemplary couple, the most successful social movers in Bullet Park, take their recreation so seriously that it collects a steady toll of their flesh and blood: "When they arrived at a party they would be impeccably dressed but her right arm would be in a sling. He would support a game leg with a gold-headed cane and wear dark glasses." Their countless accidents in the cause of sociability merely add to their success. Survivors of the good life wear scar tissue like medals.

Early one morning Nailles successfully defends his carefully clipped lawn against an enormous snapping turtle, and though the man has a shotgun, it is his persistence rather than his power that finally triumphs, the same persistence that claimed Bullet Park from the reptiles in the first place. This heroic perseverance is a characteristically middle-class quality, for the middle class must walk a very difficult and narrow path, a thin edge between two pits, bodkin between indifference and obsession. This is the way we live, with persistence and a rough temperance, rationing our cigarettes and counting our drinks. John Cheever is not interested in teetotalers or lushes, but in the human need to establish a shaky equilibrium, the desperate paradise of two-sided man, ticking along like a bad clock, passing the time through pendulum swings to either side, and perpetually in need of adjustment.

Nailles's son Tony tends to get stuck on either side: first he becomes obsessed with television, then indifferent to his French course and obsessed with football, then so indifferent to the world that he cannot be roused from bed. Doctor, psychiatrist, and physiologist all try to put Tony together again, but only a Negro guru can jolt Tony from his ennui. This contemporary holy man effects cures on wounded psyches by a process so simple it embarrasses him to perform it: he repeats hopeful words or phrases. His first cure consisted of repetition of "valor." The nobility and absurdity of man is that he responds to such an empty, but potentially full, word as though it were already stuffed with essence. At the end of "A Vision of the World," an earlier story seminal to this novel, the narrator awakes from a dream and exclaims, "Valor! Love! Virtue! Compassion! Splendor! Kindness! Wisdom! Beauty!" and announces that "the words seem to have the colors of the earth, and as I recite them I feel my hopefulness mount until I am contented and at peace with the night." It is this hopefulness that is instilled in Tony, the belief that these abstractions do exist and justify suburban life. For here is what the commuters live for, not the pink plush that so lamely represents the ideal.

In the discrepancy between reality and the vision, reality tends to become dreamlike. The wife in "A Vision of the World" has the feeling that she is "a character in a television situation comedy." "I mean I'm nice looking, I'm well-dressed, I have humorous and attractive children, but I have this terrible feeling that I'm in black-and-white and that I can be turned off by anybody." It is a frequent feeling in Cheever, one that Nailles experiences in looking at his family at the breakfast table ("they seemed to have less dimension than a comic strip") and that drains his son Tony of all resolution until he decides to stay in bed ("I feel as if the house were made of cards"). Suburban existence seems threatened with meaninglessness from all sides. Mrs. Nailles is deeply disturbed by the nudity in off-Broadway theater, by homosexuals fructifying on the bus, by the psychiatrist's questions about her family's moral norms: "'We are honest and decent people,' she said angrily, 'and I'm not going to be made to feel guilty about it.'" Their life is continually on the defensive. Nailles suddenly finds that he can no longer face his commuter train in the morning without massive doses of tranquilizers. While the Nailles family desperately persevere, they dream of a simpler past. It is John Cheever's special ability to view our healthy suburbans as a noble and dying race, their unique virtues soon to be extinct.

The penalties seem rather high, but there are also rewards for Cheever characters: swimming, trout fishing, and cutting wood--these seem to be lasting, soothing occupations that belong by right to them and temporarily make their souls whole. Religion, though dilute enough to add to their guilt feelings, can be another reward, curiously tied to the other delights just mentioned. "The trout streams open for the resurrection. The crimson cloths at Pentecost and the miracle of the tongues meant swimming." The "holy smell of new wood" is mentioned in an earlier story: in *Bullet Park* the holy man burns sandalwood for incense and is also a carpenter; Nailles thinks of scriptural quotations as he cuts down dead trees whose fragrance reminds him of "cold churches in Rome"; and even madman Hammer is free from his demons while he trims back the deadwood behind his house. When Nellie Nailles smells wood shavings, she asks herself, "Which came first, Christ the carpenter or the holy smell of new wood?" When Cheever appeared on the cover of *Time* a few years ago, we found that he was indeed both a churchgoer and a worker with chain saw and ax. What Proustian undercurrent runs here?

Cheever is placed just before Chekhov, another fine writer of short stories, in the fiction section of your public library, and the tempting criticism of the Wapshot novels is that they sometimes seem to be paste-ups of minimally connected stories. *Bullet Park*, a novel with a clean plot line, the convergence of hammer and nail, resists this temptation to digress. We are nevertheless ultimately disappointed, for while Cheever's writing retains its brilliance, his plot is not at all convincing, depending as it does upon the motivation of Hammer, a most unsuccessful character. Hammer's madness is apparent only in his plans for an absurd murder. Can it be Cheever's intention to argue that murder involves little aberration in a man's personality, or is there a previously unsuspected limitation to Cheever's imagination? This lack is made far more obvious when Hammer, for a third of the novel, tells his own story. From Poe through Faulkner and Nabokov, American authors have delighted in projecting variant images of the world through the eyes of the child, the idiot, and the lunatic. Yet the world of Hammer is pretty much the same as the world of Cheever in the rest of the novel. Nothing seems to have been gained through that first-person interlude, and a lot has been lost, including our confidence in the motivation of the character most crucial to the plot. No doubt Cheever intends to show that experiences today are fragmentary and that people no longer possess--if they ever did--a unified personality, yet if Hammer has only the vaguest of notions about why he wanted to commit murder, and discusses his actions with both detachment and distaste, we may justifiably ask why we should listen to him at all.

Curiously, the novel is more than half finished before the main plot and the character of Hammer begin to be important, and this first half is the more pleasant part. It is always strange to read a novel that weakens toward the end; we blame ourselves for its deterioration. Highly recommended for those who never finish one book before they start another.

Atlantic Monthly 223 (May 1969): 96, 98.

Cheever's People: The Retreat from Chaos

Joyce Carol Oates

Nellie Nailles, a typical inhabitant of suburban Bullet Park, takes a
course in "the modern theater," and one of her assignments is to see an
off-Broadway play. In the play an actor takes off his clothes; this
upsets Nellie tremendously, but she remains in the theater, willing to
"come to terms with the world." Afterward, she encounters New York
University students carrying signs in a filthy speech demonstration. Has
she gone mad? On a bus she sees two young men involved in amorous play.
Should she thrash them with her umbrella? She barely makes it back home
to comfortable Bullet Park, unnerved, shattered. "Falsehood, confinement, exclusion and a kind of blindness seemed to be her only means of
comprehension." Survival depends upon Bullet Park.

John Cheever's third novel, like the Wapshot chronicles, is made up of
such bizarre, comic, and yet oddly touching incidents. His people awake
to moments of acute comprehension, but such comprehension will kill
them--they subside into slumber once more, or they go mad. Cheever's
talky, fragmented, at times exasperating method of narration is a
reflection of his characters' general predicament: how to remain sane?
Cheever seems to me unique, even eccentric, in his combining of
sentimentality and brutality; one believes truly in his genuine
compassion for his characters, his desire that the world be as lovely as
they dream it should be, and yet the terror that Cheever can unleash is
as deadly, more deadly, than any promised in the glib new genre of
"black comedy." Cheever has been writing such comedy for decades.

Bullet Park should be familiar, but its suburban wastes and its
bewildered people are somehow imagined with originality and vividness.
How to combine the advertised America of beauty and simplicity with the
madness that seems to be encroaching everywhere? The novel's hero,
Eliot Nailles, visits his mother in an expensive nursing home; filled
with love for many people, Eliot loves his mother as well and is
bewildered at the way his mother must remain alive, but not quite alive,
conscious and not quite conscious. The enthusiastic director says of
his patients, "I call them my dolls. They look like people and yet
they're really not." Their hair is dyed, their faces made up, diamond
rings are slipped on their fingers for the benefit of visitors. They
look like people and yet they are not.

Everything looks one way and is another; or, perhaps, everything is
promised and nothing delivered; or, in an additional paradox, the dreams
of American adolescence somehow become available, through alcohol,
drugs, a carefully restricted range of vision, a colossal spiritual
lobotomy. Reading Cheever is a perplexing experience: one hears the

highly intelligent and highly poetic Cheever in every line, and yet one hears the repetitive, pathetic, banal voice of Americans in their attempts at speech, at justifying themselves. The novel has a plot but I think the plot is a contemptuous gesture--Cheever's homage to the traditionally wrought work, with crisis, complication, a "Perils of Pauline" ending, a crazily simple conclusion. After Nailles's problem-son Tony is very nearly burnt alive and sacrificed on the altar of Christ's Church of Bullet Park, by a madman, he returns to school on Monday, normally, and his father (tranquilized) returns to work and "everything was as wonderful, wonderful, wonderful, wonderful as it had been."

The plot involves Nailles's shadowy double, a man named Hammer, about whom pages of whimsical facts are recited but about whom we really know nothing. Hammer wants to fulfill his insane mother's dream of "crucifying" some innocent suburban inhabitant in an innocent suburban church; his victim is Nailles's son. He fails. The novel ends.

It is really not a novel at all but a series of eerie, sometimes beautiful, sometimes overwrought vignettes. Cheever's imagination leans toward the picaresque, but the "adventures" his people endure are often lyric, or adventures turned inside-out, non-events, non-happenings. Hammer's mother, living a totally senseless life in Europe, lies on her bed and talks to herself for an hour every week, since she cannot afford a psychiatrist. Similarly, all of Cheever's people--even the most incidental, accidental walk-ons--give speeches, trying to explain themselves, trying however feebly to justify themselves. They are all driven, like the disintegrating Hammer, to find paradise, a retreat from chaos and insanity; why is it they cannot make sense of their own lives or of the world? They talk. They free-associate for pages. They appear, they disappear. They have no permanent identities.

It is clear that Cheever has deliberately chosen to write about people who are sub-ideas, national traits, creatures portrayed in moments of nervous and senseless collision with one another. If there is a psychological integrity to Cheever's writing it is because of his assumption, a justified one, that his readers will bring to these people enough personal anguish to invest them with an extra dimension; otherwise they are cartoon figures, they do not exist. So much is taken for granted by Cheever that this novel, read in some distant un-Americanized culture, or perhaps read in the distant and unimagined future, will probably be incomprehensible. It is not the settings--the commuter's pastoral and high-priced hell, the various interchangeable high-priced hotels--that are peculiar to this time, but some indefinable relationship between people and setting, some mysterious infection of the brain by the times themselves, which can only be understood in relationship to what has been promised. Irony so pervades Cheever's writing that one cannot tell where whimsy begins and a real nastiness, a profound nastiness, begins. Is everything wonderful in Bullet Park? It may well be.

Chicago Tribune Book World, 20 April 1969, pp. 1, 3.

LATER CRITICISM

Witchcraft in Bullet Park

John Gardner

When in 1969 John Cheever turned from the lovable Wapshots to the weird
creatures who inhabit Bullet Park, most reviewers attacked or dismissed
him. They were, it seems to me, dead wrong. The Wapshot books, though
well made, were minor. "Bullet Park," illusive, mysteriously built, was
major--in fact, a magnificent work of fiction.

One reason the book has been misunderstood is that it lacks simple
message. No man who thinks seriously about the enormous old questions
can reduce his thought to a warning sign like BRIDGE OUT. Another
reason is that Cheever is right about evil: it comes quietly,
unannounced by thunder or screeching bats--comes like the novel's
well-dressed man getting casually off a train 10 minutes before dark.
Talking of the oldest and darkest evil, Cheever speaks softly, gently,
as if casually. Suspense is not something he fails to achieve in
"Bullet Park" but something he has avoided. The novel moves as if
purposelessly, like its bland-minded, not very likable protagonist, and
from time to time gives a nervous start at the blow of a distant axe.

Cheever's subject is chance--but more than that. Chance is a vehicle
that carries the book into darker country. The opening lines present a
setting--a train station--designed to suggest the whole human condition
in this mysterious, chance-riddled universe. A temporary planet whose
architecture, like that of the station, is "oddly informal, gloomy but
unserious"; a place of isolation where chance seems to rule even art.
"Paint me a small railroad station then," the novel begins--as if any
other setting would do as well. (But: "The setting seems in some way to
be at the heart of the matter," says Cheever, sly. Art, like life, may
start with chance, but chance shrouds something darker.)

The harmless looking man who steps from the train meets a real-estate
agent named Hazzard--"for who else will know the exact age, usefulness,
value and well-being of the houses in town." By chance, days later, the
harmless looking man will be standing on the platform with Eliot
Nailles, the novel's hero, when another man is sucked to his death by an
express train. The stranger has nothing to do with the accident; he's

buried, at the time, in his newspaper. But the skin crawls. We learn
later that by a series of accidents the stranger has become, unbeknownst
to himself, a center of demonic malevolence.

We've been told repeatedly that the universe is gloomy and frightening, random. Brute existence precedes essence and also sometimes follows it, as it does in Nailles's good Christian mother, reduced by
senility to a human doll in a nursing home. Ah, yes, ah, woe, we are
tugged by cosmic strings, dolls all! Or are we? Cheever reconsiders
the idea of chance, remembering psychic and psychological phenomena, the
claims of good and bad witches. What emerges is a world where hope does
exist (magic is real and can cure or kill), a world in a way even
grimmer than Beckett's because here love and sacrifice are realities,
like hope, but realities in flux, perpetually threatened, perishing.

The novel says yes-and-no to existentialists, who can account for all
but the paragnost. Cheever, in other words, sees the mind in its
totality--sees not only the fashionable existential darkness but the
light older than consciousness, which gives nothingness definition.
Partly for the sake of this wholeness of vision, Cheever in "Bullet
Park" abandoned the fact-bound novel of verisimilitude, which is by
nature impotent to dramatize the mind's old secrets, and turned to
dependence on *voice*, secret of the willing suspension of disbelief that
normally carries the fantasy or tale.

Cheever's voice--compassionate, troubled, humorous--controls the
action, repeatedly calling attention to itself in phrases like "at the
time of which I'm writing." Where his voice fades out, character voices
come in. Without explanation or apology, he shifts, early in the novel,
to the cry of an unnamed and never-again-to-be-heard-of adolescent, a
cry against suburban hypocrisy. ("Oh damn them all, thought the
adolescent.") Later, telling how Eliot Nailles nearly murdered his son,
Cheever shifts to Nailles's own voice as Nailles goes over the incident
in his mind. With similar abruptness he introduces the voices--or,
sometimes, centers of consciousness--of Nailles's wife, neighbors, a
zodiac-trapped French teacher, a Negro swami and the harmless looking
stranger, mad Paul Hammer.

Hammer decides to murder Nailles--at first Eliot, later his son, Tony.
The decision is without explicit motivation, based mainly on "the
mysterious binding power of nomenclature." Cheever could have explained
the whole thing, black magic as psychosis (the magic of names), and
would have done so in a Wapshot book. But how do you *render* a thing so
strange? Instead of explaining, he inserts Hammer's journal. With a
mad man's objectivity, Hammer sketches the story of his life.

The coldness of tone (even when the scene is comic), the flat description of his enfeebled quest for relationship, his survival by flight
into symbolism (yellow rooms, a dream-castle, pieces of string) explains
magically what the fact-bound novel would turn to the dry unreality of

a case study. The motive for the projected murder is coincidence--a correspondence of names, two pieces of string. We learn that Paul Hammer has murdered before, without knowing it himself, to get a yellow room. But the rendered proof of his demonic nature is his voice, a quiet stovelid on terror and rage.

As in all first-rate novels, the form of "Bullet Park" grows out of its subject. More here than in his earlier writings, Cheever depends on poetic (which is to say, magical) devices--rhythm, imagistic repetition, echo. Instead of conventional plot, an accretion of accidents. Far below consciousness, the best people in Bullet Park are mirror images of the worst: they live by magic, correspondence.

On the level of consciousness, Nailles lives by sugary, foolish opinions and declares his life "wonderful"--but he cannot ride his commuter train except drugged. Out of touch with his son, governed partly by ethical clichés and partly by the normal frustration of the blind--ruled in other words by chance--he throws out his son's beloved TV and starts the child on the way to mental illness. By the chance combination of his middle-class values, his son's slight willfulness, an argument with his wife, and an accidental meeting with black-jacketed boys whose faces he cannot see, Nailles tries--in what could pass for inexplicable rage--to murder his son on a miniature golf course. (The mechanistic universe writ small. The symbolism of place is always grim in "Bullet Park.") Though Nailles's putter misses his son's skull, the black-magic selfish rage in his attack leaves the son psychologically crippled--in fact, dying of murdered will--savable only by a swami.

An accidental meeting with a man in a bar and a chance echo when Nailles returns home makes Nailles distrust his faithful wife--faithful because, by accident, her would-be seducers were confounded by, respectively, a fire, a cold, an attack of indigestion. In short, Nailles, a tragicomic fool, is simply lucky. By accidents of his childhood, he is in touch with Nature: he cuts down diseased elms with a comically typical suburban chain-saw and shoots, in his undershorts, a century-old snapping turtle (naked man against the dinosaur). Hammer, by accidents of childhood and bastardy, is cut off from Nature and himself. Nailles's blessing is that he is married to a good woman and has a son, whereas Hammer is married to a bitch and is childless. Nailles's luck means that he's faintly in touch with the higher magic of the universe--the magic of love, creative force--whereas Hammer is in touch only with lower magic, correspondence.

Magical coincidence, echo, repetition. When images recur or correspondences appear, they are causes, benevolent or harmful. From his psychic, wholly self-centered mother, Hammer gets his witchy idea of drugging and immolating some innocent victim to "wake up" drugged America. When Rutuola, the gentle swami, makes magic, the result is ritual. Both are attempts to draw in the power of the universe. Both work, sometimes. Both are crazy. ("I know it's crazy," Tony says, raised from despair by the swami's chant of *Love, Love, Love*, "but I do feel much better.")

Benevolent witchcraft, ritual, assumes that the universe contains some good and that men in groups can reach harmony with it. (Rain or shine, Nailles drives with his windshield wiper on, because that's his silly congregation's sign of faith in the resurrection.) Malevolent witchcraft, on the other hand, assumes cosmic forces attendant to the will of the witch. Neither side wins decisively. (Selfless men contain selfishness, and even Hammer has impulses toward love.) The mainly benevolent have their marginal advantage because in times of crisis they tend to work together. Out of lonely arrogance Hammer spills his plan to the swami, and from love the swami warns Nailles.

But though Tony is rescued--Nailles rising to that strange trance-state in which nothing can go wrong (a dazzling piece of writing)--Nailles's existence is merely salvaged, not redeemed. Nailles at the start called his drab life "wonderful." When Rutuola brought Tony from despair, "everything was as wonderful as it had been." Now, when the murder has been blocked, with the help of that ridiculous chain-saw, Cheever closes: "Tony went back to school on Monday and Nailles--drugged--went off to work and everything was as wonderful, wonderful, wonderful, wonderful as it had been."

There, it may be, is the underlying reason that reviewers were annoyed by "Bullet Park." The novel is bleak, full of danger and offense, like a poisoned apple in the playpen. Good and evil are real, but are effects of mindless chance--or heartless grace. The demonology of Calvin, or Cotton Mather. Disturbing or not, the book towers high above the many recent novels that wail and feed on Sartre. A religious book, affirmation out of ashes. "Bullet Park" is a novel to pore over, move around in, live with. The image repetitions, the stark and subtle correspondences that create the book's ambiguous meaning, its uneasy courage and compassion, sink in and in, like a curative spell.

The New York Times Book Review, 24 October 1971, pp. 2, 24.

The Resurrection of BULLET PARK:
John Cheever's Curative Spell

Samuel Coale

Within two days of one another, Benjamin DeMott and John Leonard in the *New York Times* panned and praised John Cheever's third novel, *Bullet Park*. Leonard on April 29, 1969 declared that it was "Cheever's deepest, most challenging book [with] the tension and luminosity of a vision."[1]   And his position was underscored on September 14 in the London *Sunday Times* by John Updike who described the book as "a slowly revolving mobile of marvelously poeticized moments. . . . [Cheever] increasingly speaks in the accents of a visionary."[2]   But it was DeMott's front-page review in the *New York Times Book Review* on April 27 that created the most impact. For him *Bullet Park* was "broken-backed [with] parts tacked together" and was nothing more than "a collection of sketches."[3]   The style suggested a "sad, licked lyricism," and the plot involved a "grand gatherum of late 20th-century American weirdos." "DeMott's front-page Sunday assault had its effect," wrote Cheever biographer Scott Donaldson in 1988: "Sales amounted to thirty-three thousand copies only, and did not earn back the advance."[4]

The tale of DeMott's review became apocryphal in its re-telling. Both Donaldson and Benjamin Cheever, Cheever's older son and the editor of the letters published in 1988, agreed that the devastating review increased the downward spiral of Cheever's alcoholism. Cheever himself saw the book as the end of "'a method, a cadence and a perspective'" (Donaldson, 253). He explained in an interview: "The manuscript was received enthusiastically everywhere, but then Benjamin DeMott dumped on it in the *Times*, everybody picked up their marbles and ran home."[5]   In a letter written on October 3 he mused, "I may have made a mistake in using a suburb as a social metaphor."[6]   Susan Cheever summed up his response in her 1984 biography of her father, *Home Before Dark*: "'My incantation has changed,' he wrote in 1969 after *Bullet Park* had been panned by the critics and his alcoholism was worse and most of the money was spent."[7]

My own first assessment of *Bullet Park* in my 1977 book on Cheever and his work underscored the two major points. His lyric style fought with the desperation of plot and lives that he uncovered; he used it to override or at least evade that desperation and darker vision, for the novel came "too incandescently packaged."[8]   And the structure of the book was seriously fragmented and fractured, the "eccentric incidents" weakening the essential battle between Eliot Nailles and Paul Hammer (Coale, 103). Cheever's penchant for the short story had undermined any attempt at a full-fledged novel. *Bullet Park*, therefore, looked like the diminishing returns of Cheever's fiction, the end-game of his struggle with suburban mores and upper-middle-class life. As Cheever wrote in 1968 in his journals (not published until 1991): "As I came to the end of 'Bullet Park' I felt the need to overhaul my approach to things; that is, to avoid constructing fiction out of the minutiae of upper-middle-class life . . . ."[9]   And he wondered in 1972: "Is there some discernible falling off, some trace of my struggle with alcohol and age?" (*Journals*, 282).

And yet, slowly, praise for the achievement of *Bullet Park* began to grow. On October 24, 1971 the novelist John Gardner wrote in the *Times Book Review* an assessment of the book he called "Witchcraft in Bullet Park." He decided that the novel was about chance, about the novelist's voice groping with the seeming randomness of good and evil in the world. Therefore the voice relied upon "poetic . . . magical devices--rhythm, imagistic repetition, echo. Instead of conventional plot, an accretion of accidents" (*Essays*, 259). For Gardner "the novel is bleak, full of danger and offense . . . . Good and evil are real, but are effects of mindless chance--or heartless grace. The demonology of Calvin, or Cotton Mather." It is finally "a religious book, affirmation out of ashes . . . like a curative spell" (*Essays*, 261). And Walter Clemons, in his front-cover article on Cheever's *Falconer* in *Newsweek* on March 14, 1977, declared that *Bullet Park* had been "misunderstood and much maligned" (as quoted in *Letters*, 326).

Other critics picked up Gardner's clarion call. In Lynne Waldeland's *John Cheever* (1979), as in her essay for R.G. Collins' *Critical Essays on John Cheever* in 1982, she suggested that *Bullet Park* was about Nailles' initiation into the powers of evil, that the novel was carefully crafted and structured around that principle, and that "the lyricism in the novel is primarily a function of the viewpoint of Nailles" (*Essays*, 270). George Hunt in his *John Cheever: The Hobgoblin Company of Love* (1983) described 1969, the year that *Bullet Park* came out, as a devastating one in American culture. He went on to explain that critics had pigeon-holed Cheever as a kind of social realist, not allowing his developing "post-modernist" techniques to be explored. And he agreed with Gardner that the novel does not display a linear plot but suggests a certain poetic logic within which carefully crafted symbols, situations, and incidents parallel, repeat, echo, and are juxtaposed with one another, all within the vision of dynamic contradictions, itself within a genuinely redemptive (however ambiguous) Christian perspective.

Susan Cheever's 1984 biography, with its revelations of Cheever's overwhelming sense of isolation and self-doubt and his bouts with alcoholism and homosexuality, also revealed glimpses of his essential outlook on the world. In his journal he exclaimed, "life is a contest, . . . the forces of good and evil are strenuous and apparent, and that while my self-doubt is profound, nearly absolute, the only thing I have to proceed on is an invisible thread. So I proceed on this" (*Dark*, 103). He also wrote: "That bridge of language, metaphor, anecdote and imagination that I build each morning to cross the incongruities in my life seems very frail indeed" (*Dark*, 199). The bridge's crossing "incongruities" and the "invisible thread": these images suggest an approach to Cheever's narrative voice and the manner in which he uses language.

In my 1982 essay on Cheever in Collins' collection, I compared him with Hawthorne, in preparation for a book on Hawthorne's influence on modern writers of American romance, *In Hawthorne's Shadow: American Romance from Melville to Mailer*. Cheever, I decided, was more a romancer in the Hawthorne tradition than he was a novelist. Therefore the episodic structure of his fiction suggested those morally revealing "scaffold epiphanies" that can be found, for example, in *The Scarlet Letter*. Here were incidents of the self *in extremis*, a kind of moral allegory wrestling with ambiguous notions of good and evil, with the strange mixture of life as a series of random and cause-and-effect events. And the basic dualism of Cheever's character-brothers at war, whether in the *Wapshot* novels, in *Falconer*, or in the confrontation between Nailles and Hammer in *Bullet Park*, revealed the dualistic nature of much of the structure and plot of many American romances. Such a structure and plot suggested Manichean overtones, a world at war with itself, a world essentially as a prison of self-confinement with glimpses but never lasting bastions of transcendence and escape. In his biography Donaldson also played up the dualistic nature of *Bullet Park*, viewing "Hammer and Nailles [as] fragments of a single divided psyche" and Cheever as "at once the lyric transcendentalist and the bitter Calvinist" (Donaldson, 247, 241). And he quoted Stephen C. Moore's perceptive comment: "*Bullet Park* is not about a 'mystery,' it is a mystery . . . " (Donaldson, 248).

Thanks to the publication of his journals, we can now see more clearly Cheever's essential vision of things. At the heart of the matter lurk "the contradictions in my nature" (*Journals*, 129). He went on to observe that while he knew that man's very nature is "to be divided, paradoxical, wayward, and perverse," he still felt "unable to live peaceably with this fact" in his own case (*Journals*, 217). Division lies at the center of things: "And looking around for some general, some fundamental axe to grind, what do I come up with? The fundamental competitiveness of brothers" (*Journals*, 117). And yet at the same time Cheever wanted to contradict that essential confrontation: "that life . . . is a creative force [and] . . . what we lose in one exchange is more than replenished by the next, that it is only us, only our pitiful misunderstandings that make for crookedness, darkness, and anger" (*Journals*, 37). The vision of life's essential goodness, marred only by our presence in it, contradicts the equally compelling vision that confrontation and division mark the core of all essential things.

Cheever often thought of evil as some mysterious outside force that exists to thwart our creative existence. In his moral framework, life was "a creative process and . . . anything that chafes or impedes this forward thrust is evil and obscene" (*Journals*, 121). At the same time he located evil within himself: "But there are speculations and desires that seem contrary to the admirable drift of the clouds in heaven, and perhaps the deepest sadness that I know is to be absorbed in these"

(*Journals*, 122). He identified life as a battle between good and evil and at the same time, as Susan Cheever noted, for him sex revealed "the forces of good and the forces of evil combined and equal in one powerful human desire" (*Dark*, 127). Life is at once a series of "intense and profoundly broken encounters" (*Journals*, 325); it is also creative, transcendent, and almost mystically lyrical.

With contradiction piled upon contradiction--"What a struggle it is to admit the existence of evil in the world and in ourselves, how difficult it is to strike a balance between our self-expression--our extension-- and that which we know to be right" (*Journals*, 81)--Cheever sought that bridge of language, that invisible thread which would provide an equilibrium, what the poet Robert Frost once referred to as "a momentary stay against confusion." Cheever felt unable to achieve "the balance between the niceties, the stress on the appearance of things, the natural violence that lies beneath all of this, and the vision of a world where the balance is more commodious; where the sense of tragedy is not lost in anesthesia" (*Journals*, 118). Even writing, which "is allied with many splendid things--faith, inquisitiveness, and ecstasy," also suggests "diddling, drawing dirty pictures on the walls of public toilets . . . " (*Journals*, 64). As John Updike suggested in his recent review of the *Journals*, "The Waspshot Chronicle," "Cheever had no theology in which to frame and shelter his frailty; he had only inflamed, otherworldly sensations of debasement and exaltation."[10]

His attacks on the false securities and "incandescence" of suburbia were also muted or distorted by his acknowledgment of his own contradictions and divisions. He admitted as early as 1948 that "it was my decision, early in life, to insinuate myself into the middle class, like a spy, so that I would have an advantageous position of attack, but I seem now and then to have forgotten my mission and to have taken my disguises too seriously" (*Journals*, 16). He admits that his self-esteem which could shift all too readily from ecstasy to despair "at its best [reveals] a sense of fitness that approaches ecstasy--the sense of life as a privilege, the earth as something splendid to walk on. Relax, relax" (*Journals*, 245). And out of these layers of contradiction and confrontation comes yet another of his descriptions of life as "a web of creative tensions" (*Journals*, 105).

Bullet Park is the remarkably visionary novel that emerged from John Cheever's creative tensions which also mirror the tensions of his time and place and probably the dynamic dialectic at the heart of many American tensions as well. The duplicitous dualities, the opposing polarities that turn out in the end to be flip sides of the same dark coin--apparent opposites feeding off one another in some ultimately dynamic but ambiguous and unresolved manner--announce themselves in the opening paragraph:

> Paint me a small railroad station then, ten minutes before dark.
> Beyond the platform are the waters of the Wekonsett River,
> reflecting a somber afterglow. The architecture of the station
> is oddly informal, gloomy but unserious, and mostly resembles
> a pergola, cottage or summer house although this is a climate
> of harsh winters. The lamps along the platform burn with a
> nearly palpable plaintiveness. The setting seems in some
> way to be at the heart of the matter.[11]

There are the contradictions, the polarities: The somber afterglow and
gloom that are "unserious," summer and winter, the afterglow and the
burning of the lamps. And these opposites "in some way [seem] to be at
the heart of the matter." Cheever cannot be absolutely certain, but he
senses that this is so, that this is the way things "seem" to be. And
the entire paragraph suggests a dreamy state of mind, a conjuring up of
a setting at twilight almost as if in a trance, the entranced beginnings
of a moral allegory or romance, a remote but recognizable realm which,
like our own country, remains "unique, mysterious and vast."

The station itself suggests the nomadic, restless qualities of his
characters, that heart of the vision which drives them to wrap
themselves in the seemingly secure boundaries, customs and trappings of
Bullet Park: "The people of Bullet Park intend not so much to have
arrived there as to have been planted and grown there, but this of
course was untrue" (4). Cheever notes elsewhere the "confusion between
architectural decorum and moral probity . . . as if there were some
connection between real-estate values and serenity."[12]

The first chapter functions according to the dialectic of contradictions. As soon as one perspective or point of view is revealed, a
contradictory one follows it, as if one necessarily and almost
immediately generates its opposite. Thus when "some zealous and
vengeful adolescent" indicts Bullet Park for its "legions of
wife-swapping, Jew-baiting, booze-fighting spiritual bankrupts" and
among other things "their hypocrisy," Cheever suggests that adolescents
are always "mistaken" (5) and goes on to explore in detail the grim
Monday morning of the Wickwires--their celebrations, their injuries,
their "gethsemanes," their remorse--deciding that "there was nothing
hypocritical about the Wickwires' Monday mornings, and so much for the
adolescent" (9). When Mr. Elmsford sings about the mystery of
disappointment, despite the wealth and security that come with living in
Bullet Park, other singers, especially the real-estate people like
Hazzard (who is showing houses to Hammer), proclaim, "Bullet Park is
growing, growing. Bullet Park is here to stay . . ." (10). When
neighbors comfort Mrs. Heathcup about her husband's sudden suicide,
"they were so comforting that I almost forgot what had happened" (12).

At the end of the chapter the railroad station is revealed with all

its broken windows and smashed clock, all the architect's "inventions
had been stripped and defaced," and Cheever juxtaposes three stories in
the local paper: "Seventeen debutantes were presented to society. . .
Mr. Lewis Harwich was burned to death. . . School taxes expected to increase" (14). Even the references within the chapter to sacrificial
altars, tribal elders, Chinese demons, and Gethsemane suggest both the
ritualistic nature of Bullet Park, as if it were truly a kind of
religious sect, and at the same time undermine the place by calling
attention to its lack of a genuine religious vision. Upon these contra-
dictions--these reverberations, echoes, repetitions, and resonances
which are presented as individual episodes with a self at peril in every
one of them--is *Bullet Park* founded.

The basic confrontation in the book occurs between Eliot Nailles,
monogamous husband, suburban church-goer, and conventional moralist, and
Paul Hammer, social outcast, anarchic bastard, and rootless drifter
haunted by his "cafard" of melancholy and doom. "The mysterious power
of nomenclature" (19) draws them together. These "mysterious
polarities" (237) provide the central focus of the novel. And yet as
the story continues, we recognize that many things about Nailles and
Hammer are more similar than dissimilar. A fear of death haunts them;
they harbor sudden violent impulses; they each are overtaken by strange
phobias which drive Nailles to drugs and Hammer to his search for a room
with yellow walls. Each not only helps to define the other, but each
cannot exist without the other. In fact each seems to function as part
of the other, polarities that fuse and become more dialectically
interconnected than simplistically opposed. Cheever's preferred battle
between Cain and Abel produces a web of episodic events and results in
ambiguous stylistic uncertainties that implicate both of them. What
looks like a clearly demarcated confrontation turns out to be much more
complex and complicitous.

That vision of battling opposites in *Bullet Park* Cheever himself
described as "an extract of my most intimate feelings . . . " (*Journals*,
282). He also recognized the moral ambiguity of the whole, and in his
journal stated that he didn't want *Bullet Park* "to be an indictment."
Yet, he felt without such an indictment he would not seem to have a
"moral position--no position, in fact, at all." What Cheever wanted in
Bullet Park was "an uncomplicated story about a man who loved his son"
(*Journals*, 243-44). We do get the story in which Nailles rescues his
son Tony from Hammer's mad plan to execute him for the sins of suburban
America--"Nothing less than a crucifixion will wake that world . . . a
great nation singlemindedly bent on drugging itself" (166)--after Tony
himself has been rescued from a death-in-life collapse by a mysterious
Swami intoning a mysterious chant, and the complicatedness lies not in
the story but in the voice of the teller of the tale.

Cheever's style in *Bullet Park* is no mere lyric overlay. "His marvelous brightness," as Alfred Kazin tagged it years ago, is not "an effort to cheer himself up."[13]   He is not, as Updike suggests, "erecting a glowing verbal shield against . . . dismaying personal revelations . . . " (*Waspshot*, 38). Rather, the style is built upon these dynamic contradictions. It is far more tenuous and troubled than any lyric impulse would suggest. As Stephen C. Moore makes plain, "*Bullet Park* almost willfully destabilizes meanings. . . . the *telling* of this novel is notably ambivalent and is part of the not wholly resolved dialectic of the fiction . . . ."[14]

Cheever's style conjures up a multitude of experiences and feelings. In several instances the style does celebrate a certain lyricism: Nailles' sense of the inherent beauty and order of the natural world, the Swami's love prayer and chant. In others it ironically mocks and undercuts notions of Bullet Park's serenity and riches, clearly satirizing the expectations and actual events of many of the people who live there. The style also becomes a game, a way of evading darker truths, as when Nellie Nailles suggests the game, "My Grandmother's Trunk," to avoid the fact that son Tony has brought home a widow with whom he has just spent the night. In such a mode the style can act as much like a drug as the decorum and public manners for which suburbia is famous. As we have seen, the style can also indict and condemn, as in the adolescent's howl and Paul Hammer's mother's plan of crucifixion to awaken the morally bankrupt village. And again the style is itself paradoxical as in the opening paragraph: the elegiac and lyrical rhythms of its balanced and decorous cadences cannot conceal the contradictions and confrontations on display.

Cheever knew exactly what he was doing in *Bullet Park*. He wrote in a letter on May 8, 1969: "A reviewer here said that the book didn't hang together. I thought this wrong since the book is so closely constructed that it can be read backwards" (*Letters*, 273). The style and structure define and implicate one another. "The concept of man as a microcosm, containing within himself all the parts of the universe, is Babylonian," explains Hammer's soon-to-be grandfather-in-law, the alchemist Gilbert Hansen. "The elements are constant. The distillations and trans- mutations release their innate power" (202). And Hammer, armed with his mission of murder, decides finally that "the nature of man was terrifying and singular and man's environment was chaos" (230). Both voice and vision embody these essential ideas in the novel.

And yet even then Cheever cannot be certain that the bridges of language which he builds will last. Nailles, his sentimental and monogamous prototype--who ends up as a hero but heavily drugged--feels that his "sense of being alive was to bridge or link the disparate envi- ronments and rhythms of his world" (62), but his wife Nellie experiences the sense of being caught between opposing forces in a "broad river without bridges [which] seemed to give her some insight into the force of separateness in her life. She seemed to be saying goodbye to herself at a railroad station . . . " (125). The bridge must ultimately rest on resemblances; it "seems" to bridge or not bridge experience and sensibility. And as the word "seems" bridges both the connection and separation between two disparate thoughts or feelings, so Cheever's style and structure in *Bullet Park* achieve the same.

Cheever clarified his approach to art in the opening to "The Death of Justina": "Fiction is art and art is the triumph over chaos (no less) and we can accomplish this only by the most vigilant exercise of choice, but in a world that changes more swiftly than we can perceive there is always the danger that our powers of selection will be mistaken and that the vision we serve will come to nothing. We admire decency and we despise death but even the mountains seem to shift in the space of a night . . . ."[15] As Eugene Chesnick suggested, "The voice of authorial wonder in Cheever's fiction is his device for refusing to acknowledge the finality of evil" (*Essays*, 138). Perhaps, and we can sense that lyric wonder in the cadences from "Justina"--the balance of the lines, the equilibrium between "decency" and "death," the decorum of speech itself.

But we can also see the fear, the danger that any vision "will come to nothing." Atop this precarious fault line is *Bullet Park* poised. It lies at the heart of Cheever's art and vision. It is his most visionary and ambiguous book. And its "curative spell" can as easily evaporate as it solidifies. Cheever once described the style of one of his favorite writers, Hemingway: "He writes with the galvanic distortion that gives the illusion of a particular vision; that is, he breaks and re-forms the habitual rhythms of introspection" (*Journals*, 139). There lies the secret to Cheever's mysterious polarities, the contradictions and momentary stays of his constant fictional struggle and triumph.

NOTES

1. John Leonard, "Evil Comes to Suburbia," quoted by George W. Hunt, *John Cheever: The Hobgoblin Company of Love* (Grand Rapids, MI: Eerdmans, 1983), p. 153. In text and below as Hunt.

2. John Updike, "Suburban Men," quoted by Hunt, p. 153.

3. Benjamin DeMott, "A grand gatherum of some late 20th-century weirdos," *New York Times Book Review*, 27 April 1969: 40, 1.

4. Scott Donaldson, *John Cheever: A Biography* (New York: Random House, 1988), p. 248. In text as Donaldson.

5. John Cheever in an interview with Annette Grant, "John Cheever: The Art of Fiction LXII" (1981), in *Critical Essays on John Cheever*, ed. by R.G. Collins (Boston: G.K. Hall, 1982), p. 89. In text as *Essays*.

6. Benjamin Cheever, ed. of *The Letters of John Cheever* (New York: Simon and Schuster, 1988), p. 277. In text as *Letters*.

7. Susan Cheever, *Home Before Dark* (Boston: Houghton Mifflin, 1984), p. 155. In text as *Dark*.

8. Samuel Coale, *John Cheever* (New York: Frederick Ungar, 1977), p. 103. In text as Coale.

9. John Cheever, *The Journals of John Cheever*, ed. by Robert Gottlieb (New York: Knopf, 1991), p. 249. In text as *Journals*.

10. John Updike, "The Wapshot Chronicle," *The New Republic*, December 2, 1991, 38. In text as Wapshot.

11. John Cheever, *Bullet Park* (New York: Ballantine Books, 1978), p. 3. In text by page numbers only.

12. John Cheever, *The Leaves, The Lion-Fish, and The Bear* (Los Angeles: Sylvester and Orphanos, 1980), p. 16.

13. Alfred Kazin, *Bright Book of Life: American Novelists and Storytellers from Hemingway to Mailer* (Boston: Little, Brown, 1973), p. 113.

14. Stephen C. Moore, "A Text Already 'Deconstructed': *Bullet Park*," unpublished paper, University of Southern California at Los Angeles, 1985, p. 6.

15. John Cheever, "The Death of Justina," in *The Stories of John Cheever* (New York: Knopf, 1978), p. 429.

The World of Apples
1973

SELECTED REVIEWS

Victories of Happy Madness

Charles Bazerman

Since the turn of the century, quiet desperation has been the stuff of
our literary tragedies. However strong our conviction of success, we
feel a nagging dread that our achievements are hollow. We fear that as
much as Elizabethan Englishmen feared the vagaries of fortune and the
falls of monarchs; now, as in those times, stories that exercise our
fears are refreshing purgatives. The short stories of *The World of
Apples* are all in the modern American tragic mode. John Cheever
presents a collection of lives of failure, self-doubt and delusion.

In the title story, a famous poet is plagued by just such troubles. He
is known for his pleasant creations; his last volume of verse was
entitled *The World of Apples* (a good title bears repeating). But his
equanimity is disturbed when he stumbles across a couple making love in
the woods. He finds himself reduced to writing pornography, and as his
imaginings become increasingly lewd and boorish, he wonders whether he
and the world are forever consigned to filth. His sweetness of thought
returns when he makes a pilgrimage to a regional shrine on the
suggestion of his Italian housemaid. The grace of ritual reconfirms his
illusory world.

In "The Fourth Alarm," frail peace of mind is again restored by
private illusion. A suburban husband, neglected by his liberated wife
who copulates twice nightly on the New York stage, is distressed and
confused by her public lewdness. He manages to get through a lonely day

by recalling a "marvelously practical and obdurate part" of himself
which did not allow him to abandon his wallet and keys to join an
audience-participation love-pile at the end of his wife's performance.
He finds a model for his old-fashioned ways in a memory of a childhood
movie: at the last minute an almost abandoned horse-drawn fire engine is
called to put out the fire the gas-propelled ones could not. His
"marvelously practical and obdurate part" has rather romantic
antecedents.

The semi-solitude of a writer's retreat or of an affluent suburb can
keep a man satisfied in his delusions. But the depressed landscapes of
other stories weigh more heavily. In "The Chimera" a henpecked husband
waits on his back porch every night for his imaginary lover to appear
and wonders if his neighbors on their back porches are doing the same.
When his chimera comes, she produces as many problems as the rest of his
life; he is unable to carry on a successful affair even with his own
creation. One night, feeling quite guilty about abandoning his family,
he keeps his chimera waiting. The chimera in turn finds another lover
and goes on a week's binge. She returns hung-over and remorseful but is
soon off again. Having had enough of those sordid suburban affairs, his
fantasy packs up and heads for the West Coast.

The only victories Cheever allows are of a happy madness. In "The
Geometry of Love" Charley Mallory faces his personal problems with his
slide rule and the propositions of Euclid. The thought that life can be
figured out precisely is appealing. Elsewhere a gluttonous stomach
beats its master's diet. "When he ordered the *Zabaglione* I knew that I
had won." And finally there is the housewife turned sniper who takes
revenge on the superhighway that claimed the lives of her first and
second husbands and all her children. She bags four interstate trucks
before remarrying and quietly moving away.

The desire to fight back gets its most serious treatment in "Percy"
where, despite strenuous efforts to build an artistic career for herself
and her son, Aunt Percy's ambitions are always frustrated. Cast as a
reminiscence, the story creates an elegiac counterpoint of nearly
forgotten talent and the dispiriting weight of time and events. Hostile
family gatherings are temporarily relieved by the son's music, and
careers are dissipated by marriages. In this melancholy vanishing act
the family is finally left to the weakest heir, a retarded second son,
janitor at Logan Airport. Moment is added to moment and character to
character in a novelistic fashion, and in the end we are left not with
a single sad story or spot catastrophe but with a wide community of
depression.

"The Jewels of the Cabots," the most impressive story in the
collection, again in a novelistic manner, interweaves a family's decline
with the leaden depression throughout the town. Here the characters and
events are more eccentric, the catastrophes sharper. The motivating de-

ception is wealth: the wife flaunts the jewels, the daughter steals them, the wife goes mad with their loss and kills her husband. The mistress from the poor side of the river, fearing her share in the will would be contested, never files a murder complaint, and the larcenous daughter grows fat living above a restaurant in Egypt.

The story covers the rich and the poor sides of the river to create a mosaic of lost people. Between the daughter's theft and the fight between husband and wife the next evening is a 6-page excursion through all the other catastrophes of town life: Doris, a male prostitute, haunts the working-class bar, serving a world of "spiritual nomadism" and accepted with "hapless indifference." Meanwhile genteel families suffer Sunday-dinner skirmishes lured on by the promise of roast beef. The arguments are ended by the mother's change of subject. "'Feel that refreshing breeze.' There was, of course, seldom a breeze." The narrator also has a penchant for false refreshing breezes. He ends the digression with his special project of creating a newspaper that prints only good news. But even his fictitious stories have a morose ring:

> CONTROVERSIAL LEGISLATION REPEALED BY SENATE. The recently enacted bill, making it a felony to have wicked thoughts about the administration, was repealed this afternoon by a standup vote of forty-three to seven.

In the two of St. Botolphs the poor endure empty lives and the rich are brought together only by the myths of diamonds and the Sunday roast. When the story returns to the Cabots, it is only to record the final disintegration of the family.

These stories appeal to a morose part of our modern heart, the part that is convinced that we will soon end up fat, crazy or dead. It is one purpose of art to create well-turned public commiseration. It is odd, but very human, that we find delight in such things.

The Nation 217 (10 September 1973): 218-19.

Cheever to Roth to Malamud*

John Leonard

I happen to believe that John Cheever is our best living writer of short stories: a Chekhov of the exurbs. This view is not commonly shared. Critics tend to take an avuncular attitude toward Cheever; they have already written their one review of him and stashed it away in a drawer, waiting for the next book. Anyone who writes so clearly and so well, about such ordinary matters as marriage and children, cannot be presumed to be highly serious. He must be trying to glide by on charm.

See how effortlessly he goes about his business in this new collection. He enters his stories the way the rest of us leave our homes, opening the door, stepping out, getting rained on by the day. The awareness of each story seems random; it is composed of what is noticed. But watch: the noticing begins to fix on discrepancies. What is perceived is out of synch with what is felt. What is said is so often wholly inappropriate to the circumstances--women, usually, say those awful things in Cheever's fiction--that the story becomes a mugging. It's as if we had agreed to pretend that politeness is reality; then rudeness, aggression, attack not only our notion of ourselves but our notion of how the universe is supposed to be organized. Yeats asked, "How but in custom and ceremony/ Are innocence and beauty born?" Cheever was after something similar in *Bullet Park* when he talked about "that sense of sanctuary that is the essence of love." The people whom he allows to tell his stories--men, always, in *The World of Apples* (Knopf, $5.95)--find no sanctuary. Custom and ceremony are in shambles. Innocence and beauty are remembered, not experienced; and even the memories are suspect: what is being remembered is the desire for innocence, beauty, and sanctuary, rather than the fulfillment. And what remains after the stories have gone is the watermark on the day's page, the blood-vein in the mugger's eyelid: chance and terror.

And yet it is all accomplished with a casual left-handedness. Consider these beginnings, these doors opening on stories: "Reminiscence, along with the cheese boards and ugly pottery sometimes given to brides, seems to have a manifest destiny with the sea." "Artemis loved the healing sound of rain." "The first time I robbed Tiffany's, it was raining." "The subject today will be the metaphysics of obesity, and I am the belly of a man named Lawrence Farnsworth." "It was one of those rainy late afternoons when the toy department of Woolworth's on Fifth Avenue is full of women who appear to have been taken in adultery and who are now shopping for a present to carry home to their youngest child."

What is happening? We never hear about a second or third robbing of Tiffany's; we hear instead about an abusive servant and the old lady she reviles; at the moment of death, they learn that they are daughter and mother. Mr. Farnsworth's belly is a witty trifle of a story, exactly what Philip Roth could have made out of *The Breast* if he had been able to control himself and resist the silicone injections. The rain will have to heal Artemis; his Russian love is interdicted by our State Department. What began in the toy department of Woolworth's ends with the death of a man who has canceled himself out by trying to solve the problem of his wife's unhappiness with Euclidean geometry.

In other stories, a husband objects to his wife's simulating sexual acts on a stage, naked; refusing to join her and others in a "love pile," he discovers "some marvelously practical and obdurate part of myself," but he loses his wife. A middle-aged man with an unhappy marriage conjures up a phantom, a chimera of a young girl who needs his "love, strength and counsel"--only to lose even this. An expatriate returns to America to find that the walls of our public buildings are scrawled over with a new kind of graffiti, florid writing about Roman banquets, haunted manor houses, and geraniums--"What had happened, I suppose, was that, as pornography moved into the public domain, those marble walls, those immemorial repositories of such sport, had been forced, in self-defense, to take up the more refined task of literature"--and flees back to Europe. A woman who has lost three husbands to traffic accidents starts shooting truck drivers with a rifle. A kitten is ground up in a kitchen blender.

Loss, and various forms of mourning. Love, but never enough of it to "quite anneal the divisive power of pain." Here is an elderly poet remembering his boyhood on a farm in Vermont, and a natural fall of water: "He had gone there one Sunday afternoon when he was a boy and sat on a hill above the pool. While he was there he saw an old man, with hair as thick and white as his was now, come through the woods. He had watched the old man unlace his shoes and undress himself with the haste of a lover. First he had wet his hands and arms and shoulders and then he had stepped into the torrent, bellowing with joy. He had then dried himself with his underpants, dressed, and gone back into the woods and it was not until he disappeared that Bascomb had realized that the old man was his father."

Compare that with another story, a bitter vignette that breaks the heart. A man takes an aisle seat on a 707 for Rome. He is presentable, charming, likes people and is liked by them. There is a beautiful woman of his own age in the window seat. The middle seat is unoccupied. For the nine hours of the flight he tries to talk to her; she is rude and distant, refusing even the most civil of intimacies, seems actively hostile toward him. He does not understand. Neither does the reader. We come to the final paragraph. They have landed:

"But look, look. Why does he point out her bag to the porter and why, when they both have their bags, does he follow her out to the cab stand, where he bargains with a driver for the trip into Rome? Why does he join her in the cab? Is he the undiscourageable masher that she dreaded? No, no. He is her husband, she is his wife, the mother of his children, and a woman he has worshipped passionately for nearly thirty years."

I reread the story, and someone had applied the tip of a knife to my pineal gland: Cheever, touching the spot where the mind and the body were once supposed to connect, nicking it, passing on.

Now consider these desires, expressed in the stories: "Should I stand up in the theater and shout for her to return, return, return in the name of love, humor and serenity?" "But God, oh, God, how much I then wanted some kind of loveliness, softness, gentleness, humor, sweetness, kindness." "Was there such hidden balance and clemency in the universe that our needs were always requited?" "If we are any less than shrewd, courageous, and honest with ourselves we are contemptible." "Were the Littletons making for themselves, by contorting their passions into an acceptable social image, a sort of prison, or did they chance to be a man and woman whose pleasure in one another was tender, robust and invincible?" "One felt that they might live together with intelligence and ardor--giving and taking until death did them part." "No amount of ignominy or venom could make parting from [his wife and children] imaginable. As he thought of them, they seemed to be the furniture of his soul, its lintel and rooftree." "One could disparage them as homely but they were the best he knew of life--anxiety and love." "His return to Monte Carbone was triumphant and in the morning he began a long poem on the inalienable dignity of light and air."

I like these words, and the emotions they invoke--love, humor, serenity, sweetness, strength, clemency, intelligence, ardor, soul. They aren't used much, or they are not used honestly, in books by Cheever's peers. Irony has deformed these words; they have become indices of simplemindedness; their profession is excused, or traduced, as a black joke. There is, of course, no escaping irony. It is an indispensable tool for writers of twentieth-century fiction, part of the surgical bag, like sex, ennui, paranoia, and a contempt for your readers. But it isn't absolutely necessary to use irony as a club for bludgeoning your characters into submission; writers who use truncheons are fearful of themselves.

Irony *can* be used the way Cheever uses it: protectively, on behalf of ardor and intelligence and clemency, even while these words, these values really, are inadequate to cope with a world of chance, of evil. Inside Cheever's irony, love and humor are preserved, not abused. A sadness obtains. His fiction has consistently been about a certain failure of reciprocity in our relations with the rest of the universe. (Women, especially, are unknowable and chancy; I suppose someone will write a tract about it, missing the point.) What we don't know, didn't expect, and can't understand overwhelms our decent impulses. We lose. We are not, however, ugly for losing. And the rain tries to heal. . . .

Atlantic Monthly 231 (June 1973): 112-14.

The World of Apples

D. Keith Mano

There is a difference between history and nostalgia: between the 11 o'clock news and a smell recalled of leaves burnt in another year. A difference that separates the world from *The World of Apples*. Not since Proust has a writer been so concerned, and so interestingly concerned, with memory. John Cheever's present itself has a quality of the past. His people are remembered posthumously while they are alive. Not bigger than life, but set apart from it: catchy as mnemonic poems. They silhouette themselves against time's off-white blankness. They mean to be part of some future retrospection. It's their life. It's their sentiment and their morality.

"Bascomb believed, as Cocteau once said, that the writing of poetry was the exploitation of a substrata of memory that was imperfectly understood." Cheever's poet speaks. Autumn, water, marriage especially: for Cheever they are memory's substance and the catalyst of its awakening. Wordsworth's saw is pertinent: emotion recollected in tranquillity. Cheever's writing, its reflective, adult style, is charged with tranquillity. In these stories violence has been subdued, thwarted by it, made innocuous; wasps blundering to stillness in a spiderweb.

This allows us to understand eccentricity: the most charming and characteristic aspect of John Cheever's writing. People who take up residence in bathrooms; hang their diamond rings to dry on the washline; braid feathers in their hair and squat like Indians to commune with the great spirit. These are habits of another age. The eccentricity is an 18th-century invention. In the 20th we have only clinical sorts of tragic and wasteful madness. Eccentricity is private and, well-- pastoral. It's a trait of the small town: agrarian America. There are no urban eccentricities, certainly none in Cheever; they require patience, solitude, single-mindedness and, usually, at least a small independent income. Read history. Washington's false teeth last in the memory longer than Princeton or Brandywine Creek. Cheever's people are self-shaped anecdotes. Even alive, they recommend themselves to nostalgia.

One character discovers an outbreak of grafitti in the nation's lavatories. He asks a pertinent question; "Was what I had read the expression of some irrepressible love of quaintness and innocence?" We can answer: yes. These two words are perfect, concise; they denote John Cheever's intellectual business. Quaintness, for its double sense: eccentricity and anachronism. Innocence because there is no writer of Cheever's stature for whom guilt has so little fascination. He simply doesn't care to assign blame. Moreover, these attributes--quaintness

and innocence--are given preponderantly to the male. There is mild
sexual skirmishing in Cheever. The female tends to be more aggressive,
she copes; and she remembers less, cherishes less. It is in the Cheever
male, oddly, that nostalgia gets stored. The male broods. He is a
quaint, tranquil, passive instrument: nearly vestigial. And somehow
better than the female, deeper. John Cheever is a gentle chauvinist
pig.

There are robberies, a murder in *The World of Apples*. They are not
prosecuted. The perpetrators evince neither remorse nor triumph. One
story begins, "The first time I robbed Tiffany's, it was raining."
Cheever's people are not casuists, but they do have a fine weather eye.
Weather is an asset of nostalgia. Only one crime is recognized,
reproached: the failure to acknowledge and preserve memory, particularly
the joint remembrance of married couples. Wife auditions for a nude
show; husband is shocked, worried--but not by some problematical
exhibitionist sin. He is distressed because the act jeopardizes their
identity as man and wife, their several years mutual reminiscence. "Had
nakedness--its thrill--annihilated her sense of nostalgia? . . . It was
her gift gracefully to carry the memory of some experience into another
tense." America is a land of the professionally blamed; it is our
recent custom to feel responsible personally for assassinations, racial
enormities, wars. And it has been the preoccupation of literature to
present a higher morality or, anyway, a higher moralizing. In the
college anthologies of a 21st century, Cheever will suffer, I imagine.
He is not, in that public sense, an important writer. He doesn't want
to be. He refuses to be. I like his courage.

There are two halves to Cheever's St. Botolphs: East Bank and West
Bank. The East is more urban, more newsworthy and, yes, lower class.
Sensational events occur there, yet "Why would I sooner be on the West
Shore where my parents are playing bridge with Mr. and Mrs. Eliot
Pinkham in the golden light of a great gas chandelier?" Public
acts--stage performances, manslaughters, whatever--threaten nostalgia.
It is as if memory were meditation, a monastic affair. An engineer
develops "The Geometry of Love," his own mnemonic device, dry but
efficient. "Was Mallory's passionate detestation of squalor fastidious
and unmanly?" In Rome another character overhears a vicious female
harangue. "She attacks his hair, his brain and his spirit while I
observe that a light rain has begun to fall. . . ." Weather again.
That light rain, not human intemperance, will be his Roman souvenir.
Finally, "Children drown, beautiful women are mangled in automobile
accidents, cruise ships founder and men die lingering deaths in mines
and submarines, but you will find none of this in my accounts. . . Is
this an infirmity of the genteel or a conviction that there are discernible moral truths? Mr. X defecated in his wife's top drawer. This is a
fact, but I claim it is not a truth." Genteel, gentle: surely. Effete,

unmanly: could be. *The World of Apples* is a sharp repudiation of
realism. In the age of Tom Wolfe, of fiction as faction, Cheever's
restraint is heroic. He remembers for us another time, perhaps
apocryphal, when men were self-defined, not aspects of their
environment, when the sleepy interconnections between person and person
seemed commerce enough for a lifetime.

Not every tale in *The World of Apples* is pleasing. A few--"Three
Stories," "Montraldo," "The Chimera"--seem flat. But the great majority
belong with Cheever's best writing. The title story, "Percy," "The
Fourth Alarm," "The Jewels of the Cabots" are, moreover, crucial to an
understanding of the entire Cheever oeuvre. And that oeuvre, certainly,
is well worth an understanding.

The Washington Post Book World, 1 July 1973, pp. 1, 10.

The World of Apples*

Robert Phillips

In reviewing these two already widely-reviewed short story collections
late in the season, I'm tempted to review the reviewers as well as the
books. The Malamud collection has met a somewhat mixed press. (The
daily *New York Times* reviewer was by turns condescending and hostile).
The Cheever book has, on the other hand, received wild hosannas and
comparisons with Chekov. Yet I maintain that *Rembrandt's Hat* is more
important, and contains a number of stories as fine as any Malamud has
written, while *The World of Apples* is as important to the Cheever canon
as a carbon copy is to its bright original. So there appears
justification for another look at the two collections. . . .

Nowhere in *The World of Apples* do we find such levity [as we do in
Malamud's "Talking Horse"]. Even the title story, which focuses upon a
poet's loss of faith in the world and therefore in himself, does not
move the reader in the way Malamud's spiritual pilgrims do. Is this due
to Cheever's determined eccentricities? His indefatigable good humor?
With one or two exceptions, these stories chronicle the sadness and
futility of suburban and moneyed existences. In several the sound of
the rain is intended as a balm for the bruised spirits of those grown
more accustomed to the sounds of traffic. And perhaps this is one of
Cheever's shortcomings. Writing strictly of one class, his books cannot
compare with those attempting a Balzacian cross-section of humanity.
Malamud is no Balzac, and writes most often about the poor. But
Rembrandt's Hat is also populated with successful architects and
professors, doctors and students. Cheever's humor and irony make him a

greater writer than, say, Louis Auchincloss, whose humorless novels also examine the professional classes to the exclusion of all others. But the limitation is there.

Loneliness of course knows no class barrier, and it is this state which is Cheever's subject. The husband who loses his wife to the off-Broadway stage, the American tourist who loses his Russian beloved through interference of the State Department, and the husband who loses his wife to a phantom lover are all outdone by the hero of "The Chimera," whose marriage is so unhappy he conjures up a demon lover of his own, but whose masochism is also so great he loses even her. Another protagonist, in "The Geometry of Love," desperately seeks "radiance, beauty, and order, no less," and all he finds is a world in which kittens get murdered in Waring blenders.

That kitten in the blender is symptomatic of what else might be "wrong" with this collection. What formerly had been the telling detail for Cheever has, in these late stories, become a mannerism. (Would any woman *really* hang her diamonds out on the line to dry?) The eccentric actions in these rambling reminiscences have become almost Gothic: full chamberpots are thrown in husband's faces, husbands defecate in their wive's dresser drawers; daughters unwittingly murder their mothers. Moreover, in four of these twelve stories, Cheever's plots depend upon the meanest kind of trick for their denouement: a servant discerns the employer she has hated all her days is her mother; a man trying to proposition a woman on an airplane is actually her husband; etc.

Ah, but the title story! I can hear those say who already have read most of the reviews of *The World of Apples*. For it is said to be one of Cheever's best. Well, it is and it isn't. In its portrait of old Asa Bascomb, expatriate American poet comprised of 3/4 Frost and 1/4 Pound, Cheever has created a potentially remarkable character, and one quite different from his melancholy suburban husbands. Asa, whose poetry is said to contain "the pungency, diversity, color, and nostalgia of the apples of the Northern New England he had not seen for forty years," suddenly finds himself smitten by a compulsion for smut. He writes dirty limericks, ballads, finally nothing at all but dirty words. Fair enough. It is in his overnight conversion back to the pontifical Santa Claus of American poetry which strains credibility. Such rapid changes in character do, we know, sometimes occur in life. But life is, as someone said, stranger than fiction. As a cautionary tale for one man's search to recapture that which he has lost--in Asa's case, the capacity for spirituality--the story is ambitious. But ultimately lacks credibility. Just possibly the quick-change act which has become Cheever's stock-in-trade--the suburban housewife suddenly turned off-Broadway nude actress, the promising pianist who comes to hate music--has become affectation and self-imitation. *The World of Apples* is an enormously entertaining book, but it is a throwback to the somewhat trivial *The Way*

Some People Live (1943), rather than a companion volume to *The Enormous Radio*, which in retrospect is Cheever's best.

Commonweal 99 (30 November 1973): 245-47.

Fiction Chronicle*

William Peden

. . . As a longtime admirer of John Cheever I am glad to say that he has lost none of his wry understanding of contemporary manners nor his technical expertise. *The World of Apples*, his sixth collection of short fiction and his first in almost a decade, is very good Cheever, and even good Cheever is considerably better than most of the work of his contemporaries in the short fiction of manners.

Over the years Cheever's method has loosened up considerably; it is more varied, more flexible, than it was in such earlier collections as *The Enormous Radio* or *The Housebreaker of Shady Hill*. He has become increasingly fond of the leisurely, discursive, gossipy family chronicle which he has always been able to do so effectively. Characteristic is a piece like "The Jewels of the Cabots," a saga in miniature of life in the New England village of St. Botolph's which is as familiar to Cheever's followers as Polish ghettos are to [Isaac Bashevis] Singer's. Reminiscent of the author's most successful stories in this field--"The Day the Pig Fell into the Well," for example--"The Jewels of the Cabots" is Cheever at his best, a series of large and small disasters, beautifully controlled, illuminated by the effective juxtaposition of the trivial and the significant, the tragic and the comic. In the midst of reminiscences of minor childhood experiences, or recollections of love, adultery, and murder, we tend to remember most distinctly such asides as the advantages of the overhand stroke as opposed to the sidestroke: "When the ship sinks I will try to reach the life raft with an overhand and drown stylishly, whereas if I had used a Lower-Class sidestroke I would have lived forever."

The title story is a far remove from the world of St. Botolph's, a masterly depiction of an aging but still-vigorous American poet in Italy, perhaps the horniest old man in recent literature. "The Geometry of Love" and "The Fourth Alarm" are familiar Cheever territory, memorable depictions of suburban angst, anxiety, and loneliness, ranging from the essentially comic ("The Fourth Alarm" grows out of a wife's decision to perform in a New York skin show) to the disastrous (the engineer protagonist of "The Geometry of Love" is eventually devoured, eliminated, by the lack of love). Nobody does this kind of thing better than John Cheever.

The narrator of "The Jewels of the Cabots" comments that "children drown, beautiful women are mangled in automobile accidents, cruise ships founder, and men die lingering deaths in mines and submarines, but you will find none of this in my accounts." The statement is a key to Cheever's work in general. As I have commented elsewhere, in the final analysis he is a conventional moralist, albeit a highly sophisticated one. He is concerned with large problems: hypocrisy, individual and societal idiocy, the absurdity of sham and pretentiousness, the lack of love and understanding and the often disastrous effects of that lack. But in spite of the failure of so many of his people to find love and understanding, and in spite of the failures of marriage and the disruptions in family and professional life which appear and reappear from his very earliest to his most recent stories, the final effect, the pervasive mood of his work, is anything but somber. . . .

Sewanee Review 82 (Fall 1974): 719-21.

Falconer
1977

SELECTED REVIEWS

Escape Within Walls*

Hope Hale Davis

With their new novels the paths of Walker Percy and John Cheever seem curiously to cross. The two have come from very different directions, and seem on their way to very different destinations. Percy's *Lancelot* (Farrar, Straus & Giroux, 257 pp., $8.95) has deeply disappointed reviewers' great expectations, while Cheever's *Falconer* (Knopf, 211 pp., $7.95) has surprised them into hailing it as a masterpiece.

Cheever has always been accused of writing too much as an insider, as a veteran of the same frolics that scarred his wonderful Wickwires--the pair of "celebrants" in the novel *Bullet Park*--and the others who play hide and seek with horror in his six volumes of funny, terrifying short stories (most of them from the *New Yorker*). But Cheever's Farragut, literally "inside" Falconer prison, doing time for killing his brother, is really an outsider there--a wealthy professor trying to win acceptance as a fellow-convict. . . .

Cheever's message--or cluster of messages--in *Falconer* is very different [from Percy's], but in the end almost as disturbing. At first glance his need seems to have been to break out of his familiar milieu. "God preserve me from the camaraderie of commuting trains," he might be saying with his fugitive husband in the story "The Troubles of Marcie Flint." True, St. Botolphs, the home village of the family he wrote about in his big, rich novels, *The Wapshot Chronicle* and *The Wapshot Scandal*, is far from suburban. But it is very WASP indeed, as the name suggests, and the books chant a mournfully comic litany of the eccentric weaknesses and fatal strengths of an old New England blood line.

Falconer is in another country altogether, yet its story is told by our own nonchalant, witty Cheever. As only he could, he drops small, perfect tales drawn from his hero's and the other prisoners' memories--grim, droll, some with snob appeal--during Farragut's initiation, kicking of the drug habit, fulfillment in homosexual love, bereavement, and never-never-land escape.

Falconer cannot be taken as a serious attempt to bring light into the hidden hellhole of our criminal justice system, for neither the prison nor the circumstances of Farragut's confinement seem quite real. And by the time we reach the escape of his lover (disguised as an acolyte and helped by a visiting cardinal), we are tempted to take it as pure fun, a Horatio Alger story in reverse. Farragut's own flight is more sombre and symbolic, since he is borne away in place of the corpse of the saddest, most sordid murderer of them all. Still, it is just as much a fantasy.

Farragut slips into his romance with the greatest of ease, despite a prejudice against "queers" unlikely in a traveled professor. The affair is presented as an idyll unmarred by the awkward actualities of love that Cheever has made so poignant elsewhere--though the scenes here are graphic, not to say pornographic. The 48-year-old Farragut, encountering young Jody in the shower, is led--like Jesus by the Devil to the mountaintop--up to an abandoned water tower with a tremendous view. Jody explains that "Everybody's got to have a hideout." But could everybody, in a real prison?

Convicts at Falconer seem free to go almost anywhere they like. There is no sexual tyranny or homicidal jealousy, no gang rapes. The sex, like the food, is of varying quality, mostly low, but it is easy to come by. And the guard Tiny, after his one obligatory scene of sadism--he tears pet cats to pieces--is reliably benign. But the prison talk is for the most part what Cheever calls "unsavory."

Farragut's quick assimilation, his eager adoption of the speech, call for all Cheever's offhand professional *brio*. A writer of his subtlety must have found the portrayal of grossness rather tedious, even troubling. He says that "what Farragut didn't know was what importance to give unsavory matters. They existed, they were invincible, but the light they threw . . . only seemed to reinforce Farragut's ignorance, suspiciousness and his capacity for despair." This does not stop Farragut; he shows off his new vocabulary to his wife, who responds, surprisingly, with the only warmth she has ever offered him in all his trouble.

Since Cheever clearly did not intend his Falconer to be realistic, perhaps he was using the prison walls to make us feel fully what it is to be free. In one scene Farragut peers down from his cell window at the two steps leading out of the prison and marvels at the unmindful way visitors emerge into the open.   Another time, seeing the wind whirl leaflets in the prison yard, he is reminded "of the enormous and absurd pleasures he had, as a free man, taken in his environment. He liked to walk on the earth, swim in the oceans, climb the mountains and, in the autumn   watch   the   leaves   fall.   The   simple   phenomenon   of light--brightness angling across the air--struck him as a transcendent piece of good news."

Cheever goes further: Without freedom, life is still infinitely precious.   The dying Chicken II, totally friendless, about to leave the emptiest existence on earth, says that it has been "like a party, even in stir--even franks and beans taste good when you're hungry, even an iron bar feels good to touch, it feels good to sleep . . . "

The life Cheever is celebrating--make no mistake about this--is a life strictly without women.   Confinement may, in fact, be a sort of wish-fulfillment.   Only in prison can a man be safe from that baneful figure in so many Cheever stories, the vixen wife. Gifted with a talent for inventive, capricious, emasculative cruelty, she has somehow gained a hold over her husband from which he cannot free himself.

The message was not immediately apparent in Cheever's earlier work, partly because it fitted into what was thought to be the *New Yorker* formula: First dig your pit, then push your character into it.   Marriage was so universal a state that its unhappiness could be taken as a metaphor for the sadness of the human condition.   Now, though, there are "alternative life styles."   Cheever, in his own sly way, may be offering one.

The New Leader 60 (25 April 1977): 14-15.

Falconer

Joan Didion

Some of us are not Jews.   Neither are some of us Southerners, nor children of the Iroquois, nor the inheritors of any other notably dark and bloodied ground.   Some of us are even Episcopalians.   In the popular mind this absence of any particular claim on the conscience of the world is generally construed as a historical advantage, but in the small society of those who read and write it renders us "different," and a little suspect.   We are not quite accredited for suffering, nor do we have tickets for the human comedy.   We are believed to have known no poverty except that of our own life-force.   We are seen by the tolerant as carriers merely of an exhausted culture, and by the less tolerant as

carriers of some potentially demonic social virus. We are seen as
dealers in obscure manners and unwarranted pessimism. We are always
"looking back." We are always lamenting the loss of our psychic home,
a loss which is easy to dismiss--given our particular history in this
particular country--as deficient in generality and even in credibility.
Yet in a very real way the white middle-class Protestant writer in
America is in fact homeless--as absent from the world of his fathers as
he is "different" within the world of letters--and it is precisely this
note of "homelessness" that John Cheever strikes with an almost
liturgical intensity in his extraordinary new novel, "Falconer."

Of course this note of exile and estrangement has always been present
in Cheever's fiction, from the early stories on. But in the beginning
Cheever characters appeared to be exiled merely by their own errors or
passions or foolishness: lost wives and quixotic husbands, apparently
golden individuals who conceived their children at the St. Regis Hotel
and tumbled their card houses down for love of the grocery boy, love of
the plumber, love of the neighbor who came to collect for Muscular
Dystrophy and had six drinks and let her hair fall down. They tried to
behave well and they drank too much. Their best light was that which
dapples lawns on late summer afternoons, and their favorite note was
"plaintive": everything they heard was "plaintive," and served to remind
them that life and love were but fleeting shadows, to teach them to
number their days and to call them home across those summer lawns. They
yearned always after some abstraction symbolized by the word "home,"
after "tenderness," after "gentleness," after remembered houses where
the fires were laid and the silver was polished and everything could be
"decent" and "radiant" and "clear."

Such houses were hard to find in prime condition. To approach one was
to hear the quarreling inside. To reach another was to find it boarded
up, obscene with graffiti, lost for taxes. There was some gap between
what these Cheever people searching for home had been led to expect and
what they got, some error in expectations, and it became increasingly
clear that Cheever did not locate the error entirely in the hearts of
the searchers.

For a while he appeared to be locating this error in the "modern
world," and he did in fact make extravagant ironic use of the fractures
peculiar to postwar America. The demented verities and sweet wilds of
the family farm had been tamed into suburbs: Shady Hill, Bullet Park,
Proxmire Manor, where jobs and children got lost. Discharged
housekeepers and abandoned secretaries reappeared as avenging angels.
Your neighbor might take the collection at early communion on Sunday,
but he might also take a billfold from your bedroom on Saturday night.
So might you. Your child might be beautiful and fragrant, but one
morning that child might be too sad to get up. So might you. Guns kept
at home tended to get fired. Planes going home tended to crash.

Alfred Kazin* has described a Cheever story, one which opens with a non-fatal plane crash, this way: "The 'country husband' in this most brilliant of Cheever's stories returns home to find that his brush with death is not of the slightest interest to his family, so he falls in love with the baby-sitter. He does not get very far with the baby-sitter, so he goes to a therapist who prescribes woodworking. The story ends derisively on the brainwashed husband who will no longer stray from home. But who cares about this fellow?"

Actually this is not an accurate precis of "The Country Husband" (the story does not end "derisively," the husband is not "brainwashed," the story suggests not that the husband will "no longer stray from home" but rather that his "home" is a moral and economic illusion), nor does Kazin seem to have meant it to be; it is instead a deflationary reduction, the walker in the city giving a rhetorical raspberry to the kid down from Westchester in his Sunday School suit, and I quote it only to illustrate the particular irritability that Cheever provokes among some readers.

Cheever is too "brilliant" for his own good. Cheever is too smooth by half. Cheever almost makes these readers "care" about his babysitters and brainwashed husbands and bewildered women with too much money and not a thought in their heads, but not quite. (This question of "caring" about the characters in fiction is an interesting one. Sainte-Beuve complained that there were no "good and beautiful souls" in "Madame Bovary." I suspect that this secret wish to read novels in which the protagonist is an improved version of the reader--a kind of point man in history's upward spiral and someone you might want for dinner--is far from dead in fancy circles.) These readers see through Cheever's beautiful shams and glossy tricks, past his summer lawns and inherited pearls, and what they see is this: a writer who seems to them to be working out, quite stubbornly and obsessively, allegorical variations on a single and profoundly unacceptable theme, that of "nostalgia," or the particular melancholia induced by long absence from one's country or home.

"Nostalgia" is in our time a pejorative word, and the emotion it represents is widely perceived as retrograde, sentimental and even "false." Yet Cheever has persisted throughout his career in telling us a story in which nostalgia is "real," and every time he tells this story he refines it more, gets closer to the bone, elides another summer lawn and pulls the rug from under another of his own successful performances. He is like a magician who insists on revealing how every trick was done. Every time he goes on stage he sets for himself more severe limits, as if finally he might want to engrave the act on the head of a pin. "The time for banal irony, the voice-over, is long gone," reflects Ezekiel Farragut, the entirely sentient protagonist of Cheever's new novel, "Falconer." "Give me the unchanging profundity of nostalgia, love and death." In this sense of obsessive compression and abandoned artifice

"Falconer" is a better book than the "Wapshot" novels, a better book even than "Bullet Park," for in "Falconer" those summer lawns are gone altogether, and the main narrative line is only a memory.

Falconer is the name of a prison (actually the name of the prison is "Daybreak House," but this "had never caught on"), and it is at Falconer that Farragut is serving time for the murder of his brother. "I thought that my life was one hundred per cent frustration," Farragut is advised by his wife, Marcia, when she visits Falconer for the first time. "But when you killed your brother I saw that I had underestimated my problems." Marcia, who is a truer lover of Italy and of one Maria Lippincott Hastings Guglielmi than she is of Farragut, nonetheless would have visited sooner had she not been in Jamaica. "I," Marcia informs the guard who tells her the visitors' rules, "am a taxpayer. It costs me more to keep my husband in here than it costs me to send my son to a good school."

Aside from Marcia's visit, Farragut's only contact with the world he recently lost is the writing of three letters, one to his Governor ("I have never had the pleasure of your hospitality although I have twice been a guest at the White House as a delegate to conferences on higher education . . ."), one to his Bishop ("We prisoners . . . are in fact the word made flesh, but what I want to do is call your attention to a great blasphemy . . ."), and one to a woman with whom he had lived when Marcia abdicated temporarily to Carmel. "You are not the most beautiful woman I have ever known, but four of the great beauties I have known died by their own hand . . . I may be trying to explain the fact that while your beauty is not great, it is very practical. You have no nostalgia."

The rest of the incident is largely prison incident--the killing of cats, the bickering and petty blackmails, the onanism, the homosexual attachments and jealousies, the drafting of appeals and the picking of guitars--and is as cool and perfect in its pitch as those summer lawns and drunken lunches ever were. "There has to be something good at the end of every journey and that's why I wanted you to know that it's all a terrible mistake," Farragut is told by one of his blockmates. "And during the time you're waiting for them to discover this big mistake you'll have your visitors." Another prisoner, one whom Farragut loves for a while, advises him that he has ruined his face by smiling incorrectly: "Look at me, for example. I know how to smile, how to use my face. This actor taught me. He was in on a morals charge but he was very beautiful. He taught me that when you use your face you spare your face. When you throw your face recklessly into every situation you come up against, you come out looking like *you* do, you come out looking like s-----."

Cheever has a famous ear, but he is up to something more in "Falconer" than a comedy of prison manners. Events are peculiar. Farragut's beloved Jody, the one who knew how to save his face, escapes Falconer by masquerading as an acolyte when the Cardinal makes a helicopter visit. Farragut himself leaves Falconer, alive, in a body bag. On its surface "Falconer" seems at first to be a conventional novel of crime and punishment and redemption--a story about a man who kills his brother, goes to prison for it and escapes, changed for the better--and yet the "crime" in this novel bears no more relation to the "punishment" than the punishment bears to the redemption. The surface here glitters and deceives. Causes and effects run deeper.

Of course Farragut has been, all his life, afflicted with nostalgia. Of course "home" has been hard to locate. Of course he has resorted to anodynes--in this case heroin--to dull his affliction. "There is a Degas painting of a woman with a bowl of chrysanthemums that had come to represent to Farragut the great serenity of 'mother.' The world kept urging him to match his own mother, a famous arsonist, snob, gas pumper and wing shot, against this image . . . why had the universe encouraged this gap?"

At Falconer there is no heroin to blur this question and Farragut must manage with methadone. "When do you think you'll be clean," Marcia asks. "I find it hard to imagine cleanliness," Farragut answers. "I can claim to imagine this, but it would be false. It would be as though I had claimed to reinstall myself in some afternoon of my youth." "That's why you're a lightweight," Marcia says. "Yes," Farragut says.

Yes and no. Of all those Cheever characters who have suffered nostalgia, Farragut is perhaps the first to apprehend that the home from which he has been gone too long is not necessarily on the map. He seems to be undergoing a Dark Night of the Soul, a purification, a period of suffering in order to re-enter the ceremonies of innocence, and in this context the question of when he will be "clean" has considerable poignance. As a matter of fact it is this question that Cheever has been asking all along--*when will I be clean* was the question on every summer lawn--but he has never before asked it outright, and with such transcendent arrogance of style. Farragut is not the first Cheever character to survive despite his father's attempt to abort him, but in the past it took more words. Farragut is not the first Cheever character to see freedom as the option to book a seat on the Tokyo plane, but in the past the option was open. Addiction has been common, but not before to heroin. The spirit of fratricide has been general, but not until now the act. In this way "Falconer" is a kind of contemplation in shorthand, a meditation on the abstraction Cheever has always called "home" but has never before located so explicitly in the life of the spirit. I have every expectation that many people will read "Falconer" as another Cheever story about a brainwashed husband who lacked energy for the modern world, so he killed his brother and *who cares*, but let me tell you: it is not, and Cheever cares.

*[Editor's note: Alfred Kazin responded to Joan Didion's criticism in a letter to the editor, *New York Times Book Review* (10 April 1977), p. 37, in which he contended that Didion "falsifies what I meant." To this Didion replied, *in toto*, "Oh, come off it, Alfred." See also p. xxv (and n. 21) of the Introduction to this volume.

The New York Times Book Review, 6 March 1977, pp. 1, 22, 24.

Cheers for Cheever

Janet Groth

Ezekiel Farragut, the hero of John Cheever's new novel, *Falconer*, inhabits a religious and social topography roughly bounded by the contours of his name. Voices of Old Testament prophets reverberate down the corridors of his psyche, while, outwardly, he displays both the polish and the paranoia we have come to expect from Cheever's heroes. These heroes have families who--deeply implicated as they are in America's civic and military history--seem always to have fallen, just the generation before, from positions of wealth into reduced circumstances. Farragut's is no exception. Farragut himself, having turned white-collar worker, makes his living as a college professor. He has a wife, a son named Peter, and a home somewhere on the Eastern seaboard (where, customarily, a bowl of roses sits, mirrored, on a table in the front hall.)

As the novel opens, the state is in the act of appending something new to Farragut's name--the number 734-508-32. He is being incarcerated in Falconer Prison for a crime of which he feels himself to be innocent, the murder of his brother. With this fact Cheever takes his largest risk, for aside from the sheer *implausibility* of it, two other problems arise out of a Cheever novel with such a setting and such a theme. Readers are liable to expect from it either a social document, a protest of some kind over the horrors of our penal system, or, more typically, a Cheever portrait of an alienated upper-middle-class American simply translated behind bars. Both elements are in fact present, but it would be a pity to come away from this book having got no more from it than that. Those who suspend their disbelief will find that, in *Falconer*, John Cheever has written a stunning meditation on all the forms of confinement and liberation that can be visited upon the human spirit.

On the level of action, nothing very much happens. Farragut has visitors, writes letters, gets into trouble, is punished, forms a homosexual liaison, and is exhilarated to witness his lover's escape. (Disguised in the robes of an acolyte, the escapee is borne away in a visiting bishop's helicopter.) Farragut succumbs, for a time, to the lethargy the prison authorities try to induce in all the inmates, lest they catch rebellious fire from reports of an Attica-like uprising nearby--but, rousing himself, he begins to build a radio. He sits at the deathbed of the least likable of his fellow-prisoners, a wretch named Chicken Number Two. Strangely mellowed by this experience, Farragut sees Chicken safely across the bar and, in the end, slips back into the outside world in the dead man's shroud.

Take a second look at that sequence of events, however, and it begins to assume almost allegorical configurations: to prefigure a kind of divine comedy, from Farragut's doom-laden entry into the gates of Falconer, through a time in Purgatory, to a miraculous, grace-bestowed happy ending. Yet this is no allegory Cheever is giving us. Rather, he has incorporated into the novel a symbolic richness usually associated with densely imaged poetry or the best crafted short story. In this and in his willy-nilly coupling of the sacred and profane he is reminiscent of John Donne.

There is even a kind of metaphysical wit in evidence: Dante is evoked, appropriately enough, except that we read his "Abandon hope, all ye who enter here," not over the prison gates but in a tattoo on Chicken's backside.

To say that the novel proceeds in symbolic or metaphysical terms is not to deny that the flesh is involved; it is, and often in the grossest way. At Falconer the flesh is always being aroused or abused, subdued or gratified, either in reality or in recollection. Terrible scenes of cruelty, degradation and lust take place. However, when we look at these fleshly encounters of Farragut's and those of his fellow inmates, Cuckold, Jody, Chicken Number Two and the rest, the quality that distinguishes the greater portion of them is, curiously, purity. As Cuckold says of the homosexual hustler he once picked up at the One Hung Low Chinese Restaurant on the strip outside Kansas City:

> All the time he was talking I listened very carefully to him, expecting him to sound like a fairy, but he never did, not that I could hear. I have this very strong prejudice against fairies. I've always thought they were silly and feeble-minded, but he talked like anybody else. I was really very interested in what he had to say because he seemed to me very gentle and affectionate and even very pure.

The determined air of normalcy, of heterosexuality, in all of the attitudes displayed in this and other passages accounts for much of their appeal, and explains why they are to so large a degree successful in breaking down the reader's own prejudices. Yet this tolerant spirit is not earned cheaply, either by us or by Cuckold. It must stand the

severe test of watching the hustler at work and the hustler having got
mixed up with the wrong customer--of going down to the police station to
identify his dead body, complete with twenty-two knife wounds in his
back.

Neither the possibility that these encounters are mere lonely
substitutes for heterosexual love, nor the sense in which they manifest
themselves as brotherly--or, at least on some level--familial feeling is
allowed to obscure their darker components of narcissism and, even,
necrophilia. Farragut, thinking about his prison lover, a youth named
Jody, is prompted to see that "To embrace one's self, one's youth, might
be easier than to love a fair woman. . . ." "And then there was time to
think upon the courting of death and death's dark simples," he goes on,
musing that "in covering Jody's body he willingly embraced decay and
corruption." But all is bathed in a mysteriously detoxifying light.

The theology here and throughout the novel is interesting and
sophisticated. Sin is interpreted as a radical failure of love and a
consequent enthrallment (a kind of imprisonment) to fear. Love casts
out fear, as the evangelist tells us, and one of the processes Farragut
is undergoing in the Falconer "Correctional Facility" is nothing less
than the rehabilitation of his ability to love. More than anything
else, this accounts for the softening light that washes over so many of
the prison scenes.

One particular measure taken by Cheever bears remarking in this matter
of the book's strange and winning purity: it represents, I believe, both
an instance of legitimate poetic license and a profound theological
principle on Cheever's part. Though most readers will not consciously
notice that it is missing--there is more than enough obscene and
scatological language to produce convincing replicas of prison
argot--*Falconer* contains not a single instance of blasphemy. Farragut,
a methadone addict, is once heard to cry out, in the midst of a
withdrawal agony, for someone to "Get me my fix, for Jesus Christ's
sake!" But no man who describes himself in a letter to his bishop as "a
croyant" can be supposed at that moment to be taking the name of the
Lord in vain.

Cheever says nothing directly that would explain his decision to
delete this prominent feature of the vernacular. One can only suppose
that he considers swearing unsavory, and that he knows--as he tells us
that Farragut doesn't--"what importance to give unsavory matters. They
existed, they were invincible, but the light they threw was, he thought,
unequal to their prominence." Cheever, as narrator, goes on to note that
what is unsavory "only seemed to reinforce Farragut's ignorance,
suspiciousness and his capacity for despair." By daring to eschew that
kind of unsavory matter here, Cheever may actually be striving for the
opposite--a salutary effect upon all of us.

Some readers may find it difficult to place Cheever's treatment of his women characters in the context of near-universal tolerance which I have been describing as the outstanding characteristic of *Falconer*. It is true that at first the way Farragut's wife, Marcia, is pictured seems very harsh indeed. She is perilously close to a caricature of the frustrated suburban wife. She never tires of blaming Farragut for her disappointments, never stops kicking him when he is down. A rare prison visit finds her responding to Farragut's solicitous inquiry about the house with a curt "Well, . . . it's nice to have a dry toilet seat." She shows a sharp eye for Farragut's weaknesses, as well as a sharp tongue: "Do you still dream about your blonde?" she asks in the course of a later visit--"that blonde who never menstruated or shaved her legs or challenged anything you said or did?" But she would genuinely be glad to disabuse him of his wasteful dream, if she could: "Don't you understand that she never existed, Zeke, and that she never will?"

Although Farragut portrays his wife as cruelly mistreating him when he returns home from a drug cure with a seriously weakened heart, we are given this interesting comment as well: "He was in too much pain and fear to realize that the homecoming of a drug addict was not romantic." And when he is reliving his climactic scene with his brother, Eben, Marcia appears in it as a warm and sympathetic figure. We remember that she has seemed deliberately cruel only when Farragut is involved in justifying himself in her regard. She has been, in some sense, a phantasm all along--just as unreal in her implacable selfishness as his dream blonde in her docility. The soul whose progress we are following throughout *Falconer* is Farragut's.

A great deal more goes on before that soul's progress is complete, but it will be apparent from what has been said so far that this is no ordinary novel. Better say it is a new version of an old story form, a parable. In this post-Yeatsian stage of things when many of us still feel we are, as the poet says, "turning and turning in the widening gyre," the falcon unable to hear the falconer, how remarkable that John Cheever has found a way to circle back within earshot. His final word to us is an admonition to "Rejoice." *Falconer* is truly a parable for our times.

Commonweal 104 (10 June 1977): 374-76.

An Airy Insubstantial World

Joyce Carol Oates

In Cheever's imagination the concrete, visual world is transformed into emotion, and emotion into something akin to nostalgia. The senses, alerted to a patch of blue sky or swirling leaves or a sudden shaft of sunlight, are stimulated to a recollection that transcends the present and transcends, when Cheever's writing is at its most powerful, the very instrument of perception that is its vehicle. Hence the peculiar airiness of *Falconer*, the translucent quality of its protagonist Ezekiel Farragut (prisoner #734-508-32, fratricide, zip to ten years), the insubstantial quality of the narrative itself--though it purports to be located in a very real penitentiary and has been interpreted, by various critics, as a triumph of 'realism.'

The novel is a fable, a kind of fairy tale; near-structureless, it has the feel of an assemblage of short stories, and is consequently most successful in fragments: in patches of emotion. The world we glimpse through Farragut's eyes is as capricious and as alarming as a Chagall painting, and while it is occasionally beautiful it is also rather ugly, and at its worst tawdrily unconvincing--when narrative is forced to serve the demands of theme and Farragut 'escapes' prison by hiding in a dead man's shroud and afterward escapes the shroud by a maneuver that would strike us as embarrassingly awkward in a children's movie. No matter that Cheever cannot make his story probable: perhaps it is enough that it works on the level of myth, as a sort of death-and-resurrection suspense novel enriched with innumerable striking passages.

Farragut is supposedly a professor, yet we have no sense at all of his intellectual capacities; his I.Q. hovers around 119 and may even be lower. He does not seem to recall, and Cheever does not care to recall for him, his university teaching or his professional training. He is a husband and a father, but his wife is a stereotyped villainess who would be most at home in a *New Yorker* cartoon, and his son appears to be non-existent. Cheever works up a few 'memories' of wife and son but they are singularly unconvincing, as if his heart were not in it--as if the labors of conventional novelizing had grown tedious, and poetry of a whimsical, surreal nature had become more attractive. We are told too that Farragut has killed his brother Eben, an unpleasant man whom he has disliked for most of his life, but the killing is presented in a quick, truncated scene; like most physical action in *Falconer* it is hastily glossed over. What clearly appeals to Cheever is the pure action of writing itself and *Falconer* is most successful when there is nothing going on except bodiless reverie. The following passage is representative of many passages in the novel:

> . . . Farragut saw the leaves of beech trees, oaks, tulips, ash, walnut and many varieties of maple. The leaves had the power to remind Farragut, an hour or so after methadone, of the enormous and absurd pleasure he had, as a free man, taken in his environment. He liked to walk on the earth, swim in the oceans, climb the mountains and, in the autumn, watch the leaves fall.

> The simple phenomenon of light--brightness angling across the
> air--struck him as a transcendent piece of good news. He
> thought it fortunate that as the leaves fell, they turned and
> spun, presenting an illusion of facets to the light.

Such observations, lovely as they are, might belong to anyone; one feels
that they are Cheever's and not his protagonist's.

Cheever is by nature a short story writer and while in his finest
short stories (like "The Swimmer" and "The Enormous Radio") a single
surreal image is vividly developed, and draws that forward-motion called
'plot' irresistibly along with it, his novels flounder under the weight
of too many capricious, inspired, zany images. One comes away from
Falconer amused or bewildered or annoyed, recalling disparate
scenes--among them a too-brief and confused slaughter of some of the
4000 (sic) cats who dwell in the prison--that compete with one another
rather than complement one another. A prison riot at a nearby
penitentiary (called Amana or The Wall) is meant to recall the tragic
riot at Attica, but Cheever does very little with the prisoners'
uprising and their subsequent slaughter at the hands of state troopers;
it is merely an episode in the novel, a bead on the string of Farragut's
curiously soulless experience.

At the conclusion of the novel Farragut is 'resurrected' into life and
walks along the street thinking "Rejoice, rejoice." Earlier, his friend
Jody escapes by disguising himself as an altar boy; a cardinal assists
him, saying boyishly, "It is exciting, isn't it?" Of course there is no
likelihood in Cheever's airy insubstantial world of the escaped convicts
being caught. Where nothing is subjected to the laws of ordinary
earthly gravity anything is possible.

A certain visionary outrageousness in Cheever's art has often resulted
in highly successful short stories, and there are certainly a number of
powerful passages in *Falconer*, as in *Bullet Park* and the Wapshot novels;
but in general the whimsical impulse undercuts and to some extent
damages the more serious intentions of the works. This much-praised
novel is finally quite disappointing: its victories are far too easy,
its transcendence of genuine pain and misery is glib, even crude. But
one should read Cheever for the richness of his observations, perhaps,
rejoicing in his capacity to see and to feel and to value. Smallness
and even banality are not to be rejected in the 'prison' of earthly
existence:

> At a turn in the road Farragut saw a man in prison grays feeding
> bread crusts to a dozen pigeons. This image had for him an
> extraordinary reality, a promise of saneness. The man was a
> convict and he and the bread and the pigeons were all unwanted
> but for reasons unknown to Farragut the image of a man sharing

his crusts with birds had the resonance of antiquity.

Ontario Review 7 (Fall-Winter 1977): 99-101.

Up the River*

Robert Towers

America has as yet produced no important novelist who could, like Thomas Mann, publish his greatest work at the age of seventy-two and then go on to write a comic masterpiece based upon a fragmentary *jeu d'esprit* that had existed for more than forty years. Whatever the reasons adduced--thinness of the cultural humus, the isolation of individual talents, the parching glare of early success, periodic downpours of alcohol--our novelists tend to burn out or die off even sooner than our poets. At a much less Olympian level than Mann, the survival of a good American writer into his seventh decade with undiminished powers is sufficiently rare: one can hardly imagine an autumnally vigorous Scott Fitzgerald.

John Cheever has not merely survived. He has, after a successful career in St. Botolphs, the East Fifties, and suburbia, chosen to emigrate. *Falconer* is a surprising book, far stranger even than *Bullet Park* which was, in its juxtapositions and denouement, unsettling enough. The name "Falconer" is not that of the protagonist but of the prison in which the protagonist is immured. I have no idea how much first-hand knowledge Cheever--a long-term resident of Ossining, New York--has of prisons, but he has succeeded in writing a story in which the grossly tangible details of prison life interact with a series of vividly narrated but often wildly improbable events to create what seems to be the author's private version of hell. It begins with the arrival at Falconer of Ezekiel Farragut, a middle-aged, upper-middle-class professor (and drug addict) who has been convicted of fratricide; it ends with his escape, zippered into a burial sack meant for the tattooed body of a pathetic old convict known as Chicken Number Two, whose death has been labeled NKRC (No Known Relatives or Concerned).

Except for one brief episode dealing with the escape of another prisoner, the novel concentrates exhaustively upon Farragut's present and past experiences, both as he himself perceives them and as they are unflaggingly elucidated for us by the author. We are led to contemplate as well as share the outrage of a sensitive, cultivated, and wounded man who, believing himself to be essentially innocent, is subjected to the stupefying routine and progressive degradation of this new environment.

Farragut yearns poignantly (if undemocratically) for hierarchy, intelligence, and order; he is forced to submit to the bullying of his inferiors, to the senselessness of the regulations, to the ultimate chaos, not order, that underlies the system. His longing for his wife's love is met by her ferocious rejection. He is denied visits from his son on the grounds that it would be psychologically harmful for the boy to see his father as a prisoner. When he is denied--capriciously and illegally--his daily methadone fix, a deputy warden comes to watch the "floor show" of his withdrawal agony, orders him to be cut down when he attempts to strangle himself, gives him permission to go to the infirmary for the fix, and then brains him with a chair when he leaves his cell.

Though the raw material for social protest abounds here, *Falconer* is a novel with other intentions. I doubt that prison reform occupies a very high place on Cheever's list of social priorities. Even the uprising at Attica (called "Amana" in the novel), which takes place during Farragut's confinement, serves chiefly to show the fearfulness and demoralization of the guards at Falconer. Cheever's focus is upon behavior, idiosyncrasy, sudden acts of kindness, bizarre happenings, the aesthetic and other adaptive responses to a world of automatically flushing toilets, blaring radios, and diminished egos. His prisoners, known only by their nicknames (Tennis, Bumpo, the Cuckold, the Stone), recount obsessively their past exploits and humiliations. An obese guard named Tiny goes berserk when two cats steal the food off his plate, and leads a sickening massacre of the four thousand cats who inhabit the prison, kill rodents, and help assuage the loneliness of the inmates. A convict (Farragut's lover) contrives to escape disguised as an acolyte when a crimson-robed cardinal descends by helicopter to say mass and award diplomas to the prisoners who have completed a course offered by something called the Fiduciary University of Banking. Periodically the novel edges into surrealism.

It is, of course, Farragut's own adaptation (never complete) that chiefly concerns Cheever, who handles the matter with some subtlety. Before he realizes what is happening to him, Farragut finds himself involved in a love affair with the young convict named Jody--an affair that generates considerable passion and even happiness until the opportunistic Jody transfers his attentions to the chaplain's assistant, who will help him escape. Advancing further into the netherworld, Farragut begins to frequent a dim chamber called the Valley where twenty convicts at a time line up to "pump their rocks" into a cast-iron trough of a urinal. He adopts their language as well. When his wife on a visit asks if he has boyfriends, he replies, "I've had one . . . but I didn't take it up the ass. When I die you can put on my headstone: 'Here lies Ezekiel Farragut, who never took it up the ass.'" He becomes resourceful, too, in the ways of survival, improvising a radio with cop-

per wire when the sets are confiscated during the Amana uprising,
contriving his own macabre escape.

It is the tonality, even more than the subject matter, that distinguishes *Falconer* from Cheever's previous fiction. The prevailing atmosphere is one of extreme sordidness, relieved only momentarily by the old
Cheever whimsicality, tenderness, and insouciance. Cheever's stylistic
sprightliness is undiminished, but the intrusion of a coarsened vocabulary often produces grotesque effects, as in this passage where the
convicts are being photographed standing by a plastic Christmas tree:

> The irony of Christmas is always upon the poor in heart; the
> mystery of the solstice is always upon the rest of us. The
> inspired metaphor of the Prince of Peace and his countless
> lights . . . was somewhere here; here, on this asshole August
> afternoon the legend still had its stamina.

And later in the same paragraph he describes an American flag with its
"white stripes dyed by time to the yellow of hot piss." One feels that
Cheever's style has undergone, with only partial success, an adaptation
to the prevailing unpleasantness that closely parallels poor Farragut's.
Yet the continuities with the earlier fiction are almost as striking
as the obvious departures from it. From the beginning Cheever's short
stories and novels have been concerned with the precariousness of life,
with the trap doors in the polished flooring of Sutton Place apartments,
with the criminal possibilities of Shady Hill and Bullet Park. The
gracefulness of Cheever's manner, his trickiness, the snobbish
appurtenances, his lyrical and descriptive powers have all to some
degree disguised--or at least made amusing--the role played by hateful
and murderous impulse in the lives of his characters. In *The Wapshot
Chronicle* Coverly Wapshot is told by his mother--it is one of her
favorite stories--that his father had wanted him aborted, had actually
brought an abortionist out to the house during the mother's pregnancy;
we accept this as one more odd fact about the limitlessly eccentric
Wapshots.
In *Falconer* Cheever shamelessly lifts this material from the earlier
novel and applies it to Farragut and *his* father, but with much grimmer
consequences. We learn, in a flashback late in the novel, that
Farragut's imprisonment has resulted from his fatal striking of his
brother Eben with a fire iron at a moment when Eben was taunting
Farragut about their father's feticidal intentions toward him. Eben
himself--Farragut is convinced--has tried to kill his brother on at
least two occasions. There is some playfulness in Cheever's presen-
tation of even this material, but the shift in tone is unmistakable.
Farragut's mother and wife belong to a long line of tough and merciless

Cheever women, women in whom a good Freudian would have no trouble
discerning both phallic characteristics and penis-envying tendencies.
Again there is an intensification in *Falconer*. Farragut's inability to
connect his mother--"a famous arsonist, snob, gas pumper, and wing
shot"--with any traditional idea of maternal tenderness or serenity is,
he believes, a major factor in his drug addiction. His wife, whom he
once surprised in a lesbian embrace, is even more ruthless: when
Farragut, after being subjected to a tirade of abuse by his wife during
a prison visit, finally says, "And how is the house? How is Indian
Hill?" Marcia replies, "Well, it's nice to have a dry toilet seat."

The homosexual emphasis in *Falconer* will perhaps startle some Cheever
readers accustomed to his frequent and often lyrical celebrations of
heterosexual sportiveness. But a close look at his fiction during the
last decade reveals numerous occurrences of homosexual material--
occurrences to which the straight characters invariably respond with
fear or distaste. One thinks of Coverly Wapshot's worrying about
possible homosexual tendencies in himself following his wife's
desertion; or of the male prostitute in *The Wapshot Scandal*; or of the
man whom old Asa Bascomb encounters displaying his wares in a Roman
urinal in "The World of Apples." There is a striking adumbration of
Farragut's visits to the Valley in a passage in *Bullet Park* where
Nailles says to his teenage son, "You read a lot about it
[homosexuality] these days and it bothers me. I wish it didn't exist.
Before I joined the Chemists Club I used to have to pump ship in Grand
Central and I almost never went into those choppers without getting into
trouble." A dramatic shift in expressed affect has taken place--a shift
that simultaneously links *Falconer* with the earlier books and
distinguishes it from them.
    Despite the differences in subject matter and tone, Cheever's approach
to narration remains much the same. He continues to manipulate his
characters highhandedly, while commenting brightly upon their milieu,
motives, and behavior. At its best, this distancing achieves the effect
of inspired gossip. The surface is always lively and interesting, full
of arresting detail, full of surprises. The commentary is usually
intelligent and entertaining enough to compensate for its intrusiveness.
But the Cheever manner, so often brilliantly successful in his short
stories, entails disadvantages in his longer fiction. In the two
Wapshot books, surfeit results from the existence of too many cleverly
narrated episodes--a tedium not uncommon in the reading of long,
semi-picaresque novels. In *Bullet Park* and especially in *Falconer*, both
shorter and more tightly organized books, there is, I think, an
unresolved conflict between the explosive potential of the material and
the very "brightness" of its manipulation.
    Cheever quite arbitrarily makes Farragut a professor and then provides

nothing to make such an occupation credible. While Farragut's response to drug-deprivation is unforgettably vivid, the fact that he is an addict in the first place strains belief; certainly it is lent no support by the shallow psychologizing of the commentary or the claim that "His generation [Farragut is forty-eight] was the generation of addiction." Even Farragut's ingenious escape supplies not so much an ending to the novel as a nimble cop-out, for Farragut's future--to say nothing of his continued freedom--is quite simply unimaginable in view of what has been established about him. Cheever seems perfectly aware of this frivolity and half mocks it.

I am not suggesting that Cheever should struggle into a straitjacket of psychological realism, but I do wish to convey my strong sense that he has not yet discovered a fictional mode that can contain the powerful stuff with which he is now dealing. Still, whatever its shortcomings as fully achieved literary art, *Falconer* compels attention as the darkened realization of much that has been implicit in Cheever's fiction all along. It is an engrossing short novel, a notable addition to his now extensive *oeuvre*. . . .

The New York Review of Books 24 (17 March 1977): 3-4.

Two Good Fictions*

Geoffrey Wolff

John Cheever's Ezekiel Farragut is 48, a college professor, son of a well-off family that fell on hard times, married, with a son, someone you meet, you know? But different: he is also a heroin addict on methadone maintenance at Falconer, a prison up river from New York. His sentence is "zip to ten." He has killed his brother Eben with a fire poker.

"His story, Farragut knew, would be unsavory, but what Farragut didn't know was what importance to give unsavory matters. They existed, they were invincible, but the light they threw was, he thought, unequal to their prominence." Of late, Cheever's fiction have inclined increasingly toward the odd perspectives and dimensions of the dream state. He has always been preoccupied with bad luck and bad news. People call his stories and novels "sad," and they are. (In an interview in the fall, 1976, *Paris Review*, Cheever says, "All right, so I'm a sad man.") Cheever, like Magritte (whose work he used as the dustjacket illustration for his most recent collection of stories, *The World of Apples*), transports his characters into the surreal with clarity and acuity, a comprehensible grammar of purpose.

That is, Farragut's circumstances are out of the ordinary. His wife believes herself to be the most beautiful woman in the world, and she may be. She takes a lesbian lover, for a time. Ezekiel's parents, out of money, open a gas station. His brother had probably meant to murder him. In prison he takes a homosexual lover. In prison he is brutalized. One of the guards embarks upon a pogrom against the prison cats after a couple of cats eat "his steak and potatoes, shit in his plate," and begin on his dessert. The guard, Tiny, "tore the head off one of them. The other got away. When he was tearing off the cat's head he got very badly bitten." So Tiny and his comrades set out to slaughter a world of cats, and, slipping through blood and excrement and vomit, they kill many. But Tiny finally has enough: "O.K., O.K., that's enough for tonight, but it don't give me back my London broil."

There's Cheever's method, an event out of this world rendered with the precision of diction and cadence that has always been his signature. Nothing I can say can suggest how weird this book is, how disturbing. It is not merely that *Falconer* is, as Farragut concedes, an "unsavory" narrative, though it is that, indeed it is. It is that a reader expects to wake from it, or to watch Farragut awake from it: *Ezekiel woke up, and found his wife beside him, smiling. "Sleep well, dear?" she asked. "Well enough," Farragut lied.* Cheever is incapable of committing such pedestrian relief, but he creates a longing for it. The book is tense with a reader's longing for relief and Cheever's refusal to yield it.

The fiction is not, however, without its consolations, but they are measured as exactly as its language. Ezekiel's lover, Jody, escapes, and so does Farragut, like the Count of Monte Cristo. There is an insurrection at Falconer, perceived from far off. There are expressions of love, and patience, but there is also the suggestion that all people are under a kind of life sentence, and are like a prisoner known only as Chicken Number Two, "whose name was known nowhere, nowhere in the far reaches of the earth or in the far reaches of his memory, where, when he talked to himself, he talked to himself as Chicken Number Two."

Falconer is resolutely controlled, except when it once shifts its point of view to Jody, outside the prison walls. Its language is laconic, yet eloquent. There are passages that resemble echoes of Raymond Chandler, or even Bruce Jay Friedman: "The day was shit," Ezekiel thinks. Falconer is a prison, sure enough, true to prison truths as well as to the kind of prison metaphors that gather around fictions about islands and aboard ships, worlds apart from this world, yet peopled by this world's people.

The 19th century French critic Hippolyte Taine wrote that a man in an open field would rather confront a sheep than a lion, but were the beast behind bars, the man would prefer to look upon a lion; art, he maintained, provides the bars. By this measure, *Falconer*, raising bars, is art, and by creating the illusion of lowering them, is subversive and menacing art, the most bracing kind. . . .

New Times, 1 April 1977, pp. 63-64.

LATER CRITICISM

The Moral Structure of Cheever's *Falconer*

Glen M. Johnson

Writing in the *Harvard Guide to Contemporary American Writing*, Leo Braudy offers two generalizations about John Cheever's novel *Falconer*: it is "irresolutely plotted," and its mood "is more important than the matter."[1] Braudy's evaluation follows the consensus of critics who reviewed *Falconer* when it appeared in 1977. Seeking to describe the "mood" that Braudy calls "almost incantatory," these reviewers praised the "grace" of Cheever's prose, the "light . . . shin[ing] through" his style, the "transcend[ence]" of his imagination.[2] At the same time, however, there were complaints like Braudy's about the novel's "puzzling" form, its "disjointed," "haphazard," or "loose" structure.[3]

The inability of these critics to find structural coherence in *Falconer* derives from their assumption that Cheever can be categorized among (to quote the title of Braudy's essay) "Realists, Naturalists, and Novelists of Manners." In fact, Cheever's novels are effective because their plots do not serve "realistic" expectations. Cheever's imagination is fundamentally a romancer's and specifically religious, as suggested by the tendency of Braudy and others to adopt the vocabulary of religious experience when describing the mood or style of Cheever's books. A religious imagination indeed controls the mood of *Falconer*; more important, it determines the plot. This novel's structure is moral: it defines right action and then rewards it, claiming the romancer's freedom to employ "miracles" in its plotting. The specific form of *Falconer* is a secularized version of the Christian pattern of redemption: forgiveness of sins through conviction, repentance, and the receipt of grace.

Cheever prepares the reader's recognition of this redemptive structure by filling *Falconer* with religious diction and allusions. The measure of his success will be the reader's acceptance of the book's culminating imperative and last word, "rejoice." But religious references begin early. Falconer, the prison whose name is the novel's title, suggests the central symbols of two familiar poems whose subject is faith, Hopkins' "The Windhover" and Yeats' "The Second Coming." Cheever's allusion to Yeats is most obvious and most crucial, indicating from the first the focus of moral attention in this novel: the "mystery of imprisonment" symbolized by Cheever's Falconer may be the unheard Word of Yeats's falconer--a disintegrating but perhaps recoverable "center" of faith for the contemporary world. Cheever's protagonist, who will experience the mystery and recover the faith, appropriately shares the name of the Hebrew prophet Ezekiel, who "saw visions of God" while "among the captives by the river."[4] As Ezekiel Farragut enters Falconer in the novel's opening section, Cheever introduces two religiously charged symbols, both of which will reappear: "a man in prison grays feeding bread crusts to a dozen pigeons" and "a tarnished silver Christmas garland" hung on a water pipe. For Farragut, the convict St. Francis carries "resonance of great antiquity" while the Christmas garland supplies not irony but "a grain of reason."[5] From the first, then, Cheever's method supports his vision by finding--or fashioning-- transcendent value within a world of suffering and miscreancy.

Cheever's word for Farragut is "miscreant," suggesting by etymology that Farragut's wrongdoing is at base a sort of heresy--a failure of responsibility deriving from a failure of belief. The first third of *Falconer* explores the nature of its protagonist's miscreancy, developing in the process Cheever's own ethical vision. Farragut's imprisonment evidences his violation of responsibility in three areas central to Cheever's morality; in each case the miscreancy is defined by human suffering but has religious resonances as well. First, Farragut has violated his responsibility to love: he is locked with his wife in a destructive relationship marked by "ritualistic" exchanges of hurt (p. 25). Second, Farragut has violated his responsibility to his own integrity: a heroin addict for a quarter century, he has blunted his senses and damaged his body, defiling the temple of his spirit. Finally, Farragut has violated his responsibility to human brotherhood: a fratricide, he has repeated the crime by which humanity compounded the Fall. In none of these cases is Farragut's guilt unequivocal: his wife shares responsibility for their destructive marriage; his addiction began in response to the "suffocation, suppuration and murder" of war (p. 44); and his brother Eben in a sense willed the murder by calculated prodding of Ezekiel's psychic vulnerabilities. Farragut's guilt is perhaps essentially negative, an inability to act outside the bounds of a morbid preoccupation with a world in which, as he sees it, "his life had been threatened" repeatedly by intimates and strangers alike (pp. 47-51). But his guilt is not passive, and it is compounded by moral dishonesty: "I did not kill my brother," he insists early in his imprisonment (p. 25). In Cheever's view, shared responsibility is responsibility nevertheless, while dishonesty about one's own motives and actions is the fundamental miscreancy which makes all others possible. And so *Falconer* mixes a modern sensitivity to the complexities of motivation with a moral strenuousness rooted in the Christian paradox: humans enter a fallen world but are responsible for their individual falls in it.

In Christian thinking, redemption from sin involves three steps or imperatives.[6] Two are the responsibility of the sinner: *conviction*, or acceptance of guilt; and *repentance*, an implicitly active turning away from wrongdoing. To these must be added *grace*, the free gift of God which signals and constitutes salvation. Grace cannot be earned, and so is always miraculous, but for many Christians conviction and repentance are necessary conditions for its receipt. In its moral structure, *Falconer* develops a version of this Christian pattern of redemption, seeking salvation as its culmination. Farragut must, in terms of this morality, counter each of his "sins" with honest understanding of his motives and with positive action. Once he has done this he can receive God's--the novelist's--gift of grace. The novel will end with a miracle, but the miracle must be in some sense earned.

The last three of *Falconer*'s six unnumbered chapters record Farragut's redemption from, in turn, failure to love, addiction, and fratricide. First, Farragut shows himself capable of love during his affair with Jody, the prison hustler who has "meet me later" written on his palm in indelible ink. Narcissistic, shallow, and fundamentally unworthy of devotion, Jody is Falconer's equivalent of Farragut's wife, Marcia; like her, he is obsessed with physical beauty and practices calculated infidelity. These similarities between Jody and Marcia Farragut, and particularly their unworthiness as objects of love, emphasize the significance of Farragut's unselfish, redeeming love of Jody. For the essence of the *imitatio Christi* is to love the unworthy.

Cheever, who has devoted much of his career to observing how love can turn hateful, here emphasizes sexual possessiveness as the essence of Farragut's transgression. Just as Farragut praises a nameless mistress for not being "aggressive," he can see Marcia's "thrust for independence" as the primary "burden" on their marriage (pp. 79, 27). But his love for Jody is characterized by an absence of possessiveness, to the extent that Farragut, despite "radiant and aching need," renounces "any real jealousy" when Jody abandons him for another lover (pp. 106, 104) [*sic*: 101, 99]. Such renunciation, a fully conscious turning away from earlier miscreancy, is the essence of repentance, and with Farragut's renunciation and the attendant psychic suffering comes an awareness of his motives which is equivalent to religious conviction. Farragut arrives at a profound understanding of his infatuation with Jody: "If in loving Jody he loved himself, there was the chance that he might . . . have become infatuated with his lost youth. . . . And then there was to think upon the courting of death and death's dark simples, that in covering Jody's body he willingly embraced decay and corruption." And such painfully earned honesty moves backward to illuminate his past transgressions, including his failed marriage: "There was, he thought, some sameness of degree in sexual possession and sexual jealousy; and accommodations and falsehoods were needed to equate this with the inconstancy of the flesh" (pp. 104, 100-01).

Once Farragut has accepted responsibility for his and others' unhappiness in love, and has countered "possession and jealousy" with a genuinely unselfish love for Jody, he is worthy of the grace that comes in a passage which has proved problematical for critics writing on *Falconer*. Farragut's reward for unselfish love is, appropriately, unselfish joy: "the conspiratorial thrill of seeing his beloved escape" (p. 123). While Farragut watches, Jody, disguised as an acolyte, ascends from Falconer in the helicopter of a cardinal who has come to celebrate mass for the prisoners. Cheever packs his description of the "great day" with religious references, including the extended quotation of a Latin prayer for mercy and forgiveness of sins, and ends with

> glory, glory, glory! The exaltation of the bells . . . filled
> heaven and earth. They all cheered and cheered and cheered and
> some of them cried. The sound of the bells stopped, but the
> chopper went on playing its geodetic survey of the surrounding
> terrain--the shining, lost and beloved world (p. 130).

At this point Cheever pulls off the "miracle"--that is the last word of the chapter--that has bothered such critics as John Leonard, for whom *Falconer* contains "one miracle too many."[7] Arriving in New York, Jody is befriended by the cardinal himself ("'I know where you're from. . . . It is exciting, isn't it?'"), clothed, blessed, and set free (pp. 130-33).

The reference to *Les Misérables* is clear, but more to the essence of Cheever's intention is a quirk of technique: this is the only place in *Falconer* where the point of view seems to leave Farragut. But close reading suggests that the abrupt shift in perspective is only apparent; one is encouraged to read the narrative of Jody's escape as an interior monologue--as *Farragut's* imaginative construction. One hint that this is the case is provided by a woman who appears during the sequence to kiss the cardinal's ring; she is described as a television actress--an appropriate performer in a fantasy constructed by a prisoner whose only contact with the outside world is, as Cheever has noted, through television. If one considers Jody's freedom in this way, as a psychic reward for Farragut, it becomes clear that the significance of the passage lies precisely in its improbability. Jody's escape constitutes Cheever's gift of grace to Farragut, the emblem of Farragut's redemption from his offenses against love. The passage thus marks a technical and moral gamble on Cheever's part. Not only has he inserted an unabashed and unapologetic "miracle" in a fiction for this literal time, he has sought insight into love in the most unlikely circumstance possible, the infatuation of a middle-aged murderer with a prison hustler. Willfully emphasizing the paradox, Cheever seeks, even in this "grotesque bonding," a "profound" and redeeming love (p. 91).

In the chapter following Jody's escape, Farragut overcomes addiction, redeeming his offense against his own integrity. Here Cheever's emphasis is on facing dishonesty toward oneself, for the bulk of a previous chapter has been devoted to Farragut's rationalizations for his dependence on heroin:

> Farragut . . . felt that the consciousness of the opium eater was much broader, more vast and representative of the human condition than the consciousness of someone who had never experienced addiction.
>
> It was only natural that he should be an addict. He had been raised by people who dealt in contraband . . . unlicensed spiritual, intellectual and erotic stimulants.
>
> The cream of the post-Freudian generation were addicts (pp. 43, 54, 56).

Addiction here is the extreme of self-consciousness, a disease endemic to the thought-tormented post-Freudian generation. It follows that Farragut's repentance must take the form of some unself-conscious action which identifies value beyond the limits of the addict's revered consciousness. Precisely such an action comes when Farragut risks his safety to construct a forbidden radio with which to hear news of the uprising at "the Wall," an event based on the Attica riot. In constructing his radio Farragut seeks, literally and metaphorically, communication outside the prison of his own being--even if the communication must be with other prisons. And such outreaching action breaks the psychic reductiveness of his addiction: Farragut simply forgets his need for a fix.

Since Farragut's self-consciousness has fed his addiction, he can arrive at an understanding of his enthrallment only after he has broken the habit: "He could not congratulate himself on having mastered his addiction, since he had not been aware of it" (p. 187). But once he is aware, he immediately receives the novelist's gift of grace. In this case, grace shows up in the form of a transparently symbolic figure--"a young man with summery hair and immaculate clericals" who appears from nowhere and celebrates Holy Eucharist in Farragut's cell. Farragut's response (the first words of which recall his earlier "glory, glory, glory") completes the process of redemption:

> "Holy, Holy, Holy," he said in a loud and manly voice. "Heaven and earth are full of Thy Glory. Praise be to Thee, O Lord most

> high." When he had been blessed with the peace that passes all understanding, he said, "Thank you, Father," and the priest said, "God bless you, my son" (p. 188).

For an addict of the post-Freudian generation, the peace that passes all understanding is both an achievement and a gift.

On the page after Farragut receives the Eucharist, he begins the process of earning forgiveness for his sin of fratricide. Here Cheever brings together all elements of the fable of redemption that he has been developing in the previous two chapters. Farragut's crime again has strong Biblical overtones, and again is compounded by the miscreant's refusal to face his motives or accept his responsibility. But again he is able to achieve moral action and thereby to accept an imperative--here, fraternity--that he has previously violated; integral to this process is his accepting the burden of his transgression. Finally comes the gift of grace which constitutes and signals redemption; as before, Cheever emphasizes the artificiality of Farragut's deliverance, willfully asserting the possibility and necessity of miracle in the world.

As was the case in his relationship with Jody, Farragut's redemptive moral action focuses on an unworthy object--here, Chicken Number Two, a senile, "smelly" prisoner who once strangled an old woman for eighty-two dollars. A flu epidemic hits Falconer, and Farragut agrees to take the dying Chicken into his cell. His first act--he washes Chicken's body--has clear Christian overtones. Immediately after the washing, Chicken asks a key question--"'Why did you kill your brother, Zeke?'"--and the novel at last provides the details of Farragut's fratricide. Placement is essential here. Up to this point, twenty pages from the end of *Falconer*, the reader has been told nothing about the crime for which Farragut is incarcerated except the fact that it occurred. The reason is clear: Cheever keeps within Farragut's sensibility, and until now Farragut has not accepted responsibility for "the accident or what they called the murder" of his brother (p. 190). So the fratricide has been blocked from the reader as it has been blocked from Farragut's consciousness. And it is crucial to the moral structure of *Falconer* that Farragut is able to accept what has happened, thereby freeing the story for the reader, only after he has accepted fraternity by ministering to Chicken Number Two. Again, conviction and repentant action come together. This sequence culminates when, at Chicken's death, Farragut takes the dying man's "warm hand" and, paradoxically, draws from it "a deep sense of freeness" (p. 201).

In facing his responsibility as a fratricide and in ministering to the dying Chicken, Farragut achieves metaphorical conviction and repentance in the last of the three areas in which he has been miscreant. And so he is worthy of a final, saving gift of grace--release from Falconer.

Since grace is always a miracle, the "improbability" of Farragut's escape (to use John Leonard's complaining word) is its essence. Cheever emphasizes the miraculous in Farragut's deliverance by composing his escape of materials drawn from both scripture and melodrama. If Jody's escape reminds one of *Les Misérables*, Farragut's is straight out of *The Count of Monte Cristo*: he hides in a rubber body bag intended for Chicken and is carried outside the walls of the prison in "his shroud." His escape from the bag has obvious scriptural resonances: using a razor blade to slice through the rubber, Farragut cuts his fingers and his thigh. Thus marked both with stigmata and with a wound that suggests Jacob's after he wrestled with an angel and won a blessing,[8] Farragut opens the shroud and "step[s] out of his grave" (p. 206).

Moving out of Falconer's shadow and into "brightly lighted" streets, Farragut encounters a mysterious figure who, like the earlier young man who administers the Eucharist, unaccountably--thus miraculously-- provides the assistance he needs (pp. 208-11). This "stranger," who gives Farragut a coat and pays his fare on a bus away from Falconer, is the symbolic key to the final sequence of the novel. To understand his nature and function it will help to refer briefly to some earlier works by Cheever. Several of his stories end, like *Falconer*, with improbable reversals of fortune or miraculous deliverances. In almost every case, these reversals or deliverances are associated with angels--either through imagery (as in "The Housebreaker of Shady Hill") or through the presence of a character who is called "angelic" (as in "The World of Apples"). The most obvious example of this sort is "The Angel of the Bridge," where a quite literal angel--complete with harp--provides the "merciful intercession" that saves the narrator from psychic paralysis.[9]

The stranger of *Falconer* clearly belongs among Cheever's angelic intercessors. He carries a "sky blue" helmet and an electric heater "with a golden bowl shaped like the sun"; both objects--the former developing an earlier association of sky and blue with Farragut's higher aspirations, the latter suggesting both the scriptural Preacher[10] and Henry James's valedictory fable of redemption--are later "picked up" by Farragut. The stranger's significance becomes clearer when he tells his story: "'What you see here is a man who is been evicted'" by a landlady "'who can't stand life in any form.'" By raising the topic of hospitality refused and by surrounding the rejected figure with heavenly images, Cheever evokes the Biblical warning that any stranger may be an angel in disguise: "Let brotherly love continue," St. Paul wrote to the Hebrews, "be not forgetful to entertain strangers: for thereby some have entertained angels unawares."[11] And there are additional hints. When Farragut and the stranger enter the bus, Cheever points out that they make a total of seven passengers--seven being a sacred number consistently associated with angels in scripture. The earliest Biblical reference of this sort is, interestingly, in the book of Ezekiel, where an angelic figure among seven men is said to carry "a writer's inkhorn" and to record the Lord's judgments.[12] Finally, Cheever's stranger speaks of finding "a beautiful place in the morning"; in addition to its obvious connotations, this phrase may allude to the Biblical idea that angels are reborn "new every morning."[13]

Thus associated with angelic imagery, the stranger performs an angelic function: he provides the miraculous intervention that makes events in the human world conform to a divine wish to reward those who have found favor in God's sight. In *Falconer*, as in any fiction, the novelist is God, but Cheever undertakes the role more actively and transparently than most. Even though he holds the novel within Farragut's point of view throughout, he nevertheless takes care to assert his independent moral presence, beginning with a single, attention-demanding first-person pronoun on the book's second page. That moral presence oversees *Falconer* and develops its final sequence in accordance with the demands not so much of verisimilitude as of a moral structure whose end is redemption through grace. And Cheever dares to *emphasize* the artificiality of his conclusion, as if to assert, militantly, the moral novelist's right to uphold meaning beyond probability.

Using the mechanisms of fiction to illuminate a moral design, *Falconer* is in a recognizable tradition of romance--one which, in Erich Auerbach's analysis, originates in the style of sacred authority of the Hebrew scriptures.[14] Moral authority is neither an easy nor a fashionable stance in the late twentieth century, and contemporary American romancers--Vonnegut, for example, or Pynchon--have generally used their form's moral potential for ironic effects. Cheever's success lies in adapting, without undercutting, the ideologically outmoded form of religious allegory to a complex moral vision appropriate to contemporary America.

A key to understanding the moral vision is provided by a short passage of four paragraphs which separates Farragut's "resurrection" from his meeting with the angelic stranger (pp. 206-08). Farragut walks through streets so filled with "scrupulous light" that "you could read the small print in a prayerbook." He passes a dump, at which point Cheever inserts two essential sentences:

> Had he raised his head, he would have seen a good deal of velocity and confusion as the clouds hurried past the face of a nearly full moon, so chaotically and so swiftly that they might have reminded him, with his turn of mind, not of fleeing hordes but of advancing ranks and throngs, an army more swift than bellicose, a tardy regiment. But he saw nothing of what was going on in heaven because his fear of falling kept his eyes on the sidewalk, and anyhow there was nothing to be seen there that would be of any use.

At the center of this complex passage is an apparent allusion to still another poem about faith, Arnold's "Dover Beach": "And we are here as on a darkling plain/Swept with confused alarms of struggle and flight,/Where ignorant armies clash by night." There is an inversion, however, in Cheever's reference. The "darkling plain" is no longer, as in Arnold's poem, the world of human affairs--that, indeed, is now "brightly lighted." Rather, it is the *heavens* that are darkling; Cheever twice points out that clouds obscure the moon. Similarly, the "ignorant armies" are no longer earthly hordes; they are heavenly hosts. And so the seeker after salvation must now avoid the upward glance--"there was nothing to be seen there"--and keep his eyes fixed on the only source of light, the streets where humans live and die.

"Fear of falling" keeps Farragut's eyes on the earth. The diction is religiously charged, but the passage insists that "falling" be taken in a completely human sense. Cheever is not looking to heaven; there apparently is something there, but in its confusion--whether or not that confusion is, as the passage hints, in the eye of the beholder--it cannot "be of any use." Cheever's world is profoundly post-lapsarian. Or, rather, continuously lapsarian: the paragraph immediately following the one just quoted mentions "falling souls or angels," "tossed and falling, always falling." Indeed, the angelic stranger will smell of whiskey--but he will be no less the angel to Farragut for that.

In a world "always falling," where scrupulous light illuminates only the streets walked by miscreants, the standard of judgment is exclusively and profoundly humanistic. And the essence of Cheever's faith is the transfiguring power, not of divine but of human relationships. A hustler can be beloved; an addict can be cleansed; murderers can find brotherhood. What is needed, as Farragut has discovered, is the ability to love without possession or jealousy, combined with a willingness to understand and accept one's inevitably impure motivations. Human love is deeply paradoxical, and for that reason essentially miraculous. *Falconer* is a book of paradoxes: a love affair is both "grotesque" and "profound"; a "tarnished" garland is "a grain of reason"; the hand of a murderer offers "a deep sense of freeness." *Falconer* is also a book of miracles, and Cheever's accomplishment lies in daring to construct fictional miracles out of the materials of human paradox. The redemptive structure of *Falconer* is its creator's gift of grace to that ultimate paradox, "the shining, lost and beloved world."

NOTES

1. Leo Braudy, "Realists, Naturalists, and Novelists of Manners," in *Harvard Guide to Contemporary American Writing*, ed. Daniel Hoffman

(Cambridge: Harvard University Press, 1979), p. 144.

2. Walter Clemons, "Cheever's Triumph," *Newsweek* (March 14, 1977), p. 62; Dean Flower, "Fiction Chronicle," *Hud[son] R[eview]*, 30 (1977), 310; Joseph McElroy, [Review of *Falconer*], *New Republic* (March 26, 1977), p. 31.

3. John Romano, "Redemption According to Cheever," *Commentary* (May, 1977), p. 68; John B. Breslin, [Review of *Falconer*], *America* (March 12, 1977), p. 222; Bruce Allen, "Dream Journeys," *S[ewanee] R[eview]*, 85 (1977), 694; R.Z. Sheppard, "View From the Big House," *Time* (Feb. 28, 1977), p. 79.

4. Ezek. 1.1. Falconer, based on Sing Sing, is located beside the Hudson River.

5. John Cheever, *Falconer* (New York: Knopf, 1977), p. 7. Parenthetical references are to this edition.

6. See *The Oxford Dictionary of the Christian Church*, ed. F.L. Cross and E.A. Livingstone, Second Ed. (London: Oxford University Press, 1974), pp. 586-87, 1164-65, 1174; and Perry Miller, "The Marrow of Puritan Divinity," *Errand into the Wilderness* (Cambridge: Harvard University Press, 1956), for the question of grace in the context of New England culture.

7. "Crying in the Wilderness," *Harper's* (April, 1977), p. 89.

8. Gen. 32.24.

9. *The Stories of John Cheever* (New York: Knopf, 1978), pp. 268, 618, 622, 497. See also the ironic use of a guardian angel in "The Scarlet Moving Van," p. 369.

10. See Eccl. 12.

11. Heb. 13.1; cf. Gen.18 and 19 for the origin of this imperative.

12. Ezek. 9. Cf. 2 Sam 21. 6, 9, where seven sacrificial victims will atone for a broken covenant.

13. Lam. 3. 23. See Gustav Davidson, *A Dictionary of Angels* (1967; rpt. New York: Free Press, 1971), pp. 20-21.

14. *Mimesis* (1946), trans. Willard Trask (Princeton: Princeton University Press, 1953), pp. 7-23.

The Stories
of John Cheever
1978

Literary Waifs*

Pearl K. Bell

Short stories have singular virtues. They are short. They can be read in one sitting. Like a witty epigram or a clever joke, they can realize their meaning through surprise, or through an abruptly decisive ending which may be charged with ambiguity but nonetheless leaves the reader with a sense of dramatic completeness. In sum, they make a point, satisfying but not necessarily crude or simple, that eliminates any craving for further incident or explanation. And precisely because short stories are distinguished by their discrete finality, a curious difficulty arises when they are collected in book form. Reading so many stories consecutively we become surfeited with discontinuous shocks and surprises, unable to absorb all the abbreviated varieties of plot and character that are related to each other only by the consistencies of temperament and manner of one writer.

Yet writers, particularly prolific writers, *will* collect their stories, and editors reprint them in anthologies, because, deprived of the permanence of books, the separate pieces published in magazines would be consigned to oblivion. . . .

In sharp contrast to Susan Sontag's coldly axiomatic tales**, those of John Cheever, in a huge new volume that collects the stories he has written since the end of World War II, is awash in the rain of disenchantment and regret, rank with the smell of decay. Though Cheever tried, in his two Wapshot novels, to broaden his scope by endowing the poignancy of nostalgia with a local habitation and name--to portray a vanished New England blessed with social coherence, domestic stability, and moral grace--the quality of his yearning comes through with much greater power in his short stories. His temperament and talent are not at ease with the patient exploration of motives and extended personal histories, but they are flawlessly suited to the sentient moment, the rigorously foreshortened episode and isolated visual detail that suggest an unspoken fullness of feeling, a tacit sense of destiny, with highly concentrated intensity.

Peculiarly at home within the immediate present, Cheever is a master of the perfectly observed, evocative, unforgettably *fixed* moment: affluent Manhattan parents, dutiful and hung over, waiting with their children on an early-morning street corner for the private-school bus; the aging American boy hurdling sofas and tables at the end of a party that has gone on too long; the businessman model of propriety secretly baking Lady Baltimore cakes in the middle of the night to steady his nerves; the swimmer, in one of Cheever's most famous middle-class fables, making his way home from a Westchester party via a network of pools only to find his house locked, empty, forlorn. No other present-day writer can draw from the brackish smell of a rented summer house an entire life of failure and transgression, or detect and identify with Cheever's precision the ceremonial degeneracy of an Upper East Side cocktail party "where the company is never very numerous and the liquor is never very good--parties where, as you drink and talk, you feel a palpable lassitude overtaking any natural social ardor, as if the ties of family, society, school, and place that held the group together were dissolving like the ice in your drink."

In story after story, his abiding theme, however, is not so much the social and personal unraveling of his middle-class Wasp milieu as it is the private pain of disappointment, Cheever's disappointment, sometimes heartbreakingly lyrical and sometimes merely slick, with the way life has, alas, turned out. Bored and uncomfortable with analytic complexity, intimidated by the intellectual difficulties that tough scrutiny of experience and behavior might pose, Cheever prefers the soft, elegiac generalization that simulates thoughtful judgment but is really a lament, the fleeting intimation of lost hope and vanished happiness that stops short of being harsh and upsetting. Over and again he asks the same question--where did middle-class America go wrong?--but he cannot bring himself to face its disruptive implications, and he settles instead, as in "The Death of Justina," for a plangent eloquence that is brightly evasive:

> I stand, figuratively, with one wet foot on Plymouth Rock, looking with some delicacy, not into a formidable and challenging wilderness but onto a half-finished civilization em-

> bracing glass towers, oil derricks, suburban continents, and
> abandoned movie houses and wondering why, in this most
> prosperous, equitable, and accomplished world, . . . everyone
> should seem to be disappointed.

Cheever is a genteel puritan with a profound distaste for the disconcerting realities that lie beneath the melancholy beguiling surfaces of
Fifth Avenue and suburbia. Yet there are moments--in artfully facile
stories like "Torch Song" (about a woman who is an angel of death) and
"The Five-Forty-Eight" (about a deranged secretary's ugly revenge on the
boss who seduced and then fired her)--when he seems able to control his
dismay at the proliferation of so much dishonor, infidelity,
drunkenness, so much moral shabbiness, only through an artfully clever
but unpersuasive sensationalism. Nor is he convincing when, to stave
off the depression about to plunge him into the abyss, he resorts to
incantatory affirmation, as though the sound of the words alone--"Valor!
Love! Virtue! Compassion! Splendor! Kindness! Wisdom! Beauty!"--is
sufficient to make them genuine talismans of promise and redemption,
despite the admonitory lessons of experience; this is inspirational
whistling in the dark that unwittingly mocks his exaltation.

Because Cheever's enduring strength lies in his lucid grasp of social
detail, his hyper-alert eye for the telling gestures and revelations of
speech, place, dress, manner, we become exaggeratedly aware of the
constricted narrowness of the world he observes so closely. It is
strangely untouched by history, politics, war, by the need for private
accommodation to public events; it is unmoved by social change or
conflicts of class and tradition. His rare working-class characters--
cooks, doormen, janitors, baby-sitters--exist only as appendages of the
middle class that depends on the functions they perform. And when
Cheever writes about Italy, where he has spent enough time to absolve
him of a tourist's superficiality, the alien scene remains an intracta-
bly foreign accident of place in which his expatriates live out their
unchangeable American destinies; "tireless wanderers who go to bed night
after night to dream of bacon-lettuce-and-tomato sandwiches."

Cheever's America is so completely self-enclosed and detached from any
sense of history that it seems airless and timeless. But it is in the
work of Ann Beattie, another, much younger *New Yorker* writer, that we
find the dead end of his world, which was not as immune to cultural
upheaval as he would have it appear. Miss Beattie tells us what
happened to the children of Shady Hill and Proxmire Manor, those
children that Cheever wrote about with exceptional tenderness because he
was appalled by the insensitive carelessness and neglectful
self-absorption of their parents. In time those children grew up,
coming of age in the 60's, and Ann Beattie provides a bleak and chilling

account of the way they live now. It is as though her stories spell out
the legacy bequeathed to her generation by Cheever's, but in a voice
seemingly as dry and devoid of moral indignation as Cheever's is ardent
and enraged by parents who, as he wrote in "The Bus to St. James's," had
become "bewildered and confused in principle, too selfish and too
unlucky to abide by the forms that guarantee the permanence of a
society, as their fathers and mothers had done. Instead, they put the
burden of order onto their children and filled their days with specious
rites and ceremonies." . . .

**[Editor's note: *I, etcetera*, one of the five collections of short
fiction reviewed here.]

Commentary 67 (February 1979): 67, 70-71.

The Cheerless World of John Cheever

Isa Kapp

"The room was polished and tranquil, and from the windows that opened to
the west there was some late-summer sunlight, brilliant and clear as
water. Nothing here had been neglected," writes John Cheever in "The
Country Husband," one of the most characteristic pieces in his new
collection, *The Stories of John Cheever* (Knopf, 693 pp., $15). He is
describing the Shady Hill suburban home to which Francis Weed has just
returned after nearly being killed in a plane crash. "It was not the
kind of household where, after prying open a stuck cigarette box, you
would find a shirt button and a tarnished nickel. The hearth was swept,
the roses on the piano were reflected in the polish of the broad top,
and there was an album of Schubert waltzes on the rack." For three
decades the legato Cheever prose has remained as urbane and tempting as
an ad in the *New Yorker*, sharing with the magazine that has published
nearly all his stories a zealous attention to surfaces, a scrupulous
rendition of speech and, not the least of its attractions, a
supercilious tone that separates its uncommon reader from the gaucheness
and banality of common experience.
     Cheever has been called the American Chekhov, and it is true that both
writers have a ruminative manner, dwell wistfully on lost opportunities,
and are masters at conjuring up a mood, an excitation of the nerves, a
vapor of unstated emotion hanging in the air. But when they undertake
their favorite identical subject, the seesaw between tranquility and
disturbance in marriage, we see how enormous a role the accident of
disposition plays in creating the hierarchy of art. Chekhov's plain and

pliant responses make us feel that marital disharmony is only one aspect
of life, part of the natural order of things, rather than an occasion
for outrage. We sense the Russian writer's intuitive sympathy with all
of his characters. Cheever's sympathies spring unaccountably back to
the observer, as if he were personally affronted, violated in his finer
sensibilities by the shabby tales he relates. His heroes and heroines
are usually caught in a spiritual flagrante delicto, a bit awkward and
pathetic as they come into view through a light frost of derision.

In "The Season for Divorce" a busy young New York City mother receives
a gift of roses from an acquaintance, and that is enough to stir up
threatening ripples in domestic waters. Back in the suburbs, Francis
Weed (the "country husband") makes a mild bid for his family's attention
after his uncomfortable plane flight, but the children are crying, and
his wife "paints with lightning strokes the panorama of drudgery in
which her youth, beauty and wit have been lost." Almost before he knows
it, Cheever is skating along the boulevard of broken marriages, hemmed
in by wives grinding their axes or balefully slamming the bedroom doors
in the face of a man in need.

The affable husband of "The Chimera" brings his mate breakfast in bed,
only to find her haggard-eyed, avowing "I cannot any longer endure being
served . . . by a hairy man in white underwear." A reader may well
wonder whether this would have seemed sufficient provocation to Chekhov,
Henry James or even Fannie Hurst, but he will discover in this
compilation from five earlier volumes stories with no motivation at all,
like "A Vision of the World," where the hero, ensconced in a seaside
cottage with the grass freshly cut and robins flying by, unreasonably
muses: "Oh, I sometimes think of leaving her. I could conceivably make
a life without her and the children but . . . I cannot divorce myself
from the serpentine walk I have laid . . . and so, while my chains are
forged of turf and house paint, they will still bind me till I die." If
Cheever is no analyst of motive, it may be because he regards the battle
of the sexes as too ferocious for psychological interpretation, rooted
instead in some primal biological antagonism or some malevolent caprice
of the universe.

Can the author of all this domestic infelicity really believe, as he
says in his Preface, that the constants he looks for are "a love of
light and a determination to trace some moral chain of being"? We have
to suppose that he simply does not recognize his own saturnine bent of
mind, his speedy susceptibility to the faintest intimations of discord,
and to the sorrows of gin. He is like the narrator of "The Seaside
Houses," who hardly turns the key of his rented vacation home before he
discerns from the dimness of a bulb that his landlord is parsimonious,
and from the whiskey bottles in the piano bench that he is a secret
drinker and an unhappy man.

Perhaps it is to make amends to himself and us for the disproportion in his focus that so many of Cheever's stories launch into lyrical transports when the human outlook is particularly grim. The hero of "A Vision of the World," whose wife is perpetually sad, does a considerable amount of dreaming, and sits up in bed exclaiming: "'Valor! Love! Virtue! Compassion! Splendor! Kindness! Wisdom! Beauty!' The words seem to have the colors of the earth, and as I recite them I feel my hope- fulness mount until I am contented and at peace with the night." A baffling transfiguration indeed, as is the final image in the story about poor Francis Weed trying to recover from his passion for the babysitter by taking up woodwork therapy: A black dog prances through the tomato vines and "Then it is dark; it is a night where kings in golden suits ride elephants over the mountains."

Despite the rhapsodic thrill of the language, it seems to me one of the least wholesome elements in Cheever's fiction that he so often juxtaposes the pleasing prospect of nature and the disagreeable one of men and women, and lurches so readily from cynicism to exaltation. He does much better when he comes to terms with the blackness in himself, which may be why *Falconer*, for all the abrasiveness of its cat slaugh- ters and brutalities among prisoners, is a strong and plausible novel.

Similarly, because Cheever moves head-on into a harsh situation without either exaggerating or poeticizing it, "Goodbye, My Brother," written early in his career, is one of his finest stories. It takes place in a big summer house on an island off the coast of Massachusetts, and is about a family reunion dampened by the arrival of the youngest brother, a censorious New England Savonarola who sees the worst in everyone. The narrative is garnished with evocative details, such as the shadow of the maid in a dark garden and the backgammon games after coffee; and for once the landscape--dunes, coarse grass, open sea-- enhances rather than diverts us from the austere emotions.

A sense of humor can do wonders for a bilious outlook, and luckily Cheever is diverse enough a writer to give way more than once, in the midst of his disenchantments, to a comic phrase or notion. In "A Vision of the World," the narrator is in a supermarket picking up some brioches when the piped-in music changes from a love song to a cha-cha and he says to the very plain woman next to him, "Would you like to dance, Madam?" In "An Educated American Woman," a vigorous old lady with splendid white hair and a red face is designated as a humbug: "the seraphic look she assumed when she listened to music was the look of someone trying to recall an old phone number." Although several stories about feminists lay the satire on thickly, "Another Story" is easy to relish. An Italian prince despairs because his American wife insists her voice is good enough for the La Scala Opera. The narrator assures him that many American women feel that they have sacrificed career for marriage, and urges him to indulge her. The prince yields but when his

wife gives an appalling recital and then asks him to change his name, he
draws the line and, weeping, sails home to Verona. This reminds the
narrator of another friend whose wife has a musical voice yet was
sensible enough to use it to get a job as an airport announcer, and here
the denouement is even more unnerving: She begins to call her husband to
dinner and bed in the same impersonal airport voice she uses to direct
passengers to proceed to Gate Seven, and his only recourse is to take
flight.

No unhappy ending can stop Cheever's spirits from soaring, however,
once Italy enters the scene. Like himself, most of his fictional
characters have traveled in closed circuits that go from the bar of
Grand Central Station to the suburbs of New York and New England. In
1956 Cheever spent a year in Italy, and what an infusion of red blood
and charm the change in setting gives to his writing! In the Italian
stories--e.g. "The Bella Lingua" and "The Duchess"--the swimming pools
and adulteries of Shady Hill are far behind him and Cheever turns into
the most likeable of writers. He leans back, develops perspective,
takes a robust interest in other people's lives. "The Golden Age" is a
delightful memoir of an American television writer who rents a castle in
Tuscany and is known in the vicinity as "il poeta." He is embarrassed
because his situation comedy (Cheever once wrote scripts for *Life with
Father*) is to be shown that night on Italian TV and he will, in this
country of simple habits and high art, be exposed as a commercial hack,
a harbinger of barbarism and vulgarity. But when the moon comes out he
sees some figures ascending toward him. A little girl gives him flowers
and the Mayor embraces him. "Oh, we thought, signore," the Mayor says,
"that you were merely a poet."

In Italy Cheever grows more springy, outgoing and natural, and the
melancholy fog of "pain and sweetness" lifts from his fiction. His lens
to the world seems to be set at a more secure point, midway between
triumph and disappointment. What an accomplishment it would have been
if he could have added that comfortable frame of mind to the rest of his
clear and elegant prose.

The New Leader 61 (11 September 1978): 16-17.

The World of WASP

Perry Meisel

The deceptively modest self-portrait that John Cheever fashions in the
preface to his newly collected *Stories* ("Naive, provincial . . . almost
always clumsy") well accords with our customary sense of Cheever as a

natural, as a self-reliant and largely homespun historian of the manners
and morals of the upper middle class.   Despite the elegant contrivances
and highly figured language that have always called plain attention to
Cheever's exertions as a stylist in both his novels and his shorter
pieces, Cheever's image of himself as the innocent realist is a tempting
one to maintain.

One principal advantage is that it allows us to suspend our moral
exasperation with Cheever's dreamy and passive characters by shifting
the blame for their indecision and frustration away from the author. We
assign it instead to the world of WASP custom that Cheever renders with
such sympathy and exactitude in his early portraits of prewar Manhattan,
and, later on, in his sketches of the disguised Westchester suburb known
in his fiction as Shady Hill.   More abused than abusive, the usual
Cheever hero tends to be, like Ralph Whittemore in "The Pot of Gold," a
"prisoner of his schemes and expectations"; the unsuspecting and ironic
casualty of his single decisive conviction in life, "an uncompromising
loyalty," as Cheever puts it, "to the gentle manners of the middle
class."

As a result, we can attribute the loneliness of the Cheever hero to a
world of conventions no longer adequate to experience but still
impossible to break away from (a "rigid script," as Cheever calls it in
"Metamorphoses").   Such a reading shores up our sense of the Cheever
hero as the hapless or pathetic victim, different in tone from the
victim in Jewish fiction perhaps, but still consistent with the approved
modernist hero at odds, like Conrad's isolatoes, with a world of
received customs and beliefs.

The first real attempt to canonize Cheever came with the publication
of *Falconer* in 1977, for *Falconer* seemed, on the face of it at least, to
place Cheever securely in the kind of modern tradition that justifies
inaction as an indictment of society; that exploits, in short, the
familiar figure of the prison to express the way culture captures and
confines the self.   But if Falconer prison was the key to Cheever's
triumph, it was not so much because it served a vision of modern life as
a life of imprisonment and isolation, but because Cheever used it to
measure confinement as our ruling notion about ourselves.   A metaphor
about a metaphor rather than a metaphor about life, Cheever's prison
suggested that the real function of confinement was to produce, as its
necessary yield and support, the notion of freedom.

If we inquire into the arguments and architecture of the *Stories*,
here, too, we will find a very different kind of drama from the
Christian and modernist one that supposedly liberates and resurrects
Farragut as he emerges from a shroud outside Falconer's walls.   There
is, after all, no overwhelming burden or hypocrisy in the confinements
that the quotidian world places on Cheever's characters in the *Stories*
(imagine Ned Merrill in "The Swimmer" making his neighborly rounds with-

out the obligatory drinks he takes at each house along his way), for it
is a drama of accommodation to the duties of daily life that is being
played out.

It is probably even inaccurate to say that character in itself is
Cheever's particular focus. For all the richness of incident, each
affair, each frustration, each hero is a variation on another. Sometimes
whole dramatic situations are virtual contractions or extensions of one
another, as in "The Music Teacher" and "The Country Husband"; sometimes
mirror images, as in "The Cure" and "The Housebreaker of Shady Hill." In
fact, character and scene alike are memorable less for themselves than
for the particular angle of vision they provide on a world they behold
in common.

The moral corollary, of course, is that Cheever's characters are the
decided instruments of circumstance, unable and unwilling not only to
act but even to react, whether to a pathetic rival in "The Season of
Divorce," or to the regular provocation of a burned dinner and a sour
wife in "The Music Teacher." One of the most irritating examples in all
of the *Stories* comes at the start of "The Country Husband," when Francis
Weed returns to Shady Hill dazed and battered by a near calamitous crash
landing on a flight home to Idlewild from a business trip. When the
exhausted Weed tries to tell his brawling kids and distracted wife about
it, no one even hears him--the husband and father, alas, victimized by
the very household he has created. But what looks like a refusal to
engage moral questions by retreating into the fantastic turns out to be
an attempt to determine what is decisive in the formation of character
and what is not.

Even "The Enormous Radio" holds a more problematic meaning than its
rather weak moral patina suggests. Though Jim and Irene Wescott have
bought a new radio for the pleasure of listening to music, the
mysterious machine forces them instead to listen in on the sad and
sometimes brutal private lives of their neighbors, and appears to jolt
them both into the discovery of passions and pains of their own. What
is shocking about the story's final scene, however, is not the substance
of Irene's sudden moral attack on her husband for his past sins, but
that the imperturbable and virtually blank Irene (at the start of the
tale she has "a wide, fine forehead upon which nothing at all had been
written") has suddenly acquired the abusive rhetoric of intimacy from
overhearing the lives of others.

Hence the energy of plot in a Cheever story lies less with what we
think of as the customary driving force of short fiction--the moral
dilemma, the emotional tension of a conflict to be pressured or
resolved--and more with engaging the reader in a wish to uncoil the
enigmatic structure of motivation and desire, to track down the origins
of identity through the names and images that determine it. This is the
privileged obsession of Charlie Mallory in "The Geometry of Love," an

engineer whose marital squabbles and "lost . . . sense of reality" impel
him to "decipher," for each significant moment in his life, "the chain
of contingencies that had detonated the scene," and thus to express in
miniature Cheever's own enterprise in the *Stories* at large.

So in a single strategy that combines his lyric gift for the
particular with his visionary inclination for what is abstract and
paradigmatic, Cheever focuses not on character as a thing in itself, but
on what he calls in "The Sorrows of Gin" "the literal symbols of
life"--a familiar object or a scene from the past--by which a particular
character finds his own relation to life concentrated in a particular
image or situation. "The Lowboy" is a prime example of how an object
allows Cheever both to evoke a world and take apart its mechanisms in a
single stroke. Like those haunting summer houses in the more familiar
stories in the volume, the old and once forgotten piece of family
furniture that gives "The Lowboy" its title raises powerful memories of
childhood and primitive rivalry in two brothers, memories deriving from
a scene or object like those of Proust's *madeleine* or like the symptoms
of Freud's hysterics. The *Stories* might even be arranged in terms of
the "symbols" or situations that locate and define the self from tale to
tale--the allure of Broadway for Evarts Malloy in "O City of Broken
Dreams"; the ancestral summer place in "Goodbye, My Brother" or "The
Summer Farmer"; the moving van that becomes an icon of humiliation and
flight in "The Scarlet Moving Van"; even a particular day in a family's
history like the one that gives "The Day the Pig Fell into the Well" its
title, and that allows a fractured and embittered collection of
relatives to reaffirm its stamina as a unit by recalling, from various
points of view, the circumstances that surrounded the decisive event.

If there is melancholy and hesitation in Cheever's world, there is,
however, no anxiety in our recognizably modern or Jewish sense, no
struggle for self-mastery or coherence because life is already coherent
as it is. The inability of Cheever's characters to take action or even
to feel anxiety or rage about their circumstances is not, then, so much
a moral vision with problems as it is a vision beyond or apart from the
moral as we normally conceive it. For Cheever, culture precedes the
individual and subordinates him to it--makes him possible in the first
place--through the constitutive power of the "symbols" it supplies (thus
Victor and Theresa Mackenzie in "The Children," who wander from
situation to situation with no identities apart from those they can
assume by attaching themselves, for love and money alike, to a wealthy
family or an ailing estate). The Cheever of the *Stories* has a less
coherent nostalgia for the natural than the pastoral Cheever of the
Wapshot novels, and so a less coherent notion of culture itself as evil.
Indeed, the "moral chain of being" that Cheever identifies in the
preface as one of the "constants" he means to find in life is most
profitably understood as a notion of the "chain" of "mores" that links

the moments of life to one another, and that provides whatever sense life may hold for Cheever's characters. Rather than rail against the "chain" as though it represses nature and desire, Cheever prefers instead to analyze the way the "chain" of culture produces what thoughts and feelings we have. To characterize Cheever's project in this way not only suggests his links with James and Hawthorne before him, but also his less manifest links with postmodernist contemporaries like Borges or Pynchon. Despite its realist premises, after all, Cheever's art, too, is in search of a means to represent, not life itself, but the representations that structure and determine our experience of life. By remaining at the same time resolute in its obligation to render that experience in the sympathetic terms of the particular individual and his relation to the quotidian, however, Cheever's fiction wins for itself the additional distinction of maintaining two apparently antithetical modes--one realist, one antirealist or surfictional--in an equilibrium that would collapse in less knowing hands.

Partisan Review 47 (1980): 467-71.

Light Touch

Robert Towers

For years many of us have gone around with bits and pieces of John Cheever stories lodged in our minds--oddities of character or situation, brief encounters, barely remembered passages of special poignancy or beauty. But unless we have had access to a complete file of old *New Yorkers* or were provident enough to buy the collections of stories as they appeared, we have lacked a context for these fragments. A few stories ("Torch Song," "The Swimmer") have been widely anthologized, while the rest have remained in a kind of literary limbo: valued in recollection, known to exist, but difficult to reach. Though Cheever has been among the handful of contemporary writers who have sharpened our awareness and added to our arsenal of allusion, the individual volumes of his stories have been hard to come by, even in ordinarily well-stocked libraries. The success of *Falconer* has changed all that. Now we have this fat and weighty volume--sixty-one stories in all--and it comes like a splendid gift.

A reading of the entire collection usefully corrected certain misconceptions of mine that had grown up over the years. Influenced no doubt by the popularity of "The Swimmer" and by the four novels, I had come to think of Cheever's work as far more surrealistic and bizarrely plotted than it turns out to be. Of the sixteen or so stories that seem to me clearly first-rate (a high percentage, given the size of the *oeuvre*), twelve are distinctly within the bounds of realism, observing the conventions of causality, chronology, and verisimilitude, with no untoward intrusions of the arbitrary or the fantastic.

Though Cheever disclaims a documentary purpose and (rightly) resents comparison to a social nit-picker like the later John O'Hara, his stories do have a powerful documentary interest--and why not? Documentation of the way we--or some of us--live now has been historically one of those enriching impurities of fiction that only a mad theorist would wish to filter out. Less grand than Auchincloss, subtler and cleverer than Marquand, infinitely more generous than O'Hara, Cheever has written better than anyone else of that little world which upper-middle-class Protestants have contrived to maintain in their East Side apartments, in certain suburbs, in summer cottages on Nantucket, in Adirondack lodges, on New England farms. Servants are surely scarcer than when Cheever's early stories appeared, but otherwise the little world is fairly intact--a world of doormen and elevator men, of private schools, of riding lessons, skiing lessons, sailing classes, dancing classes, of cocktail parties, dinner parties, and church on Sunday.

While still influential far beyond its numbers, this world has undergone a loss of moral confidence that is clearly fascinating to Cheever. Its (generally) well-mannered inhabitants are nostalgic for--and pay lip service to--what one character describes as "the boarding-school virtues: courage, good sportsmanship, chastity, and honor," but they are constantly imperiled by alcohol, adultery, and the corrosive effects of disappointment. In that very moving story of Upper East Side adultery called "The Bus to St. James's," Mr. Bruce goes to pick up his daughter from a riding lesson and observes the other parents waiting for their children. He is struck by the notion that he and they ("all cut out of the same cloth") are "bewildered and confused in principle, too selfish or too unlucky to abide by the forms that guarantee the permanence of a society, as their fathers and mothers had done. Instead, they put the burden or order onto their children and filled their days with specious rites and ceremonies."

Many of them lack an adequate financial base for their inherited or acquired style of living. The narrator of another fine story, "The Season for Divorce," describes himself and his wife as both coming

> from that enormous stratum of the middle class that is distinguished by its ability to recall better times. Lost money is so much a part of our lives that I am sometimes reminded of expatriates, of a group who have adapted themselves energetically to some alien soil but who are reminded, now and then, of the escarpments of their native coast.

Like so many of his nineteenth-century predecessors, Cheever is authoritative in his portrayal of the shabby genteel, of those who must resort to desperate contrivances to keep up appearances, to say nothing of advancing themselves in the world.

He is also wonderfully sensitive to the rhythms of family life within this class ("The Day the Pig Fell into the Well," "The Country Husband"); to the asperities of fraternal relationships ("Goodbye, My Brother," "The Summer Farmer"); to the decorum to be maintained in one's dealing with in-laws and, by extension, with servants, babysitters, hired hands, and local inhabitants of a different class ("The Common Day," "The Summer Farmer," "The Day the Pig Fell into the Well"); and to the behavior of children disillusioned with their parents ("The Sorrows of Gin"). He catches not only the chronic irritations and disappointments but also the sudden upwelling of great tenderness and compassion.

Of course, Cheever, for all his fascination with manners, has never been primarily a documentary writer. His response to experience is essentially that of an old-fashioned lyric poet. In his preface to the new collection, he writes, "The constants that I look for in this sometimes dated paraphernalia are a love of light and a determination to trace some moral chain of being." While one might question Cheever's profundity as a moralist, there can be no doubt about his preoccupation with--and celebration of--the shifting powers of light. His stories are bathed in light, flooded with it; often his characters appear slightly drunk with it, their senses reeling.

Light, for Cheever, seems to have distinctly moral or religious properties. In the late story, "The World of Apples," the octogenarian poet, Asa Bascomb, after a demoralizing onslaught of lewd fantasies, undergoes a ritual of purification, after which he experiences that "radiance he had known when he was younger." He begins "a long poem on the inalienable dignity of light and air that, while it would not get him a Nobel Prize, would grace the last months of his life." Light seems to be associated with a blessing, with a tender maternal smile fleetingly experienced, with all that is clean, tender, and guiltless, with the barely glimpsed immanence of God within His creation. At times Cheever appears to soar like Shelley's skylark toward the source of light, a belated romantic beating his luminous wings in the void.

But while the lyric impulse sometimes leads him into a slight (and often endearing silliness--"The light was like a blow, and the air smelled as if many wonderful girls had just wandered across the lawn"--he is for the most part a precisionist of the senses. Though his imagery of light has the strongest retinal impact, Cheever's evocation of color and texture and smell is also vivid and persistent. He shares with two very different writers, Lawrence and Faulkner, an extraordinary ability to fix the sensory quality of a particular moment, a particular place, and

to make it function not as embellishment but as an essential element in
the lives and moods of his characters. Here are two young mothers, both
married to less than successful husbands, in "the sorry and touching
countryside of Central Park":

> The women talked principally about their husbands, and this was
> a game that Laura could play with an empty purse. . . . They sat
> together with their children through the sooty twilights, when
> the city to the south burns like a Bessemer furnace, and the air
> smells of coal, and the wet boulders shine like slag, and the
> Park itself seems like a strip of woods on the edge of a coal
> town.
>   "The Pot of Gold"

And here is a sorely beset husband coming home to sick children:

> It was impossible to ventilate or clean the house, and when I
> came in, after walking through the cold from the bus stop, it
> stank of cough syrups and tobacco, fruit cores and sickbeds.
>   "The Season of Divorce"

It is in such passages as these that the genuinely poetic quality of
Cheever's fiction breaks through--far more than in those flashily
"poetical" last sentences to which he is sometimes prone: "I saw them
come out and I saw that they were naked, unshy, beautiful, and full of
grace, and I watched the naked women walk out of the sea" ("Goodbye, My
Brother"). Or: "Then it is dark; it is night where kings in golden
suits ride elephants over the mountains" ("The Country Husband").

The introduction of an element of the weird into a densely realistic
setting is an old trick of Cheever's, going back to his beginnings as a
storyteller. Nowhere does it work better than in "The Enormous Radio,"
where a Sutton Place apartment house is transformed into a rancorous
hive of accusations and counteraccusations by a radio that mysteriously
allows one of Cheever's nice, upper-middle-class couples to eavesdrop
upon conversations taking place throughout the building. The social
texture is every bit as thick and as accurately rendered as in any of
the realistic stories; the husband's indictment of his wife, when at
last the contagion spreads to the couple, is as grimly factual, as
"class-specific," as if magic had nothing to do with the situation. The
stories in which the two elements are successfully interwoven are among
Cheever's most brilliant; they include not only the famous "Torch Song"
and "The Swimmer" but also that superbly macabre piece, "The Music
Teacher," in which a husband, driven to despair by a chaotic household
and regularly burned meals, resorts to an elderly piano teacher who has

been recommended by a neighbor; she gives him a musical formula with
which to tame his wife and then dies the ugly death of a witch. But on
a re-reading they seem to me to veer toward slickness, to stand up less
well than, say, a strongly felt and quietly impressive piece like "The
Summer Farmer" or "The Bus to St. James's."

Cheever is a writer whose faults have an unusually close connection to
his strengths. The imaginative identification with the upper-middle
class which allows him to depict their mores and dilemmas with such
vivacity entails a narrowness of social range and a sentimental snobbery
which can get the best of him when his guard is down. Unlike Faulkner,
whose Snopeses and Bundrages are as lovingly rendered as his Compsons,
Cheever is not at ease when he enters the thoughts and feelings of one
of those retainers—usually an Irish-Catholic—who service the elevators
and the doors of the East Side apartment houses. In "Clancy in the
Tower of Babel," "Christmas Is a Sad Season for the Poor," and "The
Superintendent," he settles for faintly embarrassing stereotypes of
those workers while displaying his usual keenness of observation and
sympathy for the apartment dwellers for whom they work. The absence of
Jews in Cheever's New York world is striking; at times it seems a
deliberate avoidance, as in "Oh, City of Broken Dreams," where a
bus-driver-turned-playwright from Indiana is brought into a thicket of
producers and theatrical agents of whom not even one has a Jewish name.

The most serious embarrassments occur when he attempts an identification with a really alien figure, as in "Clementina," his story of a
simple-hearted Italian girl who emigrates to America, or "Artemis, the
Honest Well-Digger," a late story in which he introduces a young digger
of artesian wells to a sexually predatory matron of suburbia and then
whisks him off on an implausible tour of Russia. His condescension to
these characters is well meant, full of good will, and hard to swallow.

The snobbery is fairly innocent as snobberies go, attaching itself
mostly to well-bred or even aristocratic ladies and causing little
damage beyond a maudlin blurring of Cheever's usually sharp vision. In
"The Superintendent," our sympathies (and the super's) are unduly
wrenched in behalf of nice Mrs. Bestwick, who wears diamonds as big as
filberts but can no longer afford to live in her apartment, which is
taken over by the hustling and rude upstart, Mrs. Negus. The snobbery
is intensified in several of the stories with Italian settings, where
there is a degree of sentimental obeisance to duchesses and broken-down
marchesas, one of whom wears diamonds as big as acorns.

Cheever's role as narrator is always obtrusive. He has, of course,
never had any truck with the notion—once a dogma among certain academic
critics—that an author should keep himself as invisible as possible,
that he should show rather than tell. Cheever-as-narrator is regularly
on stage, rejoicing in his own performance, commenting upon—often chat-

ting about--his characters, dispatching them on missions, granting them reprieves or firmly settling their hash. At his most effective he can tell us things about a character with such authority that we never for a moment doubt that his comprehension is total, final:

> The lackluster old woman--half between wakefulness and sleep--gathered together her bones and groped for her gray hair. It was in her nature to collect stray cats, pile the bathroom up to the ceiling with interesting and valuable newspapers, rouge, talk to herself, sleep in her underwear in case of fire, quarrel over the price of soup bones, and have it circulated around the neighborhood that when she finally died in her dusty junk heap, the mattress would be full of bankbooks and the pillow stuffed with hundred-dollar bills. She had resisted all these rich temptations in order to appear a lady, and she was repaid by being called a common thief. She began to scream at him.
>
> "The Sorrows of Gin"

He loves to generalize: "Walking in the city, we seldom turn and look back"--or: "It is true of even the best of us that if an observer can catch us boarding a train at a way station . . . ."

From these and a myriad other touches a composite image of Cheever-as-a-narrator emerges--a figure that is of course distinct from Cheever-as-a-man, though the two personalities may coincide at certain points. It is only of the former that it can be said that the style is the man; of the latter only his family, friends, and his eventual biographer have the right to make pronouncements. Cheever-as-narrator is a personable fellow--debonaire, graceful, observant, and clever. His sympathies are volatile and warm. He is a good host--one who likes to entertain, to amuse, to turn a phrase. He is also a bit of a show-off, an exhibitionist. Beneath the gaiety and charm of his discourse, deep strains of melancholy and disappointment run. He is not, however, a cynic. Nor is he a profound moralist. He has no fundamental quarrel with the family or society as they now exist. For the ills of the flesh and spirit his sovereign remedy is the repeated application of love, love, love . . . .

Cheever's highhanded way as a narrator--at its best a display of confident mastery--can degenerate into whimsicality and arbitrariness, especially in the later stories. I am not an admirer of the Wapshot novels, in which so often eccentricity--the more bizarre the better--is regarded as necessarily interesting or amusing in itself, to the detriment of sustained narrative and the sustained development of character. Something very similar is to be found in pieces like "Percy" or "The Jewels of the Cabots," which read as if they were made up of episodes

left over from the annals of St. Botolphs. In them Cheever writes as if
he couldn't care less whether we bestow a moment's credence or concern
upon a character who starves herself to death for the sake of the
starving Armenians, upon another character who washes her diamonds and
hangs them out to dry, and upon still another character who is made to
steal those diamonds and then go off to Egypt where she ends up weighing
three-hundred pounds. Sheer contrivance dominates these stories and
others like them, squeezing the little life they contain into pointless
and arbitrary shapes. Cheever's real energies during this recent period
seem to have gone into those strange, dark novels, *Bullet Park* and
Falconer, whose eccentricities--however wild--are not allowed to
undermine the powerful and moving stories they have to tell.

Thanks to this volume, the best of Cheever's stories are now spread
glitteringly before us. In our renewed pleasure in these, we can let
the others--the trivial and the miscalculated--recede to their proper
place. Cheever's accomplishment in his exacting art is proportionally
large, as solid as it is brilliant, and likely to endure--a solemn thing
to say (however true) of a writer who has so often flaunted the banner
of devil-may-care.

The New York Review of Books 25 (9 November 1978): 3-4.

Oh What a Paradise
It Seems

1982

SELECTED REVIEWS

Chance-taker

Robert M. Adams

Whether John Cheever consciously set himself the problem of making a
small piece of fiction feel like a big one, that is the most impressive
thing he's accomplished in *Oh What a Paradise It Seems*. The book is
what Henry James delighted to call (without ever condescending to define
the word) a *nouvelle*; and it would almost seem that the old master had
Mr. Cheever in his mind's eye when he wrote of "the only compactness
that has a charm, the only spareness that has a force, the only
simplicity that has a grace--those, in each order, that produce the *rich*
effect." Though the canvas is small in this new novel, it is not
miniature work; it is broad, impressionistic, at its best a poetic
narrative.

The book's central figure is a man of some years, old (we are told,
with a touch of defiance) but not yet infirm, and shaken by a sense of
the fragile beauty of vanishing things. He lives and works in what is
clearly New York City, and spends much of his time in what could be the
Connecticut suburbs--though really his world is almost limitless because
it persistently shades off into vagueness and nondefinition. His
actions hint at a parable without ever taking on the symmetry of one;
they touch on melodrama, but glancingly. Other characters encountered
by the hero are mute, almost inarticulate; with little ado they
materialize, and with even less they disappear, as into soft mist.

Lemuel Sears's affair with Renée Herndon occupies a considerable part
of the book (though less than the reader is led to anticipate); their

rendezvous are complicated by her attendance at a series of early
evening meetings to help people stop eating or drinking or smoking--just
what isn't clear. He asks her about these evenings at parish houses or
in church basements, even tries to spy on one; but she won't tell him
what they are, he never learns, and neither does the reader. Her
standard conversational gambit is, "You don't understand the first thing
about women"; and about this woman it's certainly true. Sears doesn't
understand her, she makes no effort to explain herself so the reader
doesn't understand her either; if Cheever does, he isn't letting on.
There's an enormous, charming, unreliable vacancy in and around her.

   The surface of the book is also charming and unreliable. At one point
Renée weeps in frustration at being unable to open a door; Sears takes
her in his arms, "not to solace her for the locked door of course but to
comfort her for Harold and every other disappointment in her life." She
is divorced, indeed, but her husband was named Arthur; apart from this
passage, Harold has no other existence in the book. A speed-reader will
sail blithely across the novel's glistening surfaces; if he pauses a
moment to look under his feet, the thin ice will be starring out beneath
him.

   Much of the book's action centers on Beasley's Pond, a deep body of
water actually used in winter, by Sears and others, for skating. (The
main action takes place "at the time I'm writing about," in "the
province where his daughter lived"--the nonspecification serving to
shiver ever so slightly whatever sense of solidity the reader retains.)
In any case, the pond is big as well as deep; apparently it measures
"two and a half or three miles, if one took the distance from end to
end." Yet malefactors propose to fill this entire lacustrine basin by
throwing garbage into it, and then to erect on the gigantic dump they
will have created a veterans' memorial. For no reason more mysterious
than money, mafiosi are involved in this scheme--so deeply that they
commit two outright murders of environmentalists who are trying to
protect Beasley's Pond. Neither murder has the slightest consequence,
as the village where everything takes place is largely devoid of human
beings with names, faces, or occupations. This is the stuff of
nightmare, maybe paranoia. (I use the word in a neutral, if not an
actively favorable sense.)

   The tendency of the solid surfaces to tail off into vagueness
counterpoints the way people in the story change their minds abruptly
and without explanation, the way crucial developments are determined by
coincidence. A family driving home from a day at the beach accidentally
leave their sleeping baby on the shoulder of a busy superhighway; he is
rescued and returned to his parents by the very environmentalist engaged
in saving Beasley's Pond. Sears, abruptly abandoned by Renée, makes
love with the elevator operator of her apartment building; on acquain-

tance, Eduardo proves to be a good husband and father, who explains that his younger son is a senior at Rutgers while the elder plays jazz piano in Aspen, Colorado.

That's what you call spacing it out, and it's spaced out still further by the narrator's occasional erratic interventions, leisurely and free-floating. The sense of psychic distance, inconsequence, open possibility is enhanced by the vaudeville of Cheever's style, his skill at seeming to tell a simple, unpretentious story absolutely straight, while introducing patterns of sidestep and evasion. Seeming is the theme of the book, apparent giving and real taking away. Its paradigm could be a lovely sentence from an old Irish *nouvelle* in which the narrator, describing a litigious landlord, says, "Out of forty-nine suits which he had, he never lost one but seventeen."

The truth is that Cheever's hero, though he masquerades as a technical specialist ("computer containers" are his line; he's also into "cerbical chips," and has traveled to the Carpathians where "cerb" or perhaps "cerbical" is mined), is really a poet, with persistent, intuitive feelings for the fresh, the intense, the mortal. His associations with rain run especially deep; they constitute a dimension almost as unfathomable as the mind of his mistress Renée. An open man, with a sneaking fondness for picturesque, idiotic theories and the exhilarations of a physical moment, his character invites use of the faithless adjective, "human." Like an earlier Lemuel, he travels through worlds of outsize or wrong-shaped people, looking for one of his own sort. Among the phantoms is a current and present daughter, whose relations with her father are described in the dry word "skeptical," and never mentioned again.

It has been said that satiric exaggeration is impossible in a society that already is a grotesque parody of what it pretends to be; also that paranoia in a society like our own is, on the odds, the safest approach to truth. In combining some of these dark perspectives within the frame of an idyll, Cheever has done more to create spacious and lively harmony than one would have thought possible in a small room. The ease and assurance with which the equilibrium is maintained are secondary pleasures of dealing with a practiced storyteller and chance-taker.

The New York Review of Books 29 (29 April 1982): 8.

Lonely Nomads

Ann Hulbert

"The constants that I look for," John Cheever wrote in the introduction to his collected stories in 1978,

> are a love of light and a determination to trace some moral
> chain of being. Calvin played no part at all in my religious
> education, but his presence seemed to abide in the barns of my
> childhood and to have left me with some undue bitterness.

The religious outlines of Cheever's moral world stand out clearly now,
bounding the suburban lawns and homesick heroes of the fiction he has
been writing for four decades. As the title of his last volume of
selected stories, *The World of Apples* (1974) [*sic*: 1973], suggests,
Cheever's short fiction has portrayed a fallen world, where man's body
daily betrays his spirit. In his last novel, *Falconer* (1977), he
followed a man accused of fratricide into the hell of prison. Now
Cheever is in pursuit of paradise. And with his new novella, *Oh What a
Paradise It Seems*, he takes his place in a long and illustrious line of
writers whose imaginations have lost energy, light, and warmth as they
try to map the realm of redemption.

"When I was younger, I could run all over the pasture and come back,"
Cheever recalled in an interview after *Falconer* appeared. "Now I seem
to be going much more directly to what I have to say." It's not
uncommon that artists, after gamboling among images for a time, stride
more purposefully toward statements of their underlying vision. For
years now, "pungency, diversity, color, and nostalgia"--those virtues
Cheever bestowed upon Asa Bascombe, the poet protagonist of his
masterful story, "The World of Apples"--have been the vigorous qualities
prized in his own work as well. Like Asa Bascombe, Cheever has in rare
moments "divined the voice of moral beauty in a rain wind"; and all
along, he has faithfully recorded the mundane facts of our morally
ambiguous, often intractable world--barbecue grills, radios, relatives,
genitals, and other awkward encumbrances. In *Oh What a Paradise It
Seems*, this dualistic world of facts and truths, matter and spirit, is
suddenly more starkly lit than ever before--the search for spiritual
salvation more insistent, material corruption more pervasive. The
renowned pungency, diversity, and color of Cheever's writing seem to
have faded somewhat; and the nostalgia, ever-present in his narratives
about his wandering race, has lost some of its humane, lyric tone and
echoes more remotely now.

The narrator of this eerie novella is looking back, as Cheever's
narrators usually do, but this time he's not our contemporary taking us
back with him to our common recent past--the last several decades of the
century. Instead, the narrative voice emanates from the future,
observing the close of this second millennium from a distant, and apparently idyllic, vantage point beyond us. The figure in the foreground of

the scene is Lemuel Sears as he skates up and down the black ice of
Beasley's Pond late one January afternoon. "An old man . . . but not
infirm," Sears is uneasily beginning to face the facts of approaching
old age. But, fleet and graceful on the smooth pond surface, he feels
his spirit suddenly braced by "a sense of homecoming. At long last, at
the end of a cold, long journey, he was returning to a place where his
name was known and loved and lamps burned in the rooms and fires in the
hearth." Sears's sense of spiritual comfort is rudely obliterated two
weeks later when he again collects his skates and takes the train from
his New York City apartment to the village of Janice, the site of
Beasley's Pond, only to find the icy retreat in the process of being
turned into the town dump. But shortly after that disappointment,
Sears's spirit is roused again, this time by the sight of a woman in
line at a bank, who also evokes homing instincts in him: "he thought
that perhaps it was nostalgia that made her countenance such a forceful
experience for him."

For all the familiar Cheever soulfulness with which he is endowed,
however, Sears is hardly more than a shadow after the mere ten pages it
has taken to set him off on his spiritual journey back toward love of
nature and woman. As the spare plot proceeds, it's clear the narrator
is more interested in surveying a culture and an allegorical landscape
than in probing his main character. "Here was the discharge of a
society that was inclined to nomadism without having lessened its
passion for portables," the narrator comments and then elaborates:

> Most wandering people evolve a culture of tents and saddles and
> migratory herds, but here was a wandering people with a passion
> for gigantic bedsteads and massive refrigerators. It was a
> clash between their mobility--their driftingness--and their love
> of permanence that had discharged its chaos into Beasley's Pond.

Like the water, the land has changed beyond recognition; farms have been
paved over by "that highway of merchandising that reaches across the
continent," lane upon lane of cars blurring by, row upon row of fried-
food places serving up "the food for spiritual vagrants." It was "as if
a truly adventurous people had made a wrong turning and stumbled into a
gypsy culture"; the country presents "a landscape, a people . . . who
had lost the sense of a harvest." The anthropological imagery abounds,
documenting the "barbarity and nomadism" of a contaminated civilization. In this habitat, Lemuel Sears is an interesting specimen rather
than a compelling character. The saga of his rejuvenating efforts to
purify a dirty pond and pollute a pretty woman is a schematic spiritual
progress, not an absorbing sentimental journey. Cheever's prose throughout is flatter, less highly polished and graceful than in the past. He
is aiming, evidently, to create a different fictional fabric, strands of

which have appeared in his more recent work; its cut is more contemporary and cool, with less of the often quaintly elegant style of old.

Thus Sears's love affair is farcical fantasy rather than psychologically compelling romance, reminiscent of the unlikely amorous adventures in "Artemis the Honest Well-Digger," one of Cheever's later stories. Renée, Sears's enigmatic amour, has soft lips and secrets, and next to no other notable qualities; the elevator man in her building, with whom Sears also has a brief, bizarre affair, is a phantom presence as well. Similarly, Sears's ecological mission--ostensibly a traditional suspense story, crude all-American despoilers versus poetic purifiers--turns out to be an occasion for surrealistic social satire and meditations on the state of the planet. Throughout, Cheever's depiction of a contaminated country is successfully alienating, in fact often all too dispiriting. But his protagonist never becomes a soul lit from within by a memory of love, by a yearning for some past bliss of belonging; Sears is not that soft-hearted but stalwart character of classic Cheever fiction, whom we may know all too well now but miss nonetheless.

There are two such souls, though, who play subordinate roles. And in their presence, Cheever's prose and imagination are inspired. He presents visions of wandering beings here on earth that are far more memorable than either his catalog of a contaminated hell or his paeon to a pure, natural paradise. One soul is Horace Chisholm, the environmentalist enlisted to fight for Beasley's Pond, who is graced with this rumination:

> He felt so lonely that when the car ahead of him signaled for an exit he felt as if he had been touched tenderly on the shoulder by some stranger in some place like a crowded airport, and he wanted to put on his parking lights or signal back in some way as strangers who are traveling sometimes touch one another although they will never, ever meet again. In a lonely fantasy of nomadism he imagined a world where men and women communicated with one another mostly by signal lights and where he proposed marriage to some stranger because she turned on her parking lights an hour before dusk, disclosing a supple and romantic nature.

The other soul is Betsey Logan, a Janice housewife who in the end surreptitiously saves the pond. Her unexpectedly evocative recollection after an afternoon at the beach summons up another scene of nomads in a technological nether region:

> . . . she remembered watching on TV when an astronaut went into
> space. After the countdown the camera had shown all the people
> along the beach packing up their sandwich baskets and their
> towels and their folding furniture and going back to the parking
> lot, and she remembered that this had moved her more deeply than
> the thought of a man walking around on the moon. Almost
> everybody else on the beach had gone home early, and it seemed
> to her that they had gone because they had received some urgent
> message to leave and that the beach was their home and that on
> leaving the beach they would be like the evacuees of war or much
> more recently like those people who lived near toxic dumps and
> who have to travel for years, perhaps for a lifetime, seeking a
> new home.

Out of such lonely fantasies--yellow lights blinking, black and white
figures straggling along vast highways--Cheever has created for us a
shared vision of nomadism.

The New Republic 173 (31 March 1982): 42-45.

Seeking Paradise

George Hunt

This novella begins and ends with the words, "This is a story to be read
in bed in an old house on a rainy night." These lines capture well the
story's disarming modesty but not its special magic, for they merely
hint at the delights in between. It is a story for bed, true enough,
but one narrated by a beguiling voice and shaped like the bitter-sweet
dreams we love to wake to. What is more, it is a story by John
Cheever--a yarn-spinner as gifted, though as different, as Hawthorne,
Twain and Faulkner--and so our old house (of American architecture, by
the way) is newly populated with spooky and benign ghosts who enter and
leave with seeming abandon; yet both the rain and the voice are
comforting, as only mysterious truths when shared with another are
comforting.

John Cheever is the only excellent novelist in the 20th century who
has never avoided, in fact has stressed, the superlative accent in
describing both sensation and moral aspiration. All the words the wise
avoid, like "valor, glory, virtue, paradise" and "extraordinary,
incandescent, supernatural," are those only the wiser can get away with.
Coincidentally, our finest writers know this and have never resisted
superlatives in describing Cheever himself. Ten years ago John Updike,

who continues to marvel at the "radiance" of his fiction, said that in "the coining of images and incidents, John Cheever has no peer among contemporary fiction writers. His short stories dance, skid, twirl and soar on the strength of his abundant invention." Saul Bellow was asked in a recent interview about his favorite novelists. Cheever was at the top of the list, and Bellow explained, "But here's Cheever--you read those stories, and you see his power of transformation, his power to take the elements given and work them into something new and far deeper than they were at the outset."

Updike and Bellow seem to be describing *Oh What A Paradise It Seems*. The story is extremely short by supermarket standards, and its plot is disarmingly simple. The main character is not so much a character as, like many of Cheever's creations, a place animated by bright and fallen spirits: Beasley's Pond. The pond is the centerpiece of emotional concern and, like Troy, it becomes the occasion for a host of Homeric digressions that inch us into a comically epic fable. First we meet Lemuel Sears, a man "old enough to remember when the horizons of his country were dominated by the beautiful and lachrymose wine-glass elm tree and when most of the bathtubs one stepped into had lion's claws." We discover him on skates atop Beasley's Pond, prey to noble and carnal distractions, sharing with the other skaters "a sense of homecoming" and "that extraordinary preoccupation with innocence that absorbs people on a beach before the fall of darkness."

Weeks later Sears returns, appalled to find that this pond where both mobility and permanence are celebrated has been rezoned as a dumpfill in preparation for a war memorial. He hires a lawyer to investigate the project and, when the lawyer is ominously killed, he seeks out an environmentalist to pursue the matter. Gradually we readers learn as he does that the town's politicians, in cahoots with organized crime, have determined to pollute the pond for financial gain. The subsequent story recounts all the serious and eccentric efforts of a mixed cast of characters to save Beasley's Pond.

Salvage and salvation are at the heart of this story, as they are in every Cheever novel. A convinced believer in the slippages and slides of human errancy (original sin), he is even more resolute about the first article of the Creed, "I believe in God the Father Almighty, Maker of heaven and earth." (The Creed opens the Anglican morning service, and Cheever admits he usually shouts these words rather loudly.) The two truths: the Maker and His makings along with man's makings and unmakings are the recurring themes in his work. Cheever knows well that we live in a world that denies such basic beliefs. Denial of the one would lead us to pretend that our inherited human world is ugly but *we* are potentially beautiful if only . . . and suddenly our ifs multiply, for they depend on our disconnecting all our human linkages with parentage, the race, our own personal history, severing our ties with what makes and bothers us. The other denial of makings, that of creation itself, is more subtle and even more egoistic perhaps, because if we do not care whether something like a pond, a mountain, a tree or garden in all its awesome objectivity should *last* without us, then we are blind to the grander mystery of all created life itself, expressed so simply in the Creed.

This is precisely the dramatic conflict throughout the novella, and varied efforts to save Beasley's Pond function as a metaphor for something more elusive still, the quest for spiritual salvation, achieved only by embracing both the world and what transcends it. Cheever said recently of the character Sears, "I think if he wishes to discover any purity in himself, he's not going to find it in himself; he's going to find it in some larger sphere--of which he, of course, is a part." Here, as in most of Cheever's work, every gesture, sensation, even puzzlement can be emblematic of a spiritual discovery. "A trout stream in a forest, a traverse of potable water, seemed for Sears to be the bridge that spans the mysterious abyss between our spiritual and our carnal selves." We learn of another character that he "seemed to be searching for the memory of some place, some evidence of the fact that he had once been able to put himself in a supremely creative touch with his world and his kind. He longed for this as if it were some country which he had been forced to leave."

The title, *Oh What a Paradise It Seems*, challenges us to remember the twin paradises, the one lost and the other sought. Who else but Cheever would be bold enough to have such a title and then sly enough to add "seems," eliciting our imaginative complicity? As a matter of fact all the variants on the word "seems" provide the sinews of his fiction and account for its remarkable ambiguity. On one reading you follow the realistic and bizarre circumstances and perhaps hear a plaintive tone; on another, you listen to the undertones and overtones and smile; with a third you hear both together and tear because the simultaneous extremes of human truth arrive only there. To be precious, one might say that smiles and sadness arrive at the "seams"; more truthfully, they arrive at the "seems" where all loving connections, like jokes and compassion, meet.

No other living writer enjoys simultaneously such a vivid sense of transcendence and an equally vivid sense of humor or glides so easily from the sublime to the ridiculous and back as does Cheever. This story is composed of 11 brief chapters, but it is so enriched with memorable incidents--some hilarious, others melancholy--that, on finishing it, a reader recalls a novel that *must* have been three times its length. Consider these disparate incidents: the solemn-silly murder of a pet dog, a neighborhood battle over wind chimes, a poisoning in a supermarket, the discovery of a baby, biblical fashion, in the most unlikely place by a man in nostalgic search for blackberries, a session

with a psychiatrist who is a "homosexual spinster," each recounted in a
leisurely way but with concision. Yet no incident stands by itself; it
is always allied with random memories, sober or oddball reflections,
overheard drama, while throughout everyone in it is like Beasley's Pond
itself, both fragile and worthy of redemption.

In a review one must resist dampening the delight for future readers
by citing too much. Therefore, I will select one minor event that is
typically Cheeveresque. Sears recalls his meeting with a blind
prophetess named Gallia in Eastern Europe. Gallia is famous there for
her oracular powers, most recently for prophesying that "uranium prices
would fall," and everyone speaks of her in hushed, reverent tones. Sears
arrives at her cave within a volcano, accompanied by an interpreter who
is timid in anticipating this grave encounter: "She asked to feel
something of his and he gave her his wallet. She fingered the wallet
and began to smile. Then she began to laugh. So did Sears. She
returned the wallet to him and said something to his interpreter. 'I
have no idea what she means,' said the interpreter, 'but what she said
was "La grand poésie de la vie."' The prophetess stood and so did
Sears. They were both laughing. Then she held out her arms and he
embraced her. They parted, laughing."

Mystery and laughter even conjoin to fashion the human truth, and what
else to call it but the majestic poetry of life? Years ago in his story
"The Jewels of the Cabots," the narrator (a Cheever surrogate) stated
that "My real work these days is to write an edition of The New York
Times that will bring gladness to the hearts of men. How better could I
occupy myself?"

We know how, for Cheever has.

America 146 (27 March 1982): 238-40.

LATER CRITICISM

The Optimistic Imagination:
John Cheever's *Oh What A Paradise It Seems*

Michael Byrne

For those critics who have consistently found John Cheever a sentimental, narrow chronicler of the minor epiphanies and trials of suburbia,
Oh What A Paradise It Seems will be fuel for the fire (and judging from
the tepid reviews given the book, "fire" might be too strong). This com-

plaint, usually directed against "New Yorker writers," has a corollary
in regard to a Cheever novel: structural clumsiness. With the exception
of *Falconer*, the argument suggests that the acknowledged master of the
short story fails at longer fictions, that the Cheever novel
unconsciously aspires to the condition of a short story collection. By
this estimate *Falconer* was a felicitous masterpiece and *Oh What A
Paradise It Seems* a reversion to type. Ostensibly, this criticism
applies. The novella tells the story of Lemuel Sears, an old man
outraged over the pollution of a skating pond of his youth. Sears,
despite a society unconcerned with preserving the ecology and a sinister
conspiracy concerned with turning the pond into profit, wins the day and
saves Beasley's Pond. The Yankee virtues (celebrated in *The Wapshot
Chronicle*) of breeding, tenacity and respect for nature triumph. In the
era of James Watt, Cheever's optimism seems outrageous. Moreover, in
alternating chapters of the one hundred page novella, Cheever juxtaposes
the main story with a tale of two feuding housewives, Sears' love affair
with a younger woman, Sears' first homosexual affair, and the tragic end
of an idealistic environmentalist. The story shifts and races with the
speed of a scenario rather than a novel. Finally, Cheever brings the
principals together in a town hall scene, reminiscent of the "well-made"
courtrooms of Galsworthy. And, still at a breakneck pace, Cheever
concludes: "But, you might ask, whatever became of the true criminals,
the villains who had murdered a high-minded environmentalist and
seduced, bribed and corrupted the custodians of municipal welfare? Not
to prosecute these wretches might seem to incriminate oneself with the
guilt of complicity by omission. But that is another tale, and as I said
in the beginning, this is just a story meant to be read in bed in an old
house on a rainy night."[1] A brief description of this work does seem to
evoke an image of a dying writer tossing craft aside, straining for a
final statement of affirmation, whatever the cost. Seen in the context
of Cheever's total body of work, however, *Oh What A Paradise It Seems*
actually marks the great strides his fiction was taking, thematically
and technically. Through its controlling principle of the "optimistic
imagination," the book reveals a writer closer in temperament to the
Post-Modernists than Chekhov.

That all Cheever's fiction fit the same mold never was an accurate
appraisal. The sanguine world of *The Wapshot Chronicle* quickly gave way
to *The Wapshot Scandal*'s vision of an unravelling social fabric. The
simple, good-natured, lusty town of St. Botolph's disappeared on the
last page of the second Wapshot novel, and the narrator knew "how
harshly time will bear down on this ingenuous place . . . I will never
come back, and if I do there will be nothing left, there will be nothing
left but the headstones to record what has happened; there will really
be nothing at all."[2] Of course something did remain--Bullet Park. Like
its counterparts, Remsen Park and Shady Hill, Bullet Park was a land-

scape gathering in darkness. An apparent paradise of cocktail parties,
swimming pools and upstanding citizens, Bullet Park had some problems:
spiritual paralysis, drug addiction and a homicidal madman on the loose.
When the madman is finally captured, the narrator closes with:
"everything was as wonderful, wonderful, wonderful, wonderful as it had
been."[3] The irony here prepared for a portrait of darkness that could
not be easily remedied--*Falconer*. This novel, of course, overturned the
popular conception of Cheever's fictional range. In fact, in this short
work Cheever squeezed as many unsettling scenes as one could
imagine--from the bludgeoning of the prison cats to the flashback of
fratricide. And though the novel ultimately celebrated redemption and
escape, the Cheever world would never look quite the same again.

The evolution of Cheever's settings corresponded to the evolution of
his vision. The simple piety and amusing advice of Leander Wapshot in
The Wapshot Chronicle ("Beer on whisky, very risky. Whisky on beer,
never fear . . . Stand up straight. Admire the world. Relish the love
of a good woman. Trust in the Lord.")[4] was not adequate for the
complex world that his sons inherited in *The Wapshot Scandal*. Theirs
was a world complicated by technology, bureaucracy, and the
disintegration of humanistic values. This vision dominates *Bullet Park*
also, but Cheever's tone shifts in his third novel from elegy to satire
and cynicism. By *Falconer* the pessimism that first emerged in *The
Wapshot Scandal* reached bedrock, and only through Farragut's act of
faith in the regenerative power of love could the novel reach its
ultimate position--"rejoice."

Further, as Cheever's vision had been exploring new landscapes, his
technique enlarged, creating new forms for his subjects. The earliest
evidence of Cheever's technical experiments is in the stories. If the
representative Cheever story is a seamless fabric of character, image
and action ("O Youth and Beauty!"), Cheever began to distort and exploit
elements of the traditional short story form. For example, character is
self-consciously caricatured in "The Worm in the Apple" and "A Miscellany of Characters That Will Not Appear" as Cheever playfully indulged
in selfparody. A similar self-consciousness emerged in "Boy in Rome"
and "A Vision of the World" when the typically unobtrusive Cheever narrator assumes the foreground, questioning the value and uses of fiction.
And though the early "The Enormous Radio" shows Cheever's affection for
the fantastic, later stories, such as "Three Stories," "Metamorphoses"
and "The Chimera," exploited this vein more frequently, revealing
another kind of parodic self-consciousness in which Cheever used the
"Cheever world" as a backdrop for stories bordering on the supernatural.
In short, by the time he wrote *Oh What A Paradise It Seems*, Cheever had
established selfparody, self-consciousness and the irrational as new
fictional concerns. Of course, most recently we associate these
concerns with the Post-Modernists who employ them to undermine the idea

of order (in the work of art or the world). The difference is that
Cheever used them in an optimistic assertion of order.

One recalls that Farragut's escape from prison in *Falconer* (and the
earlier escape by Jody) taxed the imagination of the reader who
approached the book as a realistic novel. A similar improbability (the
last minute rescue of Tony) concluded *Bullet Park*. These were instances
that foreshadowed the use of the "optimistic imagination" that so deeply
controls *Oh What A Paradise It Seems*. Both a statement of Cheever's
vision and the novella's technical foundation, the "optimistic
imagination" allows Cheever self-consciously to eschew the probability
of action that largely governed his prior work. In *Oh What A Paradise
It Seems*, when the narrator acknowledges the fictionality of the work,
when he himself intrudes in the action, when mysteries are left
unexplained, when subplots inexplicably evaporate, and when the main
action is resolved more quickly than the eye can read, this "optimistic
imagination" is at work.

I take the term from Cheever's description of Lemuel Sears: "[his]
imagination was inclined to be optimistic" (3) [*sic*: 16]. Indeed, after
the cozy opening of the novella ("This is a story to be read in bed in
an old house on a rainy night") (3), Sears' imagination is put to a
test. After he learns that Beasley's Pond has been declared a dump site,
he writes letters to two advocates to end the dumping. His letter is
ridiculed by the mayor (a member of the dumping conspiracy) and the two
advocates are murdered. Yet, if the conspiracy reiterates Cheever's
long concern with evil, this is an evil that remains shadowy and
abstract as is not the case in *Bullet Park* and *Falconer*). The
conspiracy is hinted at and alluded to, but never identified or shown
working. And the novella's conclusion (cited earlier) demonstrates that
Cheever intended his images of benevolence and optimism to eclipse their
dark counterparts. In this respect, a contrast between *Oh What A
Paradise It Seems* and *Bullet Park* is telling. The earlier work is
divided between the narrative of Elliot Nailles and the interior
monologue of Paul Hammer. The point of view of Nailles' story is
omniscient, cynical and tired. Nailles, the fundamentally decent
suburbanite, almost loses his son to a strange malaise and later to the
murderous imagination of Hammer. But because of the narrative tone,
Tony's rescue and the restoration of order in Bullet Park are neither
convincing nor compelling. Hammer's monologue, however, is profoundly
disturbing and real; the point of view is passionate and earnest.
Through technique Cheever's portrait of evil and chaos in *Bullet Park*
totally dominates the idea of order. In *Oh What A Paradise It Seems*
tone serves the opposite purpose. Sears' nostalgia for Beasley's Pond
is treated without sentimentality, and his naive efforts to stop the
pollution are treated affectionately rather than ironically. Likewise,
the environmentalist Horace Chisholm, eventually murdered by the con-

spiracy, is lionized without sentimentality. Cheever's delicate balance
in tone toward the optimists in his story emerges in this typical
passage on Chisholm: "Then he seemed lost. He was lost. He had lost
his crown, his kingdom, his heirs and armies, his court, his harem, his
queen and his fleet. He had, of course, never possessed any of these.
He was not in any way emotionally dishonest and so why should he feel as
if he had been cruelly stripped of what he had never claimed to possess?
He seemed to have been hurled bodily from the sanctuary of some church,
although he had never committed himself to anything that could be called
serious prayer" (77). The tonal effect of caricaturing the conspirators
(or not showing them at all) and objectively characterizing Sears and
Chisholm is that order and benevolence are made compelling; chaos and
evil, lifeless.

So total is Cheever's insistence on benevolent order that any sinister
element in the plot is summarily resolved or cryptically abandoned.
Along with the concluding dismissal of the conspirators' fates are two
unresolved subplots. The first concerns Sears' love affair with Renee,
a young, attractive woman. Her continual admonition to Sears, "You
don't understand the first thing about women" (13), is underlined by the
mysterious meetings she attends. Neither Sears nor the reader ever
learns the nature of these meetings, and Renee's departure in the middle
of the book assures Sears he never will. Similarly, the subplot
involving Betsey Logan, a housewife also enraged at the pollution of
Beasley's Pond, ends inconclusively. After the murder of Chisholm,
Betsey decides to blackmail the conspiracy by poisoning the food at the
local supermarket. Following several cases of poisoning, the dumping
ceases. Here Cheever glosses over the ethical implications of her act,
insisting only on Sears' vision of benevolent mystery as he gazes at the
restored pond: "What moved him was a sense of those worlds around us,
our knowledge however imperfect of their nature . . . The sense of that
hour was of an exquisite privilege, the great benefice of living here
and renewing ourselves with love" (100). Further, the deliberate
abandonment of the unsavory in the plot has a counterpart in Horace
Chisholm's felicitous rescue of the Logans' child (accidentally
abandoned on the turnpike!). The child lost and found is a familiar
incident for Cheever's audience. Often it figures as his analogue for
grace; in *Oh What A Paradise It Seems* it is one more instance of the
serendipitous restoration of order. A pond restored; a child saved.

If the plot of *Oh What A Paradise It Seems* trots happily along
sidestepping probability and creating more questions than answers, there
is the narrator's repeated declaration that he is reporting a plot, an
imaginative artifice. He frequently prefaces a chapter or a paragraph
with "This is a story," "At the time of which I am writing," or "this is
just a story." This insistence on fictionality urges the reader to
delight in rather than to scrutinize the narrative eccentricities.

Persons attempting to find a coherent plot will be shot.

Or will they? The question is raised in the narrator's remarkable opening of chapter three:

> I wish the story I'm telling began with the fragrance of mint growing along a stream bed where I'm lying, concealed with my rifle, waiting to assassinate a pretender who is expected to come here, fishing for trout. What I can see of the sky is blue. The smell of mint is very strong and I hear the music of water. The pretender is a well-favored young man and thinks himself quite alone. There is, he seems to think, some blessedness in fishing trout with flies. He sings while he assembles his rod and looks up at the sky and around at the trees to reassure himself of the naturalness of this garden from which, unknown to him, he is about to be dismissed. My rifle is loaded and I put it to my shoulder take the location of his heart in my cross-sights. The smell of mint seriously challenges the rightness of this or any other murder. . . . Yes I would much sooner be occupied with such matters than with the death of the Salazzos' dog Buster, but at the time of which I am writing the purity of the water was of inexorable interest--far more important than dynasties--and the Salazzos are linked to the purity of Beasley's Pond. (24)

Here the narrator's insistence on artifice is wholly realized: he (like other Post-Modern narrators) fully reveals himself. Who is the "well-favored young man"? Why is he a "pretender"? Why is he about to be dispatched? More mysteries left unanswered. But this narrative intrusion dramatizes the heart of *Oh What A Paradise It Seems*: an Edenic world (the stream bed/Beasley's Pond) is threatened with mysterious violence (the narrator/the conspiracy), a violence averted by some benevolent, imaginative imperative.

This imperative is a moral order and it forms the theme and structure of Cheever's novella. Not only does he insist throughout the book on a vision of optimism, natural order, and the "great benefice of living here" (100), he imaginatively shapes that order. It would be a serious error to call *Oh What A Paradise It Seems* a Post-Modernist work, but Cheever's improbable plot, self-conscious narrator and unresolved mysteries demonstrate the contemporaneity of his technique. That he uses these techniques for an assertion of order reveals the distance between him and many Post-Modernists. I have paraphrased Cheever in calling this order the "optimistic imagination." And I think his work as a novelist inevitably led him to this vision of regeneration and redemption. It was predicated on faith in *Falconer*; in *Oh What A Paradise It Seems* it is an act of will.

NOTES

1. John Cheever, *Oh What A Paradise It Seems* (New York: Knopf, 1982), p. 3 [*sic*: 100]. All subsequent references noted parenthetically in the text.

2. John Cheever, *The Wapshot Scandal* (New York: Harper & Row, 1973), p. 244.

3. John Cheever, *Bullet Park* (New York: Knopf, 1969), p. 245.

4. John Cheever, *The Wapshot Chronicle* (New York: Bantam, 1969), p. 310.

CEA Critic 45 (March & May 1983): 38-42.

The Letters
of John Cheever
1988

SELECTED REVIEWS

Grossness and Aspiration*

Ann Hulbert

John Cheever worked hard at burnishing the image of the artist as bourgeois. "Genius did not need to be rootless, disenfranchised, or alienated," he insisted. "A writer could have a family, a job, and even live in the suburbs." Cheever's "genteel, traditional" persona was, he observed with some satisfaction, "generally accepted." The critics who discussed his work routinely treated him as a polished *New Yorker* author, the portraitist of suburban pathos. The journalists who came to profile him went away and wrote about the charming fellow, flanked by Labrador retrievers, who scribbled and swam amid Westchester comfort.
  The revelation that Cheever's life was not exactly a traditional one introduced a seemingly discordant note into the portrait. The most dramatic discovery was that the family man had numerous homosexual affairs. He was also a serious alcoholic, not just an enthusiastic cocktail drinker. There were other, less shocking adjustments to the prevailing impression. The gentlemanly background that Cheever often suggested was his turned out to be untrue. His father had lost what money he had (from the shoe business) during the Depression, and his mother resorted to running a gift shop. Cheever was not born to the impressively leafy surroundings he and his family enjoyed in Westchester from the 1950s onward: they were at first renters of a modest house on someone else's grand estate, and only became owners of a house in Ossining relatively late in Cheever's mostly far from lucrative career.
  Instead of a *New Yorker* writer leading a *New Yorker*ish life, Cheever

suddenly was a mystery: an accomplished craftsman leading a messy, and secret, life. After numerous biographical efforts--first a memoir by his daughter, then a collection of interviews, recently a biography, and now a collection of letters edited by his son--the man still evades coherent portraiture. But that elusive life should be a spur to reconsider the work, which is itself more of a mystery than readers tend to acknowledge. The image of Cheever the fastidious miniaturist, skilled in technique but scanty on adventurous vision, is as misleading as the image of Cheever the country husband. Both his life and his art were more "rootless, disenfranchised, and alienated" than he wanted to believe and have others believe.

It was perhaps fair to label Cheever a *New Yorker* gem polisher early on in his career, as Weldon Kees did in THE NEW REPUBLIC in 1943. Cheever's first collection suffered, he complained, from the superficiality that marked the magazine as a whole, where well-wrought prose was

> expended on what is more often than not the essentially trivial; it would even seem that the magazine's character demands a patina of triviality spread over those themes and situations which its policy allows. Its writers must frequently entertain themselves by concentrating on the merely decorative qualities of a scene, a restriction brought on by an understandable hesitancy to explore their material deeply.

But the guilt by association lingered too long. Cheever didn't venture far from the circumscribed terrain--he turned from Upper East Side anxieties to a scrutiny of the suburbs--but he soon began treating it in unusual, unsettling ways. By the early 1960s, roughly half-way through his career, he had traveled too far from a traditional style for the magazine's taste. "His stories collided with the *New Yorker* idea of fiction," William Maxwell, Cheever's editor, told his daughter Susan Cheever. "Character as a confining force got less and less strong in his work. He extricated himself from ordinary realism." Only 11 of Cheever's stories appeared there after 1964. In his novels he turned to darker material and even more idiosyncratic narrative methods. Conventional, linear storytelling, Cheever explained in his notes for his second novel, *The Wapshot Scandal* (1964), was suited to "express[ing] a sense of consecutiveness," but he saw a world "distinguished principally by its curvatures."

Cheever distrusted conventional notions of character and plot not just in his fiction, but also in his life. In place of coherence of identity and consecutiveness of story, he believed in--and evidently experienced--a profound disparity between an inner and outer self. With his characters and himself, he was expert at elaborating the public persona, and reticent or elliptical about the psyche within. "He did not like to talk about human emotions. He did talk, often eloquently, about human behavior," was the way his daughter put it. "[My father] focused on the surface and texture of life, not on the emotions and motives underneath."

Acknowledging the anachronism of his approach, Cheever made it sound rather like old-fashioned discretion. He lamented "the prolonged psychoanalytic conversations many of my generation experienced, where too great an emphasis was put on our motives and too little on the thrust of life. To 'mine' was the term the doctors used. . . . As I see it, the continents of motive are far away and unknown, and their coast-lines are out of sight." But the effect of his often oblique treatment of his fictional characters--failing to round them out, omitting to trace actions to "realistic" causes or, for that matter, conse-quences--was far from old-fashioned. Instead, Cheever took his place in the company of modernists. At its best, his gaze conveyed a sense of alienation at the heart of ostensibly settled, conventional lives and a sense of disorientation about apparently well-tended places. At its less than best, it registered a disappointing flatness of scene and soul.

Cheever's obliqueness about himself was perhaps not so different, though it could at times appear simply stodgy--his evasions "reminding one once again that a WASP gentleman doesn't open his insides to casual inspection," as one frustrated interviewer, Wilfrid Sheed, wrote. In fact, his reticence seems to have been born not of confidence in his heritage, but of a feeling of spiritual homelessness he shared with his characters. Like them, he was disoriented by what he once summed up as "the conflict between grossness and aspiration" and often elaborated as a conflict between "confinement and freedom [which] is very much like Good and Evil and, to use a marvelous new metaphor we now have, it's like gravity and weightlessness."

In an interview toward the end of his life, Cheever claimed a jaunty equanimity about the predicament: "That one is in conflict with oneself--that one's erotic nature and one's social nature will everlastingly be at war with one another--is something I am happy to live with on terms as hearty and fleeting as laughter." But that attitude, which he took pains to convey--it was his social, outer nature speaking--was only part of the story, to judge by the biographical evidence that has now accumulated. The whole, darker story is still far from clear: his erotic, inner nature didn't speak much, except in journals that so far have surfaced in substantial pieces only in Susan Cheever's memoir. But within the hearty Cheever, there clearly was a character off balance, a center of gravity missing. Scott Donaldson's biography and Benjamin Cheever's edition of letters--both tedious undertakings for the most part--succeed, often unwittingly, in conveying that disequilibrium. . . .

Like his characters, Cheever managed to convey a kind of valiant dignity despite great disorder within. It's not only biographers he succeeded in keeping at a distance. His letters do not, as it turns out, raise the curtain on the private self. They're entertaining on behavior, but not much when it comes to emotions, and they don't offer any insights into his art or how he thought about it. In whimsical, self-mocking style, Cheever relayed the odd and mundane details of his days to plenty of friends, and he specialized in wittily turned anecdotes about others--often too witty to seem true. But there isn't a real confidant among the correspondents gathered here. There was a reason Cheever urged his correspondents to throw his amusing, mostly chatty mail away. "I seem to miss the Big Things, the Big Shapes; I miss them in this letter," Cheever wrote to [Malcolm] Cowley in the '50s. "I almost always miss them by a mile and since I can't get off the ground my only recourse seems, at times, to go underground."

Underground, where dignity was not so important, he was assailed by desires, and by needs. About his alcoholism and homosexuality, the secrets with which the collection culminates (and which were doubtless its selling point), the letters are somewhat more introspective. But even here his inner, erotic nature is usually less than articulate. The letters rarely illuminate the real depths of Cheever's passion and dependency, where his urges mingled with his imagination. Instead, he tended to be fatalistically flippant about his drinking: "Will John Cheever hit the bottle or the Librium or both? Stay tuned," he signs off in one letter.

There is a letter that stands out as an exception, a rare self-portrait that by ruthlessly describing behavior lays bare the emotion beneath. It's as though Cheever were writing about one of his characters, describing the body struggling with the soul in the ironic way he manages at his best, merciless and humane at the same time:

Allied to my melancholy is my struggle with Demon rum. There is a terrible sameness to the euphoria of alcohol and the euphoria of metaphor--the sense that the imagination is boundless--and I sometimes substitute or extend the one with the other. My performance is sometime comical. I leave my typewriter at quarter after ten and wander down stairs to the pantry where the bottles are. I do not touch the bottles. I do not even look at the bottles and I congratulate myself fatuously on my will-power. At eleven I make another trip to the pantry and congratulate myself once more but at twelve when the bull-horn blows I fly down the stairs and pour out a scoop. The same thing happens in the afternoon. I take long walks, split wood, paint trim and shovel snow and while I exclaim loudly over the beauty of the winter light there lurks at the back of my mind

> the image of a bottle of sour-mash. It seems to be, most of the
> time, an equal struggle.

This disparity between the will's great hopes and its weaknesses,
between noble aspirations and the needs that lurk below, is at the heart
of his fiction.

The same double vision is notably absent in the letters that touch on
homosexuality. His life was too divided to make the bridge. He wrote
frankly to his lovers and fudged with his friends, and thus, in a sense,
with himself. His work offers a far more eloquent vision of the
conflict--and the possible reconciliation--between his own desires and
his idea of the fecund natural order. "It's always been there, for all
the world to see," Cheever said of the homosexual strains in his
fiction, which should come as no surprise to Cheever readers. Just how
confused he felt about how to frame his predicament outside of his
writing becomes clear in a passing, poignant comment to a friend who
never knew of his inclinations: "Homosexuality seems to be a commonplace
in nature," he wrote to Tanya Litvinov, whom he had met on one of his
Russian trips, "and if this is so why should [a friend] seem,
spiritually, to be so ungainly. Procreative nature is surely not that
exacting and vindictive. I would like to live in a world in which there
are no homosexuals but I suppose Paradise is thronged with them."
It was a veiled self-portrait, full of ambivalence. "I have always
felt there is some ungainliness in my person, some ungainliness in my
spiritual person that I cannot master," Cheever once said of himself.
Yet he also claimed that his art established a kind of balance, that
"literature is basically an account of aspiration or hopefulness." A
grasping after grace almost always marks the close of his fiction--as it
does in a late story, "The World of Apples," about a famous old poet
determined to reject the connection "between brilliance and tragedy": he
wants to be sure that his life finishes on a note to match his work,
which is admired for its "pungency, diversity, color and nostalgia." To
his horror, the poet is suddenly overcome by a vision of human
grossness. By the end of the story, Cheever grants his character a
renewed conviction in "the inalienable dignity of light and air." It's
a lyrical conclusion, but not quite convincing--either for the poet or
for the author who clearly lurks not too far behind him. The power of
his best stories and the mystery of his life lie in the fragility of
that conviction.

*[Editor's note: also reviews Scott Donaldson's *John Cheever: A
Biography*]

The New Republic 200 (6 March 1989): 35-38.

Our Lives Are Not Well-Told Stories

Robert Kiely

"We are . . . quite comfortable, vaguely bored and frequently tight,"
John Cheever wrote to the novelist Josephine Herbst in 1947. With
disarming honesty and economy, Cheever, who died in 1982, thus sums up
his daily life and provides the reader of his letters with a natural
epigraph that captures the tone and atmosphere of "The Letters of John
Cheever." Cheever's voice in his correspondence, as in his fiction, was
established early and changed little over time. Even when writing to
very different correspondents--writers, editors, old friends, his
children--Cheever sustains a consistent persona--chipper, nonchalant,
salty, terse. He is conversational but not gabby, observant but not
given to prolonged description, occasionally philosophical in mood but
impatient of speculation and the nuances of meditation.

A writer's letters are worth publishing because of what they can tell
us not only about his private life, but about writing--as further
examples of the craft, as behind-the-scenes revelations about the
genesis of particular works, as a way into the author's mind, his
reading and working habits.

Cheever's prose does not call attention to itself. After the Spartan
reductions of Ernest Hemingway and the baroque extremes of William
Faulkner, many American writers dived for the center. No one could
accuse Cheever of being stylized or stylish, but then no one could
accuse him of being sloppy either. From the very beginning, he chose
not to be grandly literary. In 1935 he wrote to Elizabeth Ames, the
executive director of Yaddo, the artist colony in Saratoga Springs,
N.Y., that the members of his generation "have not been sustained or
constant or ordered. Our characters don't die in bed. The powerful
sense of passed and passing time that seems to be the one definable and
commendable quality of the novel is not our property. Our lives are not
long and well-told stories. But then these are not limitations. They
seem in the course of work to be exciting discoveries."

                         *   *   *

Making "exciting discoveries" and finding a supple, informal and, at
the same time, accurate language became Cheever's lifelong ambition. As
a young man he wrote, "I have no trade, no degree, no special training,"
which was his way of announcing to himself and the world that he was a
writer. He took several odd jobs and served in the Army during World
War II, but it is clear that the only thing Cheever ever wanted to do
was write. He had no patron and no easy entree into the world of
publishing; he simply sat down and wrote, and fired off short stories to
magazines until they began accepting them. His own story, like the

fiction he wrote, has a very American ring to it. He started out on his own with the single-mindedness of an entrepreneur whose business was words. Throughout his life--even after fame and considerable financial success--he thought of himself as unemployed and unemployable. His letters are full of confessions of wasted time and an inability to "work." Yet when he was writing, he had little to say about it. He often kept his longer projects secret until they were finished. There is almost no sense of work in progress in these letters. The most typical kind of Cheever comment is, "Sent off another story to The New Yorker today."

If Cheever read much, it is not especially evident in the letters. When he does comment on books, he does not come through as particularly astute or sensitive. While reading through George Eliot, he complains of "the pious and long-suffering women who appear in most English literature of the time. . . . The motivations behind the conduct of the heroines seems considerably simplified--a reflection of the position of women in the 19th century I suppose--and as I noticed in Hardy the Freudian categories that we take for granted are as far into the future as electricity."

One becomes accustomed in reading these letters to judgments, whether about books, people or places, that are impatient and dismissive. Cheever's responses were quick and impressionistic, not those of a philosopher or, despite "The Wapshot Chronicle," of a particularly good novelist, but of a born storyteller and distiller of moments. Even his brother's funeral in an 18th-century church in Hingham, Mass., provides the occasion not for a meditation on fraternal love or mortality, but for a hurried snapshot displayed with sardonic wit: "Yes, yes, Louisa Hatch did the flowers. The mourners all had sailboat tans, white hair and mannered wives. . . . The text was Tillich, Cummings and Eliot and not a tear was shed. It was splendid."

Cheever's literary self-image was in the American tradition of populism, the unprofessional tough guy, a New Englander, yes, but more Twain than Hawthorne and a lot more Hemingway than Howells. He saw himself as the antithesis of Henry James, whose complete works he began re-reading in the 1960's and then gave up on in disgust: "It was appalling. . . . I could not imagine why he had spent so much time rigging the scenery, arranging the flowers and brewing the tea. I could hear his heavy breathing behind the walls of all those so wonderfully beautiful rooms. . . . (My sort of novelist walks boldly onstage, belches, picks his teeth with a match stick and sneaks a drink of whisky from the bottle hidden in the fireplace.)"

As the winner of various honors and medals--including, eventually, the National Book Award and the Pulitzer Prize--Cheever could not completely sustain his unprofessional posture. Many of his correspondents were publishers, editors and fellow writers, including Malcolm Cowley, Philip

Roth and Saul Bellow, the last of whom he seemed especially to admire. His relations with John Updike, with whom he has most often been compared as a writer, were a muddle of affection, competitive dislike and obsessive sensitivity. Having written to various people about his intentions to snub, humiliate and embarrass Mr. Updike at writers' gatherings in Moscow or Washington, he later writes to Mr. Updike to tell a story on himself. A crank caller had telephoned Cheever in the middle of the night to report that Mr. Updike had been killed in an accident. Cheever's reaction was an outburst of grief: "'He was,' I sobbed, 'a colleague.'"

What stands out in Cheever's personal life, in the letters themselves and in the unobtrusive but intimate commentary by the author's older son, Benjamin, who edited this collection, is his domesticity, his alcoholism and his bisexuality. There were foreign travels--a year spent in Rome, cultural diplomacy in Russia, holidays in Majorca and Ireland--but Cheever felt best and worked best at home. His descriptions of exotic landscapes are trivial and unfocused, while Scarborough and Ossining, N.Y., and summer retreats in New Hampshire and Maine inhabit his prose like familiar nouns. Wife and children were not, for Cheever, a source of unmitigated bliss, but it becomes plain that despite fallings-out and periodic absences, he could not imagine himself without them.

The character that emerges from the letters is one that began by celebrating his freedom from his own parents and the narrow expectations of a New England social economy, but quickly established other kinds of dependency. Cheever not only married young, he began drinking young. The letters are full of martinis and hangovers, referred to in the early years of his career as the sophisticated accessories appropriate to a contributor to The New Yorker. As his son recalls, "Drinking had always been part of the family culture." Whatever Cheever's alcoholism may reveal about his genetic disposition or psychology, it has much to say about that "culture." For a certain class of Americans, social drinking was a sign of success, like having a maid and belonging to a golf club.

There is little question that despite a few lean early years, Cheever was throughout most of his life "quite comfortable." Drinking was one of his comforts. At least it seemed a comfort. One might even say that drink provided Cheever with his own brand of literary detachment and humor, a source of superiority over and insulation from the world that he watched but did not care soberly to inhabit. Good gin was the muse of the privileged insider who was intoxicated with the idea of the outside but could not bring himself to step into it. In his letters, he often writes as though he despises the world of private schools and private clubs and maids and gardeners, yet this is the world in which he chose to live. When he sent his daughter to the Brearley School in New

York, he was made uncomfortable by the elitism of the place: "I've never seen more well-groomed and weary women, more preternaturally shabby Harvard men, more imperious grandmothers with walking sticks, less jewelry, less perfume, and a more intense atmosphere of genteel comfort."

This is a perfect vignette, a verbal New Yorker cartoon, but, after reading the letters, one is prompted to ask where Cheever was standing at this and similar gatherings. He was there, of course, though alcohol often served to keep him from being altogether there.

Cheever's ambivalence about social class has a parallel in his ambivalence about his sexuality. Booze and a randy heterosexuality were part of his persona, even within his own family and close circle of friends. It is with a certain drama, then, that his son retraces his realization that his father not only had male "protégés" in his later years but that he had been engaged in sexual affairs with men throughout his adult life. Cheever's letters to his young male friends have the same breezy nonchalance that marks all the correspondence. In one he observes that far from being perverse, homosexual love "seems as natural and easy as passing a football on a fine October day." This is, of course, not the message he sent to his own sons or to friends, especially when he said things like, "I would like to live in a world in which there are no homosexuals." He could never quite break out of the class in which it was better to be a "drunk" than a "fairy."

"The Letters of John Cheever"--now colorful and witty, now crude and routine--has a hole at the center. Perhaps some day a cluster of unpublished documents will fill that hole. Meanwhile, one cannot help missing a sense of passion for anyone or anything. Friendships, flirtations, affections, loyalties, lusts abound, but do not seem to have been enough. Visits to Moscow and Lyndon Johnson's White House and the experience of bringing up children in the 60's yield nothing serious about the cold war, civil rights or Vietnam. Through it all Cheever seems to have sat at his typewriter in his comfortable suburban house wondering not where his next meal was coming from but when he would have his next drink: "The maid is cleaning the carpet. She stands directly between me and the gin bottle in the pantry but if I ask her to empty the ashtrays in the living room I will be able to sneak into the pantry. Will John Cheever hit the bottle or the Librium or both? Stay tuned."

That universe is too narrow, that drama too mean. It is to Cheever's credit that he knew it.

The New York Times Book Review, 18 December 1988, pp. 12-13.

The Journals
of John Cheever

1991

SELECTED REVIEWS

The Cheever Chronicle

Ted Solotaroff

A writer who maintained an intensely private profile through most of his career, John Cheever has been transformed in the decade since his death into a kind of Exhibit A for hidden damages in the trial of the literary life before the bar of publicity. In Cheever's case, the skeleton of his problems and misdeeds has flung open the closet door, with no little assistance from his family. His daughter, Susan, has expanded her cool exposure of him in *Home Before Dark* into an acerbic tour of three generations of "the family jungle" in *Treetops*, while his older son, Ben, has eagerly filled in the blanks of salacious information and innuendo in his edition of Cheever *père*'s letters. Now we have *The Journals* in which Cheever himself is thrust upon the stand to provide full disclosure of the dissolute life he bled into his fiction.

About five years ago, when the journals were put on the market, a colleague and I from Harper & Row visited Ms. Cheever to look through the twenty-eight thick notebooks that constituted the last remains of her father's vocation. Given the growing notoriety of his secret life, his relationships with such figures as Malcolm Cowley, Eleanor Clark and Robert Penn Warren, Saul Bellow, John Updike, Philip Roth et al., his frequent stays at Yaddo, his long association with *The New Yorker*, as well as his own significance as a fictional craftsman and social observer, I thought his journals might be very valuable, though hardly worth the cool $1 million the family was asking.

What this badly typed, misspelled and often unstrung prose contained was mainly a monotonous account of the Westchester round of visits and parties and a naked but less-than-riveting one of the at-home dissipations and marital distress of a mostly depressed and money-driven man. Now and then a trip into New York or elsewhere, a good morning's work at the desk or an afternoon of yard work or touch football or the opportunity to "have my way" with his wife would raise his spirits and eyes to the world and some interesting and moving passage would result. But these were few and far between: The image of Cheever that settled in my mind was of a writer who had just masturbated (he kept a record of that), doodling in the margins of his despair or boredom or occasional euphoria while waiting to hit the bottle. After a couple of hours my colleague and I shrugged and prepared to leave. I asked the noncommittal Ms. Cheever who would be editing the material and was told that she and her brother would. Well, I thought, a woman had to be pretty tough to survive the shambles of a home life I'd just glimpsed. Walking back to the office, I thought of Owl-Eyes' remark about the dead Gatsby, which Dorothy Parker repeated as she gazed at Fitzgerald's bier--"The poor son-of-a-bitch."

So I was very surprised and not a little crestfallen to find myself fascinated by the excerpts of the journals that began appearing in *The New Yorker* last year. By the magic of editing, the suppleness and precision of Cheever's style had been detected and restored, triumphing over his "forlornities," as he put it, and his moments of joy, perceptiveness, circumspection and courage had been brought out to light and lighten the reader's journey. Now we have a full version of the passages that the editor, Robert Gottlieb, has carved out--about 5 percent of the total wordage--and my admiration for his editing is even higher since he has assembled this coherent text. It presents Cheever's inner life in what might be called a final draft: concise, lucid, moving, and brimming with implications. Not since *Look Homeward, Angel* has there been an editorial feat like this.

There is one important aspect of Cheever's personality that I picked up in my reading of the original journals that has been omitted from the published ones, except for some discreet references to the "dream girls" he was wont to summon at dark times or to his "sore cod": His compulsive masturbation contributed a good deal to his sense of being unmanned and unstrung. Since I looked at only about one-fourth of the journals, I can't say how steadily and intensely it persisted. Nor do I raise it to darken his image further. The compulsion is common among writers, the last of the loves that dares not confess its name. As one novelist recently put it, "Writers jerk off more than anyone else because they're alone so much and it's such a convenient fix for all the anxiety and frustration." Its characterological and vocational significance, of course, varies from one of us to the next. In Cheever's case his intense shame points up the struggle between the adolescent and the adult in his nature that is often apparent in *The Journals* and that kept him standing on a dime, psychologically speaking, for much of his career.

The popular view of Cheever these days is that he was tormented by his bisexuality and that the drinking was his way of assuaging the frustration and anxiety it bred. There is little evidence for that in *The Journals*. His bisexuality often turns up in the more ramifying context of the standoff, embalmed in alcohol, between the boy and the man. The following passage is worth quoting at length. It comes at a point when Cheever was in his mid-50s, going through one of his brief periods of psychotherapy and yet another marital crisis:

> I drink heavily because I claim to be troubled. We talk about the shrink at the table, and I expect I talk with drunken rancor. We go to a third-rate movie and, leaving, I cry. "Why, when I asked if the bulk of our life had not been happy, did you not reply?" "My look," she said, "was my reply." . . . I have one drink, no more, and sit on the stone steps. I think myself youthful, even boyish in my misery. I stretch out on the stones, sobbing, until I realize that I am exactly in the position of a doormat.

There is much of Cheever's plight in this passage. His frequent mood swings from resentment to self-pity pivoted on his fast dependency on Mary Cheever, which was cemented by her emotional and sexual aloofness. His term for it was her *maldisposta*, which runs through *The Journals* like a leitmotif of plaintive resignation. This adhesiveness to her moods was actually a compound, one part of which came from his relationship to his mother, who was also an independent and baiting woman named Mary, and, in the words of Cheever biographer Scott Donaldson, "not given to shows of affection." Because of his father's alcoholism and improvidence she became the family breadwinner, running a gift shop that enabled the family to hang on to its shabby respectability by its fingertips, which were to remain sore and exigent in John's case--the Westchester squire even though he was renting the coach house of the estate. She resented doing the housework, which often fell to him, another early experience that he sometimes bleakly refers to in *The Journals* in the course of grumbling about his role in his marriage as a househusband. When Mary Cheever took up college teaching and began to go her own way, the two halves of Cheever's life, which he had labored to keep separate since leaving home for good at 18, ironically came together and shut.

The passage I quoted above continues:

> I sleep in my own bed, although this seems to be an indignity.

I wake at dawn, crying, "Give me the river, the river, the river," but the river that appears has willows and is winding and is not the river I want. It looks like a trout stream, so I cast with a fly and take a nice trout. A naked woman with global breasts lies on the grassy banks and I mount her. She is replaced by Adonis, and, while I fondle him briefly, it seems like an unsuitable pastime for a grown man. . . . I take a pill this morning, and it seems best for me to take full responsibility for everything that has gone wrong. There is no point in recounting to myself rebuffs, wounding quarrels, etc. One has come through much; one will come through this.

Readers of *Bullet Park* will remember the young and stricken Tony Nailles crying out in his sleep, "Give me the mountains, the mountains." The passage represents a characteristic move of Cheever's spirit from childishness to maturity and from despair to determination along the sure route of his feeling for the natural world and the tricky one of his hyperactive eroticism; his tendency to regard his gayness as immaturity, his straightness, when requited, to feeling like a man.

Donaldson raises the possibility that Cheever and his older brother Fred may have been lovers, following hints from Cheever himself. What is indisputable is their unusual intimacy. Unwanted and unloved by his feuding parents--"I have the characteristics of a bastard," he writes at one point--he improvised a succession of father figures, but his main resource was the care and support of Fred. After he left home they lived and traveled together, and it was Fred's money that enabled him to begin a second life as a writer. But there was a crucial lacuna in his adolescence when his brother was away at college that continued to haunt him and that he was condemned to refrequent psychologically. He writes of the "galling loneliness of my adolescence" that was still assailing him at the height of his career: "the sense of the voyeur, the lonely, lonely boy with no role in life but to peer in at the lighted windows of other people's contentment and vitality."

Cheever's adolescent fixations, his "damaged consecutiveness of growth," appear in various contexts. The day that his second son, Federico, was born--"I don't ever remember loving a child so much"-- and filled with paternal well-being, he finds himself gazing at some young men in an open car and "coveting their freedom." So with others--a male washing himself from a bucket or pulling off his swimming trunks or taping an oar would be glimpsed for a moment and envied for years. The furtiveness and daring of early sexuality also played a large role in his homoerotic excitements: His attraction to boys and men would often disappear as soon as any more normative social connection was made. Watching someone cunningly expose "his whatsit" in the men's room in Grand Central Station, he is tempted to throw himself into an "erotic

abyss" as well as to "make some claim for man's wayward and cat-
aclysmic nature." Then, true to form, he returns home, takes Federico
swimming and is restored to the manly virtues--"Decency, courage,
resoluteness."

His relationship to Federico also has an adolescent cast, as though he
were more like a big brother than his father. His son Ben received a
good deal of his anxiety and guilt in the name of discipline and
criticism; his daughter is typically either annoying or mystifying. But
as the younger son, like Cheever himself, Federico was a piece of
perfection: "How my whole love of life seems to gather around his form;
how he fills me with the finest ambitions," and so on for the next
fifteen years, the person, besides himself, for whom he remained married
and mostly at home. His terror of loneliness was such that he viewed
divorce as a life sentence to some sordid furnished room, and even in
the worst stretches of Mary's *maldisposta* and his own immobilizing
depressions, he could "count on touching my younger son at breakfast as
a kind of link, a means of staying alive."

Read in the light and shadow of *The Journals*, Cheever's fiction tends
to take on a certain unity until *Falconer*, when he kicked his alcoholism
and the adult in him finally triumphed over the anxious, lonely and
subversive boy. Through most of his career the conflict between them
informed his work as a kind of tense lyrical moralism in which the inner
waywardness and discontent beat against the bulwarks of propriety,
responsibility and well-being. In many of the stories his virtually
interchangeable protagonists carry the haut-bourgeois burden of
obligations which when put down results in a pratfall of panic or
humiliation--a child temporarily lost, an adulterer is shamed, a liar is
exposed, a failed businessman reduced to housebreaking is terrified--
before the beneficence of life, often borne in by the natural world,
intervenes and the moral order reasserts itself, "the obdurate truths
before which fear and horror are powerless," as he put it, whistling in
the dark of his melancholia. Cheever's typical, money-driven,
emotionally constrained story settles for a kind of wry headshake over
the vices and follies of human nature, the strain of its social
arrangements, the ironies of its providence. When he is bearing down
hard in his stories, the family man forsakes his burden, the family
pathology is exposed, the stupidity and cruelty of the ad agency or
other genteel business assert themselves. When the destructive element
Cheever knew so well is given its full say, one gets the surrealism of
the Fall through the amenities and assurances of polite society into the
hell that lurks in his best stories--such as "The Housebreaker of Shady
Hill," "Torchsong," "The Swimmer," "Goodbye, My Brother," "The Death of
Justine"--where the punishments of guilt are let loose, dreamlike, in
the daily world.

His own best critic, the Cheever of *The Journals* worried about his "confined talents." Alongside the magnitude of *The Naked and the Dead*, "my autumn roses and winter twilights [seem] not to be in the big league." Or there is Bellow's "big, wild, rowdy country . . . and here I am stuck with an old river in the twilight and the deterioration of the middle-aged businessman." As time went on he deplored his lack of development. Compared with writers who are much closer to him in milieu and temperament, such as Updike or William Trevor, his power of invention seems cruelly curtailed and his exploration of modern life hugs the shoreline of a small homogeneous community of the privileged and ungrateful, who re-enact his "wanton disappointments" ("Why should so many of us struggle to forget our happy lot?") as viewed by the old-line moralism of his New England upbringing ("Is it the ineradicable strain of guilt and vengefulness in man's nature?").

Seldom has such a sensitive and subtle observer, as evidenced by *The Journals*, written so patly so much of the time in his fiction. One could say that his money problems drove him to write for magazines that wanted mostly small and not-too-bitter doses of social and personal disturbance. But when Cheever gave himself more autonomy and scope, as in the two Wapshot novels, his imagination shows little questing power, his narrative ability weakens and one gets a series of incidents and ruminations connected by a mood. *The Wapshot Chronicle* (1957), though much praised in its time, reads today like an exercise in nostalgia, paper-thin in its social texture of the thirties and forties, a regression to the dawn of the modern novel in its technique. *The Wapshot Scandal* (1964) is also a mood novel, this time a vehicle for Cheever's mordant but mostly aesthetic response (shopping malls, subdivisions) to the rootlessness and barbarism of postwar America. Its structure is reminiscent of a man trying to hold together a bead necklace whose string has broken, and its bewildered characters portray the emptiness of the American scene mostly by lamely imitating it.

In *Bullet Park* (1969) Cheever returns to his base, and much of his earlier ease and conviction concerning the Westchester gentry are again in evidence in the first part, though hardly deepened. But structurally and dramatically the novel then becomes a botch: two novellas in different modes joined by an attempted murder that comes out of the blue. Written in a period when Cheever's alcoholism and marriage were hitting bottom, its principal interest and poignancy is in Cheever's objectification of his twin demons of drink and melancholia in the characterization of Hammer and of his guardian spirit of rectitude embodied in the troubled, addicted but upright Nailles. The absurd ending, in which Nailles rescues his son Tony with his chain saw (Cheever's favorite tool) from Hammer's mad clutches, only adds to the inadvertent pathos of the fable.

While giving much richer and more harrowing expression to his under-

standing of how "the force of life is contested," *The Journals* have some
of the same hemmed-in narrowness of Cheever's *oeuvre*. For years at a
stretch not much changes except the hour at which he begins drinking,
which grows earlier and earlier. "My best hours are from five to six,"
he writes at one point, by which he means A.M. However much personal
nuance there may be to a life at bay, it inexorably repeats itself and
one begins to long for the kind of material of literary and social
interest that the journals of an Evelyn Waugh or Edmund Wilson provide.
The fifties, the sixties, the seventies go by with seldom even a nod in
the direction of the public dramas of McCarthyism or the civil rights
movement, the cultural revolution, the Vietnam War, Watergate and so
forth. The hoax of Updike's death draws forth a splendid impromptu
eulogy that makes one regret Cheever's professional reticence otherwise.
He mentions an author he is reading such as Borges or Nabokov or
Hemingway, drops a tantalizing opinion and returns to his self-
reflections, his local and travel notes, his family's behavior, his
"chains formed by turf and house paint," his flings, his moral
temperature-taking. After a couple of hundred pages one begins trying
to keep track of the initials by which most of the people he encounters
are identified, simply to stay interested.

But there is a change of tone and a more objective focus in the last
years. His love life finally stabilizes in a guilt-free association
with the devoted M., he and Mary stop relating to each other like two
hostile porcupines, the wealth and fame he has been craving come in
abundance with *Falconer* (1977). The sobriety that enabled him finally
to sustain an entire novel; to venture deep into "the stupid pageantry
of judgment" that prison life represented and enacted--his personal
subject at last finding a new and challenging home; and to write with
the passion and empathy of self-detachment (except about Ezekiel
Farragut's wife) also finds its way into *The Journals*. His record of
his last year lived in the world of cancer is a remarkable document in
itself, climaxed by a stunning incident when he and other chemotherapy
patients are joined by a beautiful bald woman with "a look of absolute
victory on her face." Cheever's joy in her "air of having bested the
tumors and carnage of the disease" became in this reader's mind a
recognition of his victory over his own psychic tumors and carnage. Or
again, he talks to his dogs of the first snowfall of his life that he
will not be able to work or sport in, and their imperturbability prompts
him to ask himself, "Whatever made me think that I would live forever?"
This is Cheever giving up the narcissism of a lifetime, an outcropping
of the steady manliness he was always asking of himself and which, in
the last years, he made come true.

The Nation 253 (18 November 1991): 616-20.

Cheever on the Rocks*

John Updike

The Journals of John Cheever, published as a big and glossy book, make a rather different impression than the journal excerpts published in three two-part batches in *The New Yorker* over the last sixteen months. In the magazine's pages they seemed a gesture partly sentimental, a gesture that reminded its faithful readers of how luminously and jauntily Cheever's fiction had filled those same columns in bygone decades. The journals were a resurrection of sorts, and for all their fragmentariness and disconcerting emotional nakedness they shone with an ardor, an easy largeness, a swift precision that no living contributor to these columns could quite muster. No sullen minimalism or intellectual coquetry here. "How the man could write!" said we to ourselves, as the discrete paragraphs, chosen by unexplained editorial fiat, jogged from a marvellously evoked landscape to an enigmatic marital spat to a Saturday night suburban debauch to a Cheeveresque Sunday morning:

> To church: the second Sunday in Lent. From the bank president's wife behind me drifted the smell of camphor from her furs, and the stales of her breath, as she sang, "Glory be to the Father, and to the Son, and to the Holy Ghost." . . . The rector has a plain mind. If it has any charms, they are the charms of plainness. Through inheritance and cultivation he has reached an impermeable homeliness. His mind and his face are one. He spoke of the impressive historical documentation of Christ's birth, miracles, and death. The church is meant to evoke rural England. The summoning bells, the late-winter sunlight, the lancet windows, the hand-cut stone. But these are fragments of a real past. World without end, I murmur, shutting my eyes. Amen. But I seem to stand outside the realm of God's mercy.

The Cheever prose was back, and thrilling; and thrilling, too, was the scandalous frankness of his revelations, confided in many disconsolate moods to his journal, of severe marital discontent, drastic alcoholism, and repressed homosexuality. In a book of nearly 400 pages, however, the disjointedness, presented in such bulk and without a single clarifying note, begins to frazzle the brain, and the circularity of Cheever's emotions to depress the spirit. Disjointedness is to be expected in a magazine, and conclusiveness is not to be expected in *The New Yorker*, but in a book we begin to ask where we are and where we are going.

An editorial decision has been made to present the cream of the jour-

nals--one-twentieth of their bulk, we are told in an afterword by the
editor, Robert Gottlieb--as an extended prose poem, as unannotated
emanations from deep within the quiet desperation of a modern American
male.   Perhaps this was the only editorial decision that could have been
made, given the determination to expose the journals at all, less than
ten years after Cheever's death.   Many living are mentioned, often
indecorously, and must be protected.   The dates and locales of these
notations, even if knowable, would not add much, though it *is* confusing
to have a writer suddenly in Russia or Iowa or Boston with no
explanation of how he got there.   Lovers come and go so mysteriously in
these notations that we are not always certain of even their sex.   Is
the "M." of page 86, dining with Cheever at the Century Club in 1957,
the same "M." as on page 346, sharing with Cheever "a motel room of
unusual squalor" in 1978?   Certain books and stories can be glimpsed as
they go by, in the process of creation, but literary matters are among
the least of Cheever's problems, as the journals have it.   We are at
sea, amid waves of alcohol, gloom, domestic tension, and radiance from
the natural world.

A journal, even when cut to 5 percent of its bulk, reflects real time,
where we can experience how sluggishly our human adventure unravels and
how unprone people are to change.   In a novel, Cheever's alcoholism
would have been introduced, dramatized in a scene or two, and brought to
a crisis in which either it or he would have been vanquished.   In these
journals, the decades of heavy drinking, of hangovers and self-rebukes
and increasingly ominous physical and mental symptoms, just drag on. His
life is measured out in belts, or "scoops."   On a page from 1968, he
describes his preparations for an amorous tryst:

> Two scoops for the train, a scoop at the Biltmore, a scoop
> upstairs, one down--five as well as a bottle of wine with lunch
> and brandy afterward. We rip off our clothes and spend three or
> four lovely hours together moving from the sofa to the floor and
> back to the sofa again. I don't throw a proper hump, which
> disconcerts no one.

--or would have surprised, he might have added, no medical expert.   It
was a wonder he could ambulate, let alone copulate.   On the next page,
he makes a stab at bringing his drinking and his writing into meaningful
relation:

> I must convince myself that writing is not, for a man of my
> disposition, a self-destructive vocation. I hope and think it
> is not, but I am not genuinely sure. It has given me money and
> renown, but I suspect that it may have something to do with my
> drinking habits. The excitement of alcohol and the excitement

of fantasy are very similar.

In this same year he rereads two old journals and comments:

> High spirits and weather reports recede into the background, and what emerges are two astonishing contests, one with alcohol and one with my wife. With alcohol, I record my failures, but the number of mornings (over the last ten years) when I've sneaked drinks in the pantry is appalling.

Any connection between his besottedness and his wife's physical and emotional rejections is dimly descried: "Mary is depressed, although my addiction to gin may have something to do with her low spirits." At one moment, "Mary talks as if she had a cold, and when I ask if she has she says she's breathing through her mouth because I smell so horrible." He goes on, rather primly, "I seem to suffer from that degree of sensibility that crushes a man's sense of humor." Again and again in these lachrymose journals, he is innocently wounded:

> In the afternoon mail there is a letter saying that two pieces have been bought. I am jubilant, but when I speak the good tidings to Mary she asks, oh, so thinly, "I don't suppose they bothered to enclose any checks?" I think this is piss, plain piss, and I shout, "What in hell do you expect? In three weeks I made five thousand, revise a novel, and do the housework, the cooking, and the gardening, and when it all turns out successfully you say, 'I don't suppose they bothered to include any checks.'" Her voice is more in the treble than ever when she says, "I never seem able to say the right thing, do I?"

Granted, Mary Cheever, with a fine mind of her own and a formidable father, may not have been easy to impress, but what she had to cope with in the post-cocktail hour seems safely out of the diarist's line of vision. "She hates me much of the time, but naturally I can't understand why anyone should hate me." Her adverse moods baffle him: "I don't understand these sea changes, although I have been studying them for twenty-five years."

His contest with alcohol similarly remains a standoff. In 1959 he observes, "Year after year I read in here that I am drinking too much, and there can be no doubt of the fact that this is progressive. I waste no more days. I suffer deeper pangs of guilt. I wake up at three in the morning with the feelings of a temperance worker." In 1971, still drinking, he notes, "The situation is, among other things, repetitious."

Nor does he find much change in his work. As early as 1952 he writes:

> As a part of moving I have had to go through some old
> manuscripts and I have been disheartened to see that my style,
> fifteen years ago, was competent and clear and that the
> improvements on it are superficial. I fail to see any signs of
> maturity, of increased penetration; I fail to see any deepening
> of my grasp. I was always in love. I was always happy to scythe
> a field and swim in a cold lake and put on clean clothes.

Nearly twenty years later, with some marvelous fiction to his credit, he
tells his journal, "I've never much liked my work." He thought enough
of an adverse remark of his daughter's to record it: "During dinner,
Susie says, 'You have two strings to play. One is the history of the
family, the other is your childlike sense of wonder. Both of them are
broken.' We quarrel. She cries. I feel sick."

In 1970, after the disappointing reception of the rather punchy *Bullet
Park*, an entry begins with the unforgettable cry, "Whatever happened to
Johnny Cheever? Did he leave his typewriter out in the rain?" His
perversely contented stuckness, as he rotates in a mire of drink and
marital discontent, varied by rather forced spurts of child-cherishing
and nature-worship but gradually deepening into phobia, artistic
impasse, and vicious behavior, should be overwhelming, and it does tax
our patience. But in fact even at his lowest ebb Cheever can write like
an angel and startle us with offhand flashes of unblinkered acumen.

And there is, beneath the apparently futile churning of these jottings
to himself, a story, which we know not from any editorial guidance in
reading the journal excerpts but from the biographies by Susan Cheever
and Scott Donaldson and his letters as edited by his son Ben. Cheever
did, in the spring of 1975, stop drinking. The novel he then wrote,
Falconer, and the handsome volume of *Collected Stories* that he allowed
Gottlieb to assemble and to publish, won him the greatest financial and
critical success of his life. At the same time, he came out of the
closet, and the (mostly) suppressed homosexual urges so darkly alluded
to in the earlier journals blossomed into lewd romps, mostly with "M.,"
recorded as frankly and joyfully as a psychotherapist could wish: "When
we met here, not long ago, we sped into the nearest bedroom, unbuckled
each other's trousers, groped for our cocks in each other's underwear,
and drank each other's spit. I came twice, once down his throat, and I
think this is the best orgasm I have had in a year."

For those of us who faithfully followed Cheever's fiction, an oblique
announcement of this breakthrough appeared in a short story, "The
Leaves, the Lion-Fish, and the Bear," published in the November 1974
issue of *Esquire* but never collected in hardcover. Its string of feebly
connected episodes included the adventure of two married men, Larry
Estabrook and Roland Stark, who are caught overnight in a motel near
Denver by a snowstorm; they drink, get down to their underwear, do away

with the underwear, make love, and feel great about it next morning. The writer strives mightily to bring gay sex within the bounds of his accustomed moral universe:

> The ungainliness of two grown, drunken, naked men in one another's arms was manifest, but Estabrook felt that he looked onto some revelation of how lonely and unnatural man is and how bitter, deep, and well concealed in his disappointments.
>
> Estabrook knew he had done that which he should not have done, but he felt no remorse--felt instead a kind of joy seeing this much of himself and another. . . . When he returned home at the end of the week, his wife looked as lovely as ever--lovelier--and lovely were the landscapes he beheld.

On the long-stormy marital front, a relative peace set in: the alcoholic cure entailed his return to his house in Ossining, where Mary ministered to Cheever as the infirmities of old age descended upon his hard-used body and where she resigned herself not only to awareness of her husband's bisexuality but the frequent attendance of his chief homosexual lover, the loyal "M."--identified as Max Zimmer in Scott Donaldson's biography. Cheever died at home, surrounded by his family, a few weeks after having been "brought to climax" in his bathroom by this lover, while carpenters were building a studio for Mary: "Desperately ill as he was, Cheever got out of bed and into the bathroom, where, protected from the possible view of the carpenters, he was brought to climax." "Adiós," John said when Max left. "Adiós."

This sunset saga, in which selfishness and selflessness, pathos and pride inscrutably mingle, exists in the journals, as edited, in only the vaguest way. The break with drink, which involved an impulsive flight from his teaching post at Boston University that he could not afterward remember, is signaled by the abrupt entry, "On Valium for two days running, and I do feel very peculiar, but it's better, God knows, than sauce." The entry before that on the page, presumably composed as Cheever was hitting bottom, is yet one of the most evocative and complex, with its backward and forward motions:

> And I think of L. in the morning, the lovely unfreshness of her skin. It was the light scent of a young woman who has made love and slept through one more night of her life . . . but in our nearness I am keenly aware of the totality of our alienation. I really know nothing about her. We have told each other the stories of our lives--meals, summer vacations, lovers, trips, clothing, and yet if she stood at a crossroads I would have no idea of the way she would take. It is in loving her that I feel mostly our strangeness.

After he sobers up, a certain acerbity appears in his prose: "Reading Henry Adams on the Civil War. I find him distastefully enigmatic. I find him highly unsympathetic, in spite of the fact that we breathed the same air." He takes the train up the Hudson to Saratoga and Yaddo, nostalgically thinks back to how he would sneak into the toilet with his flask and says, "Alcohol at least gave me the illusion of being grounded." The alcohol, the suppressed homosexuality, the unharmonious wife perhaps made up the "knot" in himself, "some hardshell and insoluble element" that has "functioned creatively, has made of my life a web of tensions." A true artist, he feared above the ruin of his life the loss of his creativity.

And, for whatever reason, the best and indispensable John Cheever was written when all his conflicts were unresolved, in those parched morning hours stolen from the day's inebriation and the night's fretful longings. His last superb stories were "The Ocean" and "The Swimmer" from the early '60s; his best novel was the first, *The Wapshot Chronicle* of 1953 [*sic*: 1957]. *Falconer*, although a brave leap into themes hitherto sublimated--chemical addiction, homosexual love, fratricide, captivity--fails to lift its burden of bizarrerie; I myself prefer to it his last, slim fable, *Oh What a Paradise It Seems*, and I was struck, reading these journals, by how deeply Cheever, like his elderly hero in that tale, Lemuel Sears, cherished ice skating. Ice skating was his exercise, his Wordsworthian hike, his rendezvous with sky and water, his connection with elemental purity and the awesome depths above and below, while he clicked and glided along, in smooth quick strokes (I imagine) like those of his prose.

Saul Bellow is the contemporary writer he mentions most often, with affection ("He is my brother") and admiration: "Read Saul. The wonderfully controlled chop of his sentences. I read him lightly, because I don't want to get his cadence mixed up with mine." As soon confuse traffic noise with a babbling brook; Cheever's sentences dash and purl with a headlong opalescence:

> Snow lies under the apple trees. We picked very few of the apples, enough for jelly, and now the remaining fruit, withered and golden, lies on the white snow. It seems to be what I expected to see, what I had hoped for, what I remembered. Sanding the driveway with my son, I see, from the top of the hill, the color of the sky and what a paradise it seems to be this morning--the sky sapphire, a show of clouds, the sense of the world in these, its shortest days, as cornered.

His metaphors spring startlingly from a settled, instinctive reading of natural signals. Of a face: "A broad, Irish face, florid with drink. The large teeth, colored unevenly like maize. Long, dark lashes, and

what must have been fine blue eyes, all their persuasiveness lost in
rheum." Of a room: "His office is furnished with those modest antiques
you find in small hotels. His desk, or some part of it, may have come
into the world as a spinet." A sky: "It is one of those days when the
massiveness of the clouds, travelling in what appear to be a northerly
direction, gives one the feeling of a military evacuation, a hastening,
a change in campaign maneuvers." A night: "The cold air makes the dog
seem to bark into a barrel. Bright stars, house lights, rubbish fires."

   One wishes to quote on and on, erecting a glowing verbal shield
against the dismaying personal revelations of these journals. Rarely
has a gifted and creative life seemed sadder. His loneliness is
irreducible, and lifelong:

> And walking back from the river I remember the galling
> loneliness of my adolescence, from which I do not seem to have
> completely escaped. It is the sense of the voyeur, the lonely,
> lonely boy with no role in life but to peer in at the lighted
> windows of other people's contentment and vitality. It seems
> comical--farcical--that, having been treated so generously, I
> should be stuck with this image of a kid in the rain walking
> along the road shoulders of East Milton.

   He was a New Englander, and kept a Puritan ruthlessness toward himself. His journals, though used partly as workbooks for his fiction and
partly as therapy ("Rows and misunderstandings, and I put then down with
the hope of clearing my head"), primarily record his spiritual
transactions with that God whose Episcopalian manifestation, though
faithfully visited on Sunday mornings, remained discreetly hidden behind
the minister's manner and the bank president's wife's camphorous furs.
Cheever's God was a jealous God, manifest in frequently used words like
"obscene" and "unspeakable crime" and the "venereal dusk" that enwraps
one of the writer's last fictional alter egos, the old poet Asa Bascomb
in "The World of Apples." Though of a religious disposition, Cheever
had no theology in which to frame and shelter his frailty; he had only
inflamed, otherworldly sensations of debasement and exaltation. Perry
Miller, in his anthology *The American Puritans*, tells us, "Almost every
Puritan kept a diary, not so much because he was infatuated with himself
but because he needed a strict account of God's dealings with him.
. . . If he himself could not get the benefit of the final reckoning,
then his children could."

   One hopes that Cheever's three children have indeed benefitted. Like
Noah's, they have gazed upon their father naked. Ben, the older son,
has already edited, with helpful explanatory notes, a book of his
father's letters, and in a brief and engagingly honest introduction to

the *Journals* describes how, while alive, Cheever offered him a volume of the journals to read:

> I told him I liked it.
> He said he thought that the journals could not be published until after his death.
> I agreed.
> Then he said that their publication might be difficult for the rest of the family.
> I said that I thought that we could take it.

Though Ben expresses surprise at how little he appears in the journals, he and his younger brother figure benignly, as innocents who distract Cheever from his dreadful *cafarde*. Their older sibling Susan appears with a touch of menace, and their mother takes a brutal drubbing, as a romanticized love object who fails to fill her husband's bottomless needs:

> Mary says that my presence is repressive; she cannot express herself, she cannot speak the truth. I ask her what it is that she wants to say and she says, "Nothing," but what appears in some back recess of my mind is the fear that she will accuse me of being queer . . . I feel that she does not love me, that she does not even imagine a time when she might.

Ben's introduction compliments Mary on her courage in letting these journals be published; some might construe it as a long-forbearing wife's revenge.

To speak personally, this old acquaintance and longtime admirer of Cheever's had to battle, while reading these *Journals*, with the impulse to close his eyes. They tell me more about Cheever's lusts and failures and self-humiliations and crushing sense of shame and despond than I can easily reconcile with my memories of the sprightly, debonair, gracious man, often seen on the arm of his pretty, witty wife. His confessions posthumously administer a Christian lesson in the dark gulf between outward appearance and inward condition; they present, with an almost unbearable fullness, a post-Adamic man, an unreconciled bundle of cravings and complaints, whose consolations--the glory of the sky, the company of his young sons--have the ring of hollow cheer in the vastness of his dissatisfaction. Comparatively, the journals of Kierkegaard and Emerson are complacent and generalizing. And Cheever's journals make much of his fiction seem timid, arch, and falsely buoyant. (Not that the journals don't hold fiction; as Cheever's letter showed, he was an inveterate embroiderer, who would not only bend but break the truth to round out a story.)

Alfred Kazin shrewdly wrote (in *Bright Book of Life*), "My deepest feeling about Cheever is that his marvelous brightness is an effort to cheer himself up." In the light of the journals, we can be grateful for the effort. Passages here, in their unstructured emotion, reach higher and certainly descend lower than anything in the fiction, but it is the repute of his fiction that will determine if, sometime in the next century, a scholarly edition of the complete journals, as has been done for Hawthorne's notebooks, will seem warranted. It would be nice to have names and locations filled in, and a soothing undercurrent of footnotes. A leavening of duller, more dutiful daily entries might relieve the superheated, rather hellish impression this selection makes. For now, we have a literary event, a spectacular splash of bile and melancholy, clean style and magical impressionability.

[Editor's note: this review was first published as "The Waspshot Chronicle," but is reprinted here under its original title, at Mr. Updike's request.]

The New Republic 205 (2 December 1991): 36-39.

LATER CRITICISM

Tales from the Crypt(o-autobiography): A User's Guide to John Cheever's *Journals*

Robert A. Morace

> *For why or? Why in another dark or in the same? And whose voice asking this? Who asks, Whose voice asking this? And answers, His soever who devises it all. In the same dark as his creature or in another. For company. Who asks in the end, Who asks? And in the end answers as above? And adds long after to himself, Unless another still. Nowhere to be found. Nowhere to be sought. The unthinkable last of all. Unnamable. Last person. I. Quick leave him.*
>
> --Samuel Beckett, *Company* (1980)

Was he thinking of his next book, or merely expressing his innermost feelings when he wrote in his notebook: I still love Paula Hargenau and I do not love Marie-Jean Filebra. How soon after meeting Marie-Jean had he made the entry in his notebook? One month? Two? Three?

--Walter Abish, *How German Is It* (1980)

It is not a cryptogram. Samsa is not merely Kafka, and nothing else. The Metamorphosis *is not a confession, although it is--in a certain sense--an indiscretion.*

--*Conversations with Kafka*, ed. Gustav Janouch (1969)

Until the publication of *Falconer* in 1977, John Cheever remained, partly by design and partly by default, a writer who attracted surprisingly little biographical interest and no significant challenges to the version of himself as author that he was willing, in however reluctant and limited a fashion, to promote. *Falconer*--its writing and reception--changed all that. Announced in a *Newsweek* cover story as "Cheever's triumph," it brought him high praise, literary honors, economic stability, and a sufficient degree of emotional security to become a less reticent and more public literary figure. *Falconer* thus set the stage for the biographical revelations that have virtually overtaken Cheever studies since his death in 1982: two memoirs by his daughter, a selection of Cheever's correspondence edited by his elder son, a barely disguised autobiographical novel by that same son in which Cheever as father and famous writer "figures" conspicuously, a selection of the author's voluminous journals edited by Robert Gottlieb and introduced by a very busy Ben Cheever, a selection of previously published interviews edited by Scott Donaldson, an extensively researched, well written biography, also by Donaldson, along with a host of lesser items ranging from an article on/interview with Mary and Susan Cheever entitled "Life with the King of Hell" to coverage of Mary Cheever's legal battle with a small Chicago publisher over an edition of previously uncollected stories. That *Falconer* should in a sense have caused this flurry of interest in "Cheever the Man" is understandable but also ironic in that *Falconer* is neither more nor less autobiographically revealing than many of Cheever's other works, only more sensational and slightly less decorous.

Decorum would of course continue to characterize Cheever and his published writing for the years until his death just as it had his earlier self and style. Decorum also characterized his views on the art of fiction as "pontificated" (Donaldson's word), upon request, in a small

repertoire of set pieces not unlike the spiritual cheerleading which the
Swami Rutuola practices in *Bullet Park*. Fiction, Cheever liked to say,
is an "acute means of communication," "an expression of one's deepest
intuitions about life," a "revelation," an "illumination," a way to make
one's life useful and coherent, and the history of man's struggle to be
illustrious (*Conversations* 69, 45, 373, 119). He voiced these views,
often in the very same words, over and over but none quite so frequently
or adamantly as his claim that fiction was not crypto-autobiography. "I
would not like to be the kind of writer through whose work one sees the
leakage of some noisome semisecret," Cheever wrote in (confided to?) his
journal in 1956 (J 61). Why the vast majority of reviewers and critics
chose not to see any evidence of this "leakage" but to attend instead to
those features of the fiction which better and more readily satisfied
Cheever's requirements as set forth in the pontifications and why so
much attention is now being paid to this same leakage are questions well
worth asking. But the issue I wish to raise here, while related,
concerns the ways in which the journals have been used to reveal the
"real" John Cheever.

Far from clarifying the relation between Cheever's life and his
published fiction, much of what has passed itself off either explicitly
or implicitly as biographical revelation has only served to obscure that
relation, paradoxically, by simplifying it, by refusing to accept and
extend the position Donaldson adopted in writing his Cheever biography:
that the "lines of interconnection between Cheever's life and his
fiction . . . [are] rarely straight" ("State" 532). Such a seemingly
commonsensical approach strengthens his *John Cheever*, offering a
biographical background against which the fiction can now be read
without reducing it to simple biographical statement. However,
Donaldson was permitted only very limited access to Cheever's journals
("State" 531; *John Cheever* 361, 365-401), and it is the journals that
are in danger of becoming a virtual synonym for Cheever's "actual" and
"innermost" life. In order to begin the work of recognizing and
reversing the ill effects of this simplifying process, we need to
understand that much of the discussion of Cheever's life has in fact
been a discussion of a life textualized in journals, letters, and, as
some would have it, stories and novels: texts that have been first de-
and then re-contextualized.

Consider the revealing manner in which the journals were first presented for public consumption (and use) in Susan Cheever's *Home Before
Dark*. Like the *Journals* (1991), *Home Before Dark* (1984) implies
intimacy, not mediation; it is, after all, "A Biographical Memoir of
John Cheever by His Daughter." Instead of making us wary, the
acknowledgement of authorship--"by His Daughter"--makes us feel that the
account is worthy of our trust: a physically as well as emotionally
proximate account. Yet in large part *Home Before Dark* is not the inti-

mate and therefore privileged look at Cheever that it purports to be; rather it is largely a mosaic of quotations and paraphrases culled from already published sources (stories, novels, and interviews) and others not then published even in part (the correspondence and especially the journals). The former source material suggests that *Home Before Dark* depends far more on what we might loosely call the public record than on a daughter's intimate knowledge of her father's life. The latter suggests that Susan Cheever's claim to such knowledge depends largely on access, not so much to her father's hidden person, as to his hidden texts. In approaching these various sources, and through them her father's secret life, she assumes that a relation between that life and the fiction does exist, that the relation is mysterious,[1] "unfathomable," "profound and complicated beyond explanation," and of course linked to her father's "tremendous talent" (*Treetops* 168, 167, 164). And she further, and still plausibly, assumes that all her father's stories--those offered as fiction and those offered as fact--possess "an inherent truth, outside of the facts" (*Home* 31). Her claim, of the irrelevancy of factual accuracy, is valid, until we realize that it is being used to transform passages from the published stories (and, as we shall soon see, the journals) into direct autobiographical disclosures. Even as she does this, Susan Cheever castigates others for doing the same. On the one hand, she writes that "the Vanderlip family accused him of writing about Beechwood in his first novel, *The Wapshot Chronicle*. It was an absurd charge; he had certainly borrowed details and anecdotes, but the book was more his own story than anything else he had written" (*Home* 98). And on the other, she arrogates to herself the very feelings (of being betrayed, exposed, wounded) that she denies to the Vanderlips.

R.G. Collins and Scott Donaldson have both commented on the chapter in *Home Before Dark* in which Susan Cheever quite arbitrarily links an event from 1951--while walking across the Queensboro Bridge with her father her hat blew off her head and into the East River below--with a short story Cheever wrote and published ten years later, "The Angel of the Bridge." The linkage, Collins and Donaldson rightly believe, tells us little about Cheever and still less about the story (and, I would add, least of all about any "leakage" of semisecrets). It does however tell us a great deal about Susan Cheever, albeit indirectly. Her similarly lengthy discussion of another Cheever story, "The Hartleys," in *Treetops*, reveals even more of the author (Susan, not John Cheever) and her approach. She begins by recounting her reading of the story for the first time in the recently published collection, *The Enormous Radio* (1953). She then goes on to discuss the skiing trip to Vermont that the Cheevers took with two other families "the previous year" and a minor incident that occurred at that time: Ginger Reiman got her sweater caught in the tow rope and was dragged a few feet before being able to free herself. Turning to the story, Susan Cheever then notes "the eerie parallels between myself and this little girl in a book" who is dragged to her death.

> Years later, I got up the nerve to ask my father why he had written a story like that. He said that he had been expressing his anxieties about me. He told me that Ginger Reiman's accident had triggered his fears about my getting hurt while skiing. I didn't believe him. I don't think he was expressing anxieties about me; I don't think he was expressing a secret wish to see me dead, either. "The Hartleys" is fiction, a story, and I don't think my father thought about anything while he was writing it except what would make a good story, if he thought about anything at all.
>   I certainly wasn't the only member of our family or of our community to have their personal details pop up in my father's stories. Of course, the characters and events in the stories are not real, they are invented--yet scenes and details in my father's work were often completely familiar to anyone . . . who knew him. (*Treetops* 153-54)

Four paragraphs later she makes clear that this "anyone" does not include the neighbor who thought that Cash Bentley, in "O Youth and Beauty!", was based on Cheever and not, as Susan Cheever knew, on another neighbor, Dudley Schoales. "Not only did readers assume that fiction was fact, they usually even got that wrong" (*Treetops* 155). The point I wish to make here is not--or at least not only--that Susan Cheever's own grasp of the facts is less than sure: if the skiing trip on which "The Hartleys" was based took place the year before *The Enormous Radio* was published, then it also took place three years after the story originally appeared in the *New Yorker*. Nor is my point that Susan Cheever, here and elsewhere in her two biographical memoirs, fails, as Collins contends, "to account for the marvellous transforming process" by which Cheever turned life into art, and thus ends up "suggesting that the fiction is scarcely fiction at all," for Collins' high-minded view of Cheever's art proves worrisome in its own way, too rigorously and unsystematically distinguishing the very categories Susan Cheever effectively collapses. Rather, my point concerns the dismaying literal-mindedness evident throughout *Home Before Dark* and *Treetops* and implicit in the publication and reception of Cheever's *Letters* and *Journals*, a kind of annotative mentality which manifests itself most obviously in Susan Cheever's explanation of the well-known image at the end of "The Country Husband," "It is a night where kings in golden suits ride elephants over the mountains." The image, she writes, "was in fact based on a description of Hannibal, the Carthaginian general who invaded

Rome by bringing elephants over the Alps with his troops. He wore golden armor" (*Home* 126). Ludicrous as this explanation may be, it is nonetheless representative in its reductiveness of the use to which "facts" are being put. These "facts," by no means limited to the "scenes and details" mentioned above, include passages from the stories and novels deemed to be biographically relevant and more especially and more insidiously from the journals.[2] All are made to speak for Cheever without regard for the multiplicity of variously refracted voices through which he chose to speak and, even more, has come to be heard.

The *Journals* do not necessarily or especially illuminate the essential John Cheever; that is to say, they do not necessarily or especially offer a series of privileged glimpses into a heart of darkness in (intertextual) conflict with itself. Rather, the *Journals* create a textual labyrinth that the reader must negotiate by adopting a variety of interpretive strategies in order to avoid the pitfall of reducing the multiplicity and indeed at times indeterminacy of the *Journals* to the level of unified univocal discourse. Few of the entries possess the (contextualized) epistemological assurance of, for example, "Nov. 27th. Snowing" or "In *Esquire*, a piece on the New Homosexuality" (J 20, 257). Similar in texture but nonetheless occupying a quite different epistemological plane are the drafts of a letter about *Falconer*,[3] the preface for *The Stories of John Cheever*, and notes for his National Medal acceptance speech. Farther along the spectrum of *Journal* entries we find those in which Cheever acknowledges fantasizing that he is writing an advertisement for *The New York Review of Books*, making out with Mia Farrow in Leningrad, seeing his face on a postage stamp, and so forth. And finally there are the drafts of published stories and novels recognizable by anyone familiar with Cheever's major fiction. The vast majority of entries cannot be classified quite so readily, however. Passages in which Cheever appears to transcribe directly conversations heard in coffee shops, on trains, and at hospitals and AA meetings would seem to belong to the more or less "factual" end of the typological continuum just sketched. That these passages bear a striking stylistic and thematic similarity suggests, however, (1) that the original conversations have been revised (perhaps unconsciously) in the very act of transcription and/or (2) that taken together they imply a certain habit of mind in the manner Cheever registered this kind of exchange, a manner which already resembles the similarly heard or overheard monologues and conversations found in Cheever's stories and novels.[4]

Other passages from the *Journals* even more clearly suggest that the linkage--or "leakage"--between Cheever's life and his fiction is not nearly as linear and causal as some would like to believe. It makes little if any difference whether we approach this causal relation reductively, as Susan Cheever does, or transformationally, as R.G. Collins does, for both approaches figuratively situate particular texts

as links in a chain rather than, as Barthes, Eco, and Foucault have
suggested in their own ways and in different (but related) contexts, as
nodes in a network, existing outside simple temporal configurations. Put
in its simplest form, Cheever recycled material continuously. A
description of snow falling on the Vanderlip estate reappears in the
opening chapter of *The Wapshot Scandal*; a passage originally written for
Bullet Park surfaces in *Falconer* where it seems perfectly natural and
entirely unmediated. These are however fairly straightforward examples
of material which appears and then, recontextualized, reappears. But
the possibility of recycling material sometimes occurred to Cheever as
he wrote. "So my wife seems more depressed this morning than she has
seemed since my first epileptic seizure. What a sentence with which to
begin a story!" (J 383). Good, certainly, but not as good as "Absolute
candor does not suit me, but I will come as close as possible in
describing this chain of events" involving his first meeting with Max
Zimmer (J 346). In style and substance the account seems straight out
of a Cheever fiction, specifically *Falconer*, published one year
earlier.[5]   In a similar vein, the succession of domestic mishaps
suffered by Gertrude Lockhart and resulting in her suicide in *The
Wapshot Scandal* is also found in what we may be so bold as to call a
clearly autobiographical journal entry written in 1975, more than a
decade later (J 295).

To say that Cheever made a career of transforming autobiographical
experiences into crypto-autobiographical fictions is therefore to take
too limited a view, for he appears to have carried out the
transformation process in the very act of experiencing/perceiving
itself.[6]   Instead of following the experience, the "fiction," as a
perceptual mode, may be said to precede the cause of which it is
commonly judged the result. Consider two 1966 entries. The first (J
215-16) is decidedly "factual": Cheever mentions his drinking and
psychoanalysis, going to a movie, plaintively quizzing Mary about their
marriage, and then, sitting on the stone steps outside their house and
thinking himself "boyish" in his misery, "I stretch out on the stones,
sobbing, until I realize that I am in exactly the position of a doormat." The second (J 219) is just as clearly and oppositely "fictional":
"A lonely man is a lonesome thing, a stone, a bone, a stick, a
receptacle for Gilbey's gin," it begins, before going on to describe the
unhappily married Hammer whose sexual life is limited to masturbatory
fantasies. Either Hammer or the narrator wonders if Hammer's wife would
say, "You're a doormat, you're a henpecked doormat. . . ."   What
astonishes here is not that the latter entry incorporates the former's
"doormat" metaphor, recycled as it were for use in *Bullet Park*. Nor is
it that the recycled passage anticipates *Oh What a Paradise It Seems* and
(although not evident from the portion quoted here) *Falconer*, and reminds us as well of Cheever's Mia Farrow fantasy cited earlier. Rather,

what the juxtaposing of these two passages makes clear is what we might have gathered from the first one alone, that the original use of the doormat image is already the result of a fictionalizing process which the slightly later, more noticeably fictional entry only foregrounds.

Distinguishing fact from fiction in the *Journals* is therefore a difficult task made easy only if we assume that the journals are by their very nature autobiographically revealing rather than re-veiling. Once we question that assumption, the *Journals* begin to disclose less--or disclose less directly--and disguise and therefore disrupt more. Our questioning enables us to resist making those simplistic equations used in, for example, *Home Before Dark*, to strip Cheever of his narrative masks in much the same manner that the credulous audience in, and the (slightly?) less credulous readers of, Robert Coover's "The Hat Act" assume they are witnessing the unmasking of the magician whose (feigned?) incapacity (or in Cheever's case intimate revelations) may very well be his greatest deception. Approached with this possibility in mind, the *Journals* take on a new Borgesian indeterminacy which I believe an apt alternative to and antonym for the kind of intimacy to which *Home Before Dark* pretends. In one entry (J 16), for example, the markers "Rimbaud," "Zabel," "I," and the thematizing of the narrator's sense of insecurity and inferiority as well as his believing himself an imposter, a "spy" who has forgotten his mission and taken his disguises too seriously facilitate our reading this passage as direct autobiographical disclosure. The markers *facilitate* rather than *determine* our reading of this passage as autobiographical revelation because it is precisely this approach to which we are predisposed. These are, after all, John Cheever's journals: the daily record of his most intimate thoughts (intimacy, however, being a quality that the pontificating Cheever associated with fiction). Had Cheever or his editor used a different and no less descriptive word--notebooks, for example[7]--we might well have been differently predisposed ("might," not "would," because *Home Before Dark*'s approach to and use of the journals must be factored into the equation). Another entry, beginning "In town with D. His 65th birthday," poses a slightly different interpretive dilemma (J 280-81). Everything here suggests a subjective account of an actual occurrence in Cheever's life: lunch with a friend to celebrate the friend's birthday, getting his hair cut at the Biltmore, feeling dismayed that the city he once knew so well now seems so foreign to him, then the train ride home, the overheard conversations, the exhaustion. Partway through, however, Cheever describes a men's room at Grand Central Station in a manner which anticipates the Dantean description of the Valley in *Falconer*. We witness here a shift in perceptual modes, from the merely subjective to the nearly fantastic, as Cheever's sensitivity to even the slightest hint of homosexual encounter (like a whiff of sin to one of Hawthorne's puritans) results in his making the imaginative leap from mass micturation to mass masturbation.

Surely one of the most autobiographically revealing passages in the *Journals*, at least the one on which so much biographical discussion of Cheever centers, begins, "And thinking how our origins catch up with us I wonder what I will have to pay on this account. I have been a storyteller since the beginning of my life, rearranging facts in order to make them more interesting and sometimes more significant" (J 156). Then after briefly alluding to having transformed his parents into the Wapshots and having improvised for himself a "genteel," "generally accepted" background, he goes on to ask what "the bare facts" actually are. One of "the bare facts" mentioned in this entry, which we seem warranted in reading as a privileged glimpse into the human heart even though it may only be an unwitting variation on the parable of the Cretan barber, is a player piano. That player piano--or an any rate *a* player piano--reappears in a very similar entry written five years later and again dealing with Cheever's (the writer's? the speaker's?) uneasiness over his life of social imposture (or "improvisation" as it is called in the earlier entry [J 157]). If the later entry is (also?) "fact," then it is fact fleshed out in far more "Cheeveresque" fashion than the account of the "bare facts" five years earlier. If on the other hand it is fiction, or fictional, then we seem warranted in situating the earlier account not merely chronologically but epistemologically closer to Cheever's "actual life." But how would we read this later account had the earlier either not been written or (what seems the more tantalizing possibility) not included in the published *Journals*? Might not the later, more Cheeveresque entry suddenly come to occupy the position now vacated by the earlier? Stripped of any basis for comparison, would it not stand not just *closer* to the subject's actual life but *for* the life itself, as a reflection rather than an improvised variation on a theme? And would we not then be warranted in assuming that the possibility, indeed the likelihood that the later entry, restored to its supplementary position, is somehow fictional, requires that we consider that the earlier may be too? In our desperately seeking Cheever, in our rush to disclose the man himself, do we not run the risk of losing him altogether, for what we are dealing with here are not the reflected images of a recoverable point--the author as his own denotation--but instead the play of distortions in a Barthian/Barthesean funhouse.[8]

Throughout the *Journals*, "the facts" (as Philip Roth would call them) are presented in a manner perilously close to fiction. "At the edge of the swimming pool--twilight, of course--D. and I sit bare-arse, smoking, undisturbed by each other's nakedness. 'I never had an electric train,' he says. 'My father never took me to a ballgame, never once. He took me to the circus a couple of times, but he never took me to a ballgame'" (J 247). Cheever's "of course" is, from the standpoint of "pure" description (the punningly "bare facts"), an ironic and self-conscious contextualizing of an autobiographical scene in terms of a narrative convention. The rhythm of D.'s lines performs a similar function, connecting D. with the characters in Cheever's stories and novels. More intriguing are those entries in which, as Susan Cheever all too briefly notes, "The narrative shifts from recollection to fiction without notice" (*Home* 52). In one (J 204-205), Cheever writes in the present tense about cutting the grass in order to improve his spirits; then, failing that, drinking too much and reading a biography of Dylan Thomas. At first Cheever notices two similarities between his life and Thomas's: alcoholism and marriage "to a destructive woman." He immediately revises this, limiting the resemblance to the drinking only. The passage is--or may be read as--autobiographical revelation until the introduction of a "Mr Halberstrum" in the fourth sentence. Until the end of the entry two hundred and fifty words later,[9] the writing takes the form of a fantasia on the "hopeless marriage" parallel which, we recall, Cheever first posited, then rejected: self-pity giving way to self-deprecation. But if the denial is an attempt (as in the case of *Falconer*'s Farragut) to leach self-pity out of his emotional spectrum, then what are we to make of the fantasia in which Halberstrum (paralleling Cheever paralleling Thomas?) indulges in the self-pity that Cheever denies himself? "Halberstrum" clearly signals a shift in mode of discourse, but a shift whose meaning is decidedly ambiguous.

Another entry achieves a more or less similar effect but with one very significant difference, for here we cannot determine with any degree of certainty whatsoever the point at which the discourse becomes fiction. From the very first sentence? The very last? Or somewhere in-between?[10] "The train yards at Harmon on an overcast day," the passage begins. The narrative I (Cheever?) then recounts a conversation overheard on the train, mentions his desire to celebrate (used here as an intransitive verb) but acknowledges that his vision is "far from clear." After briefly considering "love's two aspects" (splendor and soiled underwear), he is met by a woman and an old friend, goes to the baths, and, a massage and a drink later, thinks back to the dreams he once had of "a good wife and lively children." "Where are my dear children?" the passage ends, "Where is Marcie?" (J 61-62). Until the final word, "Marcie," we read this entry as straightforward autobiography. It seems likely, however, that reading that name and retrospectively classifying the passage as "fiction" will not actually disabuse us of our initial "error." Rather, it will, I suspect, only confirm for us just how autobiographically revealing and indeed autobiographical Cheever's fiction "in fact" is.

This is understandable; John Cheever was, after all, his best (and only?) subject. His stories are not so much about the suburbs as they happen to be set there, just as other Cheever stories happen to be set

in New York or Italy or at Treetops or a rented seaside cottage because
these are the places where Cheever happened to be (or that he happened
to be thinking about) at the time. Contemporary events play a remarkably small role in Cheever's fiction and *Journals*, even when, as in the
case of a false report of John Updike's death, the public event impinged
on Cheever's private life. Ben Cheever, in the *Letters*, and Scott
Donaldson, in his biography, situate the report and Cheever's response
to it within the context of the death of Cheever's brother Fred a few
days before: as plausible and affecting a reading as one could wish,
until, that is, we read the full(?) entry as published in the *Journals*
(J 323). The third and shortest of the three paragraphs, apparently
written some time after the other two, acknowledges that the phone call
was a fraud, offers Susan Cheever's explanation that it was probably the
work of "an overambitious stringer," and concludes with Cheever feeling
"distempered, forlorn, and idle." Paragraph 2 (fifteen lines) eulogizes
Updike; indeed the language differs so greatly from that of paragraphs
1 and 3 as to suggest that Cheever was not so much reacting to the death
of a friend and colleague as drafting a eulogy (perhaps the eulogy
Cheever expected he would be asked to deliver). Paragraph 1 (also
fifteen lines) proves the most interesting and illuminating. Only a
little over two lines concern Updike. All the others deal with
Cheever's fear of being sent away should he try to climb in bed with
Mary, his getting up at first light to feed the dogs, and Mary's
peevishness and John's "restraint" just before and during breakfast.
What this paragraph shows, then, is that even news of his "peerless"
colleague's death serves first and foremost as the entrance line to yet
another episode in the "bitter comedy" of his life with Mary (J 128).
    But what does this preoccupation with self amount to? And how should
Cheever's autobiographical "I" be approached? In interviews Cheever
acknowledged that his narrators tend to speak in, or with, his voice,
"quite as unique as my fingerprints" (*Conversations* 111), and nowhere
does this identification seem quite so apparent as at the very end of
"The President of the Argentine," arguably Cheever's most autobiographical and narratively discontinuous story: "The man who wanted to put his
hat on the statue of the President is I." According to his daughter,
Cheever often adopted the opposite stratagem, "expressing his feelings
through a third-person narrator" (*Home* 17). However plausible her claim
may be, it begs a number of questions. Who determines when "he" is "I,"
and when this "I" is "I, John Cheever?" On what grounds? To what ends?
Switching from first to third person may, as Susan Cheever believes,
represent a change in grammatical person only; the actual person (John
Cheever) behind the "I" or "he" remains the same. However that switch
may (and in Cheever's case I would say should) lead us to question just
who this "John Cheever" is who manages to speak in and through so many
persons, first, second, and third, I, you, he, we and they (see, for ex-

ample, J 36, 49, 255, 266-67, 353-54). For a writer who so often used his journals to comment on his own physical smallness and on the metaphorical smallness--narrowness and weightlessness--of his fiction, as compared to the social and moral heft of, especially, Saul Bellow's, this ever metamorphosing "I" seems a rather slender thread upon which to hang his hopes of a useful and illustrious life. In pursuing what Paul John Eakin has aptly termed "the autobiographical imperative," Cheever, in his fiction and more especially in his journals, was doing more than "expressing" himself in various persons (grammatical and narrative); he was also, and more importantly, inventing himself (Eakin 277-78).

We should expect then, as Eugene L. Stelzig has demonstrated in his study of the confessional novels of Hermann Hesse, that the relationship between autobiographical narrative (in whatever form--fiction or journal[11]--and in whatever person) and the writer's "actual life" is one of similitude rather than correspondence, of invention and refraction rather than mere identity and referentiality. We should further expect that between John Cheever as a real or hypothesized biographical subject and all variously textualized John Cheevers there will be, as Stelzig points out, "degrees of distance and proximity, and levels of ironic detachment and sympathetic attachment" (17).[12] "Confessional fiction appeals to the modern writer because it encourages an aesthetic and psychological game-playing with fragments of the self, self-exposure as well as self-masking" (Stelzig 18). This "game-playing," as Stelzig calls it, extends well beyond the boundaries of confessional and autobiographical fiction. As Mikhail Bakhtin has explained, "The author's relationship to the various phenomena of literature and culture has a dialogical character. . . . Even had he created an autobiography or a confession of the most astonishing truthfulness, all the same he, as its creator, remains outside the world he has represented. . . . The 'image of the author'--if we are to understand by that the author-creator--is a contradiction in terms; every image is a created, and not a creating, thing" (256). Curiously enough, Cheever appears to have reached the same point intuitively that Bakhtin did theoretically. (I say "curiously" because Cheever studies have been all too free of any taint of contemporary theory.) Not only did Cheever frequently and openly distance himself from himself in his journals--imaging himself as a boy of fifty named Johnny Cheever, as an old man walking in the woods, as the John of John and Mary whose very names are talismans that will protect them from divorce, and as a self paradoxically and duplicitously confronting "the terrifying singularity of my own person" (J 222). He also understood that an image does not bear a necessary relationship to any real and recoverable antecedent. "I think of my father, but nothing is accomplished. The image of him is an invention, not a memory, and an overly gentle invention" (J 275).

We might therefore say with Paul de Man that the author, whether he be

Wordsworth or Cheever, expresses himself in tropes and only in tropes.
He can speak of himself, as Barthes does in *Roland Barthes by Roland
Barthes*, but only as a character speaking of another character. The
problem, as Barthes goes on to explain in a later (supplementary) autobiographical work, *Camera Lucida*, is that the self does not precede the
image; rather, the self exceeds the image. "[I]t's my 'me' that won't
coincide with my image; because it's the image that's stodgy, immobile
and obstinate (which is why society relies on it), and it's 'me' that's
flighty, divided and dispersed so that, like a cartesian diver in a jar,
it won't hold still" (qtd. in Smith 106). Emile Benveniste has
addressed the question of non-coincidence more specifically and less
playfully; the I who speaks (the referee), Benveniste notes, is never
the same as the I who is the subject of that speech (the referent). "I,"
he goes on to explain, refers "to something very peculiar which is
exclusively linguistic: *I* refers to the act of individual discourse in
which it is pronounced, and by this it designates the speaker. It is a
term that cannot be identified except in what we have called elsewhere
an instance of discourse and that has only a momentary reference. The
reality to which it refers is the reality of the discourse. . . . And so
it is literally true that the basis of subjectivity is in the exercise
of language" (qtd. in Silverman 43-44). As Kaja Silverman has pointed
out, "Although [Benveniste's] two subjects ['the speaking subject' and
'the subject of speech'] can only be apprehended in relation to each
other, they can never be collapsed into one unit. They remain forever
irreducible to each other, separated by the barrier between reality and
signification, or what Lacan would call 'being' and 'meaning'" (46). The
risk that Benveniste's position implies--the risk of losing the self
other than as a textual performance--is, I believe, worth taking. Only
if we do take it can we begin to challenge effectively the opposing and,
given the state of Cheever studies at this time, far more prevalent
danger posed by biographical reductivism in all its forms, from Susan
Cheever's practice in her two influential memoirs to Arthur Unger's
dismay upon discovering that "The most disconcerting thing about John
Cheever the man is that he is so much a character out of John Cheever
the author."

   It was shortly after noting the departure of interviewers like Unger
that Cheever wrote in his journal, "I become myself" (J 343). Between
the recording of their departure and the writing of the words, "I become
myself," a rather full paragraph intervenes. That intervention suggests
that the linkage between their departure and his becoming himself may
have to do more with my interpretive strategy (especially in the context
of Unger's "disconcerting" discovery) than with Cheever's authorial
intention. Cheever becomes himself not only after the interviewers
leave but after driving the maid home, walking the dogs, carrying out
the garbage, delighting in nature's beauty and vigor even in winter, all

of which seems to free him of a "highly irritable" and distorting
sexuality. But who is this "myself" that Cheever becomes? Is he the
person suddenly free of the need to perform the part of Cheever the
celebrated author of *Falconer* for his audience of interviewers? Is he
the fifty-five year-old man who takes a Leander-like delight in the
potency of the natural world even in the midst of winter? Or is he the
closet homosexual who will go on in the same entry to recount at
considerable length a liaison of a year earlier "in a squalid motel with
a young man who had none of the attributes of a sexual irregular"? Or
is he the one who, having begun by claiming to "have no perspective at
all," becomes what he is, a writer whose authorial "I" is rarely if ever
uniform and univocal, "always already" (as Derrida would add) divided
and dispersed: "disparate," to use one of Cheever's favorite words?

Cheever wanted to bring the "disparate elements" of his life together
in a utopian fantasy of "oneness," of the self coinciding with itself
and its world. This disparateness manifests itself in Cheever's writing
in various ways: in the split between the carnal and the spiritual,
between the prosaic and the lyrical, between "writing and living," as he
puts it in an early journal entry (J 23). It also evidences itself in
Cheever's divided sexual nature, in his distressing attacks of
"otherness," in his relations with his older brother Fred, and in the
recurring conflict between brothers in his stories and novels. The
journal entries which deal either directly or tangentially with brothers
prove particularly interesting, for in them we find additional evidence
of Cheever's most extensive recycling project and fullest exploitation
of the permutational possibilities[13] that *Home Before Dark* seeks to
delimit and monologize. In one 1971 entry, for example, Cheever
describes Fred in a way which recalls Blake from "The Five-Forty-Eight"
(1954) and describes himself in a way which anticipates Farragut's
brother Eben (ostensibly the "Fred" character) in *Falconer*. We could of
course side-step this confusion, or dispersal, of roles by acknowledging
that what Ben Cheever writes of his father's letters is also true of the
Journals: "It would be an exhaustive and not particularly illuminating
exercise to draw attention to every place where the image from a letter
echoes in the fiction" (*Letters* 87). But the excess of echoes ought
not to lead us either to slight or to oversimplify the relationship(s)
between the fiction on the one hand and the journals and letters on the
other, for what is illuminating about these echoes is not the fact that
they occur (and occur so frequently) but the way they contribute to the
creation of that dream-like "density" that Cheever hoped to achieve in
his fiction. Whether this density was aimed at discovery or disguise or
both is impossible to say. What is certain is that even as Cheever was
repelled by the reductivism he associated with psychoanalytical
practice, in his own writing (the journals as well as the stories and
novels) he made use of the displacement and condensation that Freud

identified as the key narrative strategies employed in dreams, strategies that make most, perhaps all, attempts to chart linearly the autobiographical trajectory of Cheever's writing misguided and misleading.

Displacement and condensation offer a useful corrective to simple equation. A still more useful approach to recurrence in Cheever's writing, considered now as a single but still largely unpublished intertextual whole, is Bakhtin's concept of reaccenting. According to Bakhtin, while the content of a particular work, or a particular author's work, may be largely "stable" and "unchanging," intentions and emphases ("accents") will vary as words are transferred "from one mouth to another," or more generally from one context to another. Bakhtin was referring specifically to the novel (as an anti-genre), but since the novel, as he defined it, is more a tendency than a form, we are warranted in approaching all of Cheever's writings dialogically, finding in them and not just in the five novels evidence of the "linguistic homelessness" which Bakhtin associated with the novel as a reflection of a "decentered" world (and that we may also associate with an equally decentered self adrift in the space between Benveniste's two I's). In such a textualized world--in such a textual space--almost every utterance is a hybrid, "an encounter, within the arena of an utterance, between two different linguistic consciousnesses, separated from one another by an epoch, by social differentiation *or by some other factor*" (emphasis added; 358).

It is Bakhtin himself who gives us the clue we need in order to understand better the nature of this "other factor" in relation to Cheever's *Journals*. "*Who* speaks and under what conditions he speaks: this is what determines the word's actual meaning. All direct meanings and direct expressions are false, and this is especially true of emotional meanings and expressions" (401). Given the nature of Cheever studies in the decade since his death, we may well say that Bakhtin's words speak with a special urgency and lead us to look at the *Journals* as the intersection of various linguistic, narrative, psychological, and socio-economic forces related to their conception and reception. In his introduction to the *Journals*, Ben Cheever makes a useful distinction: the journals "were the workbooks for his fiction. They were also the workbooks for his life" (vii). It is however a distinction he soon tries, perhaps unwittingly, to blur in order, in an effort not unlike his sister's, to strengthen the autobiographical equation linking the journals and the fiction: life was John Cheever's problem, and he dealt with it by articulating it, turning it into story, and the journals are the story of his life. Thus the journals are really just stories and the stories are autobiography and there is not much reason to distinguish between them. The *Journals* are of course confessional but to an as yet undefined and perhaps ultimately undefinable degree, and as a result we must guard against reading them as if they allow us access to Cheever's "innermost thoughts." They are not--or at least not merely or even especially--the "Puritan diaries" whose revelations have so dismayed John Updike, leading him to reevaluate the fiction, which he now views as "timid, arch, and falsely buoyant." Following a similar course, Gordon Burn claims that Cheever's Emily Dickinson-like letter-to-the-world does compromise the fiction, but only temporarily. Moreover, Burn shrewdly links the appearance of the *Journals* to the current mania for dysfunctional individuals as evidenced by television talk shows and literary/celebrity biographies such as Diane Middleton's of Anne Sexton. Hilton Kramer sees in the *Journals'* publication "the plight of American letters today" in miniature. Cheever's "guilt-wracked confession of homosexual philandering," brought to us by venal publishers and coopted by leftists, will compromise the "artistic integrity" of Cheever's "masterful short stories" as Cheever is made grist for the mill of gay studies. Betraying none of Kramer's paranoia and homophobia, Stefan Kanfer wonders why Cheever's widow and children, as his literary executors and editors, "would . . . allow him--as well as themselves--to be so unflatteringly exposed?" Reverence, perhaps? Revenge? Royalties? Or something else?

We must also keep in mind that *The Journals of John Cheever* are not the journals of John Cheever. Amounting to just one-twentieth of the total, estimated at some three to four million words, the published *Journals* offer a doubly partial (fractional and preferential) "John Cheever" and as such constitute what amounts to a synechdochic deception. The point at issue is not whether Robert Gottlieb is or is not a good editor: intelligent, honest, knowledgeable, and therefore worthy of our trust.[14] The point is not even whether the *Journals* are, as Gottlieb claims, representative. Rather, the issue is what they represent and how and by whom they are made representative. Do they, as Gottlieb contends, represent the essential John Cheever "speaking," as it were, candidly? (Recall that in "Song of Myself," candor and nakedness serve Walt Whitman as disguises.) At the very least the *Journals* represent a Cheever perpetually in crisis. Updike wishes that more purely quotidian entries had been included, not so much to reveal a different or more complete John Cheever as to protect Updike as reader against the full brunt of the *Journals'* painful disclosures. Equally important, the *Journals*, particularly as they have been introduced to the public, first by Susan Cheever and then by her brother Ben, situate their subject in a doubly paternalistic line of descent: on the one hand, as literal father and provider, and on the other as the "author" that Barthes and Foucault have, in their very different but equally useful ways, sought to demystify and dislodge. In "The Death of the Author," Barthes writes that:

> The Author, when believed in, is always conceived of as the past
> of his own book: book and author stand automatically on a single
> line divided into a *before* and an *after*. The Author is thought
> to *nourish* the book, which is to say that he exists before it,
> thinks, suffers, lives for it, is in the same relation of
> antecedence to his work as a father to his child. In complete
> contrast, the modern scriptor is born simultaneously with the
> text. . . . The fact is . . . that *writing* can no longer
> designate an operation of recording, notation, representation,
> "depiction" (as the Classics would say); rather, it designates
> exactly what linguists . . . call a performative, a rare verbal
> form . . . in which the enunciation has no other content . . .
> than the act by which it is uttered. . . . [T]he hand, cut off
> from any voice, borne by a pure gesture of inscription (and not
> of expression), traces a field without origin--or which, at
> least, has no other origin than language itself, language which
> ceaselessly calls into question all origins. (145-46)

Although Foucault agrees with Barthes that the author is not the
autonomous self who originates and authorizes his or her text, who
speaks the first and last words of its composition and interpretation,
he rejects Barthes' "death of the author" scenario as utopian and
a-historical and offers instead his own genealogical approach. For
Foucault, the author "is a certain functional principle by which, in our
culture, one limits, excludes, and chooses; in short, by which one
impedes the free circulation, the free manipulation, the free
composition, decomposition, and recomposition of fiction." Once the
author has been refigured along these lines,

> We would no longer hear the questions that have been rehashed
> for so long: "Who really spoke? Is it really he and not someone
> else? With what authenticity or originality? And what part of
> his deepest self did he express in his discourse?" Instead,
> there would be other questions, like these: "What are the modes
> of existence of this discourse? Where has it been used, how can
> it circulate, and who can appropriate it for himself? What are
> the places in it where there is room for possible subjects? Who
> can assume these various subject-functions?" And behind all
> these questions, we would hear hardly anything but the stirring
> of an indifference: "What difference does it make who is
> speaking?" (988)

Relevant as Foucault's "other questions" are to Cheever studies at any
time,[15] they are especially so now as so much new material becomes a-
vailable in a way that creates the illusion of access. By access I mean

access to the journals and more importantly to the John Cheever that the *Journals*, and the journals, are said (made) to represent. We do gain access, but it is access to a more or less private preserve operated as something of a family business.

The relevance to Cheever studies of the questions posed by Foucault does not mean that we should follow his suggestions and become indifferent to the question of who speaks. We are not in an either/or situation: either we accept that Cheever is the stable, knowable subject of conventional biographical inquiry or we see him as simply an instance of the author function whose work is interesting only insofar as it reveals the systems of constraint that characterize his particular episteme. The question that Susan Cheever and others do not consider and that Foucault chooses to leap beyond remains of vital interest, providing that we understand it in Bakhtinian terms in all its complexity.

It is in the spirit of Bakhtin that I want to close this essay by returning to the point with which it began, the epigraphs from the novels *How German Is It*, by Walter Abish, and *Company*, by Samuel Beckett. The appropriateness of these brief passages to the essay they introduce should by now be clear. Even so, the placing of Cheever in the "company" of Abish and Beckett may seem odd--as odd as the placing of Cheever in the company (or line of descent) of F. Scott Fitzgerald, another "lyrical" and auto/biographically revealing writer, has come to seem perfectly "natural." "There is no disputing the fact," Scott Donaldson has written of Cheever's contribution to *Atlantic Brief Lives*, "that in composing his brief life of Fitzgerald, Cheever was writing of himself" (352). Donaldson is very likely right; but his view is also in a way misleading insofar as linking Cheever with Fitzgerald obscures the connection between Cheever and Abish, Beckett, and a good many other, generally more accessible and more widely read contemporary writers who foreground the question of who speaks and under what conditions: Joan Didion, E.L. Doctorow, J.M. Coetzee, Salman Rushdie, and, most exhaustively, Philip Roth (in *The Counterlife*, *The Facts*, and *Deception*).[16] Read in the light (or shadow) of Fitzgerald, the *Journals* are Cheever's version of *The Crack-Up*, to which we respond with dismay, pity, and, perhaps, perverse voyeuristic pleasure. Read in the very different context of Abish and Beckett,[17] the same *Journals* resemble fictive novelist Ulrich Hargenau's notebook in *How German Is It* or Krapp in *Krapp's Last Tape*, whose narrow range of obsessive, permutating subjects and sense of tragi-farcical futility Cheever shares. There is Krapp celebrating each birthday by listening to old tapes--"post-mortems," "retrospects"--before recording a new one, appalled by what he hears, especially the aspirations, "To drink less, in particular." And then there is Cheever, "Reading old journals," realizing "that the booze fight and the *cafarde* have been going on for longer than I knew" or, on another occasion, that "what emerges are two astonishing contests, one with alcohol and one with my wife" (J 239, 245). Rather than seeing in the *Journals* Cheever at his most candid, we might choose to see him at his most alone, most like the voice in Beckett's ironically titled, dizzyingly solipsistic, and, strangely crypto-autobiographical work, *Company*, a voice made to play all the parts, I, you, and he, then and now. This is not to suggest that Beckett offers us a better way to approach Cheever and his *Journals* than does, say, Fitzgerald; only a different way, one that may lead us away from reading the *Journals* in terms of naive biographism[18] and towards a more thorough examination of the signifying practices by which both Cheever and his *Journals* are semiotically conditioned and (re)constituted. And it may lead us towards a better appreciation of the play of centrifugal and centripetal forces which, as Bakhtin has pointed out, characterize all utterances, Cheever's journals no less than his stories and novels.

NOTES

1. The word "mysterious" is Benjamin Cheever's: "The connection between his life and his work was intimate, but it was also mysterious. My father was fond of saying that fiction was not 'crypto-autobiography.' One obvious reason for this statement is that it protected him from the attacks of friends and family who felt that they'd been libeled in his prose. But his oft-repeated argument was that good writing so transcended the life it came from that an examination of the life could lead to gross misunderstandings." Nonetheless, Benjamin Cheever maintains, the letters "should shed light on both" John Cheever's life and fiction, even if they don't explain them (*Letters* 21).
2. "Insidious" here does not imply any attempt to deceive on Susan Cheever's part. I use it only because her biographical approach (to borrow the words of the *Random House College Dictionary*) "operat[es] or proceed[s] inconspicuously but with grave effects."
3. This "draft" (J 305) appears to have been written as a response to a question about *Falconer* and is of special interest for two reasons: first, because it was written in 1975 and second, because it so closely resembles the responses Cheever gave interviewers two years later when asked about *Falconer's* origins.
4. See my "From Parallels to Paradise."
5. See also the letter to Max Zimmer (?) in 1979 which sounds a good deal like *Falconer* (*Letters* 356) and the letter to Tanya Litvinov dated 21 July 1965, the opening line of which, "This is on a broken typewriter in a rented house by the sea" (*Letters* 251), is strikingly similar to that of the story "A Vision of the World" published three years earlier.

6. A 1959 entry on the infidelities of the man who delivered the Cheevers' dry cleaning seems like something out of *Falconer* (J 119).

7. In calling them "journals" Cheever was of course following a family tradition. However, because no earlier Cheever had been a fiction writer, none had reason to use his journals in quite the same way that John Cheever did.

8. "The Cheevers are very good at walking out. 'When I remember my family I always remember their backs,' he wrote in his journal" (*Home* 19). The passage also appears in Cheever's published fiction. Is the journal entry a draft of the fiction or is the fiction directly autobiographical are questions *Home* and its reviewers do not begin to address.

9. The end of the entry as published in the *Journals*. Whether this is also the end of the entry as Cheever wrote it, the reader can at best only wonder.

10. For a sampling of entries which may be fact or fiction or a mixture of the two, see J 31 ("One of the children . . . foreign country"), J 169 ("Light and shade . . . to conceal the truth"), and J 327-28 ("It will be . . . who really cares?").

11. I accept Jean Starobinski's view that "the conditions of auto-biography furnish only a large framework within which a great variety of particular styles may occur. So it is essential to avoid speaking of an autobiographical 'style' or even an autobiographical 'form' because there is no such generic style or form."

12. Post-structuralists view autobiography (in Louis A. Renza's words) "as a unique, self-defining mode of self-referential expression, one that allows, then inhibits, the project of self-representation" (qtd. in Stelzig 316).

13. See, for example, Donaldson's catalogue of Cheever's several versions of his defenestration story (*John Cheever* 118-19).

14. Donaldson has discovered an "unacknowledged deletion" from one of Cheever's letters published in the selection edited by Ben Cheever. Whether there are others in the *Letters* and the *Journals* only time and scholarly sleuthing will tell.

15. Interest in Cheever biography may be traced not only to Cheever's death in 1982 but more generally to the renewed interest in biographical study that appears to be part of a reaction against the post-structuralists' problematizing of the author and demystifying of the bourgeois self.

16. As the fictive novelist Nathan Zuckerman writes in *The Counterlife*: "If there even *is* a natural being, an irreducible self, it is rather small, I think, and may even be the root of all impersonation--the natural being may be the skill itself, the innate capacity to impersonate, I'm talking about recognizing that one is acutely a performer, rather than swallowing whole the guise of naturalness and pretending that it

isn't a performance but you."
17. For entries in which Cheever plays the part of a domesticated
Beckett see J 233 and J 262-63.
18. Kafka's fate. See Milan Kundera's "In Saint Garta's Shadow," *TLS*
24 May 1991: 3-5.

WORKS CITED

Bakhtin, M.M. *The Dialogic Imagination*. Ed. Michael Holquist. Trans.
   Caryl Emerson. Austin: University of Texas Press, 1981.
Barthes, Roland. "The Death of the Author." *Image, Music, Text*. Trans.
   Stephen Heath. New York: Hill & Wang, 1977.
Burn, Gordon. "Deterioration of the Middle-Aged Businessman." *London
   Review of Books* 14 (9 January 1992): 18-19.
Cheever, John. *The Journals of John Cheever*. Ed. Robert Gottlieb.
   Intro. Benjamin Cheever. New York: Knopf, 1991.
_____. *The Letters of John Cheever*. Ed. Benjamin Cheever. New York:
   Simon and Schuster, 1988.
_____. "The President of the Argentine." *Atlantic Monthly* 237 (April
   1976): 43-45.
Cheever, Susan. *Home Before Dark: A Biographical Memoir of John Cheever
   by His Daughter*. 1984. New York: Pocket Books, 1985.
_____. *Treetops: A Family Memoir*. New York: Bantam, 1991.
Collins, R.G. "The Dark Too Soon: John Cheever's Heritage." *Resources
   for American Literary Study* 13 (Spring 1985):   33-40.
Conversations with John Cheever. Ed. Scott Donaldson. Jackson:
   University of Mississippi Press, 1987.
Donaldson, Scott. *John Cheever: A Biography*. New York: Random House,
   1988.
_____. "The State of Letters." *Sewanee Review* 98 (Summer 1990): 527-45.
Eakin, Paul John. *Fictions in Autobiography: Studies in the Art of
   Self-Invention*. Princeton: Princeton University Press, 1985.
Foucault, Michel. "What is an Author?" *The Critical Tradition: Classic
   Texts and Contemporary Trends*. Ed. David H. Richter. New York:
   Macmillan, 1989.
Garis, Leslie. "Life with the King of Hell." *Mirabella* 2 (March 1991):
   84-88.
Kanfer, Stefan. "Jack, Wrench, Hubcap." *Time* 18 March 1991: 80.
Kramer, Hilton. "A grim scenario: The plight of American letters today."
   TLS 17 January 1992: 13.
Morace, Robert A. "From Parallels to Paradise: the Lyrical Structure of
   Cheever's Fiction." *Twentieth Century Literature* 35 (Winter 1989):
   502-28.
Silverman, Kaja. *The Subject of Semiotics*. New York: Oxford University

Press, 1983.

Smith, Paul. *Discerning the Subject*. Minneapolis: University of Minnesota Press, 1988.

Starobinski, Jean. "The Style of Autobiography." *Autobiography: Essays Theoretical and Critical*. Ed. James Olney. Princeton: Princeton University Press, 1980. 73-83.

Stelzig, Eugene L. *Hermann Hesse: Fictions of the Self: Autobiography and the Confessional Imagination*. Princeton: Princeton University Press, 1988.

Unger, Arthur. "John Cheever's Long View." *Christian Science Monitor* 24 October 1979: 17-18.

Updike, John. "The Waspshot Chronicle." *The New Republic* 205 (2 December 1991): 36-39.

Further Considerations

CRITICISM

Women in the Fiction of John Cheever

Lynne M. Waldeland

Even before the increase in attention paid to characterization of women in literature that has followed from feminist literary theory and criticism, readers and critics had noted the relatively negative view of women that pervaded the fiction of John Cheever. Cheever's memorable women characters range from Sarah Wapshot, in his first novel, who turns her husband's beloved boat into a floating gift shop, to Marcia Farragut, in *Falconer*, who comforts her imprisoned husband with the remark, "Well, it's nice to have a dry toilet seat." The wife in "O Youth and Beauty!" shoots her husband in ambiguous circumstances highly reminiscent of Hemingway's "The Short, Happy Life of Francis Macomber," and the wife and mother in "An Educated American Woman" discusses Flaubert in French with her husband during lovemaking and attends a zoning commission meeting while her son lies fatally ill at home. This gallery of women characters, along with others who poison their husbands and create chaos in their homes in a struggle for supremacy within their marriages, have led to the conclusion that Cheever had a troubled and diminishing view of women.

Yet, Cheever usually reacted with pained irritation when interviewers suggested that he was narrow or negative in his depiction of women. He would often respond with protestations of his adoration for and dependence upon women. He did admit in some interviews that he had resented the fact that his own mother, whom he identified as the model for Sarah Wapshot, had gone to work, thereby undermining his father's sense of importance and making herself less available to her son. But an example of his typical response to questions about his characterization of women is found in an interview conducted by his daughter, Susan, in which he insists: "'I really don't have any message on women. I've known a lot of women and it seems to me they are distinguished by their variety. I don't think of them as creative or destructive, serious or empty-headed.'" (Cowley 69) The question then becomes: why are so many more female characters in Cheever's work destructive or empty-headed rather than creative, serious, complex figures? Is the very devotion to women Cheever claims and with which he invests many of his male characters itself a cause of the limited perspective on women one gets from his fiction?

The publication of *Home Before Dark*, Susan Cheever's biography of her father, inevitably leads readers of Cheever's fiction to make connections between revelations about his life and aspects of his fiction. Even exercising the caution that is needed in the face of new information about an artist's life so as not to reduce the artistic production to thinly veiled autobiography, it is almost impossible not to connect the revelation that Cheever's own father had wanted him aborted to the author's use of that situation in *The Wapshot Chronicle* and in its more violent reprise in *Falconer*. Likewise, revelations in the biography and in the more recently published selections from Cheever's journals of Cheever's seriously unhappy marriage, his extra-marital affairs, and his bisexuality and his feelings about these aspects of his life may provide some basis for understanding the variance between his view of women as it emerges from reading his fiction and his avowed attitudes toward women as expressed in interviews. An examination of the relative importance assigned to the roles of women in his fiction, of the roles themselves and the relative complexity with which they are drawn, and of his rhetorical statements about women and about gender relationships in the fiction all show a troubled, often misogynous, view of women.

Women are almost never the central characters in a Cheever novel or story. Although their impact in a given narrative may be considerable, it is of interest primarily as it affects the male protagonist. Furthermore, the impact of the most important women characters on the lives of the male protagonists in the novels is negative or, at the least, constraining. Sarah Wapshot takes away her husband's pride as supporter of the family; Honora Wapshot holds the purse-strings of the family fortune and uses them to control the fate of the Wapshot men. Marietta Hammer and Marcia Farragut are cruelly unsupportive wives; and, after reading the biography and journals, it is difficult not to find significance in the similarity of their names to that of Cheever's wife, Mary, and to believe that he worked out some of his own marital anger and disappointment in the extremely negative characterizations of these fictional wives. Only Nellie Nailles, of *Bullet Park*, and the mysterious Renee Herndon, briefly the lover of Lemuel Sears in Cheever's last published fiction, *Oh What a Paradise It Seems*, bring happiness to the male protagonists of the novels.

This general pattern is found in the short stories as well. Very few of them have women as the protagonists of the narrative, and one of the few that does, "An Educated American Woman," provides one of the most negative characterizations of women in all Cheever's work. Stories such as "The Chaste Clarissa" and "The Trouble of Marcie Flint," although their titles suggest a focus on female characters, are more about their male narrators' experience and feelings than about the women.

The fact that Cheever doesn't choose to focus on women as central isn't in itself a problem. Artists, James reminded us, must be granted their choices of subject and focus; surely, this would include the choice of fictional protagonists. But the degree to which women are de-emphasized in Cheever's fiction becomes considerably more significant when we consider that he works with the material of manners, with the ways in which people live together in American society in his time. His settings, including the country clubs and cocktail parties which may be our contemporary equivalent of Jamesian drawing rooms, are almost always the locus of social interaction. In the choice of human relationships and social dynamics as his primary subjects, Cheever more resembles James than Twain, Fitzgerald than Hemingway. Thus, to note the relative absence of important women characters in Cheever's fiction is more serious than to observe that women do not line the banks of the Big Two-Hearted River. Given his social subjects and domestic settings, it is startling and dissonant to find Cheever's female characters more reminiscent of Aunt Sally and Margot Macomber than of Isabel Archer.

When women do appear in Cheever's fiction, they are important primarily for their relationships to the male characters. Very few women characters in Cheever are independent of a connection to children, husband, or lover. The meaning of their roles as mother, wife, and mistress to the women themselves is rarely explored; rather we are allowed to see how they, in these roles, affect their children, husbands, and lovers. The sense that the women characters are important primarily in terms of their impact on the lives of men is intensified by the fact that they are often rendered through the viewpoint of male characters. Although he is well-known for his use of a heavily omniscient point of view, Cheever also employs first-person narrators and makes considerable use of journals, such as Leander's in the Wapshot novels and Hammer's in *Bullet Park*. [The use of journals in the novels is more resonant for readers today who now know of Cheever's own extensive journal-keeping.] Cheever's use of omniscient point of view (often an identifiably male voice) or the first-person point of view of male protagonists functions to keep the women characters in the narrative distant from the reader and to focus the reader almost entirely on the reactions and feelings of the male characters about women.

Some critics have singled out Honora Wapshot, the controller of the Wapshot fortune, as Cheever's least negatively presented female character. She *is* given the most direct attention of any of his female characters; however, she is also a figure of almost legendary proportion and relatively genderless in Cheever's characterization. In *The Wapshot Chronicle*, there is an extended, comic description of her day, in which she uses the public bus service as a private limousine (putting the bus driver in charge of lobsters she has purchased), sneaks into a movie to enjoy a sense of sinfulness, and throws her mail into the fire unread, in case it contain something unpleasant. Her extreme eccentricity is softened somewhat in a scene in which she slips on the sidewalk and fends off help in order to preserve her sense of dignity and one in which she overhears her servant, Maggie, laughing uproariously with her sister over Honora's foibles, a moment that pulls her sense of identity out from under her. Such scenes allow us to see her as more than a comic figure. Honora has an even more central role in *The Wapshot Scandal*, in which, pursued by the I.R.S. for non-payment of taxes, she sails to Italy, befriends a stowaway, and stops the ocean liner's generators twice by plugging in her ancient curling iron. When she returns to America, she deliberately starves herself to death to avoid the impending "scandal," dying a legend in the memory of her nephew, Coverly. Her unmarried state and her entertaining eccentricities make her less negative as a character than most women in Cheever's fiction, but even she causes the Wapshot men considerable difficulty. She manipulates the lives of the Wapshots to get her way; she wants only legitimate heirs and doesn't hesitate to use her money to enforce her will, ordering her nephew, Moses, to leave home when she finds him in bed with a girl.

Honora is, however, rendered more positively than Justina, a parallel figure in *The Wapshot Chronicle*. Also, a holder of purse-strings, she controls her ward, Melissa, the woman Moses wants to marry. Unlike Honora, who had a brief, bad marriage, Justina married cynically, for money. Unlike Honora, who appreciates Europe, Justina has collected it, buying up pieces of European houses to re-assemble into the monstrous "castle" in which she lives. A bona-fide man-hater, she does all she can to thwart the romance of Melissa and Moses. Her extreme behavior causes us to see her in mythic terms as a wicked witch guarding the castle in which the beautiful damsel awaits rescue by the knight. At the end the lovers are saved, fairy-tale fashion, when the castle burns down and they can leave, escaping from Justina's spell. These two women characters--one realistic, one supernatural--stand outside the normal roles of women in Cheever's fiction, but they too use their power to control and thwart the men in these narratives.

More usually, Cheever's women characters are wives and often mothers.

Sarah Wapshot is Cheever's first extended characterization of a wife and mother. She is portrayed as a woman who lacks satisfying outlets for the fullness of her energies, and thus she turns her attention to countless civic projects. Cheever has said that she is modelled on his own mother, and some of his admitted resentment of his mother's absences from the home comes through in a passage from *The Wapshot Scandal*:

> She had exhausted herself in good works. She had founded the Women's Club, the Current Events Club, and was a director of the Animal Rescue League and the Lambert Home for Unwed Mothers. As a result of all these activities the house on River Street was always filled with dust, its cut flowers long dead, the clocks stopped. Sarah Wapshot was one of those women whose grasp of vital matters had forced them to consider the simple tasks of a house to be in some way perverted. (19)

Despite his seeming awareness that Sarah's behavior is at least partly attributable to the absence of fulfillment in the conventional roles available for women, a situation that James turned into the complex tragedy of *A Portrait of a Lady*, Cheever rails against Sarah's failure to keep up with the housework and to be an omnipresent nurturer of husband and sons.

In fact, Cheever portrays Sarah as almost willfully destructive of masculine values and relationships in the Wapshot novels. She sends her younger son, Coverly, on a long-awaited fishing trip with his father equipped with a cookbook, *Five Hundred Ways to Prepare Fish*, thereby alienating the boy from his father and this masculine ritual. Also, whenever Coverly seems to have had a good time in the company of his father, she reminds him that when she was pregnant with him, Leander had brought an abortionist to the house. Her most destructive act is the appropriation of Leander's wrecked boat, which she turns into The World's Only Floating Gift Shoppe. The boys sympathize with their father and are on the way to St. Botolphs to buy their father a new boat with their inheritance when Leander dies. The effect of Sarah Wapshot--and of Honora as well--on the Wapshot men is summed up in Coverly's statement in *The Wapshot Chronicle*: "'. . . where I come from, I think it's hard to take much pride in being a man. I mean the women are very powerful. They are kind and they mean very well, but sometimes they get very oppressive. Sometimes you feel as if it wasn't right to be a man.'" (126)

Many other mothers in Cheever's fiction are treated as oppressive or insensitive in regard to their children. Rosalie Young's mother in *The Wapshot Chronicle*, upon seeing her daughter for the first time after a serious accident, prattles on about having found a lost scarab ring. Jill Madison, in "An Educated American Woman," is blamed--by her husband

and, I suspect, most readers--for neglecting her son and perhaps con- tributing to his death. Occasionally, a mother is crazy, as is Gretchen Schurz Oxencroft, the mother of Paul Hammer in *Bullet Park*, who deserts her son at birth, fills his mind with her delusions during their infre- quent visits, and finally advises him to crucify a suburbanite to awaken the world, advice her son inexplicably takes. Nellie Nailles, also in *Bullet Park*, is an exception.   When her son seems to be dying of a mys- terious malady, she leaves her safe, orderly world to go in search of a swami whose services have been recommended. Totally out of her element, both geographically and rationally, she nevertheless manages a grace and poise in the unfamiliar situation that is attributed to her willingness to do anything to save her son's life. Most often, however, mothers in Cheever are neglectful, occasionally domineering, and rarely nurturing.

Generally, Cheever gives more attention to women in the role of wife than of mother, perhaps as an outgrowth of his own concerns about the difficulties of marriage. Cheever's portrayal of marriage--and women in the role of wife--is at best ambivalent, an ambivalence paralleled in his frequent comment in interviews that he and his wife had been married for 40 years and that, in that time, not a week had passed in which they had not considered divorce.[1] Sarah Wapshot is the first major character in whom Cheever explores the effects, mostly negative, that wives can have on their husbands. Sarah's decision to work outside the home deeply undermines her husband's sense of his prerogatives as breadwinner for the family. Turning her husband's boat into a gaily festooned gift shop is particularly diminishing of his sense of identity; and on the day of the grand opening, Leander fires a gun out the window and collapses, defeated. While the novel grants that Sarah finds in this endeavor a stimulus to "her will to live," the focus of the novel is on the disastrous consequences for Leander, who finally, after leaving the remnants of his affairs in order, swims out to sea and drowns. Her only comment: "'It was a very long association.'" (*Chronicle* 303)

The Wapshot Chronicle includes the courtship and marriage of the Wapshot sons, Moses and Coverly; *The Wapshot Scandal* deals more extensively with their marriages. Coverly falls in love with his wife in one of the instantaneous decisions that Cheever claims was his own experience and that he uses extensively in his fiction. He remains one of the most uxorious of Cheever's husbands, despite Betsy's relative unresponsiveness to him, even through her frequent nervous breakdowns during which she withdraws, cuts the buttons off his shirts, and deserts him, taking all their money. The final view we have of Coverly and Betsy at the end of *The Wapshot Scandal* suggests that they are engaged in a battle of the sexes begun in Leander and Sarah. "Coverly walked beside his wife with the slight crouch of a losing sexual combatant, while Betsy stood more erectly, held her head more sternly, seemed to seize on every crumb of self-esteem that he dropped." (299)

The relationship of Moses and Melissa is somewhat more complexly presented. After the fairy-tale aspects of their courtship and escape from the control of Justina, the real-life marriage of the two is presented in *The Wapshot Scandal*. One of several unfaithful wives in Cheever's fiction, Melissa is treated with comparative sympathy. She is, I think, Cheever's most serious attempt to understand the modern American woman of the upper middle class. Although her infidelity drives the already heavy-drinking Moses into alcoholic irresponsibility at the novel's end, this is treated at least as much as evidence of his weakness as a person as it is blamed on his wife. Melissa is portrayed in the novel as at loose ends, looking for some kind of substance and meaning in life, very much like male protagonists in Cheever's fiction. She is annoyed at cocktail party gossip about other people's sex lives and wonders why everyone in their prosperous circle seems bored and disappointed. (p. 50) It becomes clear that except for their sexual compatibility, Moses and Melissa have nothing in common. A crisis ensues when Melissa becomes ill and is hospitalized. Despite her recovery, she is convinced that she has cancer. Overcome by a fear of death, she begins to be aware of a strange man walking along the road or appearing outside her window, a harbinger similar to the beggar in *Madame Bovary*. Unsettled by her sense of meaninglessness and the fragility of life, she falls in love with the grocery delivery boy. Moses discovers their affair and leaves. The grocery boy deposits a promotional Easter egg good for a trip to Rome on Melissa's lawn. At novel's end, Moses is in a drunken stupor and Melissa is in Rome, dubbing movies. There she is reunited with Emile, the grocery boy, in a fantastic turn of events; but instead of a final scene of sexual bliss, we have a poignant picture of her in a supermarket:

> Grieving, bewildered by the blows life has dealt her, this is some solace. . . . Tears make the light in her eyes a glassy light but the market is crowded and she is not the first nor the last woman in the history of the place to buy her groceries with wet cheeks . . . . it is Ophelia she most resembles, gathering her fantastic garland not of crowflowers, nettles and long purples, but of salt, pepper, Bab-o, Kleenex, frozen codfish balls, lamb patties, hamburger, bread, butter, dressing, an American comic book for her son and for herself a bunch of carnations. She chants, like Ophelia, snatches of old tunes. "Winstons taste *good* like a cigarette should. Mr. Clean. Mr. *Clean*," and when her coronet or fantastic garland seems completed she pays her bill and carries her trophies away, no less dignified a figure of grief than any other. (*Scandal* 298)

The coupling of the domestic setting of a grocery store with the allusion to Ophelia and the final statement of the passage underscores the relative seriousness with which Cheever is prepared to treat the contemporary American woman in this instance. This is one characterization in which he seems willing to entertain the possibility that her capacity for dreams, desire for meaning, and need for fulfillment may not lie in the domestic realm to which her social class seems to assign women. He even suggests, in this story, that the failures of the male may be partly responsible for the outcome.

Consideration of the degree to which women's domestic role may be a trap is also found in the depiction of Louise Bentley, the wife in the story "O Youth and Beauty!" Her life seems to consist totally of grocery lists, child care, and household chores. She can't escape even in sleep. "Snowsuits, shoes, baths, and groceries seemed to have permeated her subconscious. Now and then she would speak in her sleep-- so loudly that she woke her husband. 'I can't *afford* veal cutlets,' she said one night." (*Housebreaker* 35-36) This story is unusual in Cheever's work for its extended view of the demands of a woman's life unmediated by the viewpoint of a male character. Ironically, it is our sympathy for Louise that creates the ambiguity of the story's ending, in which she shoots her husband as he begins to hurdle the living room furniture. She struggles with the gun's safety catch while her husband impatiently yells directions and then begins his run prematurely-- circumstances that suggest that the shooting is accidental. The reader is also aware that the husband's life has been blighted by the intimations of mortality he perceives in a broken leg sustained in a previous running of furniture hurdles, and we are tempted to an interpretation that she has compassionately put him out of his misery as one would a crippled racehorse. But the sympathetic vision of her life provided in the story also suggests the possibility that, gun in hand, she spontaneously perceived a way out of the trap their lives together have become. The story's effectiveness depends partly on this ironic reversal in which our very sympathy for the wife's situation makes us suspect her of murder at the end.

Perhaps the most disturbing of all Cheever's stories about the struggle between men and women for supremacy in marriage is "The Music Teacher." The wife in the story suddenly begins to burn dinners and create general disorder in the home, actions perceived by her husband as deliberate, "as if it was a means of expressing her resentment against him. . . . It was like some subterranean sea change, some sexual campaign or revolution stirring--unknown perhaps to her--beneath the shining and common appearance of things." (*Brigadier* 187) After entertaining the possibility in the instance of Melissa Wapshot and Louise Bentley that the domestic realm may not be fulfilling to women, Cheever here seems to fall back on the assumption that it is where women belong. The husband takes the disorder of the home as a threat to his

self-esteem and considers leaving. His only real attempt to communicate
with his wife consists of taking her to a romantic restaurant, a gesture
she counters by bringing their three small children along. A male
neighbor, perceiving the drawn battle lines, tells the husband he needs
a hobby, specifically piano lessons, specifically from a Miss Deming. He
goes to her house, noticing that all her pupils are middle-aged men like
himself. She gives him an exercise to learn, a monotonous drill, which
he practices every day for an hour, only to be sent home with the same
drill the next week and the next. One night, walking home from the
train, he thinks he hears the same piano drill coming from other houses.
His wife asks him to ask Miss Deming for a new exercise, but the teacher
replies:

> "None of the gentlemen who come here have ever complained about
> my methods. . . . Of course, Mr. Purvis went too far, Mrs.
> Purvis is still in the sanitarium, but I don't think the fault
> is mine. You want to bring her to her knees, don't you? Isn't
> that what you're here for?" (*Brigadier* 196)

Although uneasy at the possibility that he is participating in some sort
of witchcraft, the husband goes home and sits down to practice. His
wife, on her knees, begs him not to, and everything is once again fine
between them. A week later, Miss Deming's body is found, neck broken,
at a crossroads. The sudden, supernatural demise of the music teacher
is not as unsettling as the treatment of the marriage in this story.
The battle for sexual supremacy, which has been shown in other narratives, is treated as a given, one which can not be settled through communication and understanding and which can, therefore, be legitimately
carried on to the point of the subjugation of one partner. No attempt
is made to understand the wife's motives; and the story, told from the
husband's point of view, focuses on his sense of injury and asks us to
celebrate his final triumph.

The other primary role played by women in Cheever's fiction is that of
mistress. Women characters as mistresses are portrayed most simply by
Cheever, as objects of desire (as are certain wives in the fiction, such
as Nellie Nailles in *Bullet Park* and Christina Hake in "The Housebreaker
of Shady Hill"). The only negative impact on male characters that
mistresses have lies in their ability to withdraw their attention from
their lovers. Perhaps the most interesting mistress in Cheever's
fiction is Renee Herndon, in *Oh What a Paradise It Seems*, a middle-aged
woman who becomes--with minimal motivation--Lemuel Sears' mistress and
who deserts him suddenly and with as little explanation. Her role in
this last of Cheever's fictional works seems to be to create a sexual
paradise for Sears, leaving him desolate when it's withdrawn and open to
homosexual relationships. As in most Cheever narratives, the focus is

on the male character's feelings about the relationship. There are
other notable mistresses in Cheever's stories, such as Mrs. Flannagan in
"The Brigadier and the Golf Widow," who seduces Charlie Pastern to get
a key to his bomb shelter and then promptly takes a new lover, or the
heroine of "The Chaste Clarissa," a beautiful but stupid woman who is
easily seduced by a man who figures out that the one way to her bed is
to pretend to think that she is intelligent. However, most of the
mistresses in Cheever's fiction are portrayed rather simply as objects
of desire, and the focus is usually on the male characters' motives for
and feelings about the pursuit of the mistress.

Cheever's work also contains occasional rhetorical pronouncements on
women and gender relationships. For instance, *The Wapshot Chronicle*
includes an almost Jamesian delineation of the realms occupied by men
and women. Moses, the older son, realizes that the fishing camp, with
its unaired blankets, meals eaten from cans, and magazine covers nailed
to the cabin walls, is his father's realm and the house in St. Botolphs,
with linen sheets, Canton bowls, and the clock ticking in the hall, his
mother's.

> The difference seemed more strenuous than if he had crossed the
> border from one mountain country into another. . . . He stood
> . . . in a place where their absence was conspicuous and he
> smiled, thinking of how they would have attacked the camp; how
> they would have burned the furniture, buried the tin cans,
> holystoned the floors, cleaned the lamp chimneys and arranged in
> a glass slipper (or some other charming antique) nosegays of
> violets . . . . Under their administration lawns would reach
> from the camp to the lake, herbs and salad greens would flourish
> at the back door, and there would be curtains and rugs, chemical
> toilets and clocks that chimed. (56-57)

Despite the clear evidence that Sarah Wapshot (and presumably Cheever's
mother) neglected domestic activities for other interests, Cheever here
presents us with a veritable army of Aunt Sallies, doing what they can
to civilize the wilderness ways that men, left to their own devices, are
thought to prefer. The "taming" of men and their environment and
rituals is the primary image of this passage, a direct statement of the
resentment of women's effects on men that pervades so much of Cheever's
fiction.

When Cheever tries to give voice to his claimed "adoration of women"
and his sense that marital connections were entered into mysteriously
and intuitively, we hear the reflections of Farragut, the protagonist of
Falconer:

> Women possessed the greatest and the most rewarding mysterious-

> ness. . . . They were an essence, fortified and besieged, worth
> conquering and, once conquered, flowing with spoils . . . .
>   He had desired and pursued women who charmed him with their
> lies and enchanted him with their absolute irresponsibility.
> . . . When women had faults he often found them charming. When,
> while dieting rigorously and continuously talking about their
> diet, they are found eating a candy bar in a parking lot, one is
> enchanted. (100-101)

Leaving aside the images of domination, the surface flattery in this
passage is more troubling than complaints that women would, if given the
chance, domesticate a fishing camp. The passage suggests that no
personality quirks, no flaws of character matter, as long as the woman
is seen through the eyes of an attracted man. This perspective takes
away not only the individuality but the importance and dignity of women
more completely than criticism of their domesticating tendencies and
more perniciously because it can be read on the surface as "devotion."
The trouble with the view that women are "charming" in their vagaries
and lapses is that it fails to take them seriously; their flaws can only
charm because women do not ultimately matter very much.

   Cheever, for all his protestations to interviewers, does not create
various, complete, or complex women characters. They hold a relatively
unimportant place in the overall body of his fiction. As characters,
women in Cheever are defined primarily by their relationships to men.
They are most often presented through the viewpoint of male characters,
who often see them through the lens of diminished devotion or who blame
women for constraining their impulses and desires. Women in Cheever are
occasionally portrayed as goddesses who bring a kind of paradise into
men's lives, however briefly, and more often as Aunt Sally figures who
over-civilize the world of their husbands and children.

   In interviews late in his life, Cheever indicated that he had
eventually come to terms with his mother's need for independence and
fulfillment. The biographical materials published since his death
suggest that he never fully came to terms with the tensions and strains
in his marriage. In Cheever's life and work, we have an example of how
personal experience can constrict even the best artistic intentions of
a writer. In a *Paris Review* interview, Cheever said that he thought the
proper function of writing was "to enlarge people. To give them their
risk, if possible to give them their divinity, not to cut them down."
(Grant 64) This intention is behind Cheever's memorable and moving
characterizations of a number of male characters in his fiction, but it
did not influence equally his characterization of women. In Cheever's
work women's sense of risk and choice is unknown, their divinity is
largely a matter of the perception of the men in love with them, and
they are sometimes, frankly, cut down. They are portrayed primarily as

the inexplicable makers and, more often, destroyers of male happiness.

NOTE

1. This remark appears in Susan Cheever Cowley's *Newsweek* interview and in many others.

WORKS CITED

Cheever, John. *The Brigadier and the Golf Widow*. New York: Harper and Row, 1964.
_____. *Falconer*. New York: Alfred A. Knopf, 1977.
_____. *The Housebreaker of Shady Hill and Other Stories*. New York: Harper and Row, 1958.
_____. *The Wapshot Chronicle*. New York: Harper and Row, 1957.
_____. *The Wapshot Scandal*. New York: Harper and Row, 1964.
Cowley, Susan Cheever. "A Duet of Cheevers." *Newsweek* 14 March 1977, 68-70, 73.
Grant, Annette. "John Cheever: The Art of Fiction LXII." *Paris Review* 17 (Fall 1976), 39-66.

INTERVIEW

Cheever's Last Tape

Robert G. Collins

On a recent summer day I enjoyed a long afternoon's conversation with John Cheever at his rural home in Ossining, New York. It was, of course, a decade after his death. The conversation had been taped some months before he died, although the fatal cancer had already been diagnosed and a kidney removed some five weeks earlier in a futile attempt to forestall it. The visit was partly interview, partly social: the manuscript of my *Critical Essays on John Cheever* was already with the publisher, and I had been in correspondence with Cheever for some time with respect to the book, following a long interview with him a few years earlier (*Conversations*, pp. 161-172). The visit, then, had no immediate purpose other than the genial interchange that, in fact, characterized it; but with Cheever's consent, my wife--who was meeting

him for the first time--tape-recorded it. Improbably enough, it was not
until eleven years later, this summer of 1992, that I actually played
the tape through for the first time.

Modern technology is too new to pass gracefully into metaphor for the
most part, but there is something about a live tape--the very
personality of the audible voice itself, perhaps--that seems naturally
to combine the present moment and the actuality of passing life. Hearing now this tape, which in fact covered about a three-hour visit on an
afternoon when John Cheever was less than ten months short of what
became a purposefully measured death, is a strange experience, too,
precisely because I had not played it earlier. The alternating sound of
our voices, his frequent chuckle or burst of laughter--he was, it seems,
in a surprisingly amiable mood that afternoon--convey a startling
immediacy; it is as though the afternoon's visit took place just a few
days earlier this week, for there has occurred none of the steps by
which experience becomes familiar, worn, outdated.

We were traveling then. It was, in any event, too late to reopen the
manuscript on the Cheever book; the tape went into a file, a sabbatical
followed, then Cheever's death. Time passed, other projects and other
books; the tape remained unplayed by me, with Cheever's voice not
silenced there but as though he were waiting to clear his throat in that
familiar rasp, with a broad vowel and swallowed words producing an
elegant mumble.[1] As to being Cheever's last tape, at least one other
interview, long since published, (*Conversations*, pp. 224ff) took place
a few months later. The present one, however, is almost certainly the
last to be publicly heard.

August 19, 1981:[2]

When John Cheever moved into his house early in 1961, six wooded acres
on the outskirts of Ossining, New York, must have seemed a quiet retreat
that suggested Vermont or New Hampshire little more than a half an hour
from Manhattan. Today the sound of traffic on Route 9 along the Hudson
only a few hundred yards from the Cheever demesne is the roar of a busy
machine forever coming closer, constantly growing more powerful. Driving south, one sweeps off at the directed exit with that peculiarly
hurtling sensation that comes of splicing on to another divided highway
without loss of speed; then, the sudden checking internally as the Cedar
Lane sign appears to the left even as you're about to slow in search of
it. The world of out-of-control machinery only steps away from a green
bower: a tunnel opening in a wall of trees which are splotched here and
there with the seasonal blight, the deathly grey gauze of tent
caterpillars. A few yards inside the Cedar Lane roadway, a pair of
stone gateposts, a metal *New York Times* delivery cylinder, and then the
drive drops down, past a modern cottage on the right, to what looks very

much like a northern Italian rural villa with full balcony across the front and a splendid bank of trees rising behind it. The high-pitched rubber whine of the now invisible highway is the only discordant note in this peaceful enclave. By the front door stands a small, still man and a tremblingly eager yellow Labrador retriever.

It is a house with a personality, certainly. The lower level partly of stone, the second floor is fronted by its full-length covered gallery, the deck of which serves as a roof for a stone terrace on the ground floor. The entry drive curves down to a level below the house; one walks up by stone steps through the terraced garden to the level where John Cheever waits, smiling. He shuffles forward, a book in one hand, with the other gesturing as though calling our attention to our surroundings. Looking back, I see past the drive a small lawn, not so much a manicured park as rough, thick grass chopped short, interrupted here and there by a few fruit trees. Beyond is high grass, then native shrubbery swooping back down towards the highway, hiding all other signs of habitation and muffling, just enough to make its failure obvious, the speeding traffic. For a moment I think of those strange intersections that have appeared in recent years where freeways converge and swoop around each other, leaving a green overgrown captive island amid the roar, within which can sometimes be seen a stoic groundhog surveying from an earthen doorway the temporary ascendancy of screeching metal and rigid plastic, hurrying on its inevitable way to the dump. A prisoner ringed round by the unending danger of careening things, of dehumanized speed, the groundhog is any of Cheever's characters; the lovely sanctuary of his own house itself a model of isolation besieged.

It is a hot day. Sweltering in a Toyota for an hour and a half, I have been driving without my jacket. As I reach into the car for it, Cheever stops me with that crinkle-faced mixture of casual good humour and courteous formality that marks both his speech and the way he carries himself. But he has changed in the thirty-four months since I last saw him, and old age, to which he had seemed impervious at the age of 66, has leaped two decades on to the man of 69. Where he had been quick and positive in his movements, he is now bent and uncertain, turning his head to speak. But he is smiling with the Cheever charm that he could, at will, exercise to great effect, and soon he is telling us light-heartedly about the lost kidney. A very few minutes more and I forget about the change in his appearance.

Now, he urges me to forget my jacket. "I don't wear one; why should you?"

"A place to carry my wallet," I answer, thinking of one of his stories, but it is an obscure reference and, fortunately, he does not pick up on it. He is cheerfully warning my wife against being seduced by Edgar, the elderly yellow Lab, who is whimpering in a beseeching manner and holding a fuzzy green tennis ball invitingly in his/her jaws

--Edgar is actually a bitch despite the name, as he now tells us.

The book Cheever holds is a publisher's proof copy, with an anonymous red paper binding. Setting it down, still open, on a deck lounge from which he has risen on hearing our car, he tells us that it is John Updike's forthcoming novel--"He was here last week. It's a *wonderful* story, really a fine job. Come in, come in. Let me get you a drink and then we can go up and sit on the outside porch and talk."

Inside is a lovely shaded room of dark paneling and oriental rugs. A smiling young man appears; he seems powerfully built beside Cheever, whose frailty is even more obvious beside him. "This is Max," says the novelist, "he's been looking after me while Mary's in New Hampshire. But Max will be leaving tonight; my son Ben is arriving at six."

I remember, then, having read that John Updike is, this week, receiving the 1981 Edward MacDowell Medal for the Arts at the MacDowell Colony in Peterborough, New Hampshire, an event that is to be attended by many writers. As Cheever tells it, with a sort of ruefulness, Mary is representing her invalid husband. The MacDowell Medal had been awarded to Cheever himself in 1978, and Updike is, of course, one of Cheever's long-time friends, dating back to their common visit as cultural ambassadors to Russia in 1964.

Max, obviously very much at home, brings us drinks--a jug of apple juice for the invalid novelist. I find myself remembering my last meeting with John Cheever, in the late autumn of 1978, in Ottawa. He had been there under the auspices of the cultural section of the American Embassy. It had been a rigorous day for him. Following his morning activities at the Embassy, he had lunched with a group of us from the university. Then he had given me two hours in the afternoon for an interview that subsequently was published in the journal *Thalia* (*Conversations*, pp. 161-172). That evening, he had delivered one of the most successful readings in a university series that I have ever attended, reading his work with both energy and delicacy and handling scores of questions afterwards with that indescribable combination of charm and authority that kept his audience attentive to every word. Throughout, his energy, the deft assurance with which he delivered his views and responded to queries, his trimly youthful appearance--a man who could have been 45 in his tailored beige gabardine suit and polished shoes--all belied a birthdate of 1912 for this writer whose bibliography went back half a century. The collected *Stories* had just come out and was riding high on *The New York Times* best-seller list. Author of hundreds of tales, and four novels to that point, he might well be seen as the reigning master of his art--a man who was, if anything, *too* good at it, grumbled his detractors. More important still, he was, as critic John Wain and others have noted (*Critical Essays*, pp. 28ff.), a writer who handled the "large words," words such as *love, honour, generosity, goodness, valour* and used them unabashedly and well, creating a new set of expectations in us in that very area that so many serious writers have abandoned in this century. In my own view, he was nowhere near as far from skepticism as he appeared to some of his critics, while his depth was, perhaps, far greater than had yet been recognized. For instance, he is not in his art so much religious as artistically aware of the emotions, needs, and values lying behind religious impulses; his use of the "large words" was, perhaps, less optimism than the cry of a man dying of thirst and calling for water. Throughout his work, I found him superb in capturing the sense of a world gone strange in our time, that *dis*-ease that has paradoxically accompanied the achieving of physical comfort by western man, the disquieting apprehension that has slowly accreted until we now dimly realize that what we are witnessing is the birth of a new form of terror in a post-humanistic world.

And yet, even in late 1978, Cheever had revealed a personal guardedness, a briskness that stayed well short of impatience but suggested a disinclination to speak on anything other than general beliefs--the different faces of virtue in the world. While he can be a stimulating and even engrossing speaker about writing and about abstractions, in his interviews, I noted, he virtually refuses to discuss any questions of extended meaning in specific instances of his own fiction. He has none of the self-conscious satisfaction with theory that flows from writers who have spent their life in the academy; he is a pure creative writer, remote and involuted, displaying the fruit of his imagination, not its seeds, not its working-out amid fits and starts. While he has talked about the housekeeping procedures of writing, it has always been on carefully generalized terms, more apparently casual than characteristically so. On the rare occasions when he has talked about specific work, it is apt to have been in non-conclusive, almost mystic terms, as for instance in his readings when he describes the personal ordeal of writing "The Swimmer," how it grew with some kind of self-contained force to 150 pages of notes before it was beaten down to a dozen pages.

Prior to the present illness which will prove to be a terminal one, Cheever has had two previous experiences with his body which have impressed him so deeply that he has referred to them repeatedly in interviews--his apparent heart attack in 1973 (Donaldson, *John Cheever: A Biography*, p. 268) and the discovery by early 1975 that his severe alcoholism was a real and immediate threat to his life. There are men who are thoroughly religious and there are men who are deeply "religious." The first are dogmatically inclined, while the latter are disposed to view life itself with awe on one hand, with despair on the other. The first is the polemicist; the second the artist--and Cheever surely is of the latter group. Delighting in physical experience and using his body very fully, at a later point in life such a man is apt to be astonished to discover that the life in him has a life of its own beyond his will, that body can falter and fail and refuse to perform automatically as he wills it to do so. (Indeed, this was the perception that rested at the core of "The Swimmer.") A youthfulness in one's mid-60s is a blessing in one sense, but a dangerous illusion in another; when the structure crashes, when infirmity appears, it is preposterous, grotesque, rather than natural.

Cheever in 1978 and Cheever in 1981: These were the two stages of Cheever's life that I had chanced upon as an unwitting spectator. Once thoroughly convinced of the fact that the booze was a real threat to life, Cheever had quit. Now, he pours himself another glass of apple juice--he would down several that afternoon. Max has retreated with a book. Pausing at the staircase to point out to my wife a framed Chinese fan, a family heirloom that echoed the Cheever/Wapshot history, Cheever leads us upstairs through another paneled sitting room to the long open gallery. Below us are the grounds of the house; he points out how the trees now hide what was once a view of the Hudson. The angry drone of freeway traffic vibrates louder in the air, a plane roars overhead. We are talking about our recent trip to Yorkshire, where I had given a paper at a Brontë conference. Like most good writers, Cheever has partially created himself through his reading, and he has an easy familiarity with his great predecessors in the novel. Such names as Fielding, Austen, Thackeray and Brontë fall easily from his lips or his pen. He freely accords them the greatest respect--as, indeed, he does with most of his writing contemporaries. We move on, as we are seating ourselves, to a writer's involvement with public events, then the question of World War II.

JC: I was going to bring that up. It seemed to me--about the Second World War--that there was a broader and deeper current through it than in current events as such. It still seems to me--I don't know what it was. I did write . . . I wrote very little about it, of course. I was in the Army and the Pacific for just a couple of years.[3] I can say that there are deeper and broader channels, in many ways strictly ceremonial, as far as I can see. Actually, that war produced very little in any way to extend our grasp in literature, it seems to me.

RGC: Yes. For awhile, it seems that everyone was asking what the war had done to us.

JC: Also, presumably what it has produced in literature, which is a most important objective.

RGC: There was Mailer's World War II novel, *The Naked and the Dead.*

JC: Ah, yes. There was the Mailer book. Then there was a book by a fellow named John Horne Burns, called *The Gallery*. It's quite a classic book about Naples. There was Irwin Shaw's book, which I didn't like. The Mailer book, I think, as far as I'm concerned, and the Burns book were the best that I recall.

RCG: Your book of short stories, *The Way Some People Live*, came out in 1943. And some Army stories. But you've never written a great deal about the war itself, have you?

JC: No . . . no. It was never my intention to.

RGC: Was it your intention *not* to?

JC: Yes, it was my intention not to. Still it's important that there had been a war, and my intent is always to imply that there are deeper and broader currents of emotion and concern. One should get at the truth of the question . . . to tell the most traumatic experience this nation has ever encountered. It's virtually identical with the truth.

RGC: What writing was produced, perhaps, seems too purposeful. (JC: Yes.) Do you think there has been anything related to the war that changed your writing in any way?

JC: No, I was well established in my own writing by that time.

RGC: It does seem significant that you have been so continuous a writer but never really wrote about the war. . . . Speaking of continuity, I've had a great experience in the last year or two, in connection with the book, rereading everything of yours from *Homage to Shakespeare* right up to the present.

JC: I'm . . . I'm very grateful to you for saying that. I find it impossible to read my own work. When Mary was in New Hampshire--I had called her, and she had had one of those marvelous days; and I thought, well, I'll never see one again, because I won't go to her place. And I thought, well, I've got it in a story, so I don't have to worry about ever going back there. And I got started in reading it and said--I can't read this rubbish! I can't go on with it! (laughter)

RGC: Understandable, perhaps, but you're apt to be the only man in the world who would feel that about your writing. But one thing that strikes me is that, contrary to some critical views, I find your whole range remarkably integral. It's developed, there's a progress. But the things you've had to say, the way you've looked into people--what one might call the result, what's important in your work has proceeded very much in terms of what I would say was the change in the American personality over the last forty years.

JC: Do you think so?

RGC: Yes. Ironically, people at one time were saying why don't you stay in St. Botolphs as though that were reality. Then, John Leonard, for instance, asks why does John Cheever have to become a stranger in *Falconer* . . . ? I know you shy away from reviews.

JC: I don't actually shy away. I find the whole thing--well, it's impossible to describe one's attitude, of course. Someone said to me, do you know there's a cover story on you in *Time*, and I said, yes, I did. He worked for *Sports Illustrated*. I remember, he said, do you have a copy? I said no, as a matter of fact, I don't, and he said would you like one? I said, sure; I wanted it enough to see it. And so he got the *Time* cover story, and I wondered, why haven't I read this, why haven't I found it? And I started reading it and, of course, I couldn't get past the second sentence . . . and never have been able to. Basically, it's embarrassing!

RGC: Perhaps living writers have a special problem in that sense. Their fluidity. It's been an unusual experience, as I say, reading over all your work, consecutively, over the past year.

JC: I do hope it shaped up.

RGC: Beautifully, that's the thing. But I'm possibly one of the very few who don't know it in piecemeal fashion, that have had the rare experience of holding in my head the continuous development of the work.

JC: There are some Ph.D. theses . . . .

RGC: Yes, Dennis Coates, and James Valouti . . . .

JC: Well, Dennis Coates, is . . . has pretty much been disowned, I think! My brother was still alive when Coates was doing research. And my brother had been drinking very heavily, and described me as effeminate and a fag . . . and very much a shut-in [?], is what he said, which Coates took as a fight, and which wasn't the case. It wasn't at all the case. I was quite cross about that. And then Coates finally deciding that my homosexuality was the root, was what the whole work turned around . . . . Yes that is the thesis. And I said I didn't *ever* wish to see him again. (cf: *Cheever: A Biography*, pp. 280-81)

RGC: That thesis hasn't appeared in print?

JC: No, none of it is published. I'm very pleased it is known, the homosexuality . . . it's . . . it has a vague unresolved spiritual resolution. *Zen Buddhism and Motorcycle Riding* . . . . I can't remember the author; that was his favorite book. I remember thinking, how did I get mixed up in this?

RGC: Anyway, the kind of thing I wanted to talk to you about today was the way in which your overall work has changed. *Falconer*, it seems, is almost the rounding of a circle. Ezekial Wapshot, founder of the Wapshot line; his first name recurs in Ezekial Farragut, the ghost of our time who slips outside history. Is that intentionally rounding a circle?

JC: Well, there's a certain amount of family history. Ezekial Cheever founded the Cheever family in 1637, and the Cheevers have been quite prominent in Boston . . . . In the Boston Social Register, all those listed changed from, say, Ezekial Lawrence Cheever to E. Lawrence Cheever, there was a certain amount of . . . (laughter). They all changed--they all dropped the Ezekial. Ezekial is a very distinguished name; he was a very distinguished old man, lived to be 93. His Latin grammar was used until about . . . as recently as a hundred years ago. I remember, it was a first rate Latin grammar. There was a second Ezekial, who was *not* called Ezekial Junior, who testified in the Salem Witch Trials and was responsible for the drowning of several innocent women. Claiming that he had seen them talking to unicorns. It was the most *ghastly* sort of crime. It was his testimony, I think, it was in part his testimony that those poor women were drowned.

RGC: You never told that story to Samuel Coale, did you? He's written a paper on the relationship of your work and that of Hawthorne which will appear in *Critical Essays*. You'll find it interesting, though the question of conscious influence is beside the point.

JC: Yes, I've corresponded with Coale, but, no, I didn't know it then. I didn't know it until quite recently. I always thought that it was a malicious slander. I thought there was only one Ezekial.

RGC: Going back to the *changes*, and the *wholeness* of your work. John Leonard--who's a very good critic--when he hit *Falconer* didn't quite know what to do with it *because* he had enjoyed St. Botolphs. He had also enjoyed, obviously, *Bullet Park*, but I think when he got to *Falconer* the landscape was so different that he missed the earlier ones. And you have a very special definition of nostalgia, one that doesn't exclude the present. Perhaps people are not capable of dealing equally with it, in that sense. By the way, a casual question: did you by any chance give Farragut your army serial number as his convict number?

JC: No. Not that I remember.

RGC: I wondered, since you gave Tony Nailles your birthdate, May 27th.

JC: Oh, did I? I didn't know that. This is not so . . . one doesn't know what one's doing. (laughter) But I don't remember. As I say, I have difficulty reading the stuff. My son read *Bullet Park* recently, and said it was quite good.

RGC: It is very good.

JC: Occasionally I'll see one of my books. I have *Falconer* in French. And I read it in French.

RGC: The treatment that *Bullet Park* got, finally, was fairly good.

JC: Oh, I thought that DeMott review was misleading . . . .

RGC: But John Gardner, of course, changed that; he was very nice to it.

JC: *Bullet Park*, of course, was well received everywhere else in the world--except for DeMott, but it didn't really matter. The work has never been as well received in the United States as it has been, for example, in Europe.

RGC: But it seems to me that *Bullet Park* is a pivotal novel: if you look at the two Wapshots and the short stories, and then *Bullet Park*, it leads to *Falconer*. By the way, I wanted to ask you about one thing with respect to *Bullet Park*. Hammer and Nailles: you play with what you call "the mysterious power of nomenclature," which feeds the idea of the two as alter-egos. (JC: Yes.) It works very well. But you have Elliot Nailles with only a present; he has no past that's discussed in the novel. On the other hand, you have Hammer--they are both about the same age, in their forties--Hammer is a person who is suddenly in the present. But you bring him up in detail, through his childhood, his adolescence until about the age of 24, and then he has very little appearance until he shows up in Bullet Park and becomes involved with Nailles. Hammer is a first person identity, with inner emotions and thoughts, while Nailles is third person. Hammer is the one who at the end is crying in the church, just as he was the one who cried when that fellow was swept off the railway platform, or jumped, or whatever. He's the only one, in a sense, who has feelings. Nailles, when he finds his son is in the hands of Hammer, for virtually the only time in the novel becomes purposeful and effective, but without altering his drug-bound existence in the least. There's that magnificent one or two final pages . . . boom, boom, boom right to the end. But Nailles is still the *same* addict.

JC: I'm so glad you liked it. I've not read it recently, but I do remember writing it and it was very intense. And it seems to me that if one *does* feel that, then it's apparent. Perhaps, if not good, it's the best one can do. That was true in almost all of *Falconer*, which was written in rather a short period of time except for the original segment. As I say, I have not read it in English, but I was going through some papers and I came on a page or two of the notes. The voice was the best voice I have.

RGC: *Falconer*, that is, the title of it, everyone has referred to the Yeatsian imagery--the falcon and the falconer--there. Was that intentional?

JC: Not quite that intentional, no, no. Though one can't very well write without Yeats in mind. Incidentally, I had forgotten the DeMott review of *Bullet Park*, and I said it would have made absolutely no difference to me. DeMott had come out for a membership at the Century Club, and I was urged to blackball him. Which I couldn't very well have done, and I said no, I wouldn't dream of doing it. And I said, you know, it would . . . well, it made no difference to me at all. Because the book had an enormous success when it was in Europe. And I went . . . . it sold something like 100,000 copies in Moscow in one day [*sic*]. I went to Europe, I went to Russia in February of that year, or when the book came out, and I was so afraid that they had thought it a social comment. And I addressed an art gallery in Moscow and I said if you are taking this novel as a criticism of capitalism you're greatly mistaken; this has not been my intent at all. And a man asked to be recognized and he said, Mr. Cheever, we are here because we love the way you describe autumn leaves being driven in front of the headlights. Then I said, you know, then *all right!*

RGC: Lovely. There's another thing you do very well. In fact you did it in "The Night Mummy Got the Wrong Mink Coat." Snow. Coming through at night. But going back to DeMott's review of *Bullet Park*. Perhaps in a less sympathetic way he was anticipating something that Leonard would convey in his later review of *Falconer*. That is, he was hung up on the last preceding image that he had of Cheever the novelist, which did not accomodate the *Bullet Park* text. And so, that line in his review, which the *Times Book Review* used as a sub-head: a "grand gatherum of late 20th century American weirdos." This goes back to the constant critical misconception that you're a defender of American suburbia. Also, the meaningful disjunction between the totally precise language that you use and the alienated situation in which the characters find themselves seems not to have come across to critics like DeMott. They are deceived, in a sense, by the very precision of your language; as a result, I don't think such readers always understand that the characters are not supposed to be normal, realistic folk in ordinary situations. That you're not defending suburbia, that you are in fact looking at the hapless individual in a given situation suddenly identified as bizarre.

JC: DeMott, you know, had published a book on American literature some years ago--do you know it?--in which I was very favorably singled out. And I couldn't understand how he could possibly have changed his mind so swiftly. But I assumed it was a tenure battle. (laughter) At Amherst.

RGC: Before *Bullet Park* you had been safely categorized. Though, as I say, all of the changes in our collective personality, unexpected as every one has been for the past forty years, somehow are communicated in your work.

JC: I have a novel--I have completed a novel. Did you know that? And, of course, the response is that it's marvelous, but it isn't at all like what you've been doing.

RGC: That's what they've been saying for some time.

JC: Yes. I know it. The whole nature of the perfectionist, of course, is not to repeat oneself. I do it, but if I do, I try to avoid it. That, the nostalgia, nomadism, the sense of spiritual wandering is very, very strong in all the work, naturally.

RGC: Of course, repetition that is effective is called theme. You've used several things repeatedly, but you circle around them. In a way, I suppose, this is necessary in order to define anything. It's like a gemstone, or something with different facets, it's the same subject but it's approached differently and so it reveals different things about it. And as we were saying, the very criticism--let's say the potential criticism that you use the same themes is followed by the cry, why *isn't* he doing the same thing, why isn't it the same setting? Stephen Moore has said that the New York of your early stories is as remote and magical and evocative as Hemingway's Paris. Which is true, but that isn't where you are now. But it's where all of us once lived. The remarkable thing is that you haven't been stuck there. It's almost as though you had an instinct for the times, the same kind of eye or ear that you have for an image. Has there been any consciousness of yourself as deliberately changing--or have you just written the work as it came?

JC: Oh, I think that's an extremely difficult question. Of course, you're always conscious of doing badly. One writes of course to excell, you know. And so it's very genuine activity, in which to be more penetrating, or to be more useful. And as I've gotten to be an old man, it seems to me a very *important* activity, a means of communication. And then, perhaps, *to* communicate--the means of communication among literate and illiterate and serious men and women. One waits, perhaps, to communicate more . . . to *improve* one's communication. I have no idea of the merits of this last book, which here again I can't read. It's not in galleys yet, I have to go in town on Monday to go over the manuscript before it gets into galleys⁴. I trust I can do that.

RGC: What is the title?

JC: The title is *Oh, What a Paradise It Seems*. But, of course, again it alarmed everyone. They said, but you can't advertise it like that, you know. (laughter) And I said, there hasn't been an upbeat title in fiction, you know, since *Wuthering Heights*!

RGC: They might have learned that back when you published *Some People, Places, and Things That Will Not Appear in My Next Novel*. But, again, you've come up with a shift in ground: it will be interesting. Of course, even *Bullet Park* is a fantasy, but a fantasy about reality. And in *Falconer*, in that basic confinement, you have what are almost spirits surrounding Ezekial Farragut.

JC: Yes. . . .

RGC: You've said in an interview, Falconer is not a prison but confinement, the condition of confinement. And you have Farragut identify himself with the polar opposite--the blue sky.

JC: Yes, as I remember, in the first chapter, as he gets out of the van. . . . He nails himself to the sky.

RGC: To the blue sky. And at the end, he goes out, in a sense, in search of light.

JC: Yes. *Rejoice, rejoice!* I tried at the end of *Bullet Park*, happily, happily, happily, which was taken as an irony, total irony, which was not my intent[5] So when I came to the end of *Falconer* I wanted it never to be taken as irony again, and so I used "rejoice, rejoice," which is very difficult to translate as ironic. It's a big question, irony, isn't it?

RGC: But--in either book--I think that DeMott, and maybe others, found it impossible to accept an epiphany as an ending.

JC: I think that DeMott is quite incapable of accepting epiphany under any circumstances. I read very little of his work. But occasionally. . . . He writes rather like people who write cookbooks or . . . . His good opinion, of course, is something I don't want at this point.

RGC: Walter Clemons, who by the way wrote a very good review, very sound, well thought out . . . .

JC: Extremely generous, yes.

RGC: He speaks of the love in *Falconer* as relinquishing. And, of course, Farragut has to go through a cleansing. And, in fact, he is cleansed of the heroin. But also the love born there, with respect to Jody, not specifically but in the abstract, I suppose, that love extends beyond love, that love is not possessing but a relinquishing, a letting-go with tenderness. How does that relate to the love that represents desire . . . the more ordinary impulse?

JC: Yes. Well, it's not such a problem. If we once woke up to hope--and could identify it as such . . . in definitions of love. I was watching my son, my young son, drive out of the driveway on his way to California, and I was going to fly that afternoon to the MacDowell Colony and get the medal (*Cheever: a Biography*, p. 329). And I remember watching. I can't remember the *word* that I settled on, but love is simply--love is an incongruence. I can't even get the right words! Then, also, the definitions of love, you know, have thrown very little light on it. None of us can choose between one's erotic drives and one's sentimental drives that, it seems to me, are profound and almost exclusive. Ah, well, as a matter of fact, you've Adam and Eve, of course. The earliest love for anyone else.

RGC: Adam and Eve, then on to Cain and Abel. All the interviewers have referred to "the brother" being there, and in all four of your novels the brother is to varying degrees an antagonist. . . .

JC: And then, of course, I did have a brother. My feeling of it is that fiction is not crypto-autobiography, as you must have heard me say a great many times. However, the idea that my brother experiences were such *common* experiences is certainly a mistaken one.

RGC: There's very much of a love-hate relationship there.

JC: Yes, yes.

RGC: And, you said, you felt like writing him out on one occasion, and decided not to. . . .

JC: Oh, I've heard several stories. . . . He came here, he was a pure alcoholic and was dying. He was punctillious. He went to his children, his son and wife and the children in various places around the United States, he went to all of them and said goodbye, and he came here to say goodbye. I had just finished *Falconer--just*. And I said, oh Fred--he was still driving a car, I don't know how. I said--Well, I've killed you in the new book! And, I think, he did not take kindly to it. But . . . it was all quite serious, and then he went back to his home. And died.

RGC: You know, in *Falconer* one of the things about the murder is that Zeke is, in a way, perfectly justified. Is this a first stage of purification for him?

JC: I don't know. The best writing is in the story "Goodbye My Brother" when the narrator murders his brother Lawrence.[6]

RGC: And then goes off.

JC: Yes. *Goodbye*. It is the title of the story. In *Falconer*, effectively, of course, he's confined to begin with by killing his brother, that confines his sense of reality. It seems to me he is a confined man, from the community.

RGC: Because, in a way, going into the prison is the means of moving out of prison?

JC: Yes. The only way he can move. (laughter) Remember, I speak as a man who hasn't read the book!

RGC: Someone, I think it may have been John Leonard again in his review, observed that *Falconer* has a kind of valedictory character, as though it were a leave-taking.

JC: From the opening--I had written the opening paragraph, I think. The

gates of Falconer had three emblems . . . it had overtones of a Dickens
opening with two bridges around it . . . it had a particular beat
[slapping his knee, rhythmically] and this I had written when I went
down to Boston to teach a semester at Boston University. I was also
drinking very heavily, I remember. I kept, I think, no more than that
page. Then, I started to write the book in the spring, and it was done
before the next spring.

RGC: Speaking of a beat--you said once that you didn't use poetry in
yuor writing. . . .

JC: No, I think the emotions are very different.

RGC: Well, I was sent recently a manuscript on your work where the
author, by chance, when quoting you compresses the quote down to about
an inch or two as he centers it, setting it off from his text. Astonish-
ingly, it reads very well as poetry, quite as well as some of Auden.
I'll send it to you sometime so you can see the effect. Spender, for
instance, has said that a poem begins for him with an image which starts
spreading and growing. Your beginnings, of course, are famous.

JC: Everybody's beginnings should be; after all, you know, it's your
opening cue, here it is. It's certainly the responsibility of an
artist, so far as I can see, not to back on to the stage.

RGC: Do you ever find a chuckle in a line or something that you've set
down and then the story just embroiders on it?

JC: Oh yes. Yes, of course.

RGC: I suppose images are there to be unpacked, spread out, I guess.
That's what stories do. The last thing I read of yours was "The
Island," where you describe a troop of former celebrities on an island,
happily reading the classics. An image in itself. Is that the last
work? Is this a view of paradise?

JC: That's the last one that's been published. "The Island" and "The
Night That Mother Lost Her Mink Coat," or whatever it's called. They
were, of course, spinoffs, just strips thrown in. (laughter) Characters tire of eating shell-fish. I am bothered--perhaps it's that part
of my--perhaps it's my age. Or younger people telling me about the
situation . . . I worry terribly about celebrities. I see them committing suicide. Blowing out their brains at the far end of the road,
very much alone, ending up in the YMCA. I worry about the players out
there, Luis Tiant pitching a losing game. I *worry* about ball players.

And I've thought, what *is* the solution? Of course, they're all in similar neglect for selfish reasons. And some of them do survive, obviously, but then a great many of them don't. They get terribly depressed, and then they drink and suffer.

RGC: And then they write a book and make a million dollars on their disasters.

JC: I hope so!

RGC: Why are writers, American writers, so hung up on baseball? There's Coover and Mark Harris . . .

JC: Oh, I'm not actually hung up on it. I did write a short story . . . "The Best of ---." Have you ever seen it? It's never been collected. . . . Oh, it's not coming . . . it *is* coming out in a limited edition. No, I'm not really hung up on baseball. It's no more, you know, than Europeans hung up on soccer. A national sport. I'm actually very fond of football.

RGC: Have you ever met Calvino, by the way? Italo Calvino?

JC: Oh yes, I have. I intend to read more at some point in time.

[At this point a car entered the driveway. A woman, one of the Cheever neighbors, leaned part-way out of the car, and asked Cheever how he was. Did he have any tomatoes? No, he answered regretfully, and with a cordial farewell, she drove off. He sat down again.]

JC: I've been out of the hospital over three weeks. The critical weeks in which a garden can be destroyed by weeds. But they didn't destroy the tomatoes, they looked vigorous to me. Mary's been away for two weeks; when she returned . . . I picked them off and they had rotted, naturally.

RGC: Have you done much of the trimming around here?

JC: I should say I do most of it. I'm very fond of scything. I used to scythe the orchard that was over there. Not anything I learned from my father, incidentally. My father was very much a salty--he was an old line Yankee. And he gave me some very good times. Not much of a father, but . . . .

RGC: Anything like Leander?

JC: Oh very, yes. With the journal, a good deal of that was my father, that was given to me by my father. Dad was brought up to be very formal . . . at the turn of the century. My grandfather sailed to China and Ceylon on sailing ships. Dad was very much immersed in that. However, it was he who regarded New York, of course, as an absolute *sinkhole* of, you know, ordinary alien people, compared to Boston. (laughter) But he greatly appreciated the light in the sky. Which is one of the things there, however dangerous and dishonest people in New York are. It's the only city surrounded by rivers, and you find the light extraordinary, particularly in the evening sky. And this, of course, is admissable in the soul of a Yankee. The wind from the north-north-east and twilights in that part of the world are very beautiful. I was driving down the . . . now, when I remarked . . . I remember being told, I think by my mother, that loosestrife, the purple flower, is the only flower we have along the road shoulders in the United States that was mentioned in Shakespeare.

RGC: All through your work there's a very effective use of color and light; in *Falconer*, the intenseness of light is a contrast to confinement. You spoke of your father now, and his sense of light and color. One of the things about Leander that seems to be true is that he is the culmination of the past, but he's not suited to the present; his ferry boat going back and forth across to the amusement park is a grotesque version of the China trade. In the past, and you do it beautifully with the biblical form--Ezekial begat, and so on, and so on--you create there the sense of a people who, in the old legendry of New England at least, controlled the world, in short created it. Then Leander comes along, Leander comes as a transition from a time when men really created or shaped themselves through their work to a time when the world inexorably shapes us. Certainly *confinement* suggests that, and in your work that result is carefully worked out. Was that consciously done?

JC: No. It's not intentional. I assume that everything I do is, in a sense, a breaking of the mold. The novel I just completed, it's not *really* a breaking; it's meant not to be a casting off . . . it's the wish to be more penetrating. Or to be . . . as an old man, I would perhaps use the words "to be more useful."

RGC: Farragut, though, the professional academic, strikes down his brother, allows his wife her freedom; he moves away from, sheds the identities that he goes into Falconer with. As an epiphany at the end, is he modern man standing up and saying: Damn it, no?

JC: Well, I certainly hope so, yes.

RGC: Do college professors--Farragut is one--have a special character in your writing?

JC: But he's one only . . . fleetingly. That's true. My Boston University experience was disastrous. I was drinking heavily. I was on alcohol and drugs, and I thought that the university had sent me . . . kids that knew nothing but drugs.

RGC: Fiction writers generally have been extraordinarily favourable towards your writing and other professional writers have seen you as achieving something to be envied. I suspect that academics, however, tend to resent you a little, perhaps because, I think, they tend to be proprietary. That is, they like to feel they control whatever they are working with. And it seems to me that there is something in your work that academics, accordingly, bridle against.

JC: I have *no* idea what that is. I know that I'm not widely sympathized with by them. Now, Saul Bellow is. . . .

RGC: Of course, he writes about academics.

JC: But in my very short teaching experience, it seems to me that books fall into two categories very loosely--those that are taught and those that one reads. I remember teaching in Iowa, and *Gravity's Rainbow* had just come out; and they said, would you teach *Gravity's Rainbow*? And I could see where it would be a book much more easily taught than read. (laughter) And this is also true of Coover and Barthelme at that time and a couple of other writers. They don't seem to fit their responsibility *to be interesting* and so it suffers. That's to say, it's necessary to provoke the interest of students taking the course.

RGC: Perhaps you've put your finger on something there with respect to academics. One inherent problem is that an academic view of the world, is by nature, laboured. They are not willing to take life on its own terms; it always has to *mean*, always has to have a *significance*, always has to *question*. The thing about your work, about all very good writing, is that it first happens for its own sake. I've heard you say time after time that interest is . . . .

JC: . . . Is the first canon of aesthetics. Yes. I still feel that very strongly.

RGC: And significance is the first canon of aesthetics for an academic. Now, interest is there when a story is; however, significance can be there before a story, but it doesn't make creative art, it makes an essay. So perhaps academics have to have their writers finished-off, completed, packaged in one massive volume or a bound set, then they can be worked on. Because the writer can't talk back, can't write a new, unpredictable book. So with a live writer, they say, what's happened? Why is he doing this? As has been said with every succeeding novel of yours. And you came late to the novel, of course.

JC: Yes, I was in my forties when *The Wapshot Chronicle* was published. But I had waited. Well, at first I waited--I waited until I had what appeared to me a consecutive experience. I was also aware of my parents; I didn't want to distress them. Then they were both dead. And it was done. Anyhow . . . the only first-hand academic experience I had was at Boston University, where I had made myself pretty much an incompetent. I did teach a semester at Iowa, however. At the Writer's thing. However, I spent very little time with the writers and, generally, with the rest of the faculty. There were about, I should say, forty members at half-professorships[7]--from all departments, oriental languages, chemistry and everything--who were waiting for professorships at other universities, and it was fairly much the most exciting company I've ever had. I had my wife come out for part of it. I think it was something like 46 members of the faculty, all of whom I thoroughly enjoyed. And I went back perhaps two years later, and there wasn't a soul there. Occasionally they would telephone for publicity stories from, you know, Colorado, Washington State, or whatever. But that was a tremendously exciting group of applicants. Completely different.

RGC: Interesting. Writers are commonly thought of as back-biting, competitive. . . .

JC: Well, that's a bit . . . actionable! John Updike, Saul Bellow and I are the dearest of friends. I have John's new novel and it's marvelous.

RGC: That fits in, I suppose, with the respect that I mentioned all other novelists have had for your work, while writers who are less tied to creative work themselves have been less cordial. Anatole Broyard, for instance, wrote a snarky piece in the *Times* about your recent party with a tent on the lawn and an orchestra.[8]

JC: (laughter) Oh, yes, yes! You know, that party was, I think, something like eleven or twelve years ago!

RGC: And he just wrote about it this year?

JC: Yes! The only reason he was at that party was that he had given me a horrible review. And I thought--you know--what do you do? What do you do . . . invite him to a party! And also, we don't *often* have parties of *that* size, that many people, but there it was, a tent out there on the lawn. You know the way these piranhas are, and so on.

RGC: Christopher Lehmann-Haupt of the *Times* has interviewed you very well. He seems much more perceptive about you than Broyard is. On the other hand, Broyard, early on, seemed to have the potential of being a very good writer.

JC: Oh yes. Two *marvelous* short stories. I don't know whether you know it or not, I did absolutely *everything* I could about the stories. Oh, they were wonderful stories. And I met him, and. . . . However, I still think he seeks, he genuinely seeks merit, and my book was given for review. . . . Those two stories were written 35 years ago--I think it's been that long. They were published, I think, in the *Partisan Review*. And they were brilliant. And I remember speaking to my publisher about it and took it to an English publisher. And I remember meeting him in a lecture at Columbia and. . . . Oh, you asked about Calvino?

RGC: Well, yes.

JC: He was a friend of Barolini. Calvino used to visit, of course, and that's just over the hill. He spent regular time here. He had been here; I used to go up and see him. And I always thought him interesting. I think his last book is pretty much obligatory reading [*If On A Winter's Night A Traveller*]. Calvino, of course, always had the . . . the danger of being cute, exceptionally cute; he was cute as hell, and he used to be quite beautiful. The combination of cuteness and beauty is . . . well.[9] Well, I think that book is absolutely obligatory, in the tradition of Pirandello.

RGC: The relationship of the author to the reader. That's something you do well, yourself.

JC: Well, this sort of thing actually occurs at the beginning of "the Novel"; this is Fielding.

RGC: But you seem to do it less self-consciously than, say, Calvino. Frequently you identify with the central character, you even speak through his voice; but you're never simply looking at him objectively, you're relating him to the reader all the time.

JC: Well, this is broad in spectrum, what we mean by the novel, really. What we have, it began actually with Cervantes and was picked up by Richardson and Fielding. One could enjoy that much scope in the beginning days of the novel. This was no longer mythology, no longer epic character. The opening chapter in this novel, this last novel, was what I wish I were. . . . Well, I would sooner write about lying around waiting to ship canvas or something, you know, or to catch trout with flies, but unfortunately I *have* to write--it is my responsibility to write about what *counts*, which is traditional in Fielding. And the publisher, you know, said--what *is* this? And I thought, for Christ's sake, don't you know? And I suddenly realized that they *don't* know Fielding. But that variety is what, it seems to me, is what is roughly *meant* by the novel, by the end of a particular journey.

RGC: That reminds me, you wrote somewhere else about the leaves in the lights at night, about a Romanian woman who wrote to you?

JC: Oh, what I said, that was somebody in Moscow, somebody spoke to me in Moscow.

RGC: But you've had that reference elsewhere. . . .

JC: In a letter? To . . . I presumed it was from a Romanian. Then I'll have to change the Moscow line. It sounds as if I were making the whole thing up. . . . Then, I said what the hell are you talking about, and then he said I can't wait to go to pee! All right? (laughter)

RGC: One of the marvelous things that you've accomplished in your writing is that you have established a dialogue that continues outside of it. I mean you can talk to people about--or they can talk to you about--the images that you've forced on their consciousness. You've created realities for them there that mean something. That continue to mean things afterwards. There are any number of lines, situations or whatever in your writing that will flash through my head forever. You've loaded me, and others, up with a baggage of Cheever's imagination. And it's all something that you've extended into other lives, into other consciousness, as ways of seeing things. When I read things that you write, they come back to my mind afterward when I look at the world, and I see your image for that situation that I'm looking at now; you've controlled my life. And you control it for hundreds, thousands--I suppose, eventually, if your writing goes on and on--for millions of people. And, it seems to me, this is the life fulfillment that really fractures time for a writer like yourself. Here you are, in your seventieth year, you've just had a malignant kidney removed, but in an important sense your first really successful story remains every bit as

young as the very last story you've written. Not many writers actually
run through to this point.

JC: Saul Bellow has. Saul Bellow is my age, and still has a novel
coming out. It's coming out this fall. No, Saul pulled it back and
he's rewriting it. It's not coming out until February. I think that
mine is coming out in February, too. Yes. I keep telling the son of a
bitch, get the book out *this* year! Next year is Bellow's! (laughter)

RGC: These things feed each other. A book by Cheever and a book by
Bellow at the same time.

JC: Well, I don't see that it makes any difference. It seems to me
that the endurance of one's importance is a matter of relative indifference. . . . It seems to me that literature is something that one
contributes to; it is not a competitive sport. I've been reading John
Updike's book--Jesus--you know, John is 20 years younger than I am--but
this book is so marvelous! And then there have been times when I'll go
in and see, see if *I* can knock off--you know, if *I* can fix the same
thought, so to speak. But it truly isn't competitive. It seems to me
that it is a stream, and of the first importance that we make a
contribution to it--and that our prominence is roughly in the nature of
iridescence in the water. It could last ten years, it could last
hundreds of years, it doesn't matter terribly so long as it's possessive
of vitality. That *is* important. And it seems to me that John's novel
here has made a *tremendous* contribution to the vitality, the importance
of literature this year. When one opens the *Times Book Review* section,
you read--what? Reviews of something like six novels about an unhappy
childhood, about wretched marriages. What the hell, I mean, you know,
how did we *ever* get into this? What *is* this? These aren't important
books, but John's book *is* important, and dignifies the whole profession.
Now it seems to me that one's individual importance in the matter is
absolutely ridiculous.
    And by the way, I did give--you did--I did give that woman [*sic*] in
Moscow the line that I'd gotten in the letter in Romania, but there was
another recognition, in a place called Southern Bukovina, which is just
about the end of the world. Northern Bukovina is Russian, Southern
Bukovina is Romanian. And I came down for breakfast, in an Art Nouveau
hotel that was dark and--Ugh!--Oh Christ!--and I said to the waiter--I
can say in Russian "I'm the writer, John Cheever" (repeated in Russian),
and somebody shouted--"Ah, Wapshotski!" (laughter) I was *so* happy!

RGC: A great line. Do you remember Cynthia Ozick writing in a review
that what's wrong with the Wapshots is that they're not Wapsteins?
(*Critical Essays*, p. 66) It was, I believe, back in 1964.

JC: Gee, I didn't know that.

RGC: And you could have written back and said, Ah, but they are Wapshotskis! In fact, Joan Didion answered that point very well, later, pointing out that three hundred years or so of white, English culture was a foundation that had been suddenly swept away. The same culture out of which the Wapshots came. The really dispossessed at the moment are those who are not an important minority in any sense. But, to continue: In *Bullet Park*, you have a central family--Elliot Nailles and Nelly Nailles; thus, Elly and Nelly Nailles. And a son, Tony Nailles. Toenails. Now is that intentional? Surely it's not reading too much-- Elly, Nelly, and Tony Nailles? And will Tony turn into his father?

JC: No, no. I didn't do it intentionally. As I say, I haven't read the book in a long time . . . I really don't know. I assume that, writing about a father and a son, I would have been involved in the confinement of the parent, inherited by Tony. And all I remember vividly about Tony Nailles is that--well, that information is hidden at the back of my mind. And also the mantra, I'm sitting in a house by the sea, waiting for the woman that I love, that's really all I remember of this book. (See *Cheever: A Biography*, p. 237)

RGC: Paul Hammer is often spoken of as a figure of evil by critics. I found him more profound and human than Elliot Nailles. Do you ever plan to revive him or treat him again?

JC: Did you think so? No, no. No, I don't think I'll ever go back to any of the characters again. I had thought at one point of writing something called *The Wapshot Footnote*. But I never did. I never published it; I threw away notes and all. What I think--what I'd like to do--I now feel very old and quite sick, and that novel is done, and I have a television original which is being screened, which is being shot now, and then I feel my life's more or less over. Presumably it isn't, but my health isn't quite commendable. What I think I *would* like to do is to write some long stories.

RGC: You think you'll stay with the stories. . . . You know, to return to Paul Hammer, he has so much potential still at the end of *Bullet Park*. Even the idea of following his mad mother's advice and crucifying Tony, it's a desire for change, a sensitivity to whatever may be wrong with the world. The last we see of him, he's there weeping in the church. One still has questions about this. Also, you mention once his being named for a common implement, a tool. And as you concede, you always put a great deal of thought into names.

JC: Well, I suppose all of us do. It depends, if you don't care to do it, you're free not to, I suppose. The name list, the invitation that Fitzgerald uses from *Gatsby*; he gets it out of Thackeray. I don't know where Thackeray got it. There's an invitation list in the new television script.

RGC: Dickens himself, with his phonetic uses of names. . . .

JC: Yes, of course. Well, he was a little cruder than Thackeray or Fitzgerald.

RGC: You've been compared with Fitzgerald . . . and everyone else, up to Faulkner.

JC: Oh, I think there's absolutely *no* resemblance between Faulkner and me!

RGC: Well, they talk about Cheever country now--you've characterized it--just as they talk about Faulkner's terrain, Yoknapatawpha as the archetypal South. But the interesting thing is that at each stage they're comparing you with someone else.

JC: That's how we find our way to truth, to talk, isn't it? Did you, by the way, see the piece in *Harper's* on my . . . . Haven't you seen it? Oh, there's a scabrous piece; it's called "Panic Among the Philistines," and it speaks of everyone, it seems to me . . . let's see if I can find it. Oh, you haven't read it yet? Oh good! (Goes out, returns in a few seconds with a current issue of the magazine which obviously has been near at hand.) This is the piece.[10] Apart from that very commercial list for a line of watches--well, as someone pointed out, of all the errors I've made, this is the *least*. When I was asked, Rolex wanted to know if I would do a commercial. I said, no, I can't. But they asked me again. A woman I know who is a little more worldly in these matters said, No need to be bashful, ask for *two*. So I said, well, I'll do the commercial if you give me two. So they did, and I gave one to my son and one to myself. Of all my mistakes, this certainly is the *least* incriminating. That little satirical piece, actually, is contemptible. Norman Mailer, and . . . Updike and *everybody* else is listed as being a panicked philistine, which is scarcely the case! The editor of that piece resigned about a week later. I've never seen the commercial. It was shown last year, I don't quite know when.

RGC: Given commerce's use of art, perhaps you're justified in taking any advantage. You spoke about the Russians earlier. Do you know of any particularly good writing in Russian on your work? There was a Russian academic who came to Ottawa a few years ago to give a lecture, his subject was "The Fiction of John Cheever." Yuri Koslov, I think, was his name.

JC: No, I don't know of any critical writing in Russia. The last letter I had from Russia, he was asking for information. It was so god damned stupid, I didn't bother to answer it. Koslov? No. There was a Yuri . . . I don't know.

RGC: This fellow was very quick. From the University of Leningrad.

JC: Oh yes, I was at Leningrad the last time. There was a fellow there I liked very much. But I don't think. . . . It could have been he. There was one brilliant man, he was fascinating. He got the department to get some books which could, of course, have got him arrested. But nobody minds. He could do anything else that he wanted to. Now, I thought that was admirable on his part.

RGC: Speaking of foreign experience, one of the critical studies of your work by a man named John Brown pairs you with Henry James--not bad company--but he says that you don't really understand Europeans; your characters simply express bewilderment in the face of foreign experience. But that could be viewed as the disjunction or displacement, or whatever, involved when one finds himself outside his own culture. Any further thoughts on that?

JC: I went to Europe for the first time when I was seventeen. With Frederick, yup. And the European experience has always been very much a common class experience, for Americans, and I expect still is. It seems to have lost prominence at the moment, but I think it's still there.

RGC: Some of your stories seem to suggest that the American expatriate does not so much become part of a new culture as radically cut himself off from the old one. This is important in relation to tradition, one's roots, I suppose.

JC: Expatriation is sometimes a choice on both sides. The difference, of course, is between the expatriate and the exile.

RGC: Is there some of the exile in every expatriate?

JC: Well, I think not with respect to the college-style "exile," which is a term, that, at the moment, I don't take very seriously. I suppose there are exiles from what they consider to be the cultural wilderness of the United States; this is quite a keen element . . . but, I don't know.

RGC: You've referred to Fitzgerald a few times, and you've been compared to him. In some ways, he seems to me to have been more plaintive, much more. . . .

JC: Oh, well he had a different, very different voice, oh, yes! *Gatsby* I consider one of the classics, very good. Very clearly what the novel can do.

RGC: But, perhaps, the only time he absolutely separated himself from his characters, and put them out there?

JC: No. *Gatsby* is pretty much it, as far as I'm concerned. But *Gatsby* is glorious.

RGC: A little like Housman's Athlete Dying young? Gatsby's the luckiest one in the story. An American dreamer. You are a person very conscious of tradition. Do you think there is any such thing as an American identity at the moment?

JC: Oh, very definitely, yes. In fact, it seems to me that it's the nation. We possess a great deal in the way of identity, but particularly our literature. I don't think any other nation can display anything like American literature can. There must be twenty exceptionally brilliant American writers just now. . . . Although if I make lists, I'll leave *somebody* out. There's nothing comparable in Europe, or anywhere else that I know of. No. But then we will always question our identities, experience; it's rather like questioning our erotic drives. You know, they come to us rather early in time. Is it characteristic of Americans to question their identities? It's characteristic of thinking man. It is only the prude and the fool that the question doesn't occur to.

RGC: It seems to me that the English novel has been somewhat uninspired in the last forty years.

JC: Well, it seems to be--it's almost like institutions . . . the brightness seems to pass, over the whole, like the light of the sun. No one quite knows whatever happened. The Russian, the greatness of the Russian novel, of course, is the star of limits [*sic*]. Literature, as you know, music and science and arithmetic even, everything was heavily censored, but for some reason the novel was not. So for almost fifty years there was this outburst of feeling. But the greatness of the

English novel is a thing of the past. It's a thing of the past.

RGC: Are you familiar with the Soviet novelists Ilf and Petrov, the authors of the satires *The Little Golden Calf* and *The Twelve Chairs*, in the tradition of Gogol? There is something in Gogol that is very much of a piece with your writing--a precision of diction, and dialogue and at the same time an absurd disjunction of modern civilization. I can see why the Russians would appreciate you.

JC: There was a Russian, named Yuri Tripov who died about six months ago, whose work I thought was extremely good . . . and others. It seems to me that, considering censorship, they've done, actually, in the last ten years, they've currently *developed* the most exciting theatre in the world. Most of the theatre in Moscow you can't get into. My relationship with the Russians has gotten to be fairly intimate. And as soon as I get over on the plane, they tell me you have to go to the theatre. You sometimes have to go straight to the play to catch the darn thing, to see a performance, this time a performance of *Hamlet*, by a folksinger. There was the anniversary of his death about a month ago; thirty thousand people came. He used to play Hamlet; he used to give an anti-government performance of *Hamlet*. You know . . . something's rotten in the state of Denmark. As soon as I got off the plane, they said, you could only get tickets for tonight, and this can't be published. I'm just about certain this [version of the play] can't be published. But this is my rapport with the Russians. And the performance of *Hamlet*, its standards, is one of the most excitng theatrical experiences I've ever had. But . . . except for Yuri . . . I don't know of any other. Yes, Yevtuschenko is a marvelous performer.

RGC: Poets seem to have had much more publicity.

JC: Oh yes, the poetry readings. There's terrific readings, there's, you know, thousands and thousands of poets. The tradition of oral poetry in Russian is a much more older tradition. And now we have Yevtuschenko reading, you know, from a deal table on a public address system in a square in Moscow, with an audience of several thousand. And that's something we simply do not have, not in *our* powers.

RGC: And yet they've done very well. The Russian poets who have come to the U.S. have been very happily received. By the way, you make a very good distinction in one of your earlier interviews between fact and truth. You use as a launching point Truman Capote's shopping around for cheap sex in the movies. Do you remember it?

JC: No. (laughter) I have no recollection of it at all.

RGC: You said that the nature of the *fact* was obvious--Truman Capote's having had a blow job for fifty cents in the balcony of the movies, anywhere in Manhattan. You said that's a fact--but *not* a truth. A beautiful distinction. Any other comment about the truth, as you isolate it there?

JC: I was speaking to my son about my affairs and I said--roughly I expect, but it had to do with that sense of the truth--I said my concept of "the truth" perhaps would bring us closer together in the relationship. And he said, I know exactly what you mean, you don't want me to declare how often I masturbate. And I said, *precisely*. (laughter)

RGC: Reality is not truth. . . . You've several times referred to yourself as an old man. But less than three years ago, in Ottawa, when I last saw you, you were not speaking about age but you were as chipper as could be, and everyone else who has interviewed you talks about what a youthful figure you are. It's a personal question that you need not answer--but do you feel that the shock of the operation you've just had is much greater for you than was the heart attack earlier?

JC: The shock of the operation *was* . . . it's considerably . . . within a month; it's been a month since the operation, only a month. Yes, it's that . . . (pause, then laughter) and also, if my children were with me, I'd have to tell you, if I appear to be losing a game, or I've won an advantage, I then start speaking about being an old man, nearing the end of my term . . . darkness is the end of everything, and the winds of night of my life; this is generally known as the family joke. (laughter) Trying to exploit the situation.

RGC: Speaking of truth beyond fact, you've always indicated that every work of art is a kind of biblical truth, one way or another. (JC: Yes) Are certain moments of life also truths of that kind? Or does it remain true only in art?

JC: (Suddenly uneasy.) I don't really like to answer that, on tape. . . . I'm so pleased you could do all of this [preparation of *Critical Essays*] and still want to see me. . . .

RGC: Well, reading everything that you've written--I've come out of it with an altered and a very heightened sense of awe.

JC: I'm deeply grateful to you for saying that . . . I do not seek interviews. You know, I keep nothing. It has been an eccentricity, which is getting to be an impossible eccentricity. I was going to tell you this before . . . it was, it became, illegal to burn papers in Westchester (laughter), and, I must do something about my papers.

RGC: Well, I had a recent query as to whether anyone was doing a biography of you, and answered that I knew of none. Are you planning to do one yourself?

JC: Oh no. Somebody is doing a book. George Hunt of New Jersey. He wrote to tell me the book is nearly done . . . and would I read it? I don't know what to tell him. Of course, physically I would be unable to read it. I'm very fond of George.

RGC: Hunt once did a very perceptive piece on your style.

JC: It was very nice, very. He did a book on John Updike I thought first rate. And . . . maybe I will be able to read this but it's not . . . .

RGC: By the way, a fellow in North Carolina has written me to ask if I would be willing to participate if he got an NEH grant for a symposium on your work for next May, the seventieth birthday. (see *Cheever: A Biography*, p. 344)

JC: Well, all I can say to you, is for technical reasons, this is not . . . .

RGC: I suppose if I were in your shoes, I would find celebrations of myself a combination of horror and attraction.

JC: I don't get along successfully--I don't enjoy a public person's role. That's why I don't give readings, [*sic*] because I find it extreme-ly difficult to put down one role and pick up another. One of the reasons I love living in Ossining, of course, is because, frequently I can be ignored, and I can be seen as only an old man with a dog. . . .

Tape Ends.

NOTES

1. On a visit to Ottawa a year or two later, Scott Donaldson, then at work on the biography, borrowed the tape overnight, but reported that he as an outsider found it too difficult to follow the conversation and so was not able to make use of it. Certain references on the tape are verified in *John Cheever: A Biography*, however.
2. The Introduction to the conversation was written that same evening,

following my visit to Cheever's house.

3. See *Cheever: A Biography*, pp. 89-108 for Cheever's Army experiences.

4. See *Cheever: A Biography*, pp. 339-340. When interviewed by biographer Scott Donaldson, I seem to have unwittingly mentioned the galleys of *Paradise* as having been sent off; as the tape transcript makes clear here, I should have said the manuscript.

5. The ending of *Bullet Park* actually reads: ". . . and Nailles-- drugged--went off to work and everything was as wonderful, wonderful, wonderful, wonderful as it had been."

6. Actually, in that story, the narrator assaults his hateful brother, but does not kill him. See *The Stories*, pp. 1-23.

7. Cheever here, seems to be referring to graduate teaching assistants and adjunct professors.

8. See Anatole Broyard, "Mysterious Short Story," *New York Times Book Review*, 1 March 1981, p. 35.

9. In the *Journals* Cheever speaks of Calvino's "archness" with what appears to be asperity.

10. Bryan Griffin in a two-part satirical essay in the August and September, 1981 issues of *Harper's* had castigated virtually every known American writer, along with other well-known cultural personalities. He chose to attack John Cheever for having been one of several public figures who had appeared in Rolex commercials. Apparently the base remuneration was a gift of one of the very expensive watches.

WORKS CITED

Broyard, Anatole. "Mysterious Short Story." *New York Times Book Review*, 1 March 1981, p. 35.

Cheever, Benjamin, ed. *The Letters of John Cheever*. New York: Simon and Schuster, 1988.

Cheever, John. *The Stories of John Cheever*. New York: Ballantine Books, 1978.

Collins, Robert G., ed. *Critical Essays on John Cheever*. Boston: G.K. Hall, 1982.

Donaldson, Scott, ed. *Conversations with John Cheever*. Jackson: University Press of Mississippi, 1987.

Donaldson, Scott. *John Cheever: A Biography*. New York: Random House, 1988.

Gottlieb, Robert, ed. *The Journals of John Cheever*. New York: Knopf, 1991.

Griffin, Bryan F. "Panic Among the Philistines." *Harper's* 263: 1575 (August 1981): 37-52.

Hunt, George W. *John Cheever: The Hobgoblin Company of Love*. Grand Rapids: William B. Eerdmans Publishing Company, 1983.

Bibliographical Checklist

The following supplementary list includes selected reviews, essays and interviews not reprinted in either the Documentary Section of this volume or in other book-length Cheever studies. For an annotated bibliography of criticism published from 1943 through 1979, consult Francis J. Bosha, *John Cheever: A Reference Guide*; see also Dennis Coates' and Chaney and Burton's checklists, Robert Morace's bibliographic essay in *Contemporary Authors* and James E. O'Hara's bibliography in his *John Cheever*.

REVIEWS

The Way Some People Live
DuBois, William. "Tortured Souls." *New York Times Book Review*, 28 March 1943, p. 10.
Schorer, Mark. "Outstanding Novels." *The Yale Review* 32 (Summer 1943): xii, xiv.

The Enormous Radio and Other Stories
DuBois, William. "Books of The Times." *New York Times*, 1 May 1953, p. 19.
Kelly, James. "The Have-Not-Enoughs." *New York Times Book Review*, 10 May 1953, p. 21.

Stories
Martinez, Ramona Maher. "Book Reviews." *New Mexico Quarterly* 26 (Winter 1956-57): 406-07.
Nordel, Rod. "With 'a Kind of Hollow Good Cheer.'" *Christian Science Monitor*, 6 December 1956, p. 11.

Peden, William. "Four Cameos." *Saturday Review* 39 (8 December 1956): 15-16, 52.

The Wapshot Chronicle
Brennan, Maeve. "Mortal Men and Mermaids." *New Yorker* 33 (11 May 1957): 154, 156-58, 161-62.
Maddocks, Melvin. "Cheever Tries a Novel." *Christian Science Monitor*, 28 March 1957, p. 15.

The Housebreaker of Shady Hill and Other Stories
Mitgang, Herbert. "Books of The Times." *New York Times*, 6 September 1958, p. 15.
Peden, William. "How Sad It All Is." *New York Times Book Review*, 7 September 1958, 5.

Some People, Places, and Things That Will Not Appear in My Next Novel
Boroff, David. "A World Filled With Trapdoors Into Chaos." *New York Times Book Review*, 16 April 1961, p. 34.
Kapp, Isa. "Confession of a Writer." *The New Leader* 44 (18 September 1961): 29-30.
Maddocks, Melvin. "Cheever's Latest Collection." *Christian Science Monitor*, 4 May 1961, p. 11.

The Wapshot Scandal
Barrett, William. "New England Gothic." *Atlantic Monthly* 213 (February 1964): 140.
Higginson, Jeannette. "Recent Novels." *The Minnesota Review* 4 (Spring 1964): 452-54.
Janeway, Elizabeth. "Things Aren't What They Seem." *New York Times Book Review*, 5 January 1964, pp. 1, 28.
Ozick, Cynthia. "America Aglow." *Commentary* 38 (July 1964): 66-67.
Wescott, Glenway. "A Surpassing Sequel." *New York Herald Tribune Book Week*, 5 January 1964, pp. 1, 9.

The Brigadier and the Golf Widow
Elliott, George P. "Exploring the Province of the Short Story." *Harper's* 320 (April 1965): 114.
Hicks, Granville. "Slices of Life in an Age of Anxiety." *Saturday Review* 47 (17 October 1964): 33.
Mitchell, Adrian. "Haunted and Bewitched." *New York Times Book Review*, 18 October 1964, p. 5.
Prescott, Orville. "John Cheever's Comedy and Dismay." *New York Times*, 14 October 1964, p. 43.
Scully, James. "An Oracle of Subocracy." *The Nation* 200 (8 February 1965): 144-45.

Bullet Park
Bell, Pearl K.   "Taker of Notes."   *The New Leader* 52 (26 May 1969):
11-13.
Davenport, Guy.   "Elegant Botches."   *National Review* 21 (3 June 1969):
549-50.
Ellmann, Mary.   "Recent Novels: The Languages of Art."   *The Yale Review*
59 (Autumn 1969): 111-12.
Leonard, John.   "Evil Comes to Suburbia."   *New York Times*, 29 April
1969, p. 43.
Sloat, Warren.   Review of *Bullet Park*.   *Commonweal* 90 (9 May 1969):
241-42.
Updike, John.   "Suburban men."   London *Sunday Times*, 14 September 1969,
p. 62.   Reprinted as "And Yet Again Wonderful."   *Picked-Up Pieces*. New
York: Knopf, 1975, pp. 427-28.

The World of Apples
Algren, Nelson.   Review of *The World of Apples*.   *Chicago Tribune Book
World*, 13 May 1973, pp. 1, 3.
DeFeo, Ronald.   "Cheever Underachieving."   *National Review* 25 (11 May
1973): 536-37.
Edwards, Thomas R.   "Surprise, Surprise."   *New York Review of Books* 20
(17 May 1973): 35.
Woiwode, L[arry].   "The World of Apples."   *New York Times Book Review*,
20 May 1973, pp. 1, 26.
Wolff, Geoffrey.   "Cheever's Career Back in Focus with *Apples*."   *Los
Angeles Times Book Review*, 24 June 1973, pp. 1, 10-11.

Falconer
Allen, Bruce.   "Dream Journeys."   *Sewanee Review* 85 (Fall 1977): 694-95.
Clemons, Walter.   "Cheever's Triumph."   *Newsweek* 89 (14 March 1977):
61-62, 64, 67.
Lardner, Susan.   "Miscreants."   *New Yorker* 53 (2 May 1977): 141-42.
Mano, D. Keith.   "Exhaustion."   *National Review* 29 (22 July 1977):
833-34.
McPherson, William.   "Lives in a Cell."   *Washington Post Book World*, 20
March 1977, pp. 1-2.
Meisel, Perry.   "Cheever's Challenge: Find Freedom."   *Village Voice* 22
(21 March 1977): 74, 76.
Romano, John.   "Redemption According to Cheever."   *Commentary* 63 (May
1977): 66-69.
Tyler, Anne.   "Life in Prison With A Sunny Innocent."   *National Observer*
16 (12 March 1977): 19

The Stories of John Cheever
Buffington, Robert.   "Speak, Mnemosyne."   *Sewanee Review* 88 (July 1980):

423-31.

Irving, John. "Facts of Living." *Saturday Review* 5 (30 September 1978): 44-46.

Nicol, Charles. "The Truth, the Impartial Truth." *Harper's* 257 (October 1978): 93-95.

Rickenbacker, William F. "Visions of Grace." *National Review* 31 (13 April 1979): 491-93.

Shaw, Irwin. "Cheever Country." *Bookviews* 2 (October 1978): 56-57.

Shaw, Robert B. "The World in A Very Small Space." *The Nation* 227 (23 December 1978): 705-07.

Tyler, Anne. "Books Considered." *The New Republic* 179 (4 November 1978): 45-47.

Williams, Joy. "Meaningful Fiction . . . John Cheever's Stories are memorable." *Esquire* 90 (21 November 1978): 35-36.

Wolff, Geoffrey. "Cheever's Chain of Being." *New Times*, 27 November 1978, pp. 84, 86.

Oh What a Paradise It Seems
Broyard, Anatole. "Books of The Times." *New York Times*, 3 March 1982, p. C28.

Gray, Paul. "Coda." *Time* 119 (1 March 1982): 85.

Hadas, Rachel. "La Grande Poésie De La Vie." *Partisan Review* 50 (1983): 622-25.

Leonard, John. "Cheever Country." *New York Times Book Review*, 7 March 1982, pp. 1, 25-26.

Mallon, Thomas. "No Place Like Kansas." *National Review* 34 (30 April 1982): 496-97.

Updike, John. "On Such a Beautiful Green Little Planet." *New Yorker* 58 (5 April 1982): 189-90, 193. Reprinted in *Hugging the Shore*. New York: Knopf, 1983, pp. 292-96.

The Letters of John Cheever
Gray, Paul. "Grace Notes." *Time* 132 (28 November 1988): 98.

McPherson, William. "'The Geometry of Love.'" *The Nation* 247 (5 December 1988): 606-08, 610.

The Journals of John Cheever
Gates, David. "The Story He Told Himself." *Newsweek* CXVIII (14 October 1991): 66-67.

Gordon, Mary. "The Country Husband." *New York Times Book Review*, 6 October 1991, pp. 1, 21-22.

Wolcott, James. "Leave It To Cheever." *Vanity Fair*, October 1991, pp. 94-95.

LATER CRITICISM

Books

Bosha, Francis J. *John Cheever: A Reference Guide*. Boston: G.K. Hall, 1981.

Cheever, Susan. *Home Before Dark: A Biographical Memoir of John Cheever by His Daughter*. Boston: Houghton Mifflin, 1984.

-----. *Treetops: A Family Memoir*. New York: Bantam, 1991.

Coale, Samuel. *John Cheever*. New York: Ungar, 1977.

Collins, R. G., ed. *Critical Essays on John Cheever*. Boston: G.K. Hall, 1982

Donaldson, Scott., ed. *Conversations with John Cheever*. Jackson: University Press of Mississippi, 1987.

-----. *John Cheever: A Biography*. New York: Random House, 1988.

Hunt, George. *John Cheever: The Hobgoblin Company of Love*. Grand Rapids: William B. Eerdmans, 1983.

O'Hara, James. *John Cheever: A Study of the Short Fiction*. Boston: Twayne, 1989.

Waldeland, Lynne. *John Cheever*. Boston: Twayne, 1979.

Shorter Studies

Adams, Timothy Dow. "'Neither out Far nor in Deep': Religion and Suburbia in the Fiction of John Cheever, John Updike, and Walker Percy." In *Literature and the Visual Arts in Contemporary Society*. Eds. Suzanne Fergusson and Barbara Groselclose. Columbus: Ohio State University Press, 1985, pp. 47-72.

Auser, Cortland P. "John Cheever's Myth of Man and Time: 'The Swimmer.'" *CEA Critic* 29 (March 1967): 18-19.

Bell, Loren C. "'The Swimmer': A Midsummer's Nightmare." *Studies in Short Fiction* 24 (Fall 1987): 433-36.

Bellow, Saul. "On John Cheever." *New York Review of Books* 30 (17 February 1983): 38.

Bidney, Martin. "'The Common Day' and the Immortality Ode: Cheever's Wordsworthian Craft." *Studies in Short Fiction* 23 (Spring 1986): 139-51.

Bodmer, George R. "Sounding the Fourth Alarm: Identity and The Masculine Tradition in the Fiction of Cheever and Updike." In *Gender Studies: New Directions in Feminist Criticism*. Ed. Judith Spector. Bowling Green, Ohio: Popular Press, 1986, pp. 148-61.

Brans, Jo. "Stories to Comprehend Life: An Interview with John Cheever." *Southwest Review* 65 (Autumn 1980): 337-45.

Breit, Harvey. "Big Interruption." *New York Times Book Review*, 10 May 1953, p. 8.

Byrne, Michael D. "Split-level Enigma: John Cheever's *Bullet Park*." *Studies in American Fiction* 20 (Spring 1992): 85-97.

Chaney, Bev, Jr. and William Burton. John Cheever: A Bibliographical Checklist." *American Book Collector* 7 (August 1986): 22-31.

Coale, Samuel Chase. "John Cheever: Suburban Romancer." In *In Hawthorne's Shadow: American Romance from Melville to Mailer.* Lexington: University Press of Kentucky, 1985, pp. 102-22.

Coates, Dennis. "A Cheever Bibliography Supplement, 1978-1981." In *Critical Essays.*

-----. "John Cheever: A Checklist, 1930-1978." *Bulletin of Bibliography* 36 (January-March 1979): 1-13, 49.

Collins, Robert G. "Beyond Argument: Post-Marital Man in John Cheever's Later Fiction." *Mosaic* XVII, No. 2 (Spring 1984): 261-79.

-----. "The Dark Too Soon: John Cheever's Heritage. *Resources for American Literary Study* XIII, No. 1 (1983): 33-40.

-----. "From Subject to Object and Back Again: Individual Identity in John Cheever's Fiction." *Twentieth Century Literature* 28 (Summer 1982): 1-13.

-----. "Fugitive Time: Dissolving Experience in the Later Fiction of Cheever." *Studies in American Fiction* 12 (Autumn 1984): 175-88.

-----. "The Search for John Cheever." *Resources for American Literary Study* XVIII, No. 2 (1992): 194-202.

Cowley, Malcolm. "John Cheever: The Novelist's Life as a Drama." *Sewanee Review* 91 (Winter 1983): 1-16.

Detweiler, Robert. "John Cheever's *Bullet Park*: A World Beyond Madness." In *Essays in Honour of Professor Tyrus Hillway*. Ed. Erwin A. Sturzl. University of Salzburg: Institute fur Englische Sprache und Literatur, 1977, pp. 6-32.

Donaldson, Scott. "Supermarket and Superhighway: John Cheever's America." *Virginia Quarterly Review* 62 (Autumn 1986): 654-68.

-----. "Writing the *Cheever*." *Sewanee Review* 98 (Summer 1990): 527-45.

Fogelman, Bruce. "A Key Pattern of Images in John Cheever's Short Fiction." *Studies in Short Fiction* 26 (Fall 1989): 463-72.

Gerlach, John. "Closure in Modern Short Fiction: Cheever's 'The Enormous Radio' and 'Artemis, the Honest Well Digger.'" *Modern Fiction Studies* 28 (Spring 1982): 145-52.

Gilmore, Thomas B. "Drinking and Society in the Fiction of John Cheever." In *Equivocal Spirits: Alcoholism and Drinking in Twentieth-Century Literature.* Chapel Hill: University of North Carolina Press, 1987, pp. 62-80.

Gioia, Dana. "Meeting Mr. Cheever." *The Hudson Review* 39 (Autumn 1986): 419-34.

Griffin, Bryan F. "Literary Vogues: Getting Cheever while he's hot." *Harper's* 258 (June 1979): 90-93.

Gussow, Adam. "Cheever's Failed Paradise: The Short-Story Stylist as Novelist." *The Literary Review* 27 (Fall 1983): 103-16.

Hardwick, Elizabeth. "Cheever, or The Ambiguities." *New York Review of Books* 31 (20 December 1984): 3-4, 6, 8.

Hassan, Ihab. "Encounter with Possibility: Gold, Dunleavy and Cheever." In *Radical Innocence: Studies in the Contemporary American Novel*. Princeton: Princeton University Press, 1961, pp. 187-194.

Hipkiss, Robert A. "'The Country Husband'--A Model Cheever Achievement." *Studies in Short Fiction* 27 (Fall 1990): 577-85.

Hunt, George W. "John Cheever: A Life." *America* 159 (30 July 1988): 58-60.

Josyph, Peter. "The John Cheever Story: A Talk with Richard Selzer." *Twentieth Century Literature* 37 (Fall 1991): 335-42.

Kornbluth, Jesse. "The Cheever Chronicle." *New York Times Magazine*, 21 October 1979, pp. 26-29, 102-05.

[Lee, Alwyn]. "Ovid in Ossining." *Time* 83 (27 March 1964): 66-70, 72.

Magaw, Malcolm O. "Cheever's New Existential Man in *Falconer*." *The International Fiction Review* 17 (Summer 1990): 75-81.

Matthews, James W. "Peter Rugg and Cheever's Swimmer: Archetypal Missing Men." *Studies in Short Fiction* 29 (Winter 1992): 95-101.

Morace, Robert A. "John Cheever." In *Contemporary Authors: Bibliographical Series* Vol. 1. Ed. James J. Martine. Detroit: Gale Research Company, 1986, pp. 157-92.

-----. "John Cheever." In *Dictionary of Literary Biography* Vol.2: *American Novelists Since World War II*. Eds. Jeffrey Helterman and Richard Layman. Detroit: Gale Research Company, 1978, pp. 88-100.

-----. "The Religious Experience and the 'Mystery of Imprisonment' in John Cheever's *Falconer*." *Cithara* 20 (1980): 44-53.

Nash, Charles, C. "The Brothers Cheever at War and Peace." *Publications of the Missouri Philological Association* 6 (1981): 48-53.

O'Hara, James. "Cheever's *The Wapshot Chronicle*: A Narrative of Exploration." *Critique* 22 (1980): 20-30.

-----. "John Cheever." In *Dictionary of Literary Biography Yearbook: 1982*. Ed. Richard Ziegfeld. Detroit: Gale Research Company, 1983, pp. 126-33.

Pawlowski, Robert S. "Myth as Metaphor: Cheever's 'Torch Song.'" *Research Studies* 47 (June 1979): 118-21.

Peden, William. "Metropolis, Village, and Suburbia: The Short Fiction of Manners." In *The American Short Story: Continuity and Change, 1940-1975*. Boston: Houghton Mifflin, 1975, pp. 30-39.

Reilly, Edward C. "Saving Grace and Moral Balance in John Cheever's Stories." *Publications of the Mississippi Philological Association* 1 (1982): 24-29.

Robins, Natalie. *Alien Ink: The FBI's War on Freedom of Expression*. New York: Morrow, 1992, pp. 422-23.

Ross Jean W. "John Cheever." In *Dictionary of Literary Biography Yearbook: 1980.* Eds. Karen L. Rood, Jean W. Ross, and Richard Ziegfeld. Detroit: Gale Research Company, 1981, pp. 25-28.

Rupp, Richard H. "John Cheever: The Upshot of Wapshot." In *Celebration in Postwar American Fiction, 1945-1967.* Coral Gables: University of Miami Press, 1970, pp. 27-39.

Schickel, Richard. "The Cheever Chronicle." *Horizon* 21 (September 1978): 28-33.

Updike, John. "John Cheever: I, II, III, IV." In *Odd Jobs.* New York: Knopf, 1991, pp. 108-19.

Waldeland, Lynne. "Isolation and Integration: John Cheever's 'The Country Husband.'" *Ball State University Forum* XXVII (Winter 1986): 5-11.

Walkiewicz, E.P. "Cheever's 'Metamorphoses': Myth and Postmodern Short Fiction." In *Since Flannery O'Connor: Essays on the Contemporary Short Story.* Eds. Loren Logsdon and Charles W. Mayer. Macomb: Western Illinois University, 1987, pp. 32-44.

Weaver, John D. "John Cheever: Recollections of a Childlike Imagination." *Los Angeles Times Book Review*, 13 March 1977, pp. 3, 8.

Wood, Ralph C. "The Modest and Charitable Humanism of John Cheever." *The Christian Century*, 17 November 1982, pp. 1163-66.

Index

About the Editor

FRANCIS J. BOSHA is Associate Professor of American Literature at Kawamura Gakuen Woman's University in Chiba, Japan. He has previously published books on Cheever and William Faulkner, and is the author of many critical articles and essays on Ezra Pound, Saul Bellow, and Ernest Hemingway, among others.